FLESH AND STONE

FLESH
AND STONE

*The Body and the City
in Western Civilization*

RICHARD SENNETT

W · W · NORTON & COMPANY
New York   London

The text of this book is composed in Garamond #3.
Composition and manufacturing by The Maple-Vail Book Manufacturing Group.
Book design by Jacques Chazaud.

Library of Congress Cataloging-in-Publication Data
Sennett, Richard, 1943–
Flesh and stone : the body and the city in Western civilization /
Richard Sennett.
p. cm.
Includes bibliographical references and index.
1. Cities and towns—History. 2. Body, Human—Social aspects.
3. Civilization, Western. I. Title.
HT113.S45 1994
307.76′09—dc20   94-15874

ISBN 0-393-03684-7

W. W. Norton & Company, Inc., 500 Fifth Avenue, New York, N.Y. 10110
W. W. Norton & Company Ltd., 10 Coptic Street, London WC1A 1 PU

1 2 3 4 5 6 7 8 9 0

For HILARY

1&.7

CONTENTS

ACKNOWLEDGMENTS

The first draft of *Flesh and Stone* was presented at the Goethe University, Frankfurt in 1992; I would like to thank my host, Professor Jurgen Habermas, for helping me think through many problems. The work on ancient cities advanced during a stay at the American Academy in Rome in 1992–93. I would like to thank its president, Adele Chatfield-Taylor, and its professor in charge, Malcolm Bell, for their many kindnesses. I gained access to manuscripts in the Library of Congress thanks to a stay at the Woodrow Wilson International Center for Scholars in 1993, for which I would like to thank its director, Dr. Charles Blitzer.

This book was read by several friends. Professor Glen Bowersock, of the Institute for Advanced Study, gave me a key to writing the initial chapter; Professor Norman Cantor, of New York University, helped me find a context for the chapters on medieval Paris; Professor Joseph Rykwert, of the University of Pennsylvania, took me through the architectural history minutely; Professor Carl Schorske, of Princeton University, helped me with the chapter on the Enlightenment; Professor Joan Scott, of the Institute for Advanced Study, read the entire manuscript with a compassionately skeptical eye, as did Professor Charles Tilly, of the New School for Social Research.

At W. W. Norton, Edwin Barber read this book with care and understanding, as did Ann Adelman, who copy-edited the manuscript thoroughly but with due regard to the author's vanity. The book has been designed by Jacques Chazaud and produced by Andrew Marasia.

My friends Peter Brooks and Jerrold Seigel supported me with their kindness as well as their comments; they made the process of writing less lonely, as did my wife, Saskia Sassen, an avid partner in the adventure of our life. This book is dedicated to our son, whose growth has given us the greatest pleasure during the time this book has also grown.

I owe a special debt to the students who have worked with me the last few years. Molly McGarry did research on buildings, maps, and images of the body; Joseph Femia helped me understand the workings of the guillotine, and I have based my own writing on his; Anne-Sophie Cerisola helped with French translations and with the notes. I could not have written this book without my graduate assistant David Slocum; he pursued sources with a vengeance and read the endless permutations of the manuscript with great care.

Finally, my greatest debt is to my friend Michel Foucault, with whom I began investigating the history of the body fifteen years ago. After his death, I put the beginnings of a manuscript aside, taking up this work some years later in a different spirit. *Flesh and Stone* is not, I think, a book the younger Foucault would have liked; for reasons I have explained in the Introduction, it was Foucault's own last years which suggested to me another way of writing this history.

A city is composed of different kinds of men;
similar people cannot bring a city into existence.

ARISTOTLE, *The Politics*

INTRODUCTION

Body and City

F*lesh and Stone* is a history of the city told through people's bodily experience: how women and men moved, what they saw and heard, the smells that assailed their noses, where they ate, how they dressed, when they bathed, how they made love in cities from ancient Athens to modern New York. Though this book takes people's bodies as a way to understand the past, it is more than an historical catalogue of physical sensations in urban space. Western civilization has had persistent trouble in honoring the dignity of the body and diversity of human bodies; I have sought to understand how these body-troubles have been expressed in architecture, in urban design, and in planning practice.

I was prompted to write this history out of bafflement with a contemporary problem: the sensory deprivation which seems to curse most modern building; the dullness, the monotony, and the tactile sterility which afflicts the urban environment. This sensory deprivation is all the more remarkable because modern times have so privileged the sensations of the body and the freedom of physical life. When I first began to explore sensory deprivation in space, the problem seemed a professional failure—modern architects and urbanists having somehow lost an active connection to the human body in their designs. In time I came to see that the problem of sensory deprivation in space has larger causes and deeper historical origins.

1. THE PASSIVE BODY

Some years ago a friend and I went to see a film in a suburban shopping mall near New York. During the Vietnam War a bullet had shattered my friend's left hand, and the military surgeons had been obliged to amputate above the wrist. Now he wore a mechanical device fitted with metal fingers and thumb which allowed him to hold cutlery and to type. The movie we saw turned out to be a particularly gory war epic through which my friend sat impassively, occasionally offering technical comments. When it was over, we lingered outside, smoking, while waiting for some other people to join us. My friend lit his cigarette slowly; he then held up the cigarette in his claw to his lips steadily, almost proudly. The movie patrons had just sat through two hours of bodies blasted and ripped, the audience applauding particularly good hits and otherwise thoroughly enjoying the gore. People streamed out around us, glanced uneasily at the metal prosthesis, and moved away; soon we were an island in their midst.

When the psychologist Hugo Munsterberg first looked at a silent movie in 1911, he thought the modern mass media might dull the senses; in a film, "the massive outer world has lost its weight," he wrote, "it has been freed from space, time, and causality"; he feared that "moving pictures . . . reach complete isolation from the practical world."[1] Just as few soldiers taste the movie pleasures of ripping other bodies apart, filmed images of sexual pleasure have very little to do with real lovers' sexual experience. Few films show two elderly naked people making love, or naked fat people; movie sex is great the first time the stars get into bed. In the mass media, a divide opens up between represented and lived experience.

Psychologists who followed Munsterberg explained this divide by focusing on the effect of mass media on viewers as well as on the techniques of the media themselves. Watching pacifies. Though perhaps some few among the millions addicted to watching torture and rape on screen are aroused to become torturers and rapists themselves, the reaction to my friend's metal hand shows another, certainly larger response: vicarious experience of violence desensitizes the viewer to real pain. In a study of such television watchers, for instance, the psychologists Robert Kubey and Mihaly Csikszentmihalyi found that "people consistently report their experiences with television as being passive, relaxing, and involving relatively little concentration."[2] Heavy consumption of simulated pain, like simulated sex, serves to numb bodily awareness.

If we look at and speak about bodily experiences more explicitly than did our great-grandparents, perhaps our physical freedom is not therefore as great as it seems; through the mass media, at least, we experience our bodies in more passive ways than did people who feared their own sensations. What then will bring the body to moral, sensate life? What will make modern people more aware of each other, more physically responsive?

The spatial relations of human bodies obviously make a great deal of difference in how people react to each other, how they see and hear one another, whether they touch or are distant. Where we saw the war film, for instance, influenced how others reacted passively to my friend's hand. We saw the film in a vast shopping mall on the northern periphery of New York City. There is nothing special about the mall, just a string of thirty or so stores built a generation ago near a highway; it includes a movie complex and is surrounded by a jumble of large parking lots. It is one result of the great urban transformation now occurring, which is shifting population from densely packed urban centers to thinner and more amorphous spaces, suburban housing tracts, shopping malls, office campuses, and industrial parks. If a theatre in a suburban mall is a meeting place for tasting violent pleasure in air-conditioned comfort, this great geographic shift of people into fragmented spaces has had a larger effect in weakening the sense of tactile reality and pacifying the body.

This is first of all so because of the physical experience which made the new geography possible, the experience of speed. People travel today at speeds our forbears could not at all conceive. The technologies of motion—from automobiles to continuous, poured-concrete highways—made it possible for human settlements to extend beyond tight-packed centers out into peripheral space. Space has thus become a means to the end of pure motion—we now measure urban spaces in terms of how easy it is to drive through them, to get out of them. The look of urban space enslaved to these powers of motion is necessarily neutral: the driver can drive safely only with the minimum of idiosyncratic distractions; to drive well requires standard signs, dividers, and drain sewers, and also streets emptied of street life apart from other drivers. As urban space becomes a mere function of motion, it thus becomes less stimulating in itself; the driver wants to go through the space, not to be aroused by it.

The physical condition of the travelling body reinforces this sense of disconnection from space. Sheer velocity makes it hard to focus one's attention on the passing scene. Complementing the sheath of speed, the actions needed to drive a car, the slight touch on the gas pedal and the break, the flicking of the eyes to and from the rearview mirror, are micro-notions compared to the arduous physical movements involved in driving a horse-drawn coach. Navigating the geography of modern society requires very little physical effort, hence engagement; indeed, as roads become straightened and regularized, the voyager need account less and less for the people and the buildings on the street in order to move, making minute motions in an ever less complex environment. Thus the new geography reinforces the mass media. The traveler, like the television viewer, experiences the world in narcotic terms; the body moves passively, desensitized in space, to destinations set in a fragmented and discontinuous urban geography.

Both the highway engineer and the television director create what could be called "freedom from resistance." The engineer designs ways to move without obstruction, effort, or engagement; the director explores ways for people to look at anything, without becoming too uncomfortable. In watching the people withdraw from my friend after the movie, I realized he threatened them, not so much with the sight of a wounded body as with an active body marked and constrained by experience.

This desire to free the body from resistance is coupled with the fear of touching, a fear made evident in modern urban design. In siting highways, for instance, planners will often direct the river of traffic so as to seal off a residential community from a business district, or run the river through residential areas to separate rich and poor sections or ethnically divergent sections. In community development, planners will concentrate on building schools or housing at the center of the community rather than at its edge where people might come into contact with outsiders. More and more, the fenced,

William Hogarth, *Beer Street,* 1751. Engraving. *Courtesy of the Print Collection, Lewis Walpole Library, Yale University.*

gated, and guarded planned community is sold to buyers as the very image of the good life. It is thus perhaps not surprising that, in a study of the suburb near the mall where we saw the war film, the sociologist M. P. Baumgartner found "on a day-by-day basis, life is filled with efforts to deny, minimize, contain, and avoid conflict. People shun confrontations and show great distaste for the pursuit of grievances or the censure of wrongdoing."[3] Through the sense of

William Hogarth, Gin Lane, 1751. Engraving. *Courtesy of the Print Collection, Lewis Walpole Library, Yale University.*

touch we risk feeling something or someone as alien. Our technology permits us to avoid that risk.

Thus, a great pair of engravings William Hogarth made in 1751 appear strange to modern eyes. In these engravings, *Beer Street* and *Gin Lane,* Hogarth meant to depict images of order and disorder in the London of his time. *Beer Street* shows a group of people sitting close together drinking beer, the men with their arms around the women's shoulders. For Hogarth, bodies touching each other sig-

nalled social connection and orderliness, much as today in small
southern Italian towns a person will reach out and grip your hand or
forearm in order to talk seriously to you. Whereas *Gin Lane* displays
a social scene in which each main figure withdraws into him- or herself, drunk on gin; the people in *Gin Lane* have no corporeal sensation of one another, nor of the stairs, benches, and buildings in the
street. This lack of physical touch was Hogarth's image of disorder
in urban space. Hogarth's conception of bodily order and disorder
in cities was far different from that purveyed by the builder of sealed
communities to his crowd-fearing clients. Today, order means lack
of contact.

It is evidence of this sort—the stretched-out geography of the
modern city, in concert with modern technologies for desensitizing
the human body—which has led some critics of modern culture to
claim that a profound divide exists between the present and the past.
Sensate realities and bodily activity have eroded to such an extent
that modern society seems a unique historical phenomenon. The
bellwether of this historical shift can be read, these critics believe, in
the changed character of the urban crowd. Once a mass of bodies
packed tightly together in the centers of cities, the crowd today has
dispersed. It is assembled in malls for consumption rather than for
the more complex purposes of community or political power; in the
modern crowd the physical presence of other human beings feels
threatening. In social theory, these arguments have been advanced
by critics of mass society, notably Theodor Adorno and Herbert
Marcuse.[4]

Yet it is exactly this sense of a gulf between past and present I
wish to challenge. The geography of the modern city, like modern
technology, brings to the fore deepseated problems in Western civilization in imagining spaces for the human body which might make
human bodies aware of one another. The computer screen and the
islands of the periphery are spatial aftershocks of problems before
unsolved on streets and town squares, in churches and town halls, in
houses and courtyards packing people close together—old constructions in stone forcing people to touch, yet designs which failed to
arouse the awareness of flesh promised in Hogarth's engraving.

2. THE PLAN OF THE BOOK

When Lewis Mumford wrote *The City in History,* he recounted four
thousand years of urban history by tracing the evolution of the wall,

the house, the street, the central square—basic forms out of which cities have been made. My learning is lesser, my sights are narrower, and I have written this history in a different way, by making studies of individual cities at specific moments—moments when the outbreak of a war or a revolution, the inauguration of a building, the announcement of a medical discovery, or the publication of a book marked a significant point in the relation between people's experience of their own bodies and the spaces in which they lived.

Flesh and Stone begins by probing what nakedness meant to the ancient Athenians at the outbreak of the Peloponnesian War, at the height of the ancient city's glory. The naked, exposed body has often been taken as an emblem of a people entirely confident in themselves and at home in their city; I have sought to understand instead how this bodily ideal served as a source of disturbance in the relations between men and women, in the shaping of urban space, and in the practice of Athenian democracy.

The second lap of this history focuses on Rome at the time when the Emperor Hadrian completed the Pantheon. Here I have sought to explore Roman credulity in images, particularly the Romans' belief in bodily geometry, and how they translated this belief into urban design and imperial practice. The powers of the eye literally held pagan Romans in thrall and dulled their sensibilities, a thralldom which the Christians of Hadrian's time began to challenge. The early spaces made for Christian bodies I have sought to understand at the point when the Christian Emperor Constantine returned to Rome and built the Lateran Basilica.

The study then turns to how Christian beliefs about the body shaped urban design in the High Middle Ages and Early Renaissance. Christ's physical suffering on the Cross offered medieval Parisians, at the time the great Bible of St. Louis appeared in 1250, a way to think about spaces of charity and sanctuary in the city; these spaces nested uneasily, however, among streets given over to the release of physical aggression in a new market economy. By the Renaissance, urban Christians felt their ideals of community threatened as non-Christians and non-Europeans were drawn into the European urban economic orbit; I have looked at one way these threatening differences were articulated, in the creation of the Jewish Ghetto in Venice beginning in 1516.

The final part of *Flesh and Stone* explores what happened to urban space as the modern scientific understanding of the body cut free from earlier medical knowledge. This revolution began with the publication of Harvey's *De motu cordis* in the early seventeenth century, a scientific work which radically altered understanding of circulation in the body; this new image of the body as a circulating system prompted eighteenth-century attempts to circulate bodies freely in the city. In revolutionary Paris, this new imagery of bodily freedom came into conflict with the need for communal space and communal ritual, and the modern signs of sensate passivity first appeared. The triumph of individualized movement in the formation of the great cities of the nineteenth century led to the particular dilemma with which we now live, in which the freely moving individual body lacks physical awareness of other human beings. The psychological costs of that dilemma were apparent to the novelist E. M. Forster in imperial London, and the civic costs of this dilemma are apparent today in multi-cultural New York.

No one could be the master of so much. I have written this book as a dedicated amateur, and hope the reader will follow its course in the same spirit. But this short summary more urgently prompts the question of whose body is explored—"the human body" covers, after all, a kaleidoscope of ages, a division of genders and races, each of these diverse bodies having its own distinctive spaces in cities of the past, as in cities today. Instead of cataloguing these, I have sought to understand the uses made in the past of collective, generic images of "the human body." Master images of "the body" tend to repress mutual, sensate awareness, especially among those whose bodies differ. When a society or political order speaks generically about "the body," it can deny the needs of bodies which do not fit the master plan.

One need for a master image of the body is conveyed by the phrase "the body politic"; it expresses the need for social order. The philosopher John of Salisbury gave perhaps the most literal definition of the body politic, declaring in 1159 simply that "the state *(res publica)* is a body." He meant that a ruler in society functions just like a human brain, the ruler's counselors like a heart; merchants are society's stomach, soldiers its hands, peasants and menial workers its feet.[5] His was a hierarchical image; social order begins in the brain, the organ of the ruler. John of Salisbury in turn connected the shape of the human body and the form of a city: the city's palace or cathedral he thought of as its head, the central market as its stomach, the city's hands and feet as its houses. People should therefore move slowly in a cathedral because the brain is a reflective organ, rapidly in a market because digestion occurs like a quick-burning fire in the stomach.

John of Salisbury wrote as a scientist; finding out how the brain works, he believed, would tell a king how to make laws. Modern sociobiology is not too far from this medieval science in its aim; it too seeks to base how society should operate on the supposed dictates of Nature. In either medieval or modern form, the body politic founds rule in society on a ruling image of the body.

If John of Salisbury was unusual in thinking so literally about the analogy of bodily form and urban form, in the course of urban development master images of "the body" have frequently been used, in transfigured form, to define what a building or an entire city should look like. The ancient Athenians who celebrated the nakedness of the body sought to give nakedness a physical meaning in the gymnasia of Athens and a metaphoric meaning in the political spaces of the city, though the generic human form they sought was in fact limited to the male body, and idealized when the male was young. When the Renaissance Venetians spoke of the dignity of "the body" in the city, they meant Christian bodies only, an exclusion which made it logical to shut away the half-human, half-animal bodies of Jews. In these ways the body politic practices power, and creates urban form, by speaking that generic language of the body, a language which represses by exclusion.

Yet there would be something paranoiac in thinking about the generic language of the body, and the body politic, simply as a technique of power; by speaking in the singular voice, a society can also try to find what binds its people together. And this generic body language has suffered a peculiar fate when translated into urban space.

In the course of Western development, dominant images of the body have cracked apart in the process of being impressed on the city. A master image of the body inherently invites ambivalence among the people it rules, for every human body is physically idiosyncratic, and every human being feels contradictory physical desires. The bodily contradictions and ambivalences aroused by the collective master image have expressed themselves in Western cities through the alterations and smudges of urban form and the subverting uses of urban space. And it is this necessary contradictoriness and fragmenting of "the human body" in urban space which has helped to generate the rights of, and to dignify, differing human bodies.

Instead of tracing power's iron grip, *Flesh and Stone* takes up one of the great themes of Western civilization, as recounted in both the Old Testament and Greek tragedy. It is that a stressed and unhappy experience of our bodies makes us more aware of the world in which

we live. The transgressions of Adam and Eve, the shame of their
nakedness, their exile from the Garden, tell a story of what the first
humans became, as well as what they lost. In the Garden, they were
innocent, unknowing, and obedient. Out in the world, they became
aware; they knew they were flawed creatures, and so they explored,
sought to understand what was strange and unlike; they were no
longer God's children to whom all was given. Sophokles' *Oedipus the
King* tells a kindred story. Oedipus wanders, after gashing his eyes
out, newly aware of a world he can no longer see; now humbled, he
draws closer to the gods.

Our civilization, from its origins, has been challenged by the body
in pain. We have not simply accepted suffering as inevitable and
invincible as experience, self-evident in its meaning. The puzzles of
bodily pain marked Greek tragedies and early Christian efforts to
comprehend the Son of God. The issue of bodily passivity, and passive response to others, similarly has deep roots in our civilization.
The Stoics cultivated a passive relation to both pleasure and pain,
while their Christian heirs sought to combine indifference to their
own sensations with an active engagement in the pains of their breth-
ren. Western civilization has refused to "naturalize" suffering, has
either sought to treat pain as amenable to social control or to accept
it as part of a conscious higher mental scheme. I am far from arguing
that the ancients are our contemporaries. Yet these themes keep
reappearing in Western history, recast and reworked, unquiet and
persistent.

The master images of the body which have ruled in our history
would deny us knowledge of the body outside the Garden. For they
attempt to convey the completeness of the body as a system, and
its unity with the environment it dominates. Wholeness, oneness,
coherence: these are key words in the vocabulary of power. Our
civilization has combatted this language of domination through a
more sacred image of the body, a sacred image in which the body
appears at war with itself, a source of suffering and unhappiness.
People who can acknowledge this dissonance and incoherence in
themselves understand rather than dominate the world in which they
live. This is the sacred promise made in our culture.

Flesh and Stone attempts to understand how that promise has been
made, and broken, in a particular place: the city. The city has served
as a site of power, its spaces made coherent and whole in the image
of man himself. The city has also served as the space in which these
master images have cracked apart. The city brings together people

who are different, it intensifies the complexity of social life, it presents people to each other as strangers. All these aspects of urban experience—difference, complexity, strangeness—afford resistance to domination. This craggy and difficult urban geography makes a particular moral promise. It can serve as a home for those who have accepted themselves as exiles from the Garden.

3. A PERSONAL NOTE

I began studying the history of the body with the late Michel Foucault, a collaboration we started together in the late 1970s.[6] My friend's influence may be felt everywhere in these pages. When I resumed this history a few years after his death, I did not continue as we had begun.

In the books for which he is most well known, such as *Discipline and Punish*, Foucault imagined the human body almost choked by the knot of power in society. As his own body weakened, he sought to loosen this knot; in the third published volume of his *History of Sexuality*, and even more in the notes he made for the volumes he did not live to complete, he tried to explore bodily pleasures which are not society's prisoners. A certain paranoia about control which had marked much of his life left him as he began to die.

The manner of his dying made me think, among the many revisions a death prompts in minds of those who survive, about a remark Wittgenstein once made, a remark challenging the notion that built space matters to a body in pain. "Do we know the place of pain," Wittgenstein asks, "so that when we know where we have pains we know how far away from the two walls of this room, and from the floor? . . . When I have pain in the tip of my finger and touch my tooth with it, [does it matter that] the pain should be one-sixteenth of an inch away from the tip of my finger?"[7]

In writing *Flesh and Stone* I have wanted to honor the dignity of my friend as he died, for he accepted the body in pain—his own, and the pagan bodies he wrote about in his last months—as living beyond the reach of such calculation. And for this reason, I have shifted from the focus with which we began: exploring the body in society through the prism of sexuality. If liberating the body from Victorian sexual constraints was a great event in modern culture, this liberation also entailed the narrowing of physical sensibility to sexual desire. In *Flesh and Stone*, though I have sought to incorporate questions of sexuality into the theme of bodily awareness of other people, I have emphasized awareness of pain as much as promises of pleasure. This theme honors a Judeo-Christian belief in the spiritual knowledge to be gained in the body, and it is as a believer that I have written this book. I have sought to show how those who have been exiled from the Garden might find a home in the city.

PART ONE

POWERS

OF THE VOICE

AND EYE

CHAPTER ONE

Nakedness

The Citizen's Body
in Perikles' Athens

In 431 B.C. a war swept over the ancient world, pitting the cities of Athens and Sparta against each other. Athens entered the war with supreme confidence and left it twenty-seven years later in abysmal defeat. To Thucydides, the Athenian general who wrote its history, the Peloponnesian War appeared a social as well as a military conflict, a clash between the militarized life of Sparta and the open society of Athens. The values of the Athenian side Thucydides portrayed in a Funeral Oration given in the winter of 431–430 B.C. by Perikles, the leading citizen of Athens, who commemorated early casualties in the war. How close the words Thucydides wrote were to those Perikles spoke we do not know; the speech has come to seem in the course of time, however, a mirror of its age.

The Funeral Oration sought "to transmute the grief of the parents into pride," in the words of the modern historian Nicole Loraux.[1] The bleached bones of the young dead had been placed in coffins of

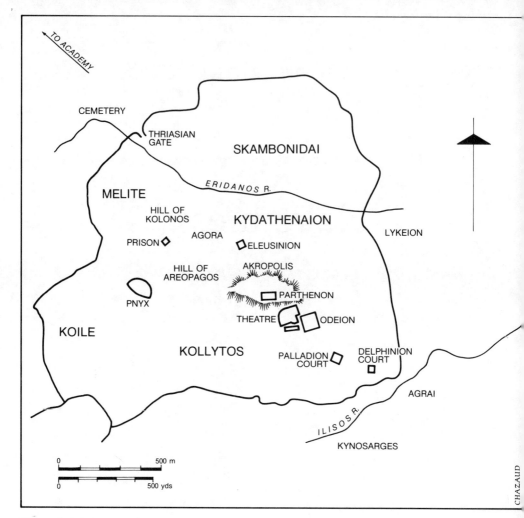

Map of Athens, ca. 400 B.C.

cypress wood, drawn in a funeral cortege to a graveyard out beyond the walls of the city, followed by an enormous crowd of mourners; the cemetery would shelter the dead under umbrella pines whose needles had formed a dense carpet over earlier graves. Here Perikles paid homage to the fallen by praising the glories of their city. "Power is in the hands not of a minority but of the whole people," he declared, "everyone is equal before the law."[2] In Greek, the word *demokratia* ("democracy") means that the "people" (the *demos*) are the "power" (the *kratos*) in the state. The Athenian people are tolerant and cosmopolitan; "our city is open to the world."[3] And unlike the Spartans, who blindly and stupidly follow orders, the Athenians debate and reason with one another; "we do not think," Perikles declares, "there is an incompatibility between words and deeds."[4]

Perikles took for granted what might most stike a modern person. The leaders of the young warriors were depicted in art as nearly naked, their unclothed bodies protected only by hand shields and spears. In the city, young men wrestled in the gymnasium naked; the loose clothes men wore on the streets and in public places freely exposed their bodies. As the art historian Kenneth Clark observes, among the ancient Greeks a nakedly exposed body marked the presence of a strong rather than vulnerable person—and more, someone who was civilized.[5] At the opening of Thucydides' account of the Peloponnesian War, for instance, he traces the progress of civilization up to the war's outbreak; as one sign of this progress, he remarks of the Spartans that they "were the first to play games naked, to take off their clothes openly," whereas among the *barbaroi* of his own day many still insisted on covering their genitals when in public at the games. (*Barbaroi* can be translated both as "foreigners" and as "barbarians.")[6] The civilized Greek had made his exposed body into an object of admiration.

To the ancient Athenian, displaying oneself affirmed one's dignity as a citizen. Athenian democracy placed great emphasis on its citizens exposing their thoughts to others, just as men exposed their bodies. These mutual acts of disclosure were meant to draw the knot between citizens ever tighter. We might call the knot today "male bonding"; the Athenians took this bond literally. In ancient Greek, the very words used to express erotic love of another man could be used to express one's attachment to the city. A politician wanted to appear like a lover or a warrior.

The insistence on showing, exposing, and revealing put its stamp on the stones of Athens. The greatest building work of the Periklean era, the temple of the Parthenon, was sited on a promontory so that it stood out exposed to view from throughout the city below. The great central square of the city, the agora, contained few places which were forbidden territory as is modern private property. In the democratic political spaces the Athenians built, most notably the theatre built into the hill of the Pnyx where the assembly of all citizens met, the organization of the crowd and the rules of voting sought to expose how individuals or small groups voted to the gaze of all. Nakedness might seem the sign of a people entirely at home in the city: the city was the place in which one could live happily exposed, unlike the barbarians who aimlessly wandered the earth without the protection of stone. Perikles celebrated an Athens in which harmony seemed to reign between flesh and stone.

The value placed on nakedness derived in part from the ways

Greeks of Perikles' time thought about the interior of the human body. Body heat was the key to human physiology: those who most concentrated and marshalled their bodily heat had no need of clothes. More, the hot body was more reactive to others, more febrile, than was a cold and sluggish body; hot bodies were strong, possessing the heat to act as well as react. These physiological precepts extended to the use of language. When people listened, spoke, or read words, their body temperatures supposedly rose, and so again their desire to act—a belief about the body which underlay Perikles' belief in the unity of words and deeds.

This Greek understanding of physiology made the idealization of nakedness far more complex than the stark contrast Thucydides drew between a Greek, proud of his body and proud of his city, and the barbarian dressed in patchy furs who lived in the forest or in the marshes. The Greek understanding of the human body suggested different rights, and differences in urban spaces, for bodies containing different degrees of heat. These differences cut most notably across the dividing line of gender, since women were thought to be colder versions of men. Women did not show themselves naked in the city; more, they were usually confined to the interiors of houses, as though the lightless interior more suited their physiology than did the open spaces of the sun. In the house, they wore tunics of thin material which extended to the knees; on the street, their tunics were ankle-length, coarse, opaque linen. The treatment of slaves similarly turned on the belief that the harsh conditions of enslavement reduced the body temperature of the slave, even if a noble-born male captive, so that he became more and more dull-witted, incapable of speech, less and less human, fit only for the labor which the masters imposed on him in the first place. The unity of word and deed celebrated by Perikles was experienced only by male citizens whose "nature" fitted them for it. The Greeks used the science of body heat, that is, to enact rules of domination and subordination.

Athens was not alone in subscribing to this ruling image of the body, in treating people in radically unequal ways based on it, and in organizing space according to its dictates. But the Athens of Perikles' time speaks to us in modern times as ancient Sparta perhaps does not in part because of how this master image of the body inaugurated crises in Athenian democracy. In his history, Thucydides returned to the themes of the Funeral Oration again and again; he feared the confidence Perikles expressed in the polity. Thucydides' history shows instead how at crucial moments men's faith in their own powers proved self-destructive; more, how Athenian bodies in pain could find no relief in the stones of the city. Nakedness provided no balm for suffering.

Thucydides tells a cautionary tale, then, about a great effort of self-display at the beginning of our civilization. In this chapter we shall pursue clues he provides about how this self-display was destroyed by the heat of words, by the flames of rhetoric. In the next chapter we shall explore the other side of the coin: how those who were cold bodies refused to suffer mutely, and instead sought to give their coldness a meaning in the city.

1. THE CITIZEN'S BODY

Perikles' Athens

To understand the city Perikles praised, we might imagine taking a walk in Athens in the first year of the war, beginning at the cemetery where he probably spoke. The cemetery lay beyond the city's walls at the northwestern edge of Athens—outside the walls because the Greeks feared the bodies of the dead: pollution oozed from those who had died violently, and all the dead might walk at night. Moving toward town, we would come to the Thriasian Gate (later named the Dipylon Gate), the main entrance to the city. The gate consisted of four monumental towers set around a central court. For the peaceful visitor arriving at Athens, a modern historian observes, the Thriasian Gate was "a symbol of the power and impregnability of the city."[7]

The walls of Athens tell the story of its rise to power. Athens originally developed around the Akropolis, a hilly outcrop which could be defended with primitive weapons. Perhaps a thousand years before Perikles, the Athenians built a wall to protect the Akropolis; Athens unfolded principally to the north of this, and somewhat incomplete evidence suggests that the Athenians walled in this new growth during the 600s B.C., but the early city was hardly a sealed fortress. Geography complicated the problem of defense because Athens, like many other ancient cities, lay near water but not on it; Piraeus, the harbor, stood four miles distant.

The lifeline connecting city and sea was fragile. In 480 B.C. the Persians overran Athens and the existing walls provided little protection; to survive, the city had to be sealed. In the 470s the fortifying of Athens began in earnest in two stages, the first girding the city itself, the second connecting the city to the sea. One wall ran down to Piraeus, the other to the smaller port of Phaleron east of Piraeus.

The walls signified a geography of bitter toil about which the Funeral Oration said nothing. The territory attached to Athens was far greater than the land enclosed by its walls. The countryside of Athens, or the *khora,* about 800 square miles, suited raising sheep and goats rather than cattle, growing barley rather than wheat. The land had been largely deforested by the 600s, which contributed to its ecological difficulties; the Greek farmer tended his olive trees and his grape vines by pruning them back sharply, a common practice throughout the Mediterranean which here further exposed the parched earth to the sun. So meager was the land that two thirds of Athens's grain had to be imported. The khora did yield silver, and after the security walls were finally in place, the countryside began to be intensively quarried for marble. But the rural economy was dominantly that of the small farm, worked by an individual land-holder with one or two slaves. The ancient world was as a whole overwhelmingly a world of agriculture, and "it is a conservative guess," writes the historian Lynn White, "that even in fairly prosperous regions over ten people were needed on the land to enable a single person to live away from the land."[8]

To Aristotle, as to other Greeks and indeed to elites in Western societies up to the modern era, the material struggle for existence seemed degrading; in fact, it has been observed, in ancient Greece there was no "word with which to express the general notion of 'labour' or the concept of labour 'as a general social function.' "[9] Perhaps one reason for this was the sheer, overwhelming need for the populace to toil, so much a condition of their lives that work was life itself. The ancient chronicler Hesiod wrote in his *Works and Days* that "Men never rest from toil and sorrow by day, and from perishing by night."[10]

This stressed economy made possible the civilization of the city. It put a bitter twist on the very meaning of the terms "urban" and "rural." In Greek these words, *asteios* and *agroikos,* can also be translated as " 'witty' and 'boorish.' "[11]

Once inside the gates, the city took on a less forbidding character. Entering the city through the Thriasian Gate, we come immediately into the heart of the Potters' Quarter *(Kerameikos)*. Potters concentrated near newer graveyards outside the walls and ancient grave sites within because the funeral urn was an essential marker of any burial. From the Thriasian Gate running in toward the center of the city lay an avenue dating from at least five hundred years before the age of Perikles; originally lined with giant vases, in the century before Perikles it began to be lined with smaller stone markers *(stelai)*, a sign of the Athenians' developing skill in carving stone. During this same century, other forms of trade and commerce developed along the avenue.

This main street was known as the *Dromos* or the Panathenaic Way. As one passes down the Panathenaic Way, the land falls, and the walker crosses the Eridanos, a small river cutting through the northern part of the city; the road then skirts the hill of Kolonos Agoraios, and one arrives in the central square of Athens, the agora. Before the Persians attacked the city, most of the buildings in the agora lay on the side of the Kolonos Agoraios; these buildings were the first to be remade after the disaster. In front of them lies a rhomboid-shaped open space of about ten acres. Here, in the open space of the agora, Athenians bartered and banked, politicked and paid obeisance to the gods.

If a tourist had strayed from the Panathenaic Way, quite another city would have appeared. The Athenian walls, about four miles in length, pierced by fifteen principal gates, ringed in a rough circle a city mostly thick with low-built houses and narrow streets. In the time of Perikles, this housing was densest in the southwest corner district called Koile. Athenian houses, usually a single story, were made of stones and high-fired bricks; if a family was affluent enough, the rooms would give out upon an interior walled courtyard or there would be a second story added. Most houses combined family and workplace, either as retail shops or as workshops. There were separate districts within the city for making or selling pots, grain, oil, silver, and marble statuary, in addition to the main market around the agora. The "grandeur that was Greece" was not to be seen in these districts smelling of urine and cooking oil, their street walls blank and dingy.

Leaving the agora by the Panathenaic Way, however, we would find the land begin to rise again, the route now ascending from the northwest below the walls of the Akropolis, the street culminating at the great entry house to the Akropolis, the Propylaia. Originally a fortress, by the early classical era the Akropolis hill had become exclusively a religious territory, a sacred preserve above the more diverse life in the agora. Aristotle believed this shift in space also made sense in terms of political changes in the city. In the *Politics,* he wrote, "A citadel [an akropolis] is suitable to oligarchy and one-man rule, level ground to democracy."[12] Aristotle supposed an equal horizontal plane between citizens. Yet the most striking building up on the Akropolis, the Parthenon, declared the glory of the city itself.

The Parthenon was begun in 447 B.C. and perhaps finally completed in 431 B.C., in place of an earlier temple. The making of the new Parthenon, in which Perikles actively participated, seemed to him an omen of Athenian virtue, for it represented a collective civic effort. The Peloponnesian enemies, he said in a speech before the war began, "cultivate their own land themselves," a condition for which he had complete contempt; "those who farm their own land are in warfare more anxious about their money than their lives." Unlike the Athenians, "they devote only a fraction of their time to their general interests, spending most of it on arranging their own separate affairs." Athens was stronger because "it never occurs [to her enemies] that the apathy of one will damage the interests of all."[13] The Greek word for city, *polis,* meant far more to an Athenian

The Acropolis of Athens, fifth century B.C. *Scala/Art Resource, N.Y.*

like Perikles than a place on the map; it meant the place where people achieved unity.

The Parthenon's placement in the city dramatized its collective civic value. Visible from many places in the city, from new or expanding districts as well as from older quarters, the icon of unity glinted in the sun. M. I. Finley has aptly called its quality of self-display, of being looked at, "out-of-doorness." He says, "In this respect nothing could be more misleading than our usual impression: we see ruins, we look through them, we walk about *inside* the Parthenon. . . . What Greeks saw was physically quite different. . . ."[14] The building exterior mattered in itself; like naked skin it was a continuous, self-sufficing, arresting surface. In an architectural object, a surface differs from a facade; a facade like the Cathedral of Notre Dame in Paris conveys the sense that the interior mass of the building has generated the exterior facade, while the Parthenon's skin of columns and roof does not look like a form pushed out from within. In this, the temple gave a clue to Athenian urban form more generally; urban volume came from the play of surfaces.

Even so, a short walk from the graveyard where Perikles spoke to the Parthenon would have shown the visitor the results of a great era of city building. This was particularly true of buildings which provided Athenians places to reveal themselves in talk. Outside the city's walls, the Athenians developed the academies in which the young were trained through debate rather than taught by rote learning. In the agora, the Athenians created a law court which could hold fifteen hundred people; built the Council House for debate about political affairs among five hundred leading citizens; constructed a building called the *tholos* in which daily business was debated among an even smaller group of fifty dignitaries. Near the agora, the Athenians had taken a natural, bowl-shaped side of the hill of the Pnyx and organized it into a meeting place for the entire citizenry.

The sheer fact of so much material improvement aroused great hope about the fortunes of the war just beginning. Some modern historians believe the Athenian idolization of the polis inseparable from the city's imperial fortunes; others that this collective whole served as a rhetorical abstraction, invoked only to punish errant individuals or control rebellious groups. But Perikles believed in it without suspicion. "Such a hope is understandable in men who had witnessed the swift growth of material prosperity after the Persian Wars," says the modern historian E. R. Dodds; "for that generation, the Golden Age was no lost paradise of the dim past, as Hesiod believed; for them it lay not behind but ahead, and not so very far ahead either."[15]

Body heat

The figures carved in stone round the outside of the Parthenon on the famous friezes called the "Elgin Marbles" revealed the beliefs about the naked human body which gave rise to these urban forms and hopes. These friezes are named in honor of the English nobleman who carted them from Athens to London in the nineteenth century, where the modern tourist sees them in the British Museum. The sculptured figures in part portrayed the Panathenaic procession during which the city of Athens paid homage to its founding and to its gods, the citizens wending through the city along the Panathenaic Way as we did and arriving at the Akropolis. The foundation of Athens was synonymous with the triumph of civilization itself over barbarism; "any Athenian . . . would naturally have thought of Athens as the protagonist in this struggle," points out the historian Evelyn Harrison.[16] The birth of Athena was depicted on the front gable of the Parthenon; on the opposite pediment the goddess struggles with Poseidon to serve as the patron of Athens; on the metopes Greeks struggle with Centaurs—half-horse, half-men—and Olympians with giants.

The Elgin Marbles were unusual because they brought together the vast crowd of human beings in the Panathenaic procession with such images of the gods. The sculptor Pheidias represented the human bodies in distinctive ways, first of all by carving them more boldly in the round than had other sculptors; this carving increases the reality of their presence near the gods. Indeed, the human beings depicted on the Parthenon friezes look more at home among the gods than they do, say, in friezes at Delphi. The Delphi sculptor emphasized the differences between gods and men, while Pheidias in Athens sculpted, in Philipp Fehls's phrase, "a subtle connection between the realms of gods and men that somehow has the appearance of an inherent necessity."[17]

The human figures on the Parthenon friezes are all young, perfect bodies, their perfections nakedly exposed, and their expressions equally serene whether they are tending an ox or mastering horses. They are generalizations about what human beings should look like, and contrasted, for instance, to a Zeus carved at Olympia a few years before; the god's body there was more an individual, his muscles

The Parthenon Sculptures: Horsemen preparing to mount, late fifth century B.C. *British Museum.*

showing signs of age and his face signs of fear. In the Parthenon friezes, the critic John Boardman has remarked, the image of the human body is "idealized rather than individualized ... other-worldly; [never was] the divine so human, the human so divine."[18] Ideal, young, naked bodies represented a human power which tested the divide between gods and men, a test the Greeks also knew could lead to tragic consequences; for love of their bodies, the Athenians risked the tragic flaw of *hubris,* of fatal pride.[19]

The source of pride in the body came from beliefs about body heat, which governed the process of making a human being. Those fetuses well heated in the womb early in pregnancy were thought to become males; fetuses lacking initial heat became females. The lack of sufficient heating in the womb produced a creature who was "more soft, more liquid, more clammy-cold, altogether more form-less than were men."[20] Diogenes of Apollonia was the first Greek to explore this inequality of heat, and Aristotle took up and expanded Diogenes' analysis, notably in his work *On the Generation of Animals.* Aristotle made a connection, for instance, between menstrual blood and sperm, believing that menstrual blood was cold blood whereas sperm was cooked blood; sperm was superior because it generated new life, whereas menstrual blood remained inert. Aristotle charac-terizes "the male as possessing the principle of movement and of generation, the female as possessing that of matter," a contrast between active and passive forces in the body.[21] The ancient physician Hippocrates made a different argument which led to the same end. He imagined two forms of sperm, strong and weak, contained in both the seminal and vaginal fluids of human beings; in Thomas Laqueur's summary of Hippocrates' view, "if both partners produce strong sperm, a male results; if both produce weak sperm, a female is born; and if in one partner the battle has gone to the weak and in the other to the strong, then the sex of the offspring is determined by the quantity of the sperm produced."[22] In this version, the result also produces a hotter male, a colder female fetus.

The Greeks did not invent the concept of body heat nor were they the first to join it to sex. The Egyptians, and perhaps even the Sumerians before them, understood the body thus; an Egyptian document, the Jumilhac Papyrus, ascribed "the bones to the male principle and the flesh to the female," bone marrow forming from semen, the fat in flesh coming from cool, female blood.[23] The Greeks refined Egyptian medicine: Aristotle thought the heat energy of the semen entered the flesh via the blood; male flesh was therefore hotter, and less likely to freeze. He thought a man's muscle was also firmer than a woman's because the male tissues were hotter.[24] The male could thus stand exposure and nakedness as female flesh could not.

The Greeks believed that "female" and "male" represented the two poles of a bodily continuum, whereas the Victorians, for example, treated menstruation and menopause as such mysterious female forces that men and women seemed almost different species. Laqueur describes this Greek view as one in which "at least two genders correspond to but one sex, where the boundaries between male and female are of degree and not of kind . . . a one-sex body."[25] Barely heated male fetuses became effeminate men; female fetuses heated beyond the norm produced butch women. Indeed, from this physiology of reproduction the Greeks derived principles for understanding the anatomies of men and women: the same organs were reversed in male and female genitalia. "Turn outward the woman's" vagina, Galen of Pergamum asked a medical student to imagine, and "turn inward . . . and fold double the man's penis, and you will find the same [structure] in both in every respect."[26] Galen's views would serve as scientific truth for nearly two thousand years, passing from Western antiquity, via Arab doctors, into Christian medicine of the Middle Ages, surviving the Renaissance, and ending only in the seventeenth century.

For most of Western history, medicine thus spoke about "the body"—one body, whose physiology moved from very cold to very hot, from very female to very male. Heat in the body seemed to govern people's power to see, to listen, to act and react, even to speak. In Perikles' time, this discourse began to cohere as a language of bodily stimulation. Two generations before him, for instance, people commonly believed that "one sees because light issues from the eye."[27] By the time of Perikles it was thought that the eye instead receives warming rays from an object. In his *On Sense and Sensible Objects,* Aristotle later argued that even the experience of transparency and empty space was such a physical experience; since light, which is a substance, impresses itself on the eye, images generate heat in the viewer.[28] Yet these warming rays are felt unequally by different human beings: the warmer the receiving body, the more intensely it responds to stimuli—as a roaring fire consumes a log more avidly than does a barely flickering fire. The cold body is sluggish in its responses, it heats more slowly.

Words seemed to make the same physical impress on the body's senses as did images, and the ability to respond to these verbal stimuli also depended on the degree of heat the receiving body contained. For Plato, phrases like "hot words" and "the heat of argument" were literal descriptions rather than metaphors; dialectic and debate warmed the bodies of the participants, while bodies which thought in solitude grew cold.[29] To be sure, by the Periklean age the Greeks had developed the habit of silent reading, a habit dramatized by the playwright Euripides in *Hippolytos;* reading required different mental habits than speaking.[30] Yet the Greeks did not have the modern, abstract experience of a "text": the Greek reader would have thought he heard the voices of real people speaking even on the page, and to revise a written text was like interrupting someone talking. Only when the body was alone, neither speaking nor reading, did its powers grow cold and sluggish.

This ancient understanding of body heat led to beliefs about shame and honor amongst human beings. The medical register passing from female, cold, passive, and weak, to male, hot, strong, and engaged formed a scale of ascending human worth; it treated males as superior to females made of the same materials. The modern historian Giulia Sissa observes that "When the feminine was included in the same sphere as the masculine . . . the result was not liberal acknowledgment of equality but dismissal of the female as 'obviously' inferior to the male."[31] This medical register also helped to contrast citizen and slave: at one end the slave's body, which has

grown dull and cold through lack of speech; at the other, the citizen
whose body has been warmed by the fires of debate in the assembly.
The fullness, serenity, and honor of those depicted naked on the
Parthenon friezes was inseparable from the shame of lesser bodies.
Honor and shame in the city derived from the Greek concept of
physiology.

To marshal the powers in a boy's naked body, his elders sent him to
the gymnasium. The modern word "gymnasium" comes from *gumnoi*
in Greek, which meant "stark naked."[32] The naked, beautiful body
seems a gift of Nature, but Thucydides, we recall, wrote about
nakedness as an achievement of civilization. The gymnasium taught
young Athenians how to become naked. In Athens there were three
gymnasia, the most important being the Academy, which a few generations after Perikles became Plato's school. To reach it on our
imaginary walk, we would have returned to the Thriasian Gate,
passed through, and walked along a broad pedestrian avenue shaded
by trees; the Academy lay about 1500 yards northwest of the gate.

   Rather than living in the Academy, students walked out to it from
the city during the day. The grounds of the Academy were ancient
shrines; during the democratic era, these grounds were transformed
into "a kind of suburban park."[33] Within the grounds was the *pal-
estra,* the rectangular building with colonnades which contained a
space for wrestling, general exercise rooms, and spaces for drinking
and talking. Some gymnasia put the wrestling school in a separate
building of its own. Aristophanes drew in *The Clouds* an idyllic picture of days spent in the gymnasia: in a modern paraphrase, "all this
healthy activity of clean-limbed young men makes a contrast with
the clever chatter of the pale, weedy, sophisticated *habitués* of the
agora."[34]

   The gymnasium sought to shape a boy's body at the point in middle to late adolescence when muscles began to tighten the skin surface but secondary sex characteristics, particularly facial hair, were
not yet advanced. This moment in the life cycle seemed critical to
marshalling the body's heat permanently in muscles. Through lifting
other boys when wrestling, the adolescent's back and shoulder muscles enlarged; the twisting and turning of the body in wrestling
cinched in the waist; when throwing the javelin or the discus, the
arm muscles stretched, when running, the leg muscles tightened, the
buttocks firmed up. Because boys coated their bodies with olive oil

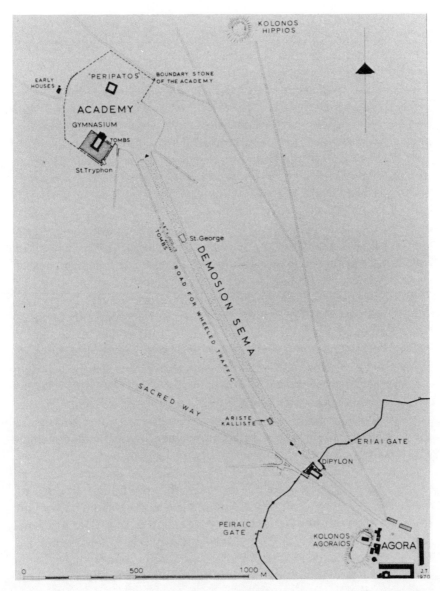

The northwest suburbs of Athens: the walk to the Academy, fourth century B.C.

when they exercised, in wrestling one another they tended to slither and slip; the grip of the hands was developed in counteracting the effects of the oil. Games served a physiological purpose also in raising body temperature through friction between bodies.

Just as the gymnasium trained male muscle, it trained the male voice, by teaching boys to compete with one another in words, a skill they would need to participate in the city's democracy. Training in debate occurred in Perikles' time through the intervention of ordinary citizens who wended their way out to the gymnasia. The first step involved showing a boy how to project his voice and articulate his words firmly. He was then taught to use words in the give and take of argument with the same economy of movement he learned in wrestling. The schools of Perikles' era had eschewed the rote learning of earlier ages; competition took the place of mechanical learning. Still, the boys were obliged to memorize vast swatches of Homeric poetry to be used as references in these debates.

Spartan gymnasia trained only the body, since the debating voice did not form part of the civic frame. Moreover, in Sparta the gymnasium aimed at developing a boy's sheer capacity to inflict body injury. For instance, the Spartan gymnasium was ringed by a moat; here, "the young Spartans fought one another ferociously and hurled one another into the water."[35] Sparta, it also should be said, was one of the few cities which encouraged girls to wrestle one another, but this was a utilitarian matter; exercise strengthened their bodies for childbirth. In Athens, the gymnasium trained boys' bodies for ends which transcended brute force.

It was in the gymnasium that a boy learned that his body was part of the larger collectivity called the *polis,* that the body belonged to the city.[36] A strong body obviously made a good warrior; a trained voice ensured the body could later participate in public affairs. The Athenian gymnasium taught a further lesson: the school trained a boy how to be naked sexually. Unlike modern moralists, the Athenians thought sexuality to be a positive element of citizenship. This was more than a matter of observing sexual prohibitions, like the belief that masturbation was fit only for slaves, with whom no one else would want to make love; more than a matter of imposing laws such as those forbidding slaves to go the gymnasia, "being in love with a boy of free status, or following him."[37] In the gymnasium a boy learned how use his body so that he could desire and be desired honorably.

As a Greek male passed through the life cycle, he would be loved by older men, then feel love for boys as he aged; he would also feel erotic love for women. The Greeks made a point of distinguishing "effeminacy," not "homosexuality" as we use the term, a distinction they based on the physiology of the body. Those with "soft" male bodies (*malthakoi* in Greek) acted like women; "they actively desire to be subjected by other men to a 'feminine' (i.e. receptive) role in sexual intercourse."[38] The malthakoi belonged to the intermediate heat zones between very male and very female. In the gymnasium, a boy was meant to learn the way to make love actively rather than passively as did the malthakoi.

A boy's tutor in love would be an older youth or adult man who had come out to the gymnasium to watch the wrestling and other games. The older male *(erastes)* sought out a younger *(eromenos)* for love; the age-line between the two usually lay in a particular second-ary sex characteristic, facial and body hair, though an eromenos had to have reached an adult height in order to be pursued. In his sixties, Socrates still had young lovers, yet more typically the erastes was a young man not yet, or just, married. The erastes paid compliments to the eromenos, gave him presents, and sought to fondle him. The public rooms of the gymnasium were not scenes of sex. Contacts were made here; when two males had reached a stage of mutual

Men making love, early fifth century B.C.

interest, they retired to the shelter of the gardens surrounding the gymnasium, or met again later at night in the city.

At this point, the sexual code dictated there should be no penetration of any orifice, neither fellatio nor anal intercourse. Instead, the boy and the man took the other's penis between their own thighs, rubbing and massaging. This rubbing was thought to raise the body heat of the lovers, and it was the heat men felt in bodily friction, rather than ejaculation, which focused sexual experience between two males. Coital friction as foreplay between a man and a woman was also thought to raise the body temperature of women, so that they had sufficient force to generate the fluids for birth.

In sex between men and women, the woman frequently crouched over, offering her buttocks to a man standing or kneeling behind

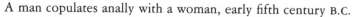

A man copulates anally with a woman, early fifth century B.C.

her. On the evidence of vase paintings, the classicist Kenneth Dover concludes that in this position, "there can be no room for doubt that it is the woman's anus, not her vagina, which is [often] being penetrated."[39] The Greeks, like many other cultures, found in anal intercourse both a distinctive pleasure and a simple, safe form of contraception. Yet it was a position which also expressed social status: the woman who lay down or bent over made herself subordinate. Similarly the effeminate male who sought to be penetrated lay in a subordinate position. In a trial brought against the Athenian Timarkhos for prostitution—a trial aiming to deprive him of citizenship—his accuser Aiskhines drew up a list of contrasts between sex unworthy of an Athenian and sex according with the future dignity of citizenship:

> adoption of a bent or lowered position, reception of another man's penis in the anus or mouth; [versus] refusal of payment, obdurate postponement of any bodily contact until the potential partner has proved his worth, abstention from any sensual enjoyment of such contact, insistence on an upright position, avoidance of meeting the partner's eye during consummation . . .[40]

Sex between men often occurred with both partners standing up. In this posture, eschewing penetration, performing the same act on one another, the male lovers are equal, despite their differing ages. In this posture, Aiskhines says, they make love as fellow citizens. Love occurs on the body's surface, parallel in value to the surfaces of urban space.

Greek culture made walking and standing expressions of character. Walking with long strides appeared manly; Homer wrote admiringly of Hector, "The Trojans drove forward in close throng, and Hector led them, advancing with long strides."[41] Whereas "when the goddesses Hera and Athena appeared before Troy to help the Greeks, they [according to Homer] resembled 'in their steps the timorous doves'—exactly the opposite of the striding heroes."[42] In the city, some of these archaic attributes persisted. Moving steadily, if slowly, marked a man as manly and well bred; "this is one trait which I regard worthy of no gentleman," the writer Alexis declared, "to walk in the streets with careless gait when one may do it gracefully."[43] Women were still to walk with short, halting steps, and a man showed himself "womanish" by doing so. Erect, equal, purposeful: in Greek, the word *orthos,* or "upright," carried the implications of male rectitude. Passivity, of the dishonorable sort thought to mark men who submitted to anal intercourse, contrasted to orthos.

This choreography of bodies in love shaped the behavior appropriate to citizens of Athens. Indeed, in the Funeral Oration, Perikles urged that citizens "should fall in love with" the city, using the erotic term for lovers, *erastai,* to express love for the city.[44] Thucydides gave Perikles a phrase to speak here which was common parlance, other Athenians employing the sexual term *erastai* to indicate those who love the city—the plays of Aristophanes also employ this usage.[45] An erotic bond between citizen and city, as between citizen and citizen, is what a boy first learned in the gymnasium, an active, upright love.

The Athenians made a direct analogy between body and building—not that they made buildings shaped like heads or fingers. Rather, they used their physiological understanding of the body to create urban form. For instance, on our imaginary walk through the agora, we passed a structure, the *stoa,* which bore the impress of this understanding. Basically a long shed, the stoa contained both cold and hot, sheltered and exposed dimensions; the back side of the stoa was walled in, the front side consisted of a colonnade which gave onto the open space of the agora. Though free-standing, the stoas were not in Perikles' day conceived as independent structures, but rather as edging for this open space. On the walled side of the shed, men gathered with a few others to talk, do business, or dine; dining rooms in public buildings were organized somewhat as in a house. Men wanted to dine and drink enclosed within solid walls, and thus people would not recline "with their backs turned to an open colonnade."[46] However, other people did not intrude, though they could perfectly well see within. When a man moved toward the unwalled side facing the agora, he could be noticed and approached; he was on the "male side, the side of exposure."[47]

Design also drew upon the lesson taught in the gymnasium that a boy's body could be molded somewhat like a work of art, the physiology of the body furnishing the raw materials. When the Parthenon's friezes were in place, they presented a scene of dramatically carved bodies which drew attention to the artistry of the sculptor and which "enabled the sculptor to compete with [dramatic] poetry," in the words of a modern commentator.[48] But the very size and shape of the Parthenon revealed more largely and politically the design implications of treating the body as a work of art.

The Parthenon built in Perikles' time was not quite like other Greek temples. It was about 230 feet long by 98 wide, which is a rough proportion of 9 to 4, a proportion that rules in many of the interior spaces as well, and a new measure in Greek temples. The columns outside also were unusual. Greek temples had a regular shape, often six columns along the front and thirteen along the side; the Parthenon had eight and seventeen. These odd measures derived from the need to house a gigantic female figure within, a statue of Athena. The sculptor Pheidias rendered Athena as a goddess of war, Athena Parthenos—from whom derives the name of the structure—rather than the Athena Polias of old, a goddess of the womb and of the soil whose sacred statue, kept elsewhere on the Akropolis, was small and made of wood. Now that Athens was a seafaring empire rather than a small city struggling to live off the land around its walls, the Parthenon celebrated the city's patron goddess in light of its own increased power in a temple whose dimensions broke with the regularities of the past.

The interior of the Parthenon divided into two rooms: in the rear, a treasury; in the front, the room containing this statue of Athena. Athena Parthenos was forty feet tall, and the impression of her height was reinforced by a reflecting pool set at the figure's base; a human being stands barely as high as the plinth on which Athena was set. She had a bronze body, but wore a dress of gold and chryselephantine, a golden dress some thirty-four feet tall; her arms and face exposed an ivory skin laid over the metal flesh. The pool kept her ivory moist as well as seeming to reflect her image deep into the earth. Perikles justified the expense of this gigantic new Athena by arguing that her golden dress could be removed and melted down, if necessary, to pay for Athens' wars—a sacred icon which could be physically violated when the state needed cash. Thus the patron body of the city put its impress on the dimensions of the most prominent building in the city.

If the gymnasium, the stoa, and the Parthenon showed the influence of the body in an urban form, these patterns do not quite show what were the consequences when Perikles asked the Athenians to become erastai of the city. The Athenians needed a spatial design which would gratify that love. More, Perikles' Funeral Oration was a hymn to democracy in Athens based upon the powers of the human voice. The Athenians sought to design spaces for the speaking voice which would strengthen its bodily force, in particular to give to the single, sustained, exposed speaking voice the honorable qualities of bodily nakedness. Yet these urban designs often failed to serve the voice in the way the designs intended; the naked voice in them became an instrument of misrule and disunity.

2. THE CITIZEN'S VOICE

Athens packed bodies together in two kinds of spaces, each of which gave the crowd a distinctive experience of spoken language. In the agora, many activities happened at once, people moving about, speaking in little knots about different things at the same time. No one voice usually dominated the whole. In the theatres of the ancient city, people sat still and listened to a single, sustained voice. Both of these spaces posed dangers to language. In the simultaneous and shifting activities of the agora, the babble of voices easily scattered words, the mass of moving bodies experiencing only fragments of sustained meaning. In the theatre, the single voice shaped itself into a work of art through the techniques of rhetoric; the spaces where people listened were so organized that the spectators often became victims of rhetoric, paralyzed and dishonored by its flow.

Spaces to speak

Although the life of the agora was open to all citizens, rich and poor, most of the ceremonial and political events that occurred here were out of bounds to the immense population of slaves and foreigners (*metics*) who supported the economy of the ancient city. One estimate puts the number of citizens in Attica during the fourth century B.C. at 20,000–30,000 out of a total population of 150,000 to 250,000; certainly throughout the classical era citizens comprised never more than 15 to 20 percent of the total population, or half the adult male population. And only a minority of those citizens possessed enough wealth to live leisurely, spending hour after hour, day after day among their fellow citizens, talking and debating: the leisure class composed from 5 to 10 percent of the citizenry. To be a member of the leisure class, a citizen needed a fortune of at least 1 talent, which was 6,000 drakhmas; a skilled laborer earned a drakhma a day.

Immersion in the fluctuating and intense life of the agora every day moreover required the citizen to live nearby. But a large slice of the members of this city-state lived far from the agora, outside the city walls in the khora; at the end of the fifth century, about 40 percent of the citizens lived further than 15 miles from the center. To live so far away meant a walk on foot of at least four hours to the agora over the pitted and uneven roads of the unloved countryside.

The agora of Athens, ca. 400 B.C.

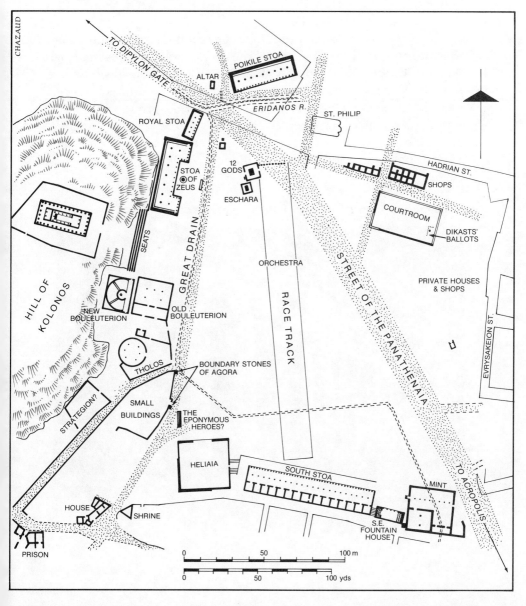

Those who could participate found in the agora many discrete and distinct activities occurring at once, rather than sheer chaos. There was religious dancing on the open flat ground, in a part of the agora called the *orkhestra;* banking took place at tables set out in the sun behind which the bankers sat facing their customers. Athenians celebrated religious rites out in the open, and within sacred ground such as a sanctuary called the "Twelve Gods" located just north of the orkhestra. Dining and dealing, gossiping and religious observance took place in the stoas, which in Periklean times lined the west and north sides of the agora. Siting the stoas on the north made them usable in winter, their walled backs turned to the wind, their colonnaded fronts open to the sun.

The most famous stoa, the Poikile or "painted" stoa, built sometime near 460 on the north side of the agora, looked across the Panathenaic Way to the Akropolis; John Camp points out that, "unlike most of the other stoas in the Agora, it was not built for any specific purpose or activity or for the use of a single group of officials. Rather, it seems to have served the needs of the populace at large, providing shelter and a place to meet just off the Agora square." Here crowds watched "sword-swallowers, jugglers, beggars, para-

A stoa in the agora of Athens, fourth century B.C.

sites, and fishmongers ... [and] philosophers."[49] And here Zeno would later found the philosophic movement called Stoicism; the suspension from worldly engagement advocated by Stoicism originated rather oddly in this place of fripperies and fun.

The evolution of Athenian democracy shaped the surfaces and the volume of the agora, for the movement possible in simultaneous space served participatory democracy well. By strolling from group to group, a person could find out what was happening in the city and discuss it. The open space also invited casual participation in legal cases. The Athenians of the democratic era were famous for their love of legal battles. A character in *The Clouds* points to a map, saying, "Here is Athens," and receives the reply, "I don't believe you, I see no jurymen sitting."[50] Although the archeological evidence is uncertain, probably the main popular law court of the city, the *Heliaia,* stood at the southwest corner of the agora. The building itself dated from an earlier era of tyranny, but benefited from the body flows of synchrony. The law court was an immense unroofed space which could hold up to fifteen hundred people. (A "jury" had to consist of at least 201, was more often 501 persons, and could comprise as many as 1,500.) The walls enclosing this large space were low, perhaps three feet high. Thus from the outside anyone could look in, and jurors and people passing by could discuss the formal arguments.

In the open space of the agora the Athenians did their most serious political business: ostracism, or sending people into exile from the city. Once a year all citizens met to decide if particular individuals were becoming so powerful that they threatened to be tyrants; speeches were made, a list was drawn up. Two months later the citizens reconvened. The prospect of ostracism, particularly during the two months allotted for reflection, offered nearly endless possibilities for horse trading, deep gossip, whispering campaigns, working dinners—the debris of political tides washing over the agora again and again. When the citizens reconvened, if any man received more than 6,000 votes, he spent the next ten years in exile.

Orthos ruled bodily behavior in the agora. A citizen sought to walk purposefully and as swiftly as he could through the swirl of other bodies; when he stood still, he made eye contact with strangers. Through such movement, posture, and body language, he sought to radiate personal composure. The art historian Johann Winckelmann said that a group of such bodies in the agora composed something like a tableau of bodily order in the midst of diversity.[51]

What happens when six thousand bodies are pressed together? By modern crowd measures this is a medium to medium-high density in a space of ten acres; it is less dense than a football crowd, more dense than the crowd in a typical shopping mall, approximate to the midday density in the square of modern Siena. In modern crowds, a mass of this size tends to separate into knots of thirty to fifty, each knot turning its back to its proximate neighbors and withdrawing from those whose backs are turned. Thus the crowd becomes many crowds, the visibility of the individual body enclosed within each subcrowd. We know the ancient Athenians found that in the agora a crowd of six thousand people could not act swiftly, a difficulty they sought to remedy in specialized buildings. The *Tholos,* for instance, housed the rotating executive committee of city, a group of fifty of the town's councilmen. This body met every day and night of the year—seventeen of the fifty were always on duty in the Tholos, so that at Athens there would be constantly a small group of people who were in charge, ready to meet all emergencies.

We know also that later ancient observers found that the diversity of the agora disturbed their sense of political decorum and gravity. In the *Politics,* for instance, Aristotle recommended that "The market square for buying and selling should be separate from the public square and at a distance from it."[52] Aristotle was no enemy of diversity; elsewhere in the *Politics* he wrote, "a city is composed of different kinds of men; similar people cannot bring a city into existence."[53] Nor did he write as a modern conservative, arguing that government shouldn't interfere with the market. On the contrary, he thought mixing economics and politics demeaned politics, particularly the administration of justice. Other later commentators argued similarly for affirming the "majesty of the law" in its own space by using the language of orthos; the magistrates in all their dignity must be seen, the dignity of their bearing apparent to the populace, not lost in a crush.[54]

We know most of all that, if order in the agora scene was imposed by bodily comportment, comportment alone could not counter the effects of simultaneous activities on the human voice. In the swirling crowd conversations fragmented as bodies moved from knot to knot, an individual's attention broke and shifted. The Athenians created a place for a more sustained experience of language in the Council House *(Bouleuterion)* on the west side of the agora, employing there a principle of design contrary to that of simultaneity.

The building housed a group of five hundred men who organized the agenda of business to be discussed by the citizens at large, and who met here every day except for the sixty public holidays of the Athenian calendar and a small number of "cursed" days when it was tempting the wrath of the gods to rule oneself. Although the Bouleuterion dated from an earlier era of tyranny, its form was put to democratic uses. The remaining evidences of the building show it had vertically raked seats, as in a theatre. The Council sat here, listening to a speaker who stood at the base. This shape made certain that a speaker could be seen by all his auditors, and that each of them could see one another. No tide of strolling bodies disturbed this confrontation of speaker and audience. The Council House was indeed somewhat insulated from the hubbub of the agora, a discreet building which "did not take the prominent place one would expect in the architecture of the agora," the archeologist R. E. Wycherley remarks, "and was a little awkward of access."[55] The walls of the Bouleuterion were high, the building roofed; someone outside could not simply peek or stroll in. The space thus sustained a single voice, its words unfolding; the seating form focused the councilors' attention upon that sound. The space which concentrated attention on the voice also created a regime of visual surveillance: because of the raked seating, councilors could be clearly identified as to how they voted. This couldn't happen as easily among a mass of people equalized at ground level, where one could see at most the reactions of one's immediate neighbors.

In 510 B.C., at the end of the reign of tyranny, almost all the words men had to speak to one another could be spoken in the agora. By 400 B.C., when democracy had been durably established in Athens, the temptations of tyranny resisted, spaces for speech had dispersed from the agora to various other parts of the city. The agora ceased, in the middle of the fifth century, to be a center for drama. In the old agora, the city erected temporary wooden stands in the open-air orkhestra when new plays were presented; sometime in the mid-fifth century these wooden stands collapsed during one of the annual festivals, and a durable theatre instead was carved out of the southern slope of the Akropolis, a theatre shaped into a bowl of seats at whose bottom the dancers and actors performed. In the same period, much of the music performed in the open-air agora shifted to the *Odeion,* a roofed hall for musical contests. The agora did not decline; it continued to fill with stoas and temples. The Assembly of all citizens still met in the agora to conduct ostracism; the law courts brimmed with people; the streets giving into the agora expanded as a central market. But now the agora was not the dominant space of the voice; in particular, its diversity no longer fully encompassed the voice of power.

Early Greek theatres were simply hills which needed only a bit of terracing to provide a place for people to sit in order to see dancers, poets, or athletes. In this position, what happens in front of a person matters much more than on the sides or behind him. Originally, the seats on the terraces were wooden benches; the theatre evolved into a system of wide aisles separating more narrow bands of stone seats. This made it easier for people not to disturb others by their comings and goings; a spectator's attention could stay focused on the frontal plane. The word "theatre" derives from the Greek *theatron,* which can be rendered literally "a place for seeing." A *theoros* is also an ambassador, and theatre indeed is a kind of ambassadorial activity, bringing a story from another time or place to the eyes and ears of the spectators.

In an outdoor theatre, the orkhestra, or dancing place, consisted of a circle of hard earth at the bottom of the fan of seats; behind this, the theatre architects in time developed a wall called the *skene,*

The theatre at Epidauros, fourth century B.C. *Scala/Art Resource, N.Y.*

originally made of cloth, later of wood, still later of stone. The action of a play by Periklean times unfolded in front of the cloth or wood skene, the actors preparing themselves behind it. The skene helped project the voice, but the greater physical power the theatre gave to the voice lay in the raking of seats. Acoustically, a voice speaking in such a raked space increases in volume two to three times compared to ground level, since the rake stops the sound from dispersing. A raked space of course also increases the clarity with which people can see over the heads of their neighbors in a crowd, but the rake doesn't magnify the size of the image as a movie camera does. The ancient theatre tied clear visual perception of a far-away figure to a voice which sounded nearer than it looked.

The magnifying of the actor's voice, and the viewer's sight of him, was related to the divide in the ancient theatre between actor and spectator. There is a purely acoustical reason for this divide: the voice of someone up in raked seats in an open-air theatre is diminished by dispersal as it travels down below, and fainter than it would sound on flat land. Moreover, by the time of Perikles, the skills of the actor had become highly refined and specialized.

The theatre at Delphi, fourth century B.C. *Scala/Art Resource, N.Y.*

This divide had great importance in theatre spaces used for politics. In Athens during the fifth century B.C., the use of a theatre for politics took place on the hill of the Pnyx, a ten-minute walk southwest from the agora. The Pnyx Hill, a bowl-shaped piece of land resembling the hillsides used for other theatres, first served for large political meetings around 500, a few years after Hippias the tyrant was overthrown. The siting of the hill meant that the audience faced into the north wind, while the speaker faced into the south sun as he stood, his face deprived of any concealing shadow. In the Periklean Pnyx, so far as is known, no backdrop existed behind the speaker: his voice came to the audience out of the immense space of the land which lay behind him, the sole mediation between the mass of citizens and that panorama of hills and sky.

The buildings of the agora were built without a master plan, and apart from retaining "an unpaved open area of about ten acres in the center, there is no discernible single idea behind [Athens'] agora architecture."[56] The theatre fan, by contrast, is a tight design, organizing a crowd in vertical rows, magnifying the lone voice below, exposing the speaker to all, his every gesture visible. It is an architecture of individual exposure. Moreover, this tight design affected the seated spectators' experience of themselves. As the historian Jan Bremmer points out, sitting carried as much value in Greek culture as did standing and walking, but a more ambivalent value. By the time of Perikles, the gods were often sculpted in sitting positions, for instance, during feasts of the gods. Yet to sit was also to submit, as when a young girl came to the house of her new husband and signified her submission to his rule in a ritual which made her sit for the first time by his hearth. Vase paintings depict urban slaves, also, performing their tasks either sitting or crouching down.[57] The theatre put this aspect of sitting to use in tragedy: the seated audience was literally in a position to empathize with a vulnerable protagonist, for both the spectators' and the actors' bodies were placed in a "humble, submissive position to higher law." The Greek tragic theatre showed the human body, the classicist Froma Zeitlin observes, "in an unnatural state of *pathos* (suffering), when it falls farthest from its ideal of strength and integrity. . . . Tragedy insists . . . on exhibiting this body."[58] In this sense, pathos was opposed to orthos.

Whereas the open-air life of the agora took place mostly among walking and standing bodies, the Pnyx made political use of such sitting, spectator bodies. They had to do the work of governing themselves, from a passive and vulnerable posture. In this posture they listened to the naked voice speaking below.

The heat of words

The consequences became evident in the meetings of the *Ekklesia,* or Assembly of all citizens, convened forty times a year on the Pnyx. Entry gates controlled access to the building; at the gates the city paid all citizens a stipend for attendance, in an effort to counteract dominance by the leisure class. Meetings started early in the morning, and lasted half the daylight hours; again, this helped the poorer citizens, who could work the rest of the day. The meetings on the Pnyx began with a prayer, then dealt with the agenda which had been set by the smaller Council in the Bouleuterion. There were prepared speeches, then voting by a show of hands as well as by ballot.

Let us suppose we are among the Ekklesia in the Pnyx on a day in 406 B.C., in the penultimate phases of the Peloponnesian War, when politic strife in the city had come to a boil.[59] During the sea battle of Arginoussai, some Athenian sailors had been left to drown by their commanders. In the Pnyx, the herald of the day asks, in the traditional fashion, "Who wishes to speak?" At a previous meeting the Athenian citizen Theramenes proposed that the city condemn the commanders. Xenophon tells us that the commanders had ably defended themselves, pleading a violent storm at sea: "with such arguments they were on the point of convincing the ekklesia; many citizens were standing up and offering to go bail for them." But then time ran out on the discussion. Today, Kallixenos, an ally of Theramenes, puts the proposal for condemnation once more.

He invokes the procedure for identifying the voters in the most serious cases of decision making, asking that "all the Athenians do now proceed to hold a ballot by tribes, that for each tribe there shall be two urns," one in which the stone ballots for forgiving the commanders be placed, the other for punishing them. Each tribe within the city can thus be held accountable for its decision based on the debate.

A feint then occurs by the commanders' supporters: the procedure is against the constitution, they say, since this is a matter for the courts. In response, "the great mass shouted out that it was monstrous if the People were not allowed to do whatever they pleased." The military partisans are intimidated by the violence of popular reaction, and they give in, all "except Socrates . . . who said he would do nothing contrary to law."

Now the defense of the commanders begins. A leading citizen, Euryptolemos, uses once again the successful arguments of the previous session. He then moves that the commanders be tried separately, going against the Council's advice in the Bouleuterion that they be tried en masse. First the citizens, by a simple show of hands, vote in favor of the proposal. However, Menekles, a prominent citizen, objects after the vote is taken, and he is able to sway the crowd, who change their vote; the commanders will be judged en masse. Debate thickens from speakers at the speaker's stand, the citizens vote to condemn the men, a flip from the popular passion on their behalf in the previous session, and those of the officers in Athens at the moment are put to death. Yet the story hasn't finished. Xenophon says that "not long afterwards, however, the Athenians repented and voted that preliminary complaints be lodged against those who had deceived the People."

What happened in this lurching, contradictory flow of events which culminated in execution followed by mutual recrimination? The event itself took place far away, outside the city. Xenophon tells us the commanders had been given less than the time legally their due, but they had argued passionately on their own behalf. They had at first succeeded in swaying the people by dramatizing the power of the storm, arousing imaginative empathy with the navy's plight. The defenders of the commanders in the second meeting of the Ekklesia, however, made a strategic error. They challenged the people's right to decide. This broke the spell, and the people began to turn against them. Then Menekles and other speakers refigured the event, so that the crowd saw human cowardice in their minds, rather than natural disaster. The commanders were killed. Having acted in this irrevocable fashion, the people sought to revoke it, and turned on those who persuaded. Theirs were deceiving voices.

To Xenophon and other ancient observers of democracy, it was the power of rhetoric which rocked the Ekklesia from side to side. The powers of rhetoric were those of *peitho*, which means gaining the acquiescence of others by force of words rather than force of arms. If this seems eminently desirable, the destructive side of rhetoric appeared in the legends told about the goddess Pandora, for instance by Hesiod: Pandora's seductive *peitho* engendered "lies and specious words and sly ways . . . to be the ruin of men and their business."[60]

Words seemed to raise the temperature of the body; the Greeks took literally expressions like "the heat of passion," or "in flaming words." Rhetoric constituted the techniques for generating verbal heat. The "lies and sly ways" of rhetoric which Hesiod feared showed the power of art to affect the human organism. This body-art deployed "tropes," or figures of speech, in such a way that a mass of people could become aroused. The Greek tropes of political rhetoric were drawn in large part from the rich store of Homeric legend and poetry, and the orator who sought to sway a crowd had to know his Homer thoroughly. The Greeks—most famously Plato but many more ordinary people as well—feared these invocations as perverse, particularly because the orator often simulated the heat of passion in order to stimulate it in others.

The orator like the actor deals in illusions, but illusion has a very different value in drama than it has in politics. At the beginning of Sophokles' *Oedipus Tyrannus,* a spectator might tell his neighbor that tonight "Oedipus will blind himself because he killed his father and slept with his mother"; knowing this, his neighbor will not then rise and leave. This plot summary is information rather than experience. In a drama, the spectator submits to verbal experience which develops through jolting confrontation, reversals, and twists. At each of these steps, meaning accumulates: gradually we understand—in an understanding which transcends plot information—that Oedipus will have to pay a terrible price, there is no going back, there is no deal he can cut to escape his fate.

In the debate over the commanders, the orators had of necessity to create an illusion through words, because the event happened somewhere else and all witnesses save the accused were dead. Yet in the passage from one rhetorical voice to another meaning did not accumulate. This lack showed as the Ekklesia lurched backward and forward over how to try the commanders; the commanders were put to death, and then the people sought to undo the undoable, blaming those who swayed them. There was no narrative accumulation, no logical flow. Instead, each speaker made the audience re-see the drowning sailors anew, so that the audience redrew their image of the abandoned men on the speaker's own terms. The better an orator, the more he cut loose from debating on his opponent's turf; through refiguration, he made the audience feel things his own way. The lone voice takes possession of an audience in political rhetoric, while in the theatre action accumulates precisely because the characters become more interdependent, even when they are in conflict.

The Athenians knew and feared the dangerous powers of a single, exposed voice possessing rhetorical skill. "The courts, like the Assembly, ran on a fuel of sophisticated rhetoric which the Athenians recognized was potentially corrosive to the machinery of the state."[61] The citizens recognized they could be manipulated by rhetoric and rhetorically skilled politicians, and in time, as Josiah Ober points out, the skilled speaker (usually a highly educated man, reading a speech commissioned from a professional writer) learned to manage the fear of his listeners so that he would manipulate them; he sought, for instance, to portray himself as a simple man of the people unaccustomed to public speaking, stuttering at first or losing his place.

The naked warriors carved on the Parthenon friezes convened an ideal serenity. The exposed voice of the orator did not lead to the same result: the powerful orator often instilled disorder among the listeners he moved, his words heating them into confusion. Perhaps the most telling incident in the trial of the commanders was the anger the citizens felt once they voted for the execution of the seven generals. The executions occurred in a secret place, as was the custom with state murders. This denouement deprived the people of experiencing anything more; their two great points of anger in the affair were when they felt they might not be allowed to hear arguments, and the day after, when action rendered all further argument pointless. After this decisive moment, the people sought to undo their decision, by arguing about who had deceived them, as though the action had cheated them. This was a common pattern in Athenian democracy: a vote taken, then taken away, an irresolution and instability in translating words into action which, in this case, could not be reversed.

The political process in the Pnyx could thus stray far from Perikles' belief in the unity of words and deeds in the polis. The powerful heat in the body, the pride in nakedness and exposure: this master image of the body did not lead to collective self-control in the body politic. The Athenians indeed suffered from *hubris,* from a bodily aspiration which stepped beyond the bounds of social control. Thucydides said in general that "what made war inevitable was the growth of Athenian power and the fear which this caused in Sparta," Athens having grown larger than was her natural measure by population, economy, or right.[62] And he saw, more finely, how the powers of rhetoric might constitute such hubris. The unravelling of Perikles' dream became evident by 427, when the entire ancient world seemed convulsed by the power of words. "To fit in with the change of events," Thucydides writes of the worsening conditions of war, "words, too, had to change their usual meanings . . . any idea of moderation was just an attempt to disguise one's *unmanly character;* ability to understand a question from all sides meant that one was totally unfitted for action." The flux of rhetoric had grown so passionate that "anyone who held violent opinions could always be trusted, and anyone who objected to them became a suspect."[63] The heat of words had made the combatants incapable of acting rationally.

Could the shaping of stones provide men some control over the heat of their flesh? Could the power to reason be *built* in the city? The Athenians grappled half-successfully with this question in the design of the place in which the stream of words was set free.

To act rationally requires one to take responsibility for one's acts. In the small Bouleuterion seated voters could be individually identified, and so held responsible for their decisions. The organizers of the Pnyx sought to do the same in the larger political theatre. The theatre's clear design, its raked fan of seats with regular terraces and aisles, made it possible for the spectators to know other men's reactions to speeches and how they voted, forming a contrast to the visual imprecision of the agora, where a person would have trouble seeing more than the few neighbors standing immediately nearby.

Moreover, in the Pnyx people had an assigned seat of some kind. The details of how seating worked are unclear; some historians have argued persuasively that throughout the Pnyx people sat according to the tribe to which they belonged. There were originally ten tribes of the city, later twelve or thirteen, and in both its early and later configurations the Pnyx was divided into wedges for them.[64] Each tribe occupied a wedge.[65] When votes were made by ballot in the Pnyx, the ballots—made of stones—were cast by tribes or by *demes* (a unit of local government), each group putting the ballots into stone urns, which were then counted and announced for that particular group.

In a democracy, responsibility and self-control are collective acts—they belong to the people. When Kleisthenes introduced democratic reforms in Athens in 508, he declared that the people possessed the power of *isegoria,* which can be translated as "equality in the agora."[66] Equality in the agora led to freedom of speech, which the Athenians called *parrhesia.* Yet this freedom would not alone

suffice democracy; it invited the perils of rhetorical flux. Another of
Kleisthenes' reforms sought to combat that peril, by making groups
of citizens collectively responsible for the decisions they took. No
matter how groups fluctuated in their opinions under the sway of
words, they were jointly responsible for whatever decision they
arrived at—even though a particular tribe might have believed the
decision was wrong. They were responsible for the decision because
they participated in the process which led to it. In practice, this
meant that after a vote, the polity's knowledge of who voted how
might be used against a tribe or a section of the city; the group could
be denied money or services, or reproached in court. The Kleis-
thenic reform aimed at making the people as a whole, not only individuals, take responsibility for the verbal process of democracy.

Yet the Pnyx, whose clear design emphasized the seriousness of
attending to words, put the people literally in a vulnerable position.
They could be responsible for their acts only if they did not move,
but in this immobile position, they became the prisoners of single
voices. The master image of bodily power did not create civic unity:
the code of sexuality affirming equality, harmony, and mutual integrity could not be recreated in politics. The citizen's body in its political posture was instead nakedly exposed to the powers of the voice
in the same way we sometimes speak of someone who is naked as
defenseless. From this political duality arose the seated "pathos" of
which Froma Zeitlin writes: the pathos of experiencing the heat of
passion in a passive body.

The story I have told here is not how Athenian democracy failed
as an ideal. Rather, it is a story of the contradictions and stresses the
people experienced in a democracy which celebrated the human
body in a particular way. The master image of a naked body fragmented in stone; the exposed voice became a force of disunity in
urban space.

This Athenian story is sometimes framed in terms of a split
between mind and body. In the modern era we often think of the
mind-body split as a matter of arid mental constructs repressing the
sensate life of the body. But at the opening of our civilization the
problem was reversed: the body ruled the word, and estranged men's
power to live rationally through the unity of word and deed which
Perikles celebrated in the Funeral Oration. The heat of the body, as
expressed in democratic rhetoric, led people to lose rational control
in argument; the heat of words in politics lacked as well the narrative
logic which it possessed in the theatre. The Athenians were unable

to create a remedial design in stone; in the Pnyx the people became responsible for their acts but not in control of them.

If the terms of this split between body and mind have altered in the course of our history, the divide itself which began at our origins has persisted; it signifies that in our history, the "human" stands for dissonant and unreconciled forces. With the advent of Christianity, this conflict will come to seem necessary and inevitable, the human animal an animal at war with itself, due to the Fall and exile from the Garden. In the ancient world, the Greeks confronted that truth by another path, in their experience of urban rituals.

CHAPTER TWO

The Cloak of Darkness

The Protections of Ritual in Athens

The Parthenon is a hymn to a female deity, a woman reigning over the city. Yet Perikles drew his Funeral Oration to an end by declaring, "Perhaps I should say a word or two on the duties of women to those among you who are now widowed. I can say all I have to say in a short word of advice." The advice was to be silent. He declared that ". . . the greatest glory of a woman is to be least talked about by men, whether they are praising you or criticizing you."[1] In returning to the city, women should again return to the shadows. No more were slaves and resident foreigners entitled to speak in the city, since they too were all cold bodies.

Although Perikles addressed the Funeral Oration to the living, he—like other Greeks—imagined he was also overheard by the ghosts of the dead. The dead had lost all body heat, yet their shades haunted the living, remaining powerful forces of good or bad fortune. Cold was allied to darkness, the underworld the home of the

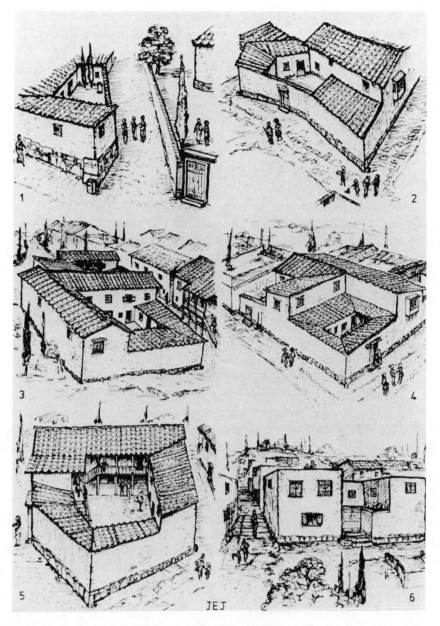

Athenian houses, late fifth and fourth centuries B.C.

shades. Yet lack of heat and light were not hopeless conditions. Those who were cursed with living cold bodies made something of their condition by practicing certain rituals, rituals which threw over themselves a cloak of darkness. These ancient rituals show an enduring aspect of our civilization: the refusal of the oppressed to suffer passively, as though pain were an unalterable fact of nature. That refusal to suffer had, however, its own limits.

1. THE POWERS OF COLD BODIES

In the Funeral Oration, Perikles spoke in a curiously offhand way about the rituals of the city. He said that "When our work is over, we are in a position to enjoy all kinds of recreation for our spirits. There are various kinds of contests and sacrifices regularly throughout the year."[2] As a modern historian has remarked, this is "a very pragmatic view of community religion"; his fellow Athenians would have taken the calendar of festivals to be the very core of their civic lives rather than "relaxation from business."[3]

Ritual may seem a static force, preserving memory through repeating gestures and words time after time. In the ancient world rituals instead modulated as old forms came to serve new needs. Rituals which honored women's place in an earlier agricultural society modulated in time so that bodily stigma was lifted from women in the city. The shift from agrarian myth into urban ritual did not violate memories of the past, nor did women use ritual to rebel against men. Though the greatest of all rituals in Athens, the *Panathenaia*, mixed men and women together, rituals which women observed alone revealed this power of modulating the past into the present more sharply. One of these, the *Thesmophoria*, aimed to dignify the cold female body; another, the *Adonia*, restored to women those powers of speech and desire Perikles denied them in the Funeral Oration.

The Thesmophoria

The Thesmophoria began as a fertility rite. It dated back to pre-Homeric times, a ritual women conducted in the late autumn when seed was to be sown. Demeter, goddess of the earth, presided as divine patron. The festival's story came from Demeter's burial and mourning for her dead daughter, Persephone; the name came from its main action, that of laying things in the earth (*thesmoi* in Greek means "laying down" in the broad sense of laying down the law). Women prepared for the Thesmophoria with a ritual act making use of pigs—treated in Greek mythology as animals of sacred value. At the end of each spring, they took slaughtered pigs down into pits, or *megara,* dug into the ground; here the dead animals were left to putrefy. This spring festival in honor of Demeter (the *Scirophoria*) served directly as a symbol of fertilizing the earth. Demeter's sanctuary at Elevsis lay outside Athens. The Thesmophoria conducted in Athens in the fall transformed this simple act of fertilizing the earth into an urban experience.

On the first of the three days of the Thesmophoria, women went into the pits containing the moist remains of the pigs, and mixed grain seed into the carcasses. This day was a matter of "going" (*kathodos*) and "rising up" (*anodos*), for the women rose from the cave to enter into special huts where they sat and slept on the ground. On the second day, the women fasted, to commemorate Persephone's death; they mourned by swearing and cursing. On the third day, they retrieved the grain-rich piglets, and this stinking mush was sown into the earth later as a kind of sacred compost.[4]

The Thesmophoria seemed to represent directly the story of Demeter as the Perikleans knew it, a story of death and rebirth, of the goddess who gives up her own daughter to the soil, a surrender paralleled by the slaughter and burial of the piglets. Yet the ritual as practiced in Athens altered the original, agricultural myth. Instead of opposing fertility and sterility, the Thesmophoria invoked sexual abstinence as opposed to fertility. For three days before the Thesmophoria the women did not sleep with their husbands, as well as being sexually abstinent during the festival. The ritual thus changed from the mourning of a daughter whose dead body nourishes the earth to a drama organized around the theme of self-control.

In a haunting passage, the classicist Jean-Pierre Vernant has evoked the ritual as practiced in Athens:

> The time of sowing marks the beginning of the period that is propitious for marriage; married women, mothers of families, celebrating as citizens accompanied by their legitimate daughters an official ceremony in which they are, for the time being, separated from their husbands; silence, fasting and sexual abstinence; they take up an immobile position, crouching down on the ground; they climb down into underground *megara* to collect talismans of fertility to be mixed in with seeds; a slightly nauseous smell prevails, and instead of aromatic plants

there are clumps of willow branches, the willow being a plant with anti-aphrodisiac qualities.[5]

The smell of the desire-deadening willow was important during the rite, as was the foul odor and the darkness of the huts in which the women crouched on the ground. Their bodies became still and cold, almost lifeless. In this chilled, passive condition the ritual began to transform them: they became dignified bodies enacting the story of Demeter's mourning.

While the Demeter myth related women to the earth, the Thesmophoria in Athens linked women to one another. This new bond appeared in the formal organization of the Thesmophoria; the officers of the ritual were chosen by the women themselves. "Men were involved only to the extent," Sarah Pomeroy writes, "that, if they were wealthy, they were compelled to bear the expense of the festival as a liturgy or tax in behalf of their wives."[6] Moreover, the women celebrated the rite, Vernant says, "as citizens," though they withdrew from the world of men to do so. Only at the end of the third day did they return to the husbands who awaited them outside, emerging from the huts with their birth-burden of dead flesh and grain. The cloak of darkness in the earth, the cold of the pits, the closeness to death, transformed the status of their bodies. The women made a journey during the Thesmophoria through darkness, emerging into the light, their dignity affirmed.

To be sure, the metamorphosis from country to city left its mark on many other rituals as well, since the calendar of urban festivals was originally tied to rural life, to the cycle of the seasons, and to farming. But the transformation of the Demeter myth into urban ritual had a special meaning for women because of the specific place it occurred in Athens. Fragmentary evidence suggests that, when first practiced, the laying down of the piglets occurred in natural caves. The urban archeologist Homer Thompson has identified where this Neolithic rite was reconstructed in the city. The pits were dug out and the huts built on the Pnyx hill, behind the seats where the men sat in the Ekklesia. Through ritual, the women had thus established a civic space for themselves in Athens near the space of power occupied by men.

The technical name for the changes that occurred in the Thesmophoria is "metonymy," a Greek word for one of the tools of rhetoric. A metonymy substitutes one word for another; sailors can be called sharks or seagulls, depending on the effect a speaker or writer seeks.

Each of these substitutions makes an explanation: by calling a sailor a shark, we immediately explain the viciousness of his actions; by calling him a seagull, we explain his prowess to rise, like a gull, above the turmoil of the sea.[7] Metonymy does something like throw a cloak over original meanings, by transforming the original through association. Of all the weapons in the poet's arsenal, metonymy most varies language, transmuting the meaning of a word further and further from its origins.

During the course of the three days of the Thesmophoria, the women—smelling pig stench and willow, crouching in the ground—experienced ritual transformation thanks to the powers of metonymy. "Cold" and "passive" came to mean, by the second day, self-discipline and fortitude, rather than weakness and inferiority as they did outside. These changes culminated on the third day when the women emerged. They had not become like men. The light shone on cloaked bodies transformed in a ritual—mysterious and unknowable by men—which had somehow dignified these bodies.

Ritual metonymies, unlike a poet's phrases, make use of space to effect such changes. These spaces alter the condition of the bodies which step within ritual's magic circle. Such an alteration occurred in the Thesmophoria, the ritual pit, cold and dark, giving the cold bodies whom Perikles counseled to live unnoticed a new civic value. The shape of the huts concentrated the fumes of the willow, which aided women in this transformation by deadening their desires. The location of the huts in urban space emphasized the nearness of this dignifying site to the place where men ruled as citizens.

The Adonia

The Adonia festivals were agricultural rites tied to death. Their urban transformations occurred in domestic space. Greeks women were confined to houses because of their supposed physiological defects. The Greek historian Herodotus contrasted the reasonableness of his civilization in doing so to the strangeness of the Egyptians, observing that "in their manners and customs the Egyptians seem to have reversed the ordinary practices of mankind. For instance, women go to market and engage in trade, while men stay home and do the weaving."[8] In Xenophon's *Oikonomikos,* a husband enjoins his wife, "your business will be to stay indoors."[9]

The ancient Greek house had high walls and few windows; when money permitted, its rooms were oriented around an inner court-

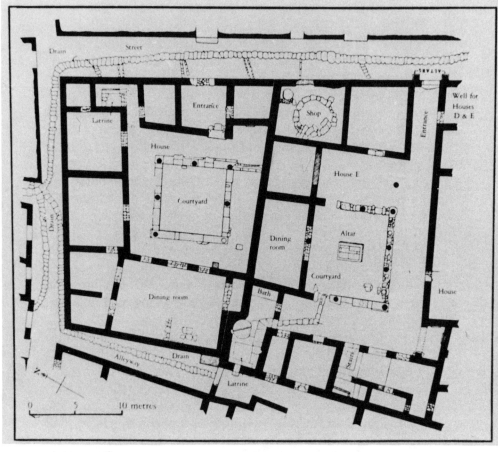

Athenian house plans, from Delos, fifth century B.C.

yard. Within the house, something like the purdah system of the classic Muslim household prevailed. Married women never appeared in the *andron,* the room in which guests were entertained. At the drinking parties given in the andron, only women slaves, prostitutes, or foreigners appeared. Wives and daughters lived in the room or rooms known as the *gunaikeion;* if the household was prosperous enough, these occupied the second story, a further remove from the daily intrusions of the street upon the courtyard.

The Adonia differed significantly from male celebrations (the *symposia*) occurring throughout the year beneath the roof in the andron. In a moderately prosperous house, this usually square room might have three couches on the side walls and one couch at the end; fourteen diners could recline here, eating and drinking, fondling both male and female prostitutes. The symposion provided an occa-

excite."[10] In the Thesmophoria, an anti-pheromone, the willow smell, pervaded the huts, a smell supposedly deadening desire; the Adonia, on the other hand, made use of aromatic spices which seemed to arouse desire. "The contrast between the Thesmophoria and the Adonia," writes the anthropologist Marcel Detienne, "is like that between Lent and Shrove Tuesday." The Adonia celebrated women's sexual desire; sweetly fragrant, drunken and bawdy, this aromatic festival set free female powers to speak about their desires in an odd and normally unused space of the house, the roof.

The Adonia derived from mythological stories surrounding the god Adonis. He stood at one extreme of the Greek imagination of masculinity; at the other end stood Herakles, the exemplary warrior. Herakles was famous, Homer said in the *Odyssey*, "for his gluttonous gut that never stopped eating and drinking." His sexual hunger equalled his gluttony; in the *Lysistrata*, a horny husband bursts out, "my cock is Herakles invited to dinner." Herakles was reputed to have sired seventy-two sons and one daughter.[11] By contrast, the graceful Adonis was neither gluttonous nor greedy. Unlike Herakles, he died before he could father a child, at the end of his adolescence gored to death by a wild boar. And most unlike Herakles, Adonis gave pleasure to women, rather than sating his lust in their bodies. Adonis was a figure of *hedone,* the Greek word for sensual pleasure, and Aphrodite mourned him as a lover of women.

In the ritual of the Adonia, women in Athens drew on this myth, lamenting the death of a youth who knew how to give women pleasure. A week preceding the festival in his honor every July, women planted seeds of lettuce in little pots on the roofs of their houses; these seeds are quick-germinating, and the women watered and fertilized the pots carefully until young green shoots appeared. At this moment, though, they deprived the plants of water. When the seedlings began to die, it was time for the festival to begin. Now the pots on the rooftops were called "gardens of Adonis," the withered plants mirroring his death.

One might expect the ritual to follow closely the story told by the myth; indeed, the time of year seemed to reinforce the symbolism of the dying garden, July being a month of scorching sun. Yet the women of Athens contrived a ritual that was a funeral in name only. Instead of grieving, they stayed up all night, dancing, drinking, and singing with each other. They threw balls of myrrh and other spices into incense burners (Adonis was the son of Myrrha, the nymph of myrrh) in order to arouse themselves sexually. The festival acquired

Young women mime the mourning of Adonis during the Adonia.

a reputation for lewd joking and illicit sex: one fictional Roman text of several centuries later has a courtesan writing to a friend, "We are going to arrange a banquet to celebrate the [Adonia] at the house of Thessala's lover. . . . Remember to bring a little garden and a statuette with you. And also bring along your Adonis [evidently a dildo] whom you smother with kisses. We will get drunk with all our lovers."[12]

The very plants women had sown in their little "gardens of Adonis" affirmed this sexual celebration. The poet Sappho wrote that Aphrodite had laid Adonis out in a field of lettuce after he was gored; if the image seems odd to us, it made perfect sense to the Greeks, who considered lettuce to be a potent anti-aphrodisiac: "its juice is of use to those who have wet dreams and it distracts a man from the subject of love-making," Dioscorides wrote.[13] Lettuce appeared in ancient literature as a symbol of impotence and more generally of a deadly "lack of vital force."[14] It was thought indeed a plant that thrived among the shades, and was eaten by dead mothers. During the Adonia, women started to celebrate when lettuce wilted, turned brown, and shrivelled in the pots of parched earth. They began to celebrate, that is, when a plant dies whose juices supposedly dry up living sexual desire.

The Adonia seems a celebration of desires not otherwise fulfilled in women's lives. Sexual deprivation was not due to men's infatuation with those boys destined to become citizens; that would suppose homosexuality on the modern model, as though one kind of erotic desire excludes another. As the jurist Eva Cantarella has remarked, "The real rivals of wives were . . . other 'respectable' women who could induce their husbands to divorce them."[15] The plants and spices of the Adonia helped women confront a more fundamental problem: their desires were inseparable from their submission to the will of men. The aromas of the Adonia attempted to provide a breathing space from that submission.

The Adonia, like the Thesmophoria, transformed an agricultural rite into an urban experience. The ancient myth associated the death of pleasure with the fertility of the earth, as the blood of the dying Adonis spilled out into the soil; this signified that the land draws its nourishment from human suffering. In the urban ritual, the drying of the land and the wilting of its plants brings the sensual body back to life. It was to make an old rite serve this end that women transformed the space of the house.

The Adonia differed significantly from male celebrations (the *symposia*) occurring throughout the year beneath the roof in the andron. In a moderately prosperous house, this usually square room might have three couches on the side walls and one couch at the end; fourteen diners could recline here, eating and drinking, fondling both male and female prostitutes. The symposion provided an occasion for men to let themselves go, engaging in raucous fun "fundamentally opposed to those [decorous conventions] within the polis as a whole."[16] The symposion was, L. E. Rossi has written, "a spectacle unto itself," as the men drank, flirted, talked and boasted, but the spectacle retained one convention of bodily comportment from the outside.[17] Just as at the gymnasium, competition suffused the male bonding of the symposion. Men prepared poems, jokes, and boasts in advance, so that they could show off their skills during the banquet. The balance between competition and camaraderie sometimes tipped out of control and the symposion degenerated into a violent brawl.

Upstairs on the roof, during the Adonia there was equal lewdness, but the women did not compete with each other; there were no prepared jokes. The Adonia also avoided the privacy and exclusiveness which marked the symposion. Women wandered from neighborhood to neighborhood, heard voices calling them above in the dark, ascended the roofs on ladders to meet strangers. In the ancient city, rooftops were usually empty. Moreover, this festival occurred at night in residential districts with no street lighting. The dominant spaces—the agora, gymnasium, Akropolis, and Pnyx—were spaces of daylight exposure. The few candles lit on the rooftops during the Adonia made it difficult to see others sitting nearby, let alone down in the street. It thus threw a cloak of darkness over transformations wrought on the space of the house. Filled with laughter in the dark, the roof became an anonymous, friendly territory.

It was in this space that women, under the cloak of darkness, recovered their powers of speech, spoke their desires. Just as the Thesmophoria transformed images of cold, the Adonia transmuted images of heat; exposure to the heat of the sun became deadly to their lettuce plants, while darkness set the women free.

Up to recent times, scholars thought the Adonia to be a lesbian rite, simply assuming that when women gathered for autonomous pleasure, they must have given each other sexual stimulation. The famous love lyrics Sappho wrote have often been cited in relation to the Adonia:

> For when I look at you for a moment, then it is no longer possible for me to speak; my tongue has snapped, at once a subtle fire has stolen beneath my flesh, I see nothing with my eyes, my ears hum, sweat pours from me, a trembling seizes me all over, I am greener than grass, and it seems to me that I am little short of dying.[18]

It now seems a more complicated event: whatever the mixture of sexual preferences, the ritual lacked the moving intensity of Sappho's lyrics, for this was an occasion for temporary pleasure among strangers in the dark, not deep and sustained erotic bonding.

The city did not formally recognize the Adonia; it did not appear on the official calendar as did most other festivals, which were scheduled, supervised, and financed by the city. It was a festival as informal in organization as spontaneous in feeling. And, unsurprisingly, the Adonia made men uncomfortable. Contemporary writers like Aristophanes in the *Lysistrata* derided the sheer noisiness, wailing racket, and drunkenness of the event, treating with contempt women who had departed from their accustomed silence. But the most consequent charge against the Adonia was made by Plato in the *Phaedrus*. Plato has Socrates say:

> Now tell me this. Would a sensible farmer take seed which he valued and wished to produce a crop, and sow it in sober earnest in gardens of Adonis, at midsummer, and take pleasure in seeing it reach its full course in eight days? Isn't this something that he might do in a holiday mood by way of diversion, if he did it at all? But where he is serious he will follow the true principles of agriculture and sow his seed in the soil that suits it, and be well satisfied if what he has sown comes to maturity eight months later.[19]

Plato saw in the Adonia a revelation of the barrenness of momentary pleasure, as opposed to the ancient agricultural story of the nourishing of the earth. Desire, alone, is barren.

Against Plato it could be said that, if the Adonia gave back to women the language of desire, it did so in a particular way. Like the Thesmophoria, this ritual made use of one of the poet's tools in spatial rather than verbal form. The Adonia drew on the powers of metaphor. A metaphor binds separate things together in a single image, as in the expression "the rosy-fingered dawn." In such a metaphor, the meaning of the whole is greater than its parts. Metaphor works differently from metonymy: in a metonymy, one can substitute various words for "sailor"—shark, gull, porpoise, albatross—but once "rosy fingers" and "dawn" are put together, they take on a character which is greater than an analogy of the parts, dawn and fingers. Moreover, strong metaphors resist literalizing. If you say "the rosy-fingered dawn" suggests that barrel-shaped, pink-colored clouds appear in the sky at daybreak, you lose the evocativeness of the image; the poet created an image which dies in explanation.

In the ritual of the Adonia, space made the metaphor work. Normally, fertility and childbearing legitimated women's sexuality. That a person should feel free while on a roof in July at night surrounded by dead plants to speak to strangers about her intimate desires *is* a bit odd; to combine these unlikely elements together was metaphor's spatial power. A "space of metaphor" refers, in a ritual, to a place in which people can join unlike elements. They do so through how they use their bodies, rather than through explaining themselves. In the Adonia, dancing and drinking take the place of complaint, or of analysis of the condition of women in Athens. This explains a certain bafflement in Aristophanes' and Plato's comments on the Adonia, their inability to make sense of what was going on; the rooftop rite defies analytic reasoning.

The classicist John Winkler, in a memorable phrase, calls the Adonia the "laughter of the oppressed."[20] But this ritual did not say no to the male yes. It did not prompt women to commandeer the agora, the Pnyx, or other male bastions for a night. The roof was not a launching pad for rebellion. Instead, it was a space in which women momentarily and bodily stepped out of the conditions imposed on them by the dominant order of the city. The Adonia could have easily been suppressed by husbands or the guardians of the polis, yet no civic power sought to prevent women from observing it, and perhaps this also was metaphor's gift in a festival of resistance too odd to invite direct reprisal. If the Thesmophoria legitimated cold bodies within the stones of the city, the Adonia lifted, for a few nights, their weight.

Logos and mythos

These two ancient festivals illustrate a simple social truth: Ritual heals. Ritual is one way the oppressed—men as well as women—can respond to the slights and contempt they otherwise suffer in society, and rituals more generally can make the pains of living and dying bearable. Ritual constitutes the *social* form in which human beings seek to deal with denial as active agents, rather than as passive victims.

Western civilization has had, however, an ambivalent relation to these powers of ritual. Reason and science have seemed to promise victory over human suffering, victory rather than simply ritual's active engagement with it. And reason, of the kind which shaped our culture, has suspected the foundations of ritual, its metonymies and metaphors in space, its bodily practices, which refuse logical justification or explanation.

That ambivalent Western relation of reason and ritual took form in the ancient world. It appeared in the distinction the Greeks drew between *logos* and *mythos*. The historian of religion Walter Burkert has summarized this contrast as follows:

> *Mythos* as contrasted with *logos*: *logos* from *legein*, "to put together," is assembling single bits of evidence, of verifiable facts: *logon didonai*, to

render account in front of a critical and suspicious audience; *mythos* is telling a tale while disclaiming responsibility: *ouk emos ho mythos,* this is not my tale, but I have heard it elsewhere.[21]

The language of logos connects things. The *logon didonai* sets the stage for a person making connections: there is an audience judging the person arguing, and the audience is suspicious. Logos can become impure; as in the debate over the commanders, a speaker may arouse sympathy and identification with his pictures of individual facts, persons, or events. These images flow one after another, the word pictures feel connected, though they could not withstand the scrutiny of pure deductive analysis.

In all forms of logos, however, the speaker is identified with his words; they belong to him and he is responsible for them. Greek political thought shaped ideas of democracy around aspects of logos. As first asserted by Kleisthenes, freedom of expression and debate makes sense only if people take responsibility for their words, otherwise argument is weightless, words have no importance. The Pnyx made logos work spatially in this way; you could see and hear who applauded or jeered a speech, and account how they voted.

In mythos, a speaker is not responsible for his or her words. Instead, the language of myth turns on the belief embodied in the Greek remark, "This is not my tale, but I have heard it elsewhere." Most myths, certainly Greek ones, concern the doings of magical beings or the gods, so that it makes good sense to think that the gods shape these stories, not the men and women who recount them to others. Thus the audience hearing someone recount a myth will be free of suspicions it might harbor toward a speaker in the political assembly, a speaker who claims credit for his words. The anthropologist Meyer Fortas once spoke of myth in this way, as a "ratification of the social bond."[22] Or again, Aristotle famously defined the drama as a "willing suspension of disbelief"; myth, from which the early dramas derived, sets the true context for that statement. Mythos is about trust in words, in themselves.

The distinction between logos and mythos teaches a harsh lesson. The words for which people claim responsibility create mutual distrust and suspicions that need to be deflected and manipulated. This harsh truth shed a terrifying light on Kleisthenes' belief that people should be free to speak and responsible for what they say. Democracy deals in the politics of mutual mistrust. The words for which the speakers seem not responsible create a bond of trust; trust is forged by people only under the sway of myth, under the sway of language external to the speakers themselves, as in the paeans in homage to Demeter spoken in the huts on the Pnyx and to Adonis on the roofs of the Athenian house. The cloak of darkness thrown over both places reinforced the impersonal, trustworthy character of these words, since the individual speaker could not easily be seen—the words came out of the dark. The spaces of rituals created magic zones of mutual affirmation. And all these powers of mythos affected the celebrating body, endowing it with new value. In ritual, words are consummated by bodily gestures: dancing, crouching, or drinking together become signs of mutual trust, deeply bonding acts. Ritual threw a cloak of darkness over the suspicions individuals might have harbored of one another in the ancient city, quite unlike the mixture of admiration and suspicion elicited by naked display.

Athenian culture thus formed parallel contrasts: hot versus clothed bodies; naked men versus clothed women; light, "out-of-door" spaces versus the darkened spaces of the pit and the roof at night; the challenging exposures of the *logos didonai* and the healing cloak of the mythos; the body of power often losing self-control by the very force of its words versus the oppressed bodies united in ritual, even if that bond could not be articulated, justified, or explained.

But Thucydides will not let us celebrate in quite this way, at least about the Athens he knew. Reason has cause to suspect ritual, for ritual contained its own fatal defect in binding people together. Thucydides showed how ritual gave the Athenians no sufficient understanding of *why* they suffered at a moment of great civic disaster; without that understanding, their lives together could unravel.

2. THE SUFFERING BODY

Perikles' Funeral Oration ends one scene of Thucydides' *History;* the next recounts a great plague which befell Athens in the winter and spring of 430. Under the impact of the plague, people acted in ways which contradicted the shining confidence expressed in the Funeral Oration: the institutions of democracy broke down, sick bodies unravelled the bonds of ritual in the city, and Perikles himself was destroyed.

The doctors of ancient Athens knew little about how to cope with a massive outbreak of cholera, and Thucydides describes the bodily symptoms of plague with bewildered awe:

Their eyes became red and inflamed; inside their mouths there was bleeding from the throat and tongue, and the breath became unnatural and unpleasant . . . there were attacks of ineffectual retching, producing violent spasms . . . though there were many dead bodies lying about unburied, the birds and animals that eat human flesh either did not come near them or, if they did taste the flesh, died of it afterwards.[23]

The plague struck first and most fatally at the social fabric of the city, by destroying those rituals which paid homage to the sanctity of death. The Greeks started to violate one another's dead: "they would arrive first at a funeral pyre that had been made by others, put their own dead upon it and set it alight; or, finding another pyre burning, they would throw the corpse that they were carrying on top of the other one and go away." Though some people did act honorably, tending the sick and so becoming infected themselves, ". . . the catastrophe was so overwhelming that men, not knowing what would happen next to them, became indifferent to every rule of religion. . . ."[24]

Once ritual had sickened, the plague struck at politics. "No one expected to live long enough to be brought to trial and punished." The Athenians lost their powers of self-discipline and self-governance; instead, faced with plague, they gave themselves over to momentary or forbidden pleasures: "People now began openly to venture on acts of self-indulgence which before then they used to keep dark . . . they resolved to spend their money quickly and to spend it on pleasure . . . the pleasure of the moment."[25] Sickness rendered the hierarchies of politics meaningless, for the plague made no distinctions between citizen and non-citizen, Athenian and slave, men and women. At this moment when the Athenians could no longer control their own lives, their enemies seized the advantage, advancing upon the city through the countryside in the spring of 430 B.C.

Only a few months after he had delivered the Funeral Oration, Perikles' dream of a self-governing city lay in ruins, and he himself was menaced as an architect of that dream. Before the war, Perikles had suggested the Piraeus wall be doubled, so that traffic could pass protected from city to port, and this was done; a space of about 150 yards separated these two parallel walls, and they were thus large enough to contain people from the countryside seeking shelter during time of war. Now, as the Spartans under Archidamus invaded the plains of Attica near Athens in 430, masses from the countryside crowded behind the walls he had created, particularly into the channel walls linking the port of Piraeus and Athens. This corridor became a plague trap for refugees. The Athenians then turned on Perikles. "The man responsible for all this," Plutarch later said, "was Perikles: because of the war he had compelled the country people to crowd inside the walls, and he had then given them no employment, but left them penned up like cattle to infect each other. . . ."[26]

Yet these same Athenians were hardly cowards afraid of pain or death; they were physically courageous on the battlefield and at sea. When Thucydides reached his account of the final land battle fought by the Athenians, at Cynossema in 411, he described exhausted and weak soldiers still fighting valiantly, still hoping: "they came to believe that, if they did their part resolutely, final victory was still possible."[27]

Rituals should have held the city together. Ritual comes "from somewhere else," and that place is often the place of the dead. The Thesmophoria and Adonia resembled other rituals of the city in drawing their mythic themes from death, burial, and mourning, linking the living and the dead. In the Funeral Oration, Nicole Loraux observes, Perikles wanted to convince his listeners that the fallen soldiers had died "fine deaths," because their deaths had occurred according to the rules and for the sake of the entire city; Perikles says that "every one of us who has survived would naturally exhaust himself in her [Athens'] service."[28] In the same way, the Thesmophoria and the Adonia assured women that Demeter's daughter and Adonis had died "fine deaths," deaths which served the needs of urban women. Sophokles' *Oedipus Tyrannus* told a story about plague, again, whose denouement lies in the king blinding himself in order to relieve the plague, to restore his city; it was a self-sacrificial story which had a civic meaning to its contemporary audience beyond the Freudian story of forbidden lust and guilt.

The plague offered no parallel civic opportunity. Thucydides tells us that this plague did cause Athenian and non-Athenian alike to "consult old oracles," but that the oracles gave a confusing response; the clearest could have been no comfort to the Athenians, for it told the Spartans that, "if they fought with all their might, victory would be theirs and that the god himself would be on their side."[29] To be sure, the Athenians, like all the ancients, had a profound sense of the smallness, limits, and darkness of human action in the larger cosmic order; many of their rituals attested to these limits. But these rituals spoke of human despair rather than civic redemption and cohesion in the face of disaster.

A ritual's self-contained powers which come "from somewhere else" mean it is not a tool people can use to investigate and reason about the unknown and unforeseen. And this is because ritual is not like a tool or an instrument which one manipulates to explore different possibilities and outcomes, as one might in a scientific experiment. Nor is a ritual like a work of art, its materials consciously exploited for greatest effect. The essence of any ritual practice, at the moment people perform it, is that they enter into something which both already exists and which seems outside themselves. The magic of ritual which comes "from somewhere else" depends on seeming outside the frame of being *willed*. Like all the urban rituals of the city, the Thesmophoria and the Adonia had evolved very slowly, over the course of centuries, old meanings gradually melting tranformed into new ones. In any particular year, women practiced these rituals in a spirit of re-enacting what had come before, not analyzing the changes they might be subtly making in a received rite.

During the plague, the Athenians suffered the fate of other highly ritualized cultures, that of finding the repertoire of past magic practices lacking a sufficient explanatory scope to make sense of crises in the present. The Athenians came closest to a mythic understanding of the plague, if Plutarch's later description is accurate, in interpreting Perikles' great efforts at city building as something like the hubris of Oedipus. This interpretation did not however tell them what to do. Thucydides emphasizes this inadequacy, portraying ritual's cloak of darkness over human agency as a cloak of confusion.

Yet Athenian culture was distinctive in believing that people could create and understand their own condition. In Greek the word *poiein* means "making"; *poiesis* is derived from that root, and means the creative act; far more than Sparta, the culture of Periklean Athens formed a sustained hymn to the ideal of poiesis, the city conceived as a work of art. Reasoning is a part of that creative act, both scientific and political reasoning; some ancient writers called democratic politics an *auto-poiesis*, an ever-changing political self-creation.

A few modern interpreters have taken Thucydides' tight pairing of the Funeral Oration and the Plague of Athens as a sign that the historian disbelieved the fine phrases of his contemporary leader. But this is too simple. Rather than siding in sympathy with the Spartan enemy, Thucydides sought to understand the complex and often unstable forces which had created the culture of the polis. The powers of auto-poiesis dramatized on the Parthenon friezes represented a danger to the city, but so did the powers of ritual alone, unaided by the exercise of experiment, inquiry, and debate.

These forces converged in the human body, the city's greatest work of art. "The Greek body of Antiquity did not appear as a group morphology of fitted organs in the manner of an anatomical drawing," Jean-Pierre Vernant writes, "nor in the form of physical particularities proper to each one of us, as in a portrait. Rather, it appears in the manner of a coat of arms."[30] Of all the cities of Greek antiquity, Athens displayed this heraldic body: displayed the body's nakedness as a civilized creation; trained the male body in the gymnasium as a work of art; made men's bodies loving each other into civic signs; trained and exposed the speaking voice, transforming a place originally devoted to drama for the political purposes of autopoiesis. The complex rituals of Athens drew on the poetic powers of metaphor and metonymy consummated in the body and in urban space.

"Our city is an education to Greece," Perikles boasted.[31] The legacy of Perikles' Athens consists, in part, in darker lessons, revealed by the pains of this civic body. From Athens' art of the body came one source of the divide between mental understanding and bodily freedom which has dogged Western civilization, and an intimation of the limits of ritual to bind and to heal a society in crisis.

CHAPTER THREE

The Obsessive Image

Place and Time in Hadrian's Rome

In A.D. 118 the Emperor Hadrian began a new building on the site of the old Pantheon in the Campus Martius section of Rome. The original Roman Pantheon had been designed by Agrippa in 25 B.C. as a shrine devoted to all the Roman gods. Hadrian's Pantheon gathered the deities together in a remarkable new building, an enormous half dome resting on a cylindrical base. Perhaps its most striking feature then, as today, is the light entering the Pantheon through the top of the dome. On sunny summer days, a lightshaft searches the interior, moving from the edge of the dome down the cylinder onto the floor and then up the cylinder again, as the sun outside moves in its orbit; on cloudy days, the light becomes a gray fog tinted by the concrete of the shell. At night the building mass vanishes; through the opening at the top of the dome a circle of stars looms out of the darkness.

In Hadrian's time, the light in the Pantheon shone on an interior

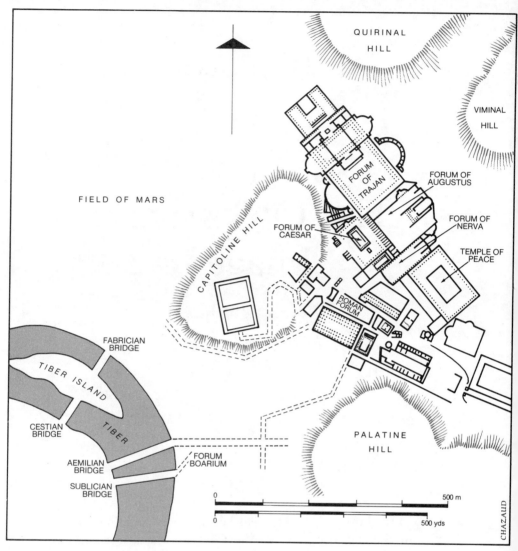

Map of Rome, ca. A.D. 120.

saturated with political symbols. The floor of the Pantheon had been laid out as an immense checkerboard of stones; this same pattern the Romans used to design new cities in the Empire. The circular wall contained niches for statues of gods; the gathering of gods were thought to sponsor in mutual harmony Rome's quest for world domination. The Romans indeed came close to worshipping them as idols possessed of life. The Pantheon celebrated, in the words of the modern historian Frank Brown, "the imperial idea and all the gods of the Empire who stood for it."[1]

Five hundred years after Hadrian built the Pantheon it became a Christian church, Sancta Maria ad Martyres, consecrated by Pope Boniface IV in A.D. 609. It was one of the first pagan temples in Rome used for Christian worship, and owes its survival to that fact; while other ancient Roman monuments crumbled into mere stone quarries for builders during the Middle Ages, the church could not be pillaged. Sancta Maria ad Martyres took on a new life as a martyrium, devoted particularly to Christians who suffered for their faith. Once a temple devoted to a crowd of gods who smiled on the Empire, Sancta Maria ad Martyres served now one god only, a god of the weak and the oppressed. The building stands thus as a landmark of the great passage in Western civilization from polytheism to monotheism.

The building of the Pantheon marked as well a drama in its own time. The Roman Empire had made visual order and imperial power inseparable: the emperor depended upon making his power *seen* in monuments and public works. Power needed stone. Yet the Pantheon appeared, one of its historians remarks, "when rites and rules drawn from a very long past were not yet abandoned, but when the surge of a new and utterly different age was already being felt."[2] In Hadrian's time cults filled the Roman Empire, new cults like Mithraism and Christianity, and these cults "made far more of a world unseen than of this one."[3] To be sure, Romans did not believe they could directly see the pagan gods who ruled them; it was thought that when the gods came to earth to walk among men and women, they disguised themselves so that they could not be recognized. Yet people had believed the old gods made everywhere visible signs of their presence, and the rulers of Rome had drawn upon these visible traces to mobilize and to justify their own reign, building imperial monuments throughout the Western world in the name of the gods. The Pantheon was such an effort, in Rome itself, to make men and women look, believe, and obey.

The uneasy relations between the seen and the unseen in Hadrian's Rome came from a deeper and more general malaise about the human body. Though the Athenians knew the darkness and frailty of human life, they celebrated the sheer strength of muscle and bone. By the time Hadrian built the Pantheon, a strong Roman did not stand in light. The gladiators swore an oath which ends, "What difference will it make if you gain a few more days or years? We are born into a world in which no quarter is given." The Roman writer Seneca proclaimed that this—the gladiator's "most loathsome of contracts" *(turpissimum auctoramentum)*—also expressed the most honorable bond among soldiers and citizens.[4] The Latin word *gravitas* means "dignity," and also sheer, grim determination. The gladiator's oath, taken by men swearing to kill one another, asserts this determination in a terrible contradiction: "You must die erect and invincible." Physical strength was tinged with darkness and despair.

The arousal of sheer bodily desire terrified pagan and Christian Roman alike. "As the Romans feared disabling hope," the historian Carlin Barton writes, "so they feared desire and its awful consequences," yet pagans and Christians feared bodily desire for different reasons. For the Christian, desire debased the soul; for the pagan, it meant "the flouting of social conventions, the dismantling of hierarchy, the confusion of categories . . . the unleashing of chaos, of conflagration, of the *universus interitus*."[5] If the ruler had need of visual order, so did his subjects. In this grim world of dark strength and unruly desire, the pagan sought reassurance by willing himself to believe in what he saw on the streets of the city, at the baths, the amphitheatre, the forums. He needed to go further, believing in stone idols, in painted images, in theatrical costumes, all as literally real. He would look and believe.

The Roman obsession with images made use of a particular kind of visual order. This was a geometric order, and the principles of this reassuring geometry the Romans sensed not so much on paper as in their own bodies. More than a century before Hadrian, the architect Vitruvius had demonstrated that the human body is structured by geometrical relationships, principally by the bilateral symmetries of the bones and the muscles, the ears and the eyes. By studying these symmetries, Vitruvius then showed how the body's structure could be translated into the architecture of a temple. Other Romans used similar geometrical imagery to plan cities, following the rules of bilateral symmetry and privileging linear visual perception. From the geometer's ruler thus came Rule; the lines of bodies, temples, and cities seemed to reveal the principles of a well-ordered society.

Unlike the painting of an historical scene, abstract geometric figures impart no sense of time to the viewer. The timeless quality of geometry served the Romans well in reassuring themselves about the times in which they lived. When the Romans founded new cities in the Empire, for instance, they sought to measure and rule out dimensions of a place so that the Roman urban design could be immediately impressed onto the conquered territory. This geometric imprint, frequently requiring the destruction of old shrines, streets, or public buildings, denied the histories of those whom the Romans conquered.

It is true, as the art historian E. H. Gombrich has observed, that both Greek and Roman art sought to make public art tell stories, in contrast to the Egyptian art they knew.[6] But the Romans particularly liked to look at story images which emphasized the continuity of the city, the durability and unchanging core of her essence. Roman visual narratives repeat the same story over and over; they depict civic disasters or threatening events in such a way that these crises are resolved by the appearance of a great senator, general, or emperor.

The Roman would look and believe; he would look and obey an enduring regime. The durability of Rome ran counter to time in the human body, a time of growth and decay, of plans defeated or forgotten, the memory of faces obscured by ageing or despair. As Hadrian himself had acknowledged in a poem, the experience a Roman had of his own body conflicted with the fiction of the place called "Rome."

The Roman Christians sought, as Christians, to affirm by contrast a particular experience of time in their own bodies, bodies transformed in the course of adulthood. The Christians hoped that through religious conversion the chaos of bodily desires would cease to afflict them; the weight of the flesh would lighten as a Christian moved to union with a higher, immaterial Power. For change to occur, believers like St. Augustine emphasized St. John's horror of the "lust of the eyes"; compelling visual images created attachment to the world.[7] A Christian's visual imagination was to form around the experience of light, God's Light, which blinds the beholder, effacing the ability to see the world or look into a mirror.

As their faith in God grew stronger, the early Christians believed in turn they would feel ever less attached to the places in which they lived. In this they drew on the long Judaic heritage affirming dispossession, Jews who saw themselves as spiritual wanderers in the world, in it but not of it. Yet the devoted Christians eventually ceased to wander; they came to pray in Hadrian's temple. The civic fiction of Roman place reappeared, "the old became new," the art historian Richard Brilliant writes, "the past the present."[8] And with that resurgent sense of place Christians felt less urgently the need to transform their bodies.

The passage from pantheism to monotheism thus unveiled a great drama about body, place, and time. The intense polis-love of the Greeks had already given way by Hadrian's era to a more anxious desire for security and an uneasy obsession with images, among people troubled about their traditional gods and their place in the world. The passage to monotheism now emphasized inner change at the expense of urban continuity, put greater value on personal history than on civic membership. Yet if the pagan would not give himself over to the realm of stone without nagging doubts, the Christian could no more entirely give his body over to God.

1. LOOK AND BELIEVE

The fears of an emperor

Over the entrance of the Pantheon a Roman read: *M. Agrippa L. f. cos. III fecit,* which means "Marcus Agrippa, son of Lucius, consul for the third time, had this building made." The inscription puzzles a modern visitor, for Hadrian had carved on his temple the name of the builder of the old Pantheon, erected a hundred and fifty years earlier. But the inscription explains Hadrian's own need for the civic fiction of "Rome."

Hadrian became an emperor under ambiguous circumstances. It was not certain that his predecessor Trajan had adopted Hadrian as son and heir, following the normal imperial practice. The young Hadrian felt dwarfed by Trajan's great popularity, the people awarding Trajan the title of best emperor *(optimus princeps).* The moment Hadrian took power, he caused the murder of four popular members of the Senate whom he thought were rivals. In A.D. 118, soon after he succeeded Trajan, Hadrian sought to walk out of these shadows. He made an apology of sorts to the Senate for the killings; he handed out gold to the people and forgave their debts to the state, the bills burned in a great bonfire. Rather than fight against people's memories of Trajan, Hadrian sought to appropriate these memories. He did so by carrying out Trajan's desire to be buried at the base of Trajan's Column, a column depicting in bas-reliefs the achievements of the *optimus princeps.* More, Hadrian sought to link himself to the first emperor, the divine Augustus; Hadrianic coins showed a phoenix rising from the ashes, an emblem of the restoration of order and unity in Rome under Augustus. After his initial missteps, all these acts signalled Hadrian's desire to emphasize that the past would flow smoothly forward, to minimize the sense of change. In the same spirit Hadrian began to build the Pantheon.

The Pantheon emphasized continuity in many ways. Hadrian placed statues of Augustus, the first emperor, and Agrippa, the

Republican architect, on either side of the entrance. Like Augustus, he asked the Roman Senate to serve as official sponsor for his own effort. This was purely for form's sake, a fiction of enduring Republican values, since for a hundred and thirty years the institutions of the old Republic had withered under the rule of the emperors—yet at this point in Hadrian's life such fictions were useful. Throughout his reign Hadrian would pursue this path of least resistance; as a builder, he tried not to destroy the work of others, instead constructing on empty land in Rome as much as possible.

For a ruler who wanted to reassure his subjects, the artist in the emperor may have made a misstep, for the Pantheon is an immensely striking object. Romans had seen domes before, but the size and engineering perfection of this one made it special. One critic remarks that "there seems to be have been an effort to disguise from the front the unconventionality of Hadrian's new building."[9] A perfectly ordinary forecourt faced the front of the Pantheon, complemented by the conventional shape of a slice of temple front *(pronaos)* shoved against the cylindrical body to serve as an entrance. Opposite, on the east side of the Pantheon, another boxy building, the Septa Julia, shoved up against it. Far from being apparent in all its roundness, the Pantheon was held like a cylinder in a vise. Moreover, the Pantheon occupied a very different place in Rome than did, say, the Parthenon in Athens. The Parthenon stood out boldly exposed. The Pantheon had been woven into a dense fabric of surrounding buildings; one came upon it in walking down a street.

Older Romans had painful memories of how an emperor could violate the city through building. They would have thought of Nero, for instance Nero's "Golden House," the *Domus Aurea,* which served as his palace. Architecturally, the great vaulted spaces in the Domus Aurea foreshadowed Hadrian's dome. This vast construction built two generations before Hadrian destroyed much of the fabric of central Rome, its walled and guarded gardens preventing ordinary Romans from walking about the city center. Romans hated signs of Nero's megalomanic genius: a 120-foot-high statue of himself, a mile-long arcade enclosing its gardens, a ton of gold leaf. "When the palace had been decorated throughout in this lavish style," Suetonius wrote in the next generation, "Nero dedicated it, and condescended to remark: 'Good, now I can at last begin to live like a human being!' "[10] Chased from his Golden House, Nero ended his reign as a still young man falling upon his sword in a squalid dwelling in the Roman suburbs in A.D. 68.

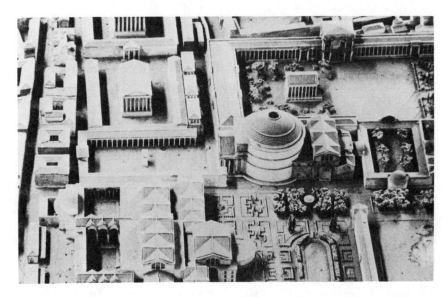

Model of the Pantheon district in Rome, ca. A.D. 300.

Nero bequeathed to Hadrian a cautionary tale about rulers who nakedly display their power, yet "the emperor was what the emperor did," in the words of the historian Fergus Millar.[11] Making daunting, impressive buildings was among the most important of these acts, for the emperor's own prestige and for the Empire; through their buildings, the emperors literally constructed their legitimacy in the eyes of their subjects. The Roman architect Vitruvius, addressing Augustus, declared that "The majesty of the Empire [is] expressed through the eminent dignity of its public buildings."[12]

Hadrian needed to build, Hadrian needed to be discreet: like other successful emperors, Hadrian resolved this tension through the civic fiction that the monumental growth of the city revealed its essential and unchanging character as "Rome." No matter that subjects rebelled, senators plunged into civil wars, emperors stripped the polity of power, the glory of the buildings made manifest the essential character of the city from its very moment of birth. The fiction of an essential character drew, indeed, upon the mythology of Rome's unique virtues at that moment of birth. "Not without reason have gods and man chosen this site for the founding of a city," Livy declared, ". . . health-giving hills, a navigable river . . . a position where the sea is near enough for profitable use, but not exposed unduly to the attacks of foreign fleets."[13] Factually Livy was not far off the mark; the Tiber River flowing through Rome "has a stable delta that could be developed as a port," the modern urbanist Spiro Kostof observes; "this fact, and the clear passage upriver . . . secured Rome's overseas reach."[14]

Belief in something fixedly Roman then proved ever more necessary as Roman power extended over the world. Ovid wrote that "other peoples have been allotted a certain defined portion of the earth; for the Romans, the space of the City is the space of the world {Romanae spatium est urbis et orbis idem}."[15] In the paraphrase of the historian Lidia Mazzolani, Virgil in the *Aeneid* aimed to show "the City of Rome's right to supremacy, which heaven had been preparing for hundreds of years."[16] These boasts had a different implication from Perikles' claim five hundred years before that "Athens is an education to Greece." Athens had no intention of making any of the people it conquered into Athenians. Rome did.

The city attracted like a magnet all those whom it dominated, swelling with immigrants who wanted to be close to the source of the center of wealth and power. Except for the Jews, whom he ruthlessly persecuted, Hadrian had shown tolerance for the immense diversity of sects and tribes throughout the Empire and in the city. It was in his reign that captured territories were included in the definition of "Rome" itself, as members of a "commonwealth in which each individual province and nation possessed its own proud identity."[17] By the time Hadrian came to power, nearly a million people filled Rome, most of them living in dense quarters that approximated the most crowded sections of modern Bombay. The massive human stream deformed street lines, as buildings cut into or even filled up the streets. The pressure of population was vertical as well as horizontal, forcing poorer Romans into *insulae,* the first apartment houses, which were irregular structures built over time story by story, sometimes rising as high as 100 feet.

Like Perikles' Athens, Hadrian's Rome was a city composed in the vast majority by poor people. Unlike Perikles' Athens, slaves in Hadrian's Rome could somewhat more easily gain their freedom, as a gift from the master, or by purchasing it themselves, which made for a new source of diversity. The precincts of poverty in the city also contained imperial soldiers, who eked out a living only when they were fighting on the frontier. The population was volatile: violence ruled the unlit city at night. The very economics of imperialism made for an unstable city.

The historian Michael Grant estimates that "the entire commerce and industry of all the empire together probably never amounted to more than ten percent of its total revenue."[18] Manufacturing occurred in the Empire on a local scale, as did trade in grains and food; fuel was scarce; wealth came from conquest. Most people depended for survival on an intricate web of client relationships with more powerful individuals, a web which distributed the spoils but which also tore frequently during the tremblings of Empire. An upper servant had lower servants as clients, a shopkeeper had a retinue of upper servants, a minor local official had a retinue of shopkeepers, and so on. The Roman day took form in attending the risings and daily receptions of those upon whom one depended, personal flattery mixed in between favors, tips, and little deals.

For all these reasons, the ideal of an essential and continuing Rome was a necessary fiction for Romans; it asserted that stable values underlay the insecurity, misery, and humiliation of everyday life. However, simply asserting that the city was "Eternal" would hardly suffice; the vast urban agglomeration looked nothing like the little village which first took form along the Tiber, nor was the political history of Rome anything like a story of conservation and continuity. To make the fiction of an "Eternal City" credible, the emperor had to dramatize his powers in a certain way, and the people had to treat city life as a kind of theatrical experience.

Hadrian murders Apollodorus

An emperor might survive military defeat, famine, or even his own dull wits. But he needed to act with iron firmness and intelligence as the set designer of that stage for human folly and glory called "Rome." A story, probably untrue but widely believed, about Hadrian's murder of an architect in his service, dramatized that pressure to make no false moves.

By the time, in the middle years of his reign, when Hadrian began to build there, the Roman forum had filled with monuments testifying to the glory of earlier emperors. To counter these dynastic shrines, Hadrian made the Temple of Venus and Roma, just east of the *Forum Romanum;* he built it over part of Nero's ill-fated "Golden House," and the Temple of Venus and Roma loomed over the forum. Hadrian dedicated this shrine to civic worship of the city itself. "Hadrian's new Temple (and cult) of Venus and Roma . . . exalt[ed] the strength and origins of Rome and the Roman people above those of an individual family."[19] At the beginning of his reign Hadrian had promised *populi rem esse, non propriam,* the state "belongs to the people, not to me." The Temple of Venus and Roma symbolized his keeping that promise.[20]

Supposedly the emperor sent the plans for this temple to the professional architect Apollodorus. Apollodorus, one of the great architects of Imperial Rome, had previously served Trajan, and known Hadrian for perhaps twenty years; the modern historian William MacDonald describes the architect as "a man of considerable consequence, a writer and a cosmopolitan citizen."[21] When Hadrian sent him the plans for this new work, Apollodorus criticized the technical construction and the proportions of both the building and its statues. Hadrian reacted, according to later gossip, by having Apollodorus killed.

Some thought Hadrian was jealous of the architect, in an echo of Hadrian's relations with Trajan. Dio Cassius thought so, who wrote down this story a hundred years later in his *Roman History.* Yet Dio Cassius also mentions a popular belief which explained the murder differently. When Hadrian received Apollodorus' criticism, "the emperor was both vexed and exceedingly grieved because he had fallen into a mistake that could not be righted," Dio reported, "and he restrained neither his anger nor his grief, but slew the man."[22] The popular belief made sense, given the dictum that the emperor is what the emperor does. The emperor's works were his claim to legitimacy. Apollodorus told Hadrian that the Temple of Venus and Roma, meant to convey the emperor's unity with the Roman people, was flawed. An emperor who built badly did not commit merely an architectural error; he broke his most important bond to the people. There would be nothing inconsistent about an emperor who protected that bond by murdering a critic of his design.

The people also gained from believing that their ruler's building works bore the stamp of absolute authority. To the Romans we owe the phrase *teatrum mundi,* later rendered by Shakespeare as "all the world's a stage." A Roman could give him- or herself over to that willing suspension of disbelief which is the essence of theater, assured that power guaranteed as consequent and correct those places in which the spectacle of life unfolded. The realm of certified stone in the city literally set the stage for Romans believing the evidence of their eyes.

Teatrum mundi

The Roman experience of the *teatrum mundi* relied on what seems, to a modern person, an absurdly literal-minded belief in appearances. In a famous anecdote, for instance, Pliny recounted the following story about the artist Zeuxis:

> Zeuxis [painted] a picture of grapes so dexterously represented that birds began to fly down to eat from the painted vine. Whereupon Parrhasius designed so lifelike a picture of a curtain that Zeuxis, proud of the verdict of the birds, requested that the curtain should now be drawn back and [his own] picture displayed.[23]

A modern reader might take this to be a story about the artist's powers of illusion. A Roman thought it showed art's relation to reality: Parrhasius' addition to his painting made it more real to Zeuxis. Taking appearances so literally marked an institution in Rome which also may to us seem far away from Hadrian's home for the gods, the gladiator's home in the amphitheatre.

A Roman amphitheatre was in form two Greek semicircular theatres put together, so that the theatre space was entirely enclosed. In these vast circular or oval spaces, the Romans had for centuries observed gladiators fighting each other to the death; enjoyed lions, bears, and elephants ripping one another and men to shreds; watched criminals, religious heretics, and deserters from the army tortured, crucified, or burned alive. Carlin Barton estimates a trained gladiator had about a 1 in 10 chance of being killed each time he went out, whereas the slaves, criminals, and Christians had almost no chance of surviving their first encounter. The odds dropped when the emperors arranged "mock" battles in which armies of gladiators contended in the amphitheatre; Trajan once had ten thousand men fight to the death there over a four-month period.[24]

This theatre of cruelty was more than sadistic entertainment. The shows accustomed people to the carnage necessary for imperial conquest, as the historian Keith Hopkins has shown.[25] More, in the amphitheatre Romans willed the gods into appearing, when real human beings were forced to impersonate them. The writer Martial described one such summoning in which " 'Orpheus' appears in a rustic though sumptuous setting. He stands alone, wearing an animal skin loin cloth and carrying a lyre. . . . He is suddenly attacked and killed by a bear that materializes 'spontaneously' through a trap door from the arena basement. . . ."[26] Officials waited in the background

Death by wild beasts in the amphitheatre, from a mosaic found in a villa near Leptis Magna, North Africa.

armed with branding irons and whips to make sure the condemned wretch acted out his role. Or again, the Christian Tertullian testified, "We once saw Atys [a figure from Greek mythology] castrated . . . and a man who was being burned alive played the role of Hercules."[27] The gladiators and martyrs in the amphitheatre conveyed the literal reality of appearances, just as Zeuxis the painter did. Martial declared, "Whatever fame sings of, the arena makes real for you"; the Romans, Katherine Welch observes, " 'improved' on myth by actually making it happen."[28]

In the gladiatorial shows, as in the formal theatre, this literal-minded appetite took a particular form, as mime and pantomime in which the silent image rules. Roman pantomime was popular because it made constant literal allusions to real life. For instance, in Suetonius' life of Nero, the Roman historian describes a pantomime by Datus in which the actor

> illustrated the first line of the song "Goodbye Father, goodbye Mother" with gestures of drinking and swimming—Claudius had been poisoned, Agrippina nearly drowned—and the last line, "Hell guides your feet" . . . [was directed] with a wave of his hands towards the senators whom Nero intended to massacre.[29]

The pantomime showed what had happened to Nero's forbears, and what was likely to happen to Nero's enemies. Having seen it on the stage, Nero supposedly decided it was indeed time to kill the senators; the emperor, who himself acted in pantomimes, believed more generally that all power was a matter of acting as well as a mime. Suetonius even claims that at his squalid death Nero first struck various poses he had learned in performing pantomimes, then fell on his sword, "[muttering] through his tears: 'Dead! And so great an artist!' "[30] So powerful was the impact of pantomimes of living political leaders that the early Emperor Domitian banished them. Trajan, however, "allowed the pantomimes back on the stage around A.D. 100, and his successor, Hadrian, who was particularly fond of the theater and its artists, took all the pantomimes associated with the court into state ownership."[31]

Pantomime entered the world of actual political behavior in terms of bodily gesture. Raising a hand, pointing a finger, turning the torso, formed a precise body language. Here, for instance, is how the Roman orator Quintillian instructed others to express *admiratio* (which means both surprise and admiration): "the right hand turns slightly upwards and the fingers are brought in to the palm, one after the other, beginning with the little finger; the hand is then reopened and turned round by a reversal of this motion"; a simpler gesture to express regret should be made by pressing a clenched fist to one's breast.[32] The orator, like the martyr acting out the castrated Atys, must go through a sequence of pantomimes; without them, his words lack force.

These political gestures became more simple and concise in Hadrian's era, as we see in Roman coins. Coins played an important role in the far-flung Empire, providing on their faces hard bits of information; the arts of pantomime were deployed in making the coins eloquent. The historian Richard Brilliant observes that makers of coins during Trajan's reign stamped on them imperial images which "abstract[ed] the royal image from situations in which his masterful character had been revealed," while the makers of Hadrianic coins "simplified . . . and abbreviated" the emperor's gestures; one coin depicting a royal decree contrasts "the stark lucidity of his image against the neutral ground" of the coin.[33] Rather than the unity of democratic words and deeds celebrated by Perikles, coin pantomime created a unity of imperial images and acts.

These were the elements of the *teatrum mundi:* a scene stamped with authority; an actor who crossed the line between illusion and reality;

acting based on the silent body language of pantomime. Such theatre had direct and immediate meaning. Anyone handling one of Hadrian's coins could at once understand the import of the coin by looking at the gestures on its two faces. The Roman in the amphitheatre knew immediately that the wretch dressed in a certain way was Orpheus, and that he was about to be eaten alive by a bear. In politics, gestures like *admiratio* could be simplified, as on Hadrianic coins, but the gesture itself was unproblematic, its essence fixed.

The teatrum mundi thus departed from rituals like the Greek Thesmophoria, which transformed a story through gesture and in space so that a new meaning emerged by metonymy from an old one. The teatrum mundi sought to make literal references, to repeat known meanings. The Romans gratified their taste for novelty in the amphitheatre by slaughtering a hundred Orpheuses with a hundred bears, by multiplying the image, rather than by contriving a new, strange death. This very taste for repetition impressed the image ever more strongly on a spectator's mind.

The teatrum mundi inspired St. Augustine with particular horror; its visual power could overwhelm even faith in God. To show the force of this evil, St. Augustine related the experience of a Christian friend who went to the Colosseum to test his faith. The Christian initially kept his head turned away from the violent show taking place in the arena below, praying for inner strength; slowly, as though a vise twisted his head, he began to look and succumbed to the spectacle, its bloody images entrancing him until he shouted and cheered like the mass of people around him. In the visual prison constructed in the pagan world, the Christian will weakened, then surrendered to images.

Some modern commentators think the Romans suffered from a dearth of visual imagery because they viewed the world so literally.[34] Rather than an absence of imagination, the Roman may have suffered from its graphic excess. Troubled by the dark forebodings conveyed in the gladiator's oath, living in a society where power fathered disorder, in a city choking on its growth, Hadrian's Romans entered into a "willing suspension of disbelief" through their eyes.

2. LOOK AND OBEY

We do not usually think of actors and geometricians as engaged in the same line of work. Yet bodily gestures were founded on a more systematic imagery, on the system of symmetries and visual balances which the Romans thought they had discovered in the human body. This bodily geometry the Romans in turn used to impose order on the world they ruled as imperial conquerors and as city builders. The Romans thus merged the desire to look and believe with the command to look and obey.

The geometry of the body

The Pantheon offers some clues about how they did so. The Pantheon is ruled by symmetry. The interior of the Pantheon is composed of three parts, a circular floor, a cylindrical wall, and the dome. The horizontal diameter is almost exactly equal to the vertical height. From outside to inside, the Pantheon is divided into three zones, a temple front, a middle passage, and the interior. From the middle passage one sees ahead straight lines inlaid on the floor which show one how to move forward; the floor lines lead the eye ahead to a large niche in the wall directly opposite the entrance, containing the most important cult statue in the building. Though the geometry is abstract, some architectural writers have spoken of the central floor lines as the building's "spine" and the large niche as its "head"; other writers, looking from floor to ceiling, have imagined the building as something like a Roman bust, the bottom cylindrical slice like the shoulders of a general, the statues like the carvings on a warrior's breastplate, the dome like his head—a somewhat awkward image because the opening at the top, the *oculus,* is literally the eye of the building.

Still, the geometry inspires these organic allusions for good reason. Vast as the Pantheon is, the building seems uncannily to be an extension of the human body. In particular the Pantheon's symmetrical play of curves and squares recalls famous drawings made by Leonardo and Serlio during the Renaissance. These drawings show a man's naked body, the arms and legs extended. In one, Leonardo da Vinci drew (circa A.D. 1490) a perfect circle around the outstretched limbs, with its center the man's navel; a perfect square connects the four points at the tips of the same man's fingers.

In the third of his *Ten Books of Architecture,* called "On Symmetry: In Temples and in the Human Body," Vitruvius directly connected the proportions of the human body to the proportions that should govern the architecture of a temple. "Nature has designed the human body so that its members are duly proportioned to the frame as a

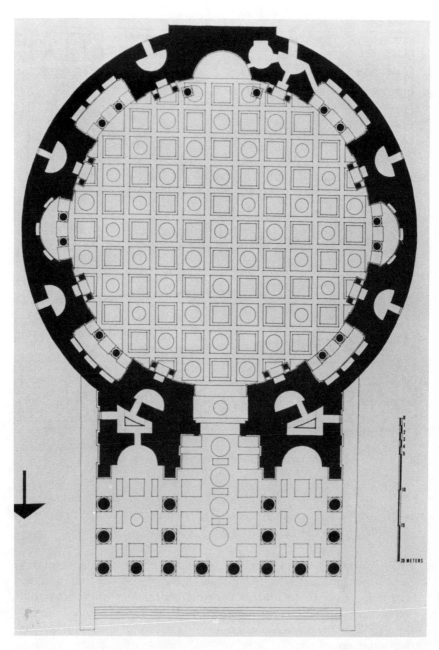

The Pantheon in Rome, modern drawing.

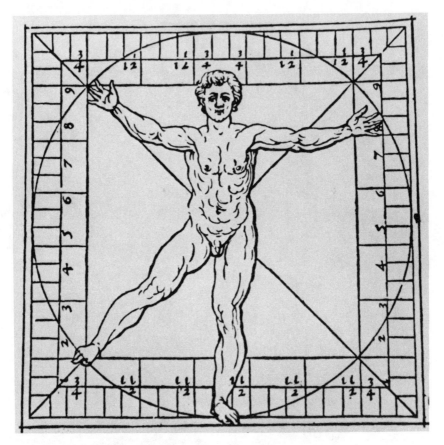

Sebastian Serlio's drawing of a man's body.

whole," he wrote,[35] and it is this that the maker of a building should emulate through the relation of the circle and square:

> If . . . there is a symmetrical correspondence between the members separately and the entire form of the body . . . we can have nothing but respect for those who, in constructing temples of the immortal gods, have so arranged the members of the works that both the separate parts and the whole design may harmonize in their proportions and symmetry.[36]

A temple should have equal and opposite parts just like the sides of the body. This is obvious in a square building, but the Romans were arch and dome makers. The genius of the Pantheon was to

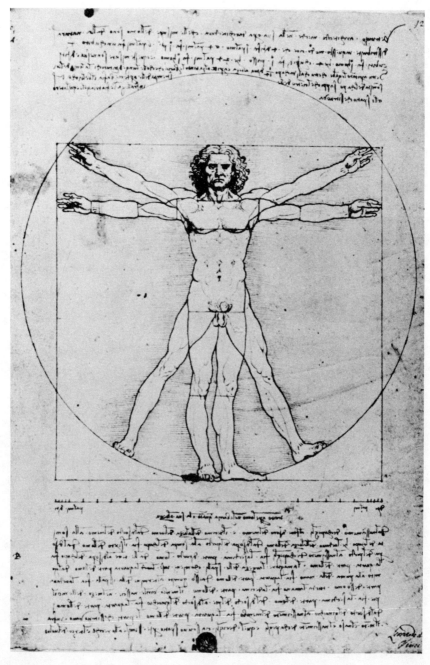

Leonardo da Vinci, *Human Figure in Circle, Illustrating Proportions,* 1485–90.

make bilateral symmetry rule within a spherical space: for instance, the two niches, one on either side of the main niche opposite the entrance, are bilaterally symmetrical. Vitruvius further believed that the architect must derive scale and proportion in a building from the scale and proportion of the body's parts. Vitruvius imagined the body's arms relate to its legs via the navel, and so to the umbilical cord, the source of life. The limbs can be extended so that arms and legs make lines: the two lines of limbs will intersect at the belly button. The tips of the fingers then establish the lines of a square. This is the Vitruvian body, as Leonardo and Serlio later drew it, the square inscribed within a circle, and this Vitruvian principle shapes the interior of the Pantheon.

This was the Roman master image of the body, as codified by Vitruvius from many diverse sources and long-established practices, as we shall see. By following this ideal order, an architect could make buildings on a human scale. More, this human geometry revealed something about what a city should look like.

The creation of a Roman city

Renaissance artists like Albrecht Dürer who studied Vitruvius' writings were struck by the possibilities for drawing a grid of smaller squares within his original square-within-a-circle, so that parts of the body could be defined within the general geometric system. The floor of the Pantheon shows that same division: it is a checkerboard, defined by squares made of marble, porphyry, and granite, aligned on the north-south axis to which the building as a whole is oriented. Stone circles are inlaid on alternating squares. The imperial designers of Vitruvius' own time planned entire towns making use of this system, creating a checkerboard of streets enclosing plots of land.

Commonly this urban design is called the Roman "grid plan," but it is not a Roman invention. The oldest known cities in Sumer were built according to it, as were Egyptian and Chinese cities thousands of years before Roman dominance. In Greece, Hippodamus designed checkerboard cities, as on the Italian mainland did the Etruscans. What matters about grids, as about any elemental image, is the way a particular culture uses them.

To start a city, or refound an existing city wrecked in the process of conquest, the Romans tried to establish the point they called the *umbilicus,* a center of the city approximating the navel of the body;

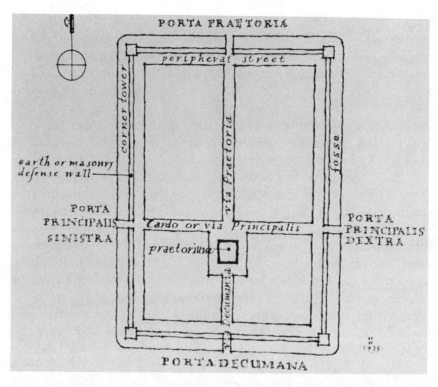

Plan of a Roman castrum, drawn by the monks of St. Gall. *Walter Horn and Ernest Born, from* The Plan of St. Gall *(University of California Press, 1980). All rights reserved.*

from this urban belly button the planners drew all measurements for spaces in the city. The floor of the Pantheon contains such an umbilicus. As in a game of checkers or chess the central square has great strategic value, so in the Pantheon: the central square of the Pantheon floor lies directly underneath the circular oculus opening up a view of the sky through the dome.

The planners also pinpointed the umbilicus of a city by studying the sky. The passage of the sun seemed to divide the sky in two; other measurements of stars at night seemed to cut this division at right angles, so that the heavens were composed of four parts. To found a town, one sought on the ground a spot that reflected directly below the point where the four parts of the sky met, as if the map of the sky were mirrored on the earth. Knowing its center, the planners could define the town's edge; here they tilled a furrow in the earth called the *pomerium,* which was a sacred boundary. To violate the pomerium, Livy said, was like deforming the human body by stretching it too far. Having now a center and an edge, the settlers drew the two principal right-angle streets which would intersect at the umbilicus; the streets were called the *decumanus maximus* and the *cardo maximus.* These street lines created a space of four symmetrical quadrants; surveyors next divided each quadrant in four. Now the city had sixteen sections. It would be divided again and again until it looked like the floor of the Pantheon.

The umbilicus had immense religious value. Below this point, the Romans thought the city was connected to the gods interred in the earth; above it, to the gods of light in the sky—the deities who controlled human affairs. Near it, the planner dug a hole in the earth, a hole called the *mundus* which was "a . . . chamber, or two such chambers, one above the other . . . consecrated to infernal gods" below the earth's crust.[37] It was literally a hellhole. In making a city, the settlers laid fruit and other offerings from their homes into the mundus, a ritual to propitiate these "infernal gods." Then they covered over the mundus, set up a square stone, and lit a fire. Now they had "given birth" to a city. Writing three hundred years before Hadrian, the Roman Polybius declared that the Roman military camp must consist of "a square, with streets and other constructions regularly planned like a town"; conquest was meant to induce that birth.[38]

Vitruvius thought of the legs and the arms of the human body connected to each other via the navel; the umbilical cord had greater symbolic importance in his architectural thinking than the genitals. So too the umbilicus of a city served as the point for calculating its geometries. Yet the navel was a highly emotionally charged marker of birth. The founding rites of a Roman town took cognizance of the terrifying powers of the unseen gods in the earth, whom the city planners sought to propitiate below the center. The terror associated with giving birth to a city marked the story of Rome's own founding.

Romulus, according to one legend, founded Rome on April 21, 753 B.C., by digging a mundus on the hill of the Palatine. A fire cult existed on the Palatine from earliest times, and from this fire cult came the first Temple of Vesta, a round building; food was stored in it, like the food stored in the earth in the mundus. Later the Temple of Vesta moved to the Roman forum, where the vestal virgins were charged with keeping the fire of the temple ever alight, save for one day a year; if it went out longer, Rome would perish, so powerful and deadly were the gods below the city. The dread of unseen powers which became so marked in Hadrian's time had its origins deep in Roman culture, felt at the very urban center.

It would not be surprising therefore that the seemingly rational geometry uniting the body and the city did not operate quite rationally. The Romans wrote about the places they conquered using very down-to-earth precepts: put a city where there are good harbors, a flourishing market, natural defenses, and so on. Yet often the town planners chose not to follow these rules. About ten miles north of Nîmes, in Roman Gaul and modern France, for instance, there is a site that would have made an excellent bastion, full of hilly outcrops, and containing at the time of Roman settlement a thriving market; the conquerors chose the more exposed, less economically active area to the south because here a deep mundus could be dug and filled with great quantities of food, in order to keep the gods of the underworld at bay.

Just as the gladiator's oath expresses both fear and resolution, so did the town planners' map. The digging of the mundus in a new town on the frontier declared that, here, Roman civilization would be born again; the disciplined and determined violence of the Roman legions balanced the fears represented by the hole the victors dug in the ground to propitiate their infernal gods. Because the Romans used the same geometry again and again in giving birth to cities, the urbanist Joyce Reynolds criticizes them as "notorious for their retention of thought-patterns appropriate to [Rome], despite the ever-increasing irrelevance of that civic ideology to their new imperial circumstances."[39] Yet these repetitive settlements reflected and arose from an essential aspect of Roman culture: the teatrum mundi.

In Rome, the people watched gladiators and martyrs slaughter and be slaughtered in pantomimes obsessively repeated; on the frontier, the troops gathered to watch the surveyors act out for them in elaborate ceremonies the acts of locating the umbilicus, digging the mundus, and tilling the pomerium at the new town's edge. The surveyors repeated the ceremonies whenever and wherever the legions advanced; in Gaul, on the Danube, in Britain, the same words and gestures conjuring the same image of place.

Like the theatre director, the Roman planner worked with fixed images. Roman imperial planning sought to map out a city at a single stroke, Roman geography imposed the moment a conquering army gained territory. The urban grid aided in this because such a geometric image stands out of time. Yet to plan in this way assumes there is nothing "there" in the conquered territory. It seemed to the Roman

conquerors, indeed, that they marched into emptiness, though in fact
the landscape might have been dotted with settlement. "If I look
upon the country, 'tis devoid of charm, nothing in the whole world
can be more cheerless," wrote the poet Ovid in exile; "if I look upon
the men, they are scarce men worthy the name; they have more of
cruel savagery than wolves. . . . With skins and loose breeches they
keep off the evils of the cold; their shaggy faces are protected with
long locks."[40] If Romans on the march remained Romans, in the grip
of a repetition compulsion, there was also a great divide between
home and frontier: at the edge of the Empire mundi, these pantomimes of refounding Rome threatened to destroy the lives of the
conquered.

Of course the conquered people seldom fit the stereotype of histo-
ryless and characterless brutes. In Gaul and Britain, the native tribes
often in fact were townmakers on their own, and the Roman elabora-
tion of a city might co-exist with continuing native growth—the town
center Romanized, the residential areas and peripheral markets elab-
orating local traditions. In the Greek city-states which the Romans
conquered, these prejudices fell entirely flat, since so much of
Roman high culture derived from the Greeks. The imposition of
"Rome" was more like the overlaying of a memory of "home" in
order to legitimate rule.

The conquerors hoped that urban form would help assimilate barbarians quickly into Roman ways. The ancient historian Tacitus provided a picture of just how this happened when Agricola governed
Britain:

> He would exhort individuals, assist communities, to erect temples,
> market-places, houses: he praised the energetic, rebuked the indolent,
> and the rivalry for his compliments took the place of coercion. More-
> over he began to train the sons of the chieftains in a [Roman] liberal
> education. . . . As a result, the nation which used to reject the Latin
> language began to aspire to rhetoric: further, the wearing of our dress
> became a distinction, and the toga came into fashion.[41]

The geometry of the new city had economic consequences for the
conquerors themselves. Carving up the city quadrants continued
until the blocks of land were small enough to be given to individuals.
In the army, the number of plots a soldier received depended on his
rank. The conquered countryside was apportioned in the same way,
soldiers receiving shares of land finely calculated to their rank. The

mathematical boundaries mattered immensely to a Roman, not simply because he owned land, but also because his possession had been *rationalized* by the process of subdivision. The owner could defend his property rights against stronger individuals, since his ownership of a part derived from the very logic which generated the whole. Bronze tablets called *formae* described where the land was and showed its size and shape. These pieces of bronze were the most precious objects a soldier carried with him. "No other civilization," Joseph Rykwert writes, "had practised, as the Romans did during the late republic and the empire, the imposition of a constant, uniform pattern on the towns, on the countryside, and also on their military establishments, with almost obsessional persistence."[42]

This then was the design of "Rome" impressed into other places; it was, precisely, an organic geometric design. What meaning could this design have in Hadrian's Rome itself, a city which had long since effaced whatever general plan governed its birth?

The Roman forum

The old Roman forum *(Forum Romanum)* was a town center much like the Athenian agora of Perikles' time, mixing politics, economics, religion, and sociability. Amid the milling crowd, special groups had each their own turf. Plautus, the Roman playwright, sardonically described these territories during the early second century B.C. according to various sexual tastes:

> . . . rich married loungers, hang around the Basilica. A good supply of harlots, too, if not in prime condition; also men for hire-purchase . . . in the Lower Forum respectable and well-to-do citizens out for a walk: flashier types in the middle Forum. By the Old Shops, the money changers—loans negotiated or accepted. . . . In the Vicus Tuscus, homosexuals, very versatile, flounce about.[43]

The forum differed from the agora in framing this diverse crowd in a more rectangular space, lined on all four sides with buildings. Particularly important was a religious building, the Portico of the Twelve Gods, which abutted the old forum at the base of the Capitoline Hill. Whereas the Greek gods continually fought one another, here, in something like an early pantheon, the deities met peaceably. The Twelve Gods were known as *Di Consentes et Complices*—agreeing and harmonious. The early Romans imagined that "there were agreed-upon ranks of supernatural power" in the heavens and in the underworld.[44] That same image of gods lined up in proper order suggested the form Romans sought to build on earth, in the forum.

The Romans sought to make their architecture ever more agreeing, harmonious, and linear through the development of two forms: the peristyle and the basilica. As we understand these building forms today, the peristyle is a long colonnade running ground a central court or joining buildings; the basilica is a rectangular building in which people enter at one end and move toward the other. In their Roman origins, these two architectural forms were not nearly so distinct. The Romans sought to create a space in which a person was meant to move forward, rather than be distracted by sideways movement; Roman space had a spine. This was how the first modern

The Roman forum in the fourth century B.C.

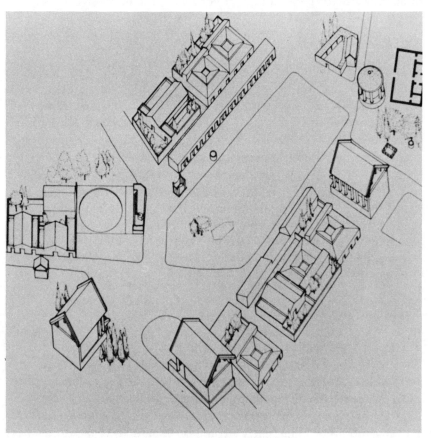

museum worked. In 318 B.C., above a row of shops lining one side of the forum, the city built a long second story (the *Maeniana*), in which souvenirs of Roman conquests were laid out in historical order. By moving along the spine, the visitor could follow the history of Roman military might.

"A basilica was but a large meeting hall."[45] The form originated in Greece as a hall of judgment, the judge sitting at one end. In the Roman world, basilicas were long, tall structures, often flanked by strips of building with lower roofs attached to the sides. The central hall was lit at both ends, as well as by windows above the line where the side strips of building attached to the main body. The basilica contained hundreds or sometimes thousands of people, moving along its spine in one end and out the other. The first fully documented basilica in the Forum Romanum appeared in 184 B.C.; the Romans then added ever larger structures made on the same principles, as giant, directional boxes.

A modern history has described what these buildings might have looked like to a Roman standing outside in the open air of the Forum Romanum: "you saw the colonnades and porticoes of temples and basilicas on each side, and as a backdrop at the far end, the facade of the Temple of Concordia."[46] But you, as a Roman, did not idly saunter by. The great buildings seemed to command you to place yourself squarely in front of them.

We recall that the surfaces of the Greek Parthenon were designed to be seen from many different points in the city, and that the viewer's eye travelled round the building's exterior. The early Roman temple, by contrast, sought to station the viewer only in front. Its roof extended in eaves on the sides; its ceremonial decoration lay all on the front face; the paving and planting around it was oriented to a person looking at the front.[47] Inside the temple, the building similarly gave directions: look forward, move forward. These bossy boxes were the origins of the visual directives made in Hadrian's Pantheon, with its spine and bilateral symmetries on the walls and on the floor.

The geometry of Roman space disciplined bodily movement, and in this sense issued the command, look and obey. This command intersected with the other Roman dictum, look and believe, for instance at a famous turning point in Rome's history. While fighting in Gaul, Julius Caesar hoped to remind Romans of his existence by creating a new forum, under the Capitoline Hill, just west of the Forum Romanum. Though its stated purpose was to provide addi-

tional space for the legal business of the Republic, its real purpose
was to make Romans literally face Caesar's power while he was away.
Here he built a Temple of Venus Genetrix. Venus was supposedly
the goddess who gave birth to Caesar's family, the Julians; Caesar's
construction "was in effect a temple to the Julian family."[48] This single monument dominated, as the head of the building complex; sub-
sidiary buildings or walls extended out from it precisely to create
bilateral symmetry along the sides of a rectangle. By positioning the
viewer squarely in front of the main temple, as in front of a shrine
to the gods, Julius Caesar sought to underline his family's supposedly
divine origins, and so make his own awesome presence felt.

As in the provincial cities, the geometry of power in Rome's center eroded the display of human diversities. As the Forum Romanum
became more regular, the city's butchers, grocers, fishmongers, and
merchants took themselves off to separate quarters of the city, leaving the business of the forum, in later Republican times, to lawyers
and bureaucrats; then, as the emperors built their own forums, these
political pets left the Forum Romanum to follow their masters into
new spaces. The buildings became, in modern planning jargon, more
"mono-functional," and by Hadrian's time many were largely empty.
"Many of the political and commercial activities that in the agora
required free space have been displaced to the periphery," the archeologist Malcolm Bell writes; "in this well-planned world . . . there
was little need for the ambiguous values of the stoa."[49]

As diversity ebbed, this ancient center of Rome became a place
given over to the ceremonial, the Forum Romanum becoming a
point at which power donned the reassuring robes and roles of pantomime. For instance, until about 150 B.C. both trials by jury and
certain voting by citizens occurred within a building at the side of
the Forum Romanum, the Comitium. As urgent appeals to buy a
rare apricot from Smyrna or to make a good deal on bulls' testicles
faded from the Forum Romanum, voting and political discussion
moved outside. Speakers harangued the crowd from the Rostra,
originally a curved platform jutting out from the Comitium, the
voice of the speaker reinforced by a solid building behind him.
When Julius Caesar moved the old Rostra to a new site in the Forum
Romanum, from the side in to the northwest end, he meant this new
speaker's stand to be a place for ceremonial declaration rather than
participatory politics. The speaker no longer spoke surrounded by
people on three sides; instead, he was placed like a judge within the
earliest basilicas. Outside, his voice now projected poorly, but no

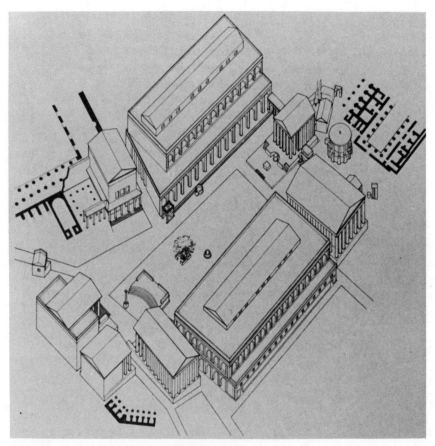

The Roman forum in the first century A.D.

matter. The orator was meant to appear, to point a finger, to clutch his breast, to spread out his arms: he was to look like a statesman to the vast throng who could not hear him, and who had lost the power to act on his words in any event.

Visual order also put its stamp on the buildings housing the Roman Senate, as that supreme institution of the Roman Republic declined into a largely ceremonial body with the coming of the emperors. Until near the end of the Republic, the Senate fronted prominently on the Forum Romanum, in the Curia Hostilia, accommodating the three hundred Senators of Rome in a building terraced inward in a series of steps. Julius Caesar pushed the Curia out of the forum, so that it stood hidden behind another large building, the Basilica Aemilia. Here, in the Julian Curia (the Curia Iulia), an aisle led from the entrance to a podium for Senate officials. Rows of seats gave off at right angles from this spine; seating by rows was by rank, seniors at front, juniors at back. Voting was not like the Greek Pnyx, however. Senators moved from one side of the main aisle to the other, staying within their linear rank, and the presiding officer decided an issue had been judged when he saw a greater crowd at one side than the other. The serried ranks of order among the gods had now been reproduced in a Senate ever more impotent to control the affairs of state.

The political leech Velleius Paterculus evoked the result of these visual changes, in words meant to praise the first emperor, Augustus:

> Credit has been restored in the forum, strife has been banished from the Forum, canvassing for office from the Campus Martius, discord from the senate house; justice, equity, and industry, long buried in oblivion, have been restored to the state . . . rioting in the theater has been suppressed. All have either been imbued with the wish to do right or have been forced to do so.[50]

A ceremonial space, dignified, empty of business, unseemly sex, plain sociability, the Forum Romanum became ever more deadly by Hadrian's day, the old urban center a place in which, in Vellieus' telling words, "All have either been imbued with the wish to do right or have been forced to do so."

The history of the Forum Romanum foreshadowed the sequence of great imperial forums which would be built under the Empire. By the end of the Imperial era, these composed immense ceremonial spaces through which Romans moved as along a spine, facing enormous, cowing buildings which represented the majesty of the living gods who ruled their lives. No scheming Supreme Mathematician presided over the fortunes of the Forum Romanum, the birth of the Forum Iulium, and the growth of the imperial forums, making these spaces ever more daunting as the voices of citizens grew weaker. Instead, the visual control which the Romans practiced in making cities on the frontier had now come home. Though cosmopolitan

The Imperial Forums of Rome, ca. A.D. 120.

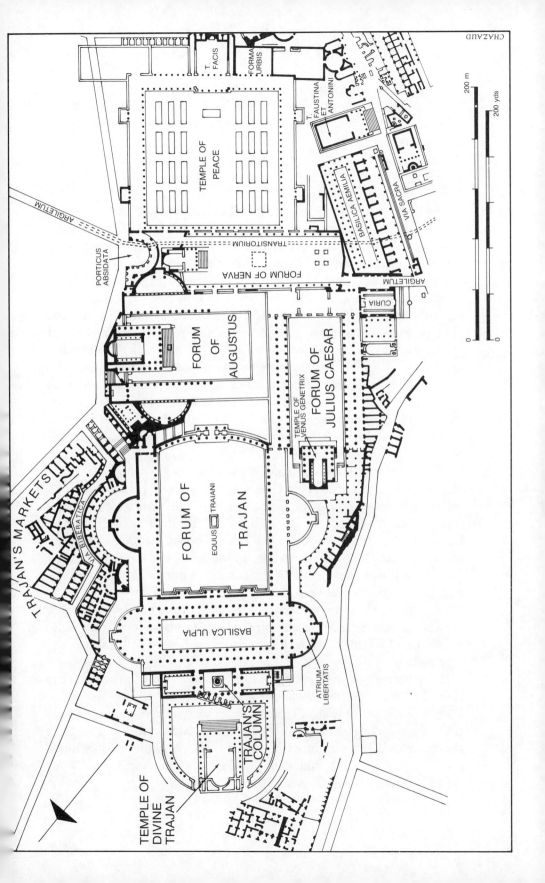

Romans loathed the provinces, by Hadrian's time the visual orders Romans gave to conquered peoples ruled their own lives as well.

By Hadrian's time, the geometries of power ruled intimate space as much as the public realm.

The Roman house

The Roman house contained families remarkably unlike Greek families in one respect, for there was much greater equality between the sexes. Wives could retain their own property, if they married *sine manu,* that is, without coming under the complete authority, the manus, of the husband. Daughters could share with sons some types of inheritance. Men and women dined together; in the earliest days of Rome men reclined on couches while women stood, but by the time of Hadrian, married couples reclined together—a sight that would have been inconceivable to a Periklean Greek. To be sure, the family group was strongly hierarchical and patriarchal, with the oldest male its ruling authority. Yet the more complex relations between men and women signalled ways in which the Roman household, the *domus,* mirrored the city outside household walls. Geometry in the house made sense of the classes, clients, ages, and property of the people it contained.

The exterior of the old Roman domus was no more important that the exterior of the Periklean Greek house, a set of blank walls. The interiors of some houses might at first sight look quite similar, with rooms ranged around an open courtyard. Yet from its beginnings, linearity ruled. One entered an old Roman house through a vestibule and came into the open-air atrium; to the sides, one saw rooms used for sleeping and storage; ahead, across the pool or fountain, one saw a niche containing the patron gods of the house. This was the place of the father, where he sat sometimes on a raised chair like a throne, flanked on either side by ancestral portraits made into masks; the visitor faced a tableau of authority composed of masks, statues, and a living man.

If the house was sufficiently wealthy, linearity ruled as well on the side: one moved from room to room in terms of who and what should dominate in each. There was a "clear spatial statement of precedence, the clear shape of before, behind, and beside, and of great and small" in the ordering of household spaces, so that people knew to a fine point who should walk first into a room and in what order others should follow, or which rooms should be used, depending on

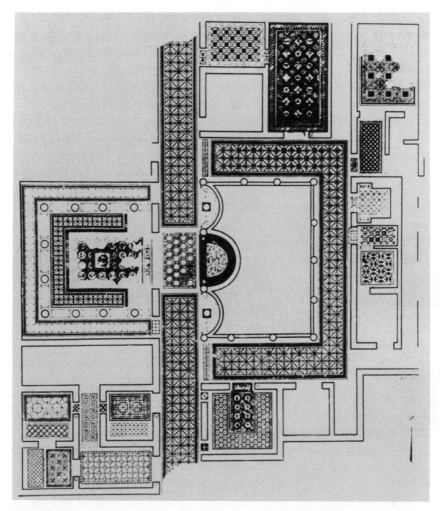

The House of Neptune in Acholla with *oecus* to the west, *triclinium* to the south, and bedrooms abutting antechambers or corridors in the southwestern corner.

the importance of the guests.[51] This supposes, of course, that a family could afford a house of many rooms, and most Romans obviously could not. Yet domestic order at the top of the social pyramid served as a standard for how others should live.

We could imagine visiting such an ideal home in Hadrian's time, one belonging to a family of the upper middle class, probably comparable to the home of a doctor or judge in the nineteenth century, staffed by eight to ten servants. It may be useful in making this mental visit to keep in mind that the price of a healthy human slave in Roman times was a third to a quarter the price of a horse. We arrive at the entrance to the house, whose gate (or gates, for frequently there was a progression of three gates) lead to a covered vestibule in which we and other visitors are first scrutinized. The vestibule is meant to impress us with the family's wealth; Vitruvius recommended it be as lavish as possible. The vestibule gives onto the colonnaded court. The recession of rooms off the main courtyard would have been more evident in Roman times than in modern designs based on the same principle, for the Roman house usually lacked inner doors; there were instead cloth hangings. An upper servant signals how far we can penetrate into the house by how many of these hangings are drawn back.

We would then enter the open courtyard of the house, standing at the edge of its pool, waiting. In some ways the open court functioned like an agora: "it was a space in which a variety of activities took place, from solitary pursuits to great receptions befitting the master's high social station—to say nothing of the work of the servants, for whom the peristyle served as passageway, work space, and water supply."[52] And in some ways it worked more like a forum: here the throng of people around us will be sorted out in order of importance to be received by the master within. Those drawn into the further rooms of the domus have, generally, a closer tie to the family than those kept in the open space of the peristyle. Everything in the house conveys sequence and progression. In the very grandest houses, the main court leads to smaller peristyles which in turn had rooms radiating off them. Where a particular member of the household receives us will depend on that person's importance in the domus as well as our own. This hierarchy extends to the servants, who controlled spaces in the Roman house rather as they did in English houses of the nineteenth century—the major domo with his own offices, the butler and housekeeper's dining room, and so on.[53]

Lines order social life in the dining room, or *triclinium*. If we have been invited to dinner, we see that the members of the house take their places on the couches depending on their rank, in a straight sequence along the walls culminating in the master's place on the right end of the principal couch. Married women rest on their sides on the couches along with the men, yet no one is entirely relaxed. Juvenal railed against the pomposity of these dinners, the paterfamilias lecturing the guests who became ever more fawning in their replies, the further away they sat from the host—and yet Juvenal, consummate Roman, also reckoned to an exact degree the standing of each member of the house by where he or she reclined.

The lines of power culminated in the master bedroom, where we are not welcome. "At the moment of intercourse," the historian Peter Brown observes, "the bodies of the [Roman] elite must not be allowed to set up so much as a single, random eddy in the solemn stream that flowed from generation to generation through the marriage bed."[54] The image of a "blood line" is a figure of speech now; to the ancient Romans it was a literal measure. Plutarch declared that the marriage chamber should be "a school of orderly behavior,"[55] for once married, the nuclear pair was governed by these blood lines: an illicit child became a legal claim upon the family's property, as was not the case in Periklean Athens.

Body, house, forum, city, empire: all are based on linear imagery. Architectural criticism speaks of the Roman concern for clear and precise orientation in space, spaces with well-defined orthogonals, like the grid plan, structures with strict forms, like the Roman arch, a half-circle, or buildings with severely defined volumes, like the domes which result from rotating that half-circle in a three-dimensional space. The desire for precise orientation spoke of a deeply felt need, akin to the greed for images which could be repeated over and over, and taken literally as truth. This visual language expressed the need of an uneasy, unequal, and unwieldy people seeking the reassurance of place; the forms sought to convey that a durable, essential Rome stood somehow outside the ruptures of history. And though Hadrian spoke this language masterfully, he may have known it was all a fiction.

3. THE IMPOSSIBLE OBSESSION

Sometime in his reign—given its subject matter, I suspect when he was an old man—Hadrian composed the following short poem, "To his Soul," which reads in Latin:

> *Animula uagula blandula,*
> *hospes comesque corporis,*
> *quae nunc abibis in loca*

pallidula rigida nudula,
nec ut soles dabis iocos!

Here is the translation the young Byron made of it:

Ah! gentle, fleeting, wav'ring sprite,
Friend and associate of this clay!
To what unknown region borne
Wilt thou now wing thy distant flight?
No more with wonted humour gay,
    But pallid, cheerless, and forlorn.[56]

    A relentless builder of place, here Hadrian attests to the dissolutions of time. The poem can be read as more a bittersweet than despairing lyric, as the historian G. W. Bowersock thinks it should be, for the tone is informal, the diction affectionate.[57] The poem could also be read as the novelist Marguerite Yourcenar chose, based on a sentence she found in the letters of Flaubert about Hadrian's era: "Just when the gods had ceased to be, and the Christ had not yet come, there was a unique moment in history, between Cicero and Marcus Aurelius, when man stood alone."[58] Certainly, Hadrian's poem is far from a boast.

    The "clay" in Byron's translation is in Hadrian's Latin "the body"; Byron mistranslates *soles* to suggest loneliness in the world. But perhaps the modern poet understood the spirit of the ancient emperor-poet, an emperor who stamped his reign throughout the Western world, and who built on the fear that man indeed stands alone. To modern critics of the Pantheon like William MacDonald, taking that liberty with Hadrian's words would not be foreign to the building. Saturated with Vitruvian, religious, and imperial symbols as the Pantheon is; controlled, almost over-determined, as is its visual form; still the building arouses a profound and mysterious sense of solitude.

    The very different spirit in which a Christian might have written a testament to the power of time is suggested in a poem by Alexander Pope whose title as well as general subject resembles Hadrian's.[59] Pope's "Dying Christian to his Soul" ends with the following stanza:

The world recedes; it disappears!
    Heaven opens on my eyes! my ears
    With sounds seraphic ring:

> *Lend, lend your wings! I mount! I fly!*
> *O Grave, where is thy victory?*
> *O Death, where is thy sting?*

Beginning with the small cell of Christians in Hadrian's Rome, our ancestors found this affirmation of time more compelling than Hadrian's pagan solitude.

CHAPTER FOUR

Time
in the Body

Early Christians in Rome

I n the pagan world, bodily suffering seldom appeared as a human opportunity. Men and women may have confronted it, may have learned from it, but did not seek it out. With the coming of Christianity, bodily suffering acquired a new spiritual value. Coping with pain perhaps mattered more than confronting pleasure; pain was harder to transcend, a lesson Christ taught through His own sufferings. The Christian's journey in life took shape through transcending *all* physical stimulation; as a Christian became indifferent to the body, he or she hoped to draw closer to God.

If the Christian's journey in time succeeded, away from the body and toward God, the believer would also withdraw from attachments to place. The pagan commands to look and believe, look and obey would not arouse faith; no orientation in space would reveal where God is. God is everywhere and nowhere; Jesus was a wanderer, as were Jewish prophets before Him. The believer following in the

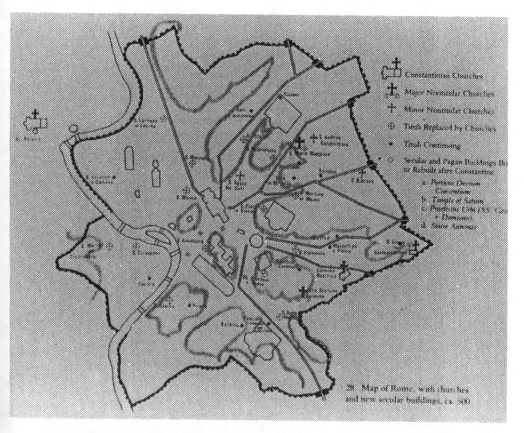

Map of Christian Rome, ca. A.D. 500.

prophet's path would leave the city, at least spiritually. In uprooting him- or herself, the Christian would re-enact the Exile from the Garden, becoming more aware and more compassionate towards other human beings in pain.

This Christian journey made heroic demands on its followers. A religion aimed at the poor and the weak asked them to find within themselves a superhuman strength. The story of the early Christians in Rome was of a people who clung to that faith yet discovered they, only human, needed ground under their feet. They needed a city.

1. THE ALIEN BODY OF CHRIST

Antinous and Christ

One of the most dramatic passages in early Church history arose from the charge a Christian brought against Hadrian's most personal building project, a city the emperor built in honor of his follower Antinous. Little is certain about the personal relations of Antinous and Hadrian. They probably met when Hadrian visited Athens or another Hellenic city in the early 120s; Antinous was then a boy of twelve to fourteen. A few years later, Roman coins showed Antinous among the emperor's hunting parties, and so part of his intimate entourage. In the late 120s, when Antinous was nineteen or twenty, he suddenly died; his body was found washed up in the Nile. The emperor paid tribute to the young man by erecting a city in his honor on the shore of the Nile where Antinous died, called Antinöpolis; Hadrian filled his own retreat at Tivoli with statues of the youth. That Hadrian and Antinous were lovers is a logical reading of this fragmentary record. The love Hadrian bore Antinous would explain not only his desire to build an entire city in the boy's honor, but also Hadrian's decree, shortly after the boy died, that Antinous was a god.

The French novelist and classicist Marguerite Yourcenar wrote a novel about Hadrian and Antinous—*The Memoirs of Hadrian*—which turns on the puzzle of why Antinous drowned. The novelist chose to confront various Victorian explanations of this event, explanations that either steered clear of male love, Antinous simply drowning by accident in the river, or made male love the cause of death, Hadrian drowning Antinous for being unfaithful. Yourcenar shaped her story upon another explanation which was at once more sexually open and more historically probable. She had Hadrian consider the possibility that Antinous committed suicide. It was commonly believed in the eastern Mediterranean at this time that one could, through suicide committed using the proper ritual, save the life of a person one loved; the life force would then pass from the dead into the living. Hadrian had been perilously ill shortly before Antinous' death, and Yourcenar conjectured that the young man had killed himself in order to preserve the emperor. In the 130s the dead Antinous indeed became a popular cult figure as a new Osiris, the young, healing Egyptian god whose death passed his life force into others.

Because the Antinous cult referred to Osiris, some Romans compared Antinous to other gods who had sacrificed themselves for men. The most famous of these comparisons was made by Celsus, a Roman who wrote a generation after Hadrian in the latter third of the second century; he compared Antinous to Christ. Celsus had declared, probably in a text dating from 177–180, that since Anti-

Antinous of Eleusis.

nous' suicide to save Hadrian's life was comparable to the martyrdom of Christ, "the honour which [Christians] give to Jesus is no different from that paid to Hadrian's favourite."[1]

This comparison provoked a generation later a counterattack by Origen, one of the first great Christian intellectuals. He sought to disparage a loving bond between men as weak and unstable: "What is there in common between the noble life of our Jesus and the life of the favourite of Hadrian who did not even keep the man from a morbid lust for women?"[2] But in responding to Celsus, and in challenging the comparison between Antinous and Christ, Origen had a far deeper goal in mind: he wanted to show that the body of Christ is unlike a human body.

Unlike Antinous, Origen maintained, Jesus cannot be accused "of having had the slightest contact with the least licentiousness," because Christ is not like a pagan god with desires and bodily longings.[3] The pagan gods of Hadrian's time appeared as magnified human beings, endowed with supernatural powers and eternal life. They knew pleasure and fear, jealousy and rage; many of them were monsters of egotism. Jesus, Origen wrote, was different; just as He had no sexual desires, He suffered upon the cross only out of compassion for His earthly followers. Christ may well seem strange to pagans for lacking bodily sensations, but this is because He is God; His body is an alien body, unfathomable by human beings.

Origen dismissed the magical powers of the dead Antinous as mere "Egyptian magic and spells," mocked Hadrian's construction of Antinöpolis, and declared that "the case of Jesus is very different from this." Here Origen took a second, immensely challenging step. He declared that faith in Jesus cannot be created by the state. Christians did not "oblige some king who commanded them to come or to obey the order of a governor."[4] In the Pantheon the gods gathered in their niches to attest to the fortunes of the Empire, as they had gathered four hundred years before in the Portico of the Twelve Gods to smile, "agreeing and harmonious," on the felicity of Rome; politics and religion were inseparable. Now the state could not decree faith, and all monuments and temples were mere hollow shells.

The early Christians did not so much publicly challenge the state-controlled forms of worship as recoil from them personally. Yet the new religion drew a line which even the most cosmopolitan and accommodating Christian could not cross. He or she was obliged by the rules of faith, the historian Arthur Darby Nock writes, "to renounce the public cult of the Emperor"; this meant that the Christian "could not swear by the Emperor's genius, the life-spirit of his family; he could not take part in the celebrations of the days of his birth and of his accession; he could not as a soldier or as a municipal magistrate take part in those acts of worship in which either would participate."[5] Such a divide between politics and faith arose from the very conception of time which marked early Christian belief.

This belief asserted people are not born Christian, they *become* Christian—a self-transformation which does not occur by following orders. Faith has to be created in the course of an individual's life, and conversion is not a one-time event; once it starts, it never stops unfolding. Such spiritual time was expressed in theological language by the assertion that believing is an experience of becoming. Conversion separates the person ever further away from dependence on the commands of a dominant power, and so drives a wedge between state and religion.

When William James came to write about the psychological experience of conversion in *The Varieties of Religious Experience,* he noted that conversion could take two forms; the first form of conversion is psychologically "cool," James thought, rather like changing political parties. One may well include bits and pieces of what one believed before in converting, and one preserves a certain measure of detachment about the new doctrine even in subscribing to it. One does not lose one's place in the world; such an experience is usually a discrete, one-time event. James had in mind people who converted to Unitarianism in New England; reform Judaism might also fit this picture.

The other experience of conversion, James wrote, is much more impassioned; it comes from a sense that the way one lives now is all wrong, that fundamental change is necessary. But in this form of conversion, "the sense of our present wrongness is a far more distinct piece of our consciousness than is the imagination of any positive ideal that we can aim at." This form of conversion has been expressed by Arthur Darby Nock as a "turning away . . . as much as a turning towards."[6] Because it does not resemble changing political parties, this turning away is never finished in the course of a lifetime. The early Christians converted in the second manner, that of turning away. In the pagan world, the body belonged to the city; yet free from this bondage, where did one go?[7] There was no clear roadmap; the maps of worldly power were useless. And the confusions of becoming were especially potent among early Christians because in the Judaic origins of Christianity a devout person wandered, uprooted, from place to place.[8]

The people of the Old Testament thought of themselves as wanderers, and the Yahweh of the Old Testament was himself a wandering god, his Ark of the Covenant portable. In the theologian Harvey Cox's words, "When the Ark was finally captured by the Philistines, the Hebrews began to realize that Yahweh was not localized even in it. . . . He traveled with His people and elsewhere."[9] Yahweh was a god of time rather than of place, a god who promised to his followers a divine meaning for their unhappy travels.

Early Christians drew on these Old Testament values. The author of the "Epistle to Diognatus" at the height of the Roman Empire's glory, for instance, declared that

> Christians are not distinguished from the rest of humanity either in locality or in speech or in customs. For they do not dwell off somewhere in cities of their own . . . nor do they practice an extraordinary style of life. . . . They dwell in their own countries, but only as sojourners. . . . Every foreign country is a fatherland to them, and every fatherland is a foreign country.[10]

Even if one does not wander physically, one must lose one's attachments to where one lives. St. Augustine expressed this injunction as the Christian's obligation to make "a pilgrimage through time." He wrote in *The City of God:*

> Now, it is recorded of Cain that he built a city, while Abel, as though he were merely a pilgrim on earth, built none. For, the true City of the saints is in heaven, though here on earth it produces citizens in which it wanders as on a pilgrimage through time looking for the Kingdom of eternity.[11]

This "pilgrimage through time" rather than loyalty to physical places drew its authority from Jesus' refusal to allow His disciples to build monuments to Him, and His promise to destroy the Temple of Jerusalem. To be an ardent citizen, engaged in the life around oneself, conflicted with the values of faith in another world. For the sake of one's spiritual welfare, one had to break the emotional bonds of place.

That effort began in one's own body. Origen's attack on Celsus, Antinous, and Hadrian meant to show that Christianity had revolutionized the pagan experience of the body. Origen sought in his writings against Celsus and in his own life to exemplify that revolution. He wrote that conversion may start intellectually, in pondering how Christ's body is so unlike our own. The convert learns not to identify his or her own sufferings with the sufferings of Jesus, nor to imagine that divine love resembles human desire. For this reason, Hadrian's sin in deifying Antinous, and Antinous' sin in dying for Hadrian, lay in connecting physical passion to divinity. Pagan Romans like Celsus, who could make little sense of these assertions, thought the secrecy practiced by Christians came from the fact that they conducted orgies in private—perfectly acceptable behavior, and not foreign to the occasional wild parties staged by the gods themselves.

The Christian's next step in conversion would be more radical, a step Origen took to an extreme. In a fit of religious ecstasy, he castrated himself with a knife. Again, pagans frequently accused Christians of mutilating their bodies in the secret rites. If few actually did, Origen saw his own passion as more generally significant in following the Passion of Christ, for the effort to confront and overcome pain is a far more decisive step than the mere resolve to abstain from pleasure. We cannot simply decide to abstain from pain. Origen's self-mutilation had resonances in ancient paganism, moreover, for instance the self-blinding of Oedipus, which led the pagan king to a new moral understanding; or again in other monotheistic cults like early Zoroastrianism, whose followers sometimes stared at the sun until they went blind; as their bodies transformed, they thought they began to sense God.

A modern person may honor these acts as truly ascetic, yet explain them as deriving from a sense of bodily shame, in the Christian case a shame traceable back to the transgressions of Adam and Eve. For Origen, bodily shame could not be an end in itself. The body of the Christian must step beyond the very limits of pleasure and pain, in order to feel *nothing,* to lose sensation, to transcend desire. Thus Origen reacted most strongly against the charge made by Celsus, who himself turned a gimlet eye on the orgiastic practices of many of the Eastern cults devoted to Osiris, that Christian discipline of the body was a form of masochism. Celsus wrote that Christians "go astray in evil ways and wander about in great darkness more iniquitous and impure than that of the revellers of Antinous in Egypt."[12]

By describing this arduous and unnatural bodily journey, Origen came to affirm the two social foundations of Christianity. The first was the Christian doctrine of equality between human beings. In the sight of this God, all human bodies are alike, neither beautiful nor ugly, superior nor inferior. Images and visual forms no longer matter. Thus did the Christian principle challenge the Greek celebration of nakedness, the Roman formulas, "Look and believe," "Look and obey." Moreover, though Christianity for a long time held to ancient ideas about body heat and physiology, early Christianity broke in principle with the conclusion about the inequality between men and women based on that physiology. The bodies of men and women are equal, among believers there will be no more "male and female." St. Paul in First Corinthians argued for strict dress codes separating the appearance of men from women; yet he also maintained that male and female prophets are filled with "one Spirit," and in this sense gender-free.[13] It was thanks to the alien, revolutionary body of Christ that His followers freed themselves from the prison of worldly appearances based on sex or wealth—or any other visible measure. These had no compelling value in this religion of the Other.

Secondly, Christianity allied itself ethically with poverty, with the weak, and with the oppressed—with all those who are vulnerable bodies. Of prostitutes, John Chrysostom declared, "For say not this, that she that is stripped is a harlot; but that the nature is the same, and they are bodies alike, both that of the harlot and that of the free woman."[14] The Christian emphasis on the equality of the humble and the power of poverty derived directly from the religion's understanding of Christ's body. Perceived as a low-born, weak man by others, His martyrdom was meant in part to restore honor to those who most were like Him in the world. The historian Peter Brown summarizes this connection of Christ's vulnerable body and the bodies of the oppressed by saying that "The two great themes of sexuality and poverty gravitated together, in the rhetoric of John and of many other Christians. Both spoke of a universal vulnerability of the body, to which all men and women were liable, independent of class and civic status."[15]

Logos is Light

"How then can I know God? . . . And how can you show him to me?" the pagan Celsus demanded, to which the Christian Origen replied, "The Creator of all . . . is Light."[16] When Christians sought to explain the process of becoming, they invoked the experience of light. They described conversion as a process of Illumination; in Judeo-Christian usage, the Logos, the divine connection between

The Passion of Christ becomes a triumph, as in St. John's Gospel. The Cross is merged into Constantine's victorious standard and the crown of thorns is replaced with a laurel wreath.

words, means words on which light has been cast. Origen declared that light showed Christ "as he was before he became flesh" and after He left the flesh.[17]

Light, pure light, divine light, shows no image. It was for this reason that St. Augustine "condemned astronomers for their efforts to master the heavens . . . [and] offered the analogy of a spider entangling its victim in its web, calling [such] curiosity the 'lust of the eye.' "[18] Heaven is not visible in the heavens.

Light is everywhere. Theologically, this means that the immaterial God is everywhere, invisible but never absent. The process of becoming to Origen, as to St. Matthew and St. Augustine, was the process of transforming one's bodily desires so that one could appreciate this invisible force which fills the world. It meant stepping out of one's body into the light.

Yet just at this point, when the new theology seemed to reach its immaterial conclusion, the physical world intruded. Just because light is everywhere, to experience it requires a construction, a building, a special place. A Christian of Hadrian's time entering the temple which would later become a Christian shrine knew this. In the Pantheon the concrete dome gives shape to light. When there is direct sunlight overhead, the oculus open at the top of the dome focuses the light into a definite shaft. When there is no direct sunlight above on cloudy days, the light coming through the oculus is diffused and appears to impregnate the shell.

The pagan Dio Cassius thought that, "because of its vaulted roof, [the Pantheon] resembles the heavens." The poet Shelley, himself an atheist, had a more Christian reaction when entering the building in the early nineteenth century; looking upward, it seemed to Shelley that, "as when you regard the unmeasured dome of Heaven, the idea of magnitude is swallowed up & lost."[19] Yet he could not, and did not, have this same experience walking around outside, where the sky was equally apparent to him in all its infinitude.

This was the dilemma the early Christians faced. They needed to create places where they could make their "pilgrimage through time." Conversion was an urgent matter. The Christian could not remain content with Suetonius' respectful if somewhat ironic relation to the gods. Indeed, this need to convert seemed almost paralyzing in its immensity: all sensory stimulations would have to cease for the body no longer to desire, touch, taste, and smell, a body indifferent to its own physiology. There were dramatic examples of conversion through bodily renunciation, like Origen's castration; but this self-mutilation required extraordinary physical courage. More ordinary individuals needed a place where they stood out of their bodies as pilgrims through time. More, that place would have to be well made, with art, if it was to help those who were weak and vulnerable to see the light.

2. CHRISTIAN PLACES

In practice, early Christianity was a cult of the eastern Mediterranean whose message was spread by travellers in the East who carried letters from town to town defining the faith and bringing news of the faithful. The cities in which Christianity first took root were small, mostly centers of trade within the Empire. The Younger Pliny's letters to Trajan were early signs that official circles began to take note of Christians as a different group from Jews; Romans began first to note this difference in A.D. 64 when Nero made Christians scape-

The interior of the Pantheon in Rome.

goats for the great fire that destroyed much of Rome. Still, by Hadrian's reign they would have scarcely been visible in the city.

In their early years, urban Christians in some ways resembled the adherents of revolutionary communism in the early twentieth century. Both were organized into little cells of believers meeting in houses, spreading news by word of mouth or by reading aloud secret documents; lacking a unifying structure of command, schism and conflict between cells was rife in both early Christianity and communism. But the first communists discounted the house as a significant scene of action; their beliefs focused on infiltrating the public sphere of the city, its factories, newspapers, and government institutions. For the first Christians, the house was the place where their "pilgrimage through time" began.

The Christian house

The house began to serve Christian fellowship from the generation after Jesus' death to about the middle of the second century, when Christians moved out of houses into other buildings. In Hadrian's reign, Christianity was entirely confined to domestic space; the state forbade public practice of the religion, and the faithful also protected themselves against harassment by staying within walls. Because of these restrictions, it had long seemed to Church historians that early Christians were powerless, if not poor. We now know better: urban Christianity drew converts from a wide economic spectrum. They seem absent from the middle and upper classes of society because these Christians had to engage in evasion when others were *en fête;* to compromise themselves in public if they hadn't the strength for martyrdom; above all, to practice secrecy.

Within the shelter of the house, their journey of faith began in the dining room. The small Christian cell shared a common meal, during which the faithful talked, prayed, and read out letters from Christians elsewhere in the Empire. Though the experience of conversion was intensely individual, this social setting gave a particular kind of emotional support. As St. Paul explained, gathering around a common table echoed the gathering of the Last Supper.[20] Moreover, a modern Church historian observes, "dining in individual house church groups was fundamental" because "eating was a sign of social relations with others. The extension of hospitality through the meal setting was the central act that served to define the worshipping community."[21] Christians as a whole were called by St. Paul an *Ekklesia,* using the Greek usage for the body politic. Christians called this meeting-dinner *agape,* which can be translated as "a celebration of fellowship," the latter word in the Bible being *koionia.* But agape also had connotations of passionate love—which is why, when pagans heard about these feasts, they imagined they were orgies.

The Christian feast sought to break the patterns of pagan sociability, of the sort Petronius described in his novel *Satyricon* illustrated with almost cartoonlike exaggeration. Petronius writes about a feast given by Trimalchio, an immensely rich ex-slave, who almost buried his guests under mountains of rich food and drowned them in expensive wines. After several courses had been served, they fell into a stupefied trance, while Trimalchio's energy never faded and he never stopped talking. The dinner became a kind of theatre of cruelty, as the guests farted, gagged, and vomited their way through the evening. In place of the commonality at the Greek symposion, Trimalchio's feast dramatized the dominance of a single individual over those around him. There was no mutual competition, instead an active host and his passive, fawning guests. Yet Trimalchio's guests were not unwilling victims; their gullets always had a little space left for another mouthful of oysters in cream, the guests managed just enough energy to hold out their cups for another glass of wine. If everything at the dinner drew attention to Trimalchio's own wealth and power, if Trimalchio's luxury literally took possession of the guests' bodies, still they came back for more, they gave him their bodies to fill, they ate themselves into submission.

Agape sought to break the impulse of clientage. The feast shared equally by all sought to mark that "there is neither Jew nor Greek, there is neither bond [slave] nor free, there is neither male nor female."[22] Whereas people mostly attended pagan banquets by invitation, strangers bearing Christian news were openly and easily welcomed at the table. It was to Romans gathered around a dining-room table that St. Paul sent his great Letter to the Romans, setting out the principles which would later define the structure of the Church. This letter dates from about A.D. 60, which is also the time when St. Peter preached in Rome. Phoebe, his envoy, carried the letter into the household cells of the Christians at Rome, each time reading out Paul's propositions to the faithful, who in turn debated and discussed the letter, and other discussions of it followed in other houses. In these discussions, unlike Trimalchio's feast, no one voice dominated, by right, as host.

In the early house gatherings, the Christian ethos changed where people sat. The Roman code of linear seating placed the more important person at the head, people ranged around him in descending rank. The Christian gathering broke this order, instead placing people in the room according to the strength of their faith. Postulants, who were individuals interested in Christian teaching but not yet Christian, and catechumens, who were converted but not yet baptized, stood at the door or along the sides of the dining room, while full Christians sat together around the table. Although the evidence is sketchy, all the faithful seemed to sit directly at table together for the crucial moments of the meal, at least until about A.D. 200, when formal rituals replaced the informal common meal.

"The impulses of nature and the impulses of the spirit are at war with one another," St. Augustine wrote in his *Confessions* about what he felt during such a feast when the smell of food, the kick of alcohol in his blood, aroused him.[23] "Time and again I force my body to obey me, but the pain which this causes me is cancelled by the pleasure of eating and drinking."[24] Augustine sought comfort in the words of Luke 21:34: "And take heed to yourselves, lest at any time your hearts be overcharged with surfeiting, and drunkenness, and cares of this life." Yet agape served to test him, a test which would first lead him to understanding the meaning of the phrase "the alien body of Christ."

Both fellowship and test culminated in the Eucharist, drinking the wine and eating the bread which symbolized the blood and flesh of Christ. By the time St. Paul wrote his First Letter to the Corinthians, the ritual of the Eucharist had become defined in its enduring form: "And when he had given thanks, he brake it, and said, Take, eat: this is my body, which is broken for you: this do in remembrance of me. After the same manner, also he took the cup, when he had supped, saying, This cup is the new testament in my blood: this do ye, as oft as ye drink it, in remembrance of me."[25] The cannibalistic overtones of the Eucharist joined early Christianity to many other cults which also sought to eat the bodies of their gods. Yet the Christian who "partakes" of the god's blood and flesh did not feel imbued with a god's power, as the Aztec priests felt when drinking the actual blood of a sacrificial victim. The test lay in resisting the surge of bodily energy provided by bread and wine. As Origen preached, the soul triumphed when the senses tasted *nothing*. In this way, writes the Church historian Wayne Meeks, the Eucharist gave ritual meaning to the biblical adage to "strip off the old human" and put on "the new human, Christ."[26]

* * *

The ritual of baptism was the other way Christians sought in the house to "strip off the old human" and put on "the new human, Christ." In this ritual, as in dining, they also radically departed from pagan sociability. The importance of baptism lay in the challenge it indeed posed to one of the most important pagan Roman civic experiences, the experience of bathing together.

By Hadrian's time, Rome had filled with public and private bathing establishments; the baths were great domed structures, covering pools and exercise halls. Institutions in which all Romans met, usually in groups, the baths, unlike Greek gymnasia, accommodated women as well as men, old as well as young. Until Hadrian's era, men and women bathed at the same time; he was the first to segregate the sexes, the women bathing before the men. Bathing occurred in the afternoon and early evening, after the day's visits and labors had concluded. Very wealthy people had their own private baths, and went to the public ones only when they needed to curry favor or make a point to the general populace. Hadrian himself often bathed in public with his subjects, which earned him their immense regard. The poor lingered inside the public baths, finding there a refuge from the squalor of their own homes until the buildings closed at sunset.

Pagan bathing was organized in a regular sequence: the bather, after paying a small fee and undressing in a common room called the *apodyterium,* moved first to a large pool filled with hot water, the *caldarium,* where he scraped his sweating pores with a bone brush; then he moved to the pool of warm water called the *tepidarium,* and finally plunged into a cold pool called the *frigidarium.* As in a modern public swimming pool, people lolled around the edges of the pools, chatting, flirting, and showing off.

Seneca scorned the bath as a scene of noisy self-regard, for instance, "the hair plucker keeping up a constant chatter in his thin and strident voice, to attract more attention, and never silent except when he is plucking armpits and making the customer yell instead of yelling himself," or the "cries of the sausage dealer and confectioner and of all the peddlers of the cook shops, hawking their wares."[27] Procurers for boy and girl prostitutes worked the baths, and baths more generally released people from the harshness of the life outside, as in the Roman saying that "baths, wine, and women corrupt our bodies—but these things make life itself."[28]

Yet people also felt that bathing dignified their bodies; Roman descriptions of barbarians obsessively stereotyped the foreigners as unwashed. Cleanliness was a shared civic experience, and a public bath was the most popular building a ruler could erect. The baths mixed the enormous diversity of the city together in a common nakedness.

Christians frequented public baths just like other Romans. But their religious immersion in water had a personal and religious, rather than civic, importance. Baptism in water signified that the individual felt he or she had come sufficiently far in the struggle with bodily desire to make a life-long commitment to the faith. As practiced in the early Christian house, someone who felt ready for baptism undressed completely, then plunged into a tub of water in a room or space separated from the space of the ritual feast. Upon emerging from the pool, the celebrant put on entirely new clothes to signify that he or she was now a changed person. "The bath [became] a permanent threshold between the 'clean' group and the 'dirty' world."[29]

The Baths of Caracalla in Rome. A modern rendering of the interior.

This water ritual helped set the Christians off as well from their Jewish ancestors. In ancient as in modern Judaism, women bathe in mikveh pools to purify themselves symbolically, particularly to wash away menstrual blood. As the Hebrew scholar Jacob Neusner notes, the mikveh pool has no connotation of the washing away of sins; it is a purifying but not self-transforming ritual.[30] The women who leave it have not become different human beings; rather, their bodies are ready to participate in rituals. Baptism was instead a permanent threshold, one the believer crossed when he or she felt a life-long commitment to the religion. The cleansed, transformed Christian body reflected the story of Christ's own death and Resurrection: Paul writes in his Letter to the Romans, we are "baptized into his death."[31]

In the early Church, baptism was for adults rather than for infants; it could have no meaning for babies because baptism entailed making a decision, the most serious decision of one's life. For this same reason, the early Christians renounced the Jewish practice of circumcision. One source in the New Testament does speak of baptism as "the circumcision of Christ," but in this Christian "circumcision" the penis would not have been altered.[32] St. Paul, in writing against circumcision, sought to erase any *predicate* on the body, any marking of those persons who from birth were automatically included within the faith. The refusal of circumcision arose again from the early Christian belief that people were not born as Christians; they came to be Christian.

Baptism sharply broke the command to "Look and believe" which ruled pagan Rome. The baptized Christian carried a secret within which could not be seen. Male Jews could be identified and persecuted by stripping them naked and examining their genitals, while "the circumcision of Christ" left no mark on the body. More generally, it was impossible to understand what Christianity meant by looking at a Christian; his or her appearance was meaningless. And yet the practices of house worship began to root Christians to the cities in which they worshipped.

The first churches

Estimates are difficult to make of the number of Christians in Rome in Hadrian's time; at most there were a few thousand believers. Some generations later, Christians began to be persecuted in the Roman amphitheatre and elsewhere in the city, culminating in a great slaughter between 250 and 260, yet the sect steadily grew. Richard Krautheimer puts the numbers of Christians in Rome at thirty to fifty thousand in A.D. 250.[33] By the time the Emperor Constantine converted to Christianity in the early fourth century, the followers of his new religion comprised a third of the Roman populace.

Constantine's Edict of Milan, in A.D. 313, served as a turning point in this growth, for it made Christianity a legal religion throughout the Empire. The Roman Bishop Dionysius (259–268) established the form of Church governance which would continue to prevail, a bishop who guided the affairs of Christians in the city. As Christianity took root, it received urban property through bequests and wills, the property controlled by voluntary associations, which also bought land for cemeteries and created community centers in public buildings.

Constantine entered Rome in 312 as its first Christian emperor, and the Lateran Basilica which he began in 313 showed this re-entry at work. The Lateran Basilica was an imperial possession. Basilica and Baptistery "rose on ground that was at the emperor's free disposal, among mansions and gardens, all or mostly imperial property, tucked away at the edge of the city."[34] A building of stone with a wooden roof, its central hall was flanked by two smaller aisles on either side; a semicircular apse capped one end. Before the apse, the bishop or other presiding priest stood on a raised platform facing the rows of parishioners. The form of the ancient court of justice had been recreated. The Baptistery was attached behind and to one side. A silver screen sheltered a statue of Christ, and paintings depicting the Christian story abounded on the walls. The walls of the Lateran Basilica were further sheathed with precious materials, fine marble and porphyry; real jewels glinted in the eyes of the Virgin Mother and her crucified Son.

The growth of Christianity as a public force partially transformed the image of Christ: "Christ was no longer . . . primarily the god of the humble, the miracle-worker and saviour. As Constantine viewed himself as God's vicar on earth, so God was viewed increasingly as the Emperor of Heaven."[35] A modern scholar, Thomas Mathews, argues that Christ did not simply become a new version of the emperor; He remained a strange and wonder-working magician. Yet the places in which the new god was now publicly worshipped drew Christianity into the orbit of older forms of worship.[36] The linear and axial order of the Roman basilica, its sensual and expensive decor, now served an imperial vision of Christ.

Worship took a form that befitted an imperial building. Between

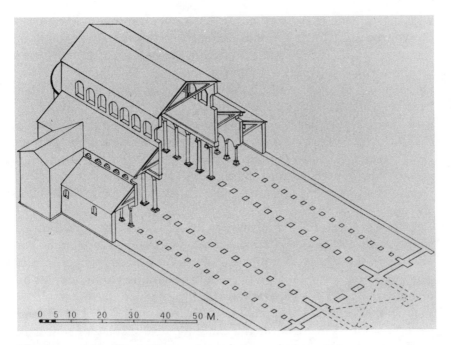

The Lateran Basilica in Rome. A modern rendering.

the rulers of the Church and the believers a great divide opened. The bishop wore the robes and carried the lights of a Roman magistrate, he entered the Lateran Basilica surrounded by lesser Church officials who accompanied him as he made a ceremonial entrance down the central aisle, watched by the parishioners; his journey ended when he seated himself on a throne set in front of the apse, facing the congregation, men on one side, women on the other. The hierarchy of faith was now also reflected in the order of service, a Mass of the Catechumens, in which common prayers were said, then readings from Scripture, followed by a Mass of the Faithful. Those who were baptized began this second mass by parading down the central aisle bearing gifts which they placed at the foot of the bishop seated on his throne. Then the wafer and the wine, the Flesh and the Blood, were tasted, the prayer of communion was read, and the bishop left, descending from his throne and passing through the lines of believers who bore witness to him in silence. In these ways the Church had re-entered the world.

In the view of some scholars, the spaces in the Lateran Basilica were a long time in the making. In this view (drawing on researches on synagogues in Dura-Europas rather than in Rome), the communities of Hadrian's time had already begun the process of spatial segregation: a separate, private room for the ritual of baptism, and the enlargement of the dining room by knocking down a wall so that rows of congregants could face an altar. The pressure of numbers may have dictated this, as well as an early separation of the rituals of the Eucharist from those of common prayer.[37] In the Lateran Baptistery, these changes, to the extent they occurred, were transformed in this Christian emperor's monument. It was a space in which "Rome" had its stamp, in order that Christian Romans would look and obey.

To be sure, commands to the eye in the Lateran Basilica did not simply copy those of the religious temples of Hadrian's time. For one thing, the Christian basilicas gathered a mass of people inside. The Pantheon may well have been unusual among pagan temples by making it possible for a crowd to gather within; in other pagan places such as the Temple of Venus Genetrix, the masses looked at, and were positioned in front of, the building. The display of power in the Lateran Basilica was all inside; the outside was a dull, unadorned, looming mass of brick and concrete.

If the physical splendor and eroticized idols hidden within the Lateran Basilica compromised the early Christian urge to transcend the realm of the senses, Christians tried to preserve their bond to that earlier faith in another kind of space, meant for more individual religious experience. This was the *martyrium.* Here light was molded in a special place.

Because of the Crucifixion, Christian theology put a strong emphasis on death. In Constantine's time, Christians sought to be buried near the tombs of Christian martyrs; through elaborate if sometimes dubious archeological research they located the graves of martyrs and dug out shafts, called cataracts, down which they poured offerings of wine and scented olive oil—much as the pagan Romans had fed the gods of the earth in the mundus. The martyrium first served as a place for massive Christian burials near the cataract of a martyr. Originally it was a large, rectangular shed attached to the basilica of a church; St. Peter's in Rome began this way, supposedly on the site where Peter was buried. In time, however, the martyrium became a cylindrical or eight-sided space, with the tomb of the venerated saint, or an individual worthy of veneration, at the center. Symbolically, the altar is the tomb of Christ, His five wounds signified by five crosses on the altar stone.

San Costanza was such a martyrium, built for the tomb of Constantine's daughter Costanza in about 350, and still stands, though in an altered state. The form is of a double cylinder, the smaller inner cylinder raised up on twelve double columns. It was as sumptuous inside as the Lateran Baptistery, filled with precious stones and statues, but the emphasis was on funereal rather than triumphal display. In other, less ornate martyria, a sacramental font was placed on the floor under the dome, the light illuminating this shrine, the human beings moving around it cast into relative shadow. However ornate, martyria were contemplative structures, meant for individual reflection on the lives of Christians who suffered for the faith.

San Costanza foreshadowed the conversion of the Pantheon into the martyrium, Sancta Maria ad Martyres. A shrine was placed on the mundus at the central point of the Pantheon's floor, the round walls focusing the mourner's sight on that center, the eye moving from that human plane of suffering upward toward the light. The very name of Hadrian's monument took on a new meaning. Up to the fourth century, Romans viewed their city as a meeting ground for the gods of Empire. Christians "colluded with this myth: just as Rome had assembled the gods of all nations to act as talismans, so Roman Christians had come to believe that Peter and Paul had travelled from the East to lay their holy bodies in the city."[38] The Christian name for the Pantheon, Sancta Maria ad Martyres, continued that pantheonic tradition, for it means the place where all martyrs are gathered in the presence of Mary.

The light in the martyria made certain symbolic suggestions about the Christian's journey. In San Costanza, the raised cylinder is lit by twelve windows, flooding the center with light, leaving the aisles in darkness. Shadow was thought to define the space where one looked inward and contemplated. Looking toward the light from the shadows symbolized the narrative of conversion, because this church light did not illuminate a face, or make the details of a landscape easier to see. Sancta Maria ad Martyres dramatized this play of light and shadow on those very days when the sunlight outside was strongest, its rays entering the building like a searchlight, a beam of light which never came to rest in one place, which had no destination. Here one could look and believe, as a Christian.

The basilica and the martyrium came to represent the two sides of

Christianity, Christ the King and Christ the Saviour of the martyred and the weak. Yet the martyrium and the basilica also represented Christianity's uneasy accommodation to the place in which Christians lived, the city, particularly to Rome. The Christianization of Rome occurred as the imperial city declined. Pagans interpreted this as cause and effect. When the barbarian Alaric sacked Rome in 410, pagans blamed Christian indifference to worldly affairs as a contributing cause of the city's weakness. Throughout the *City of God* St. Augustine sought to counter these charges that Christianity sickened the Empire. The Christian is also a Roman, Augustine argued, and observes the rules of the city so long and so far as they do not conflict with the dictates of faith; Christian Romans defended the city against Alaric, and were no enemies within the gates. The contrast Augustine drew between the City of Man and the City of God was indeed, in the words of Peter Brown, "a universal explanation of men's basic motives . . . in every age, of a single fundamental tension" between the pilgrimage through time and allegiance to place, not a specific repudiation of their own city.[39]

In a way, Augustine's defense accorded with the earliest Christian doctrine, for the City of God is not a place. Augustine made the distinction between the two cities in the following words:

> For all the difference of the many and very great nations throughout the world in religion and morals, language, weapons, and dress, there exist no more than two kinds of society, which, according to our Scriptures, we have rightly called the two cities.[40]

The Lateran Baptistery represented one way in which this distinction was no longer possible. When the religion grew powerful and institutional, its initial austerities did not mesh easily with its dominion. Power required place. But the martyrium represented for Christian faith something else, a redemption of place. For only in some places, made carefully, with art, could the meaning of conversion be *seen*. The Christian here renounced the flesh but recovered the value of stone.

3. NIETZSCHE'S HAWKS AND LAMBS

Of all modern writers who have pondered the earliest Christian desire to transcend both flesh and stone, none disliked it more than the young Friedrich Nietzsche. He dismissed it as a ruse, a mere tactic of power. A passage from Nietzsche's *On the Genealogy of Morals,* published in 1887, perhaps best expresses his belief about the deceitfulness of Christianity. It is a parable about lambs and the "great birds of prey" who feed upon them.[41] Nietzsche chose his animals with care: the lamb is of course a Christian symbol, and predatory birds figure in Nietzsche's writings as particularly Roman animals, imperial birds; he thought the Romans flew over the world hunting and dominating everywhere they found prey.

In the parable, he begins by explaining why these birds of prey are stronger than lambs. Their strength is greater than their talons and beaks; the birds are strong because they are unconscious of their powers. They do not *decide* to kill the lambs, they simply go after meat whenever hungry. Similarly, men with strong appetites no more choose to drink, to kill, or to make love; they simply do it. Like Schopenhauer, Nietzsche conceived of the strong body as blind to itself, unburdened by self-consciousness, by mind. Philosophically, this means that "there is no 'being' behind doing, effecting, [or] becoming" for the sensually empowered man.[42] Such a person does not judge his own behavior, nor rein himself in by thinking about the other, reckoning what lambs (animal or human) might suffer due to his desires.

The only defense the weak have is "to make the bird of prey *accountable* for being a bird of prey."[43] The human lambs—the weak—weave a web of social relationships and moral judgments around the strong body, tying it down in doubts and second thoughts. The reason Nietzsche scorns the weak is not that they are weak, but that they lie about what they are doing. Instead of admitting, "I am afraid," the lamb bleats, "I have a soul." Soul talk of the Christian sort is all about how terrible it is to want to eat or make love freely, how good is the person beset by doubts and second thoughts about bodily desires. Thus, Nietzsche concludes, the soul "has perhaps been believed in hitherto more firmly than anything else on earth because it makes possible to the majority of mortals, the weak and oppressed of every kind, the sublime self-deception that interprets weakness as freedom. . . ."[44] Christians had to tell this necessary lie if the meek were indeed to inherit the earth.

In this parable of Christian lambs and pagan birds of prey, Nietzsche did not intend to be fair or historically accurate. The parable could explain neither the gladiator's conscious mixture of resolution and pessimism nor the physical courage of a Christian who castrates himself. Nor was the split between mind and body a Christian creation. As we have seen, the origins of that split can be traced back to the naked Greeks whom Nietzsche celebrated as free men. The error of this parable lies elsewhere, in Nietzsche's misunderstanding of power. Nietzsche fails to recognize that brute strength does not suffice for domination. Were brute force enough, the powerful would never seek to legitimate their strength, for legitimation is a language of self-justification spoken *by* the powerful, not *to* them. Moreover, Nietzsche's parable leaves out the behavior of the weak, who do not act like lambs; weak human beings try to control their own bodies in order to resist those who are strong.

The history of the body in the spaces of the pagan city, Athenian and Roman, speaks against this parable written in the name of "the pagan." The idealized Periklean body proved vulnerable to its own vocal strengths. The rituals of women in Perikles' Athens resisted the dominant order by dramatizing both their powers of sexual restraint and sexual desire. The visual order implied in the Vitruvian body, realized in Hadrian's Rome, imprisoned Romans in appearances. Resisting this visual order gave Christians the strength to uproot themselves, to make the pilgrimage through time, a strength they derived from despising their own flesh. In the ancient world, the lamb was the human hawk's double, not his victim.

Rather than destroy the "natural" man, Christianity changed the consolations people sought for the contradictions they lived. Writing on the genesis of religions, the anthropologist Louis Dumont has observed that religions can either establish individuals as fulfilled within the world or outside it.[45] Hadrian's Pantheon promised the first of these fulfillments; the Church of Sancta Maria ad Martyres promised the second. When monotheism began to rule Western civilization, it broke with the body as conceived in the pagan, pantheistic past, but it did not entirely break with the spaces of pantheism, at least in their Roman versions. The lamb, too, could not free itself from its need for the hawk; the soul could not cut free from its need of a place in the world.

PART TWO

MOVEMENTS

OF THE HEART

CHAPTER FIVE

Community

The Paris of
Jehan de Chelles

1. "STADT LUFT MACHT FREI"

For roughly five hundred years, from A.D. 500 to 1000, the great Roman cities withered. Most of Europe reverted to a primitive agricultural economy; the lives of ordinary men and women lay poised on the edge of starvation, subject to violent attack by warring, migratory tribes against which most people who worked the land had no defense. Only isolated, walled monasteries and abbeys dotting the countryside offered refuge to the few who could reach them when in danger. The European landscape of fear and scarcity began to grow greener in the late 900s. The countryside where most people lived became more secure thanks to the building of castles and the rise of feudalism, in which local lords gave their subjects some measure of military protection in exchange for perpetual service. Medieval cities as well began to grow; though they contained a small fraction of the

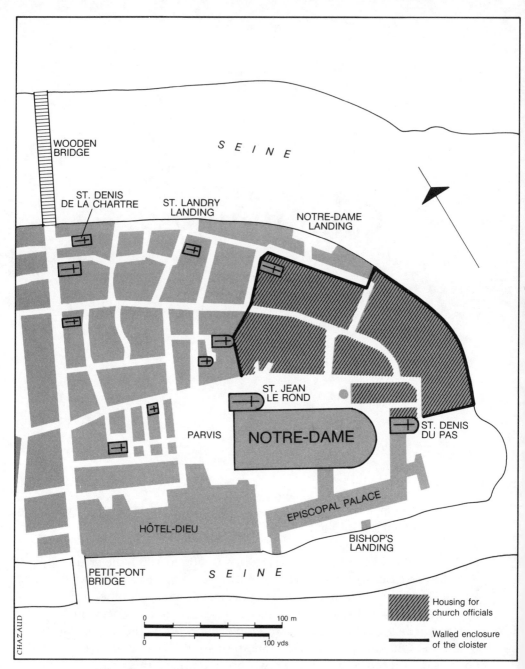

Map of parish surrounding Notre-Dame in Paris, ca. 1300.

SEINE

WOODEN
BRIDGE

ST. DENIS
DE LA CHARTRE

ST. LANDRY
LANDING

NOTRE-DAME
LANDING

ST. JEAN
LE ROND

PARVIS

NOTRE-DAME

ST. DENIS
DU PAS

EPISCOPAL PALACE

HÔTEL-DIEU

BISHOP'S
LANDING

PETIT-PONT
BRIDGE

SEINE

CHAZAUD

0   100 m

0   100 yds

Housing for
church officials

Walled enclosure
of the cloister

European population, behind their walls these towns gathered in food, cloth, and luxury goods acquired through trade.

In medieval Paris, the year 1250 saw two landmarks of this rebirth. In that year Jehan de Chelles began the final phase of work on the Cathedral of Notre-Dame. Beautifully sited in the center of the city on the eastern end of an island with branches of the Seine River flowing around and behind it, a tall mountain of exquisitely carved stone, the Cathedral testified to the power of Christianity in this new center of Western civilization. Yet Parisians did not mark its erection as Romans had inaugurated Constantine's Lateran Basilica centuries before. Although both the King of France and the Bishop of Paris basked in the event, representing Church and State, Parisians celebrated Notre-Dame also as a triumph of the building trades, fêting the carvers, glassblowers, weavers, and carpenters who did the manual labor, and the bankers who financed the work. A third party, Economy, made its debut on the stage of civilization.

In 1250 the greatest illustrated Bible of the Middle Ages appeared

The garden side of Notre-Dame in Paris today.

The St. Louis Bible, ca. 1250. *Trustees of the Pierpont Morgan Library, 1987.*

in Paris, sponsored by the King later known as St. Louis. In its coloring and elaborate script, the book was as sensuous an object as the Lateran Basilica. Here too that third party appeared in the celebrations. Thanks in large part to the growth of trade, masses of students had swarmed into Paris from all of Europe. "Because scholastic activity shifted from the [rural] monasteries to the cathedrals," the historian Georges Duby writes, "the principal centers of artistic creativity moved to the heart of the city."[1] The professional editing and production of the St. Louis Bible depended on the presence of this large and flourishing university. The St. Louis Bible, a supreme work of art, appeared at the end of a chain of events which began in the fish and grain markets on the banks of the Seine River.

The economic foundations of civilization received scant acknowledgment in the ancient world; both trade and manual labor seemed little more than dismal, bestial activity. The medieval city made this beast into a human being. "The medieval citizen [was] on the way toward becoming an economic man," in the words of the sociologist Max Weber, whereas "the ancient citizen was a political man."[2] Beyond material abundance, the forces of the economy promised two distinct freedoms to those few who lived behind the city's walls. Today the visitor can see above the city gates, in cities which belonged to the medieval trade network called the Hanseatic League, the motto *Stadt Luft macht frei* ("The air of a city makes people free"). In Paris, as in the Hanseatic cities, the economy promised to set them free from the inherited dependence embodied in the feudal labor contract. More, the city promised people new individual rights of property; John of Paris in the mid-thirteenth century asserted that individuals "had a right to property which was not with impunity to be interfered with by superior authority—because it was acquired by [the individual's] own efforts."[3]

The medieval economy, the state, and religion did not live in a happy *mariage à trois*—nor could the celebration of Jehan de Chelles' Notre-Dame and the publication of the St. Louis Bible obscure the tensions among these three great forces. The power of St. Louis rested in large part on feudal obligations he exacted from his own vassal, lesser lords; the Church often conflated the possession of individual thoughts and rights with heresy. More, those possessing economic power, particularly the urban merchants and bankers, frequently affronted the sensibility of their partners.

The year 1250 culminates the era the historian R. W. Southern has called "scientific humanism." For more than a hundred years

medieval thinkers had sought to apply human knowledge systematically to the problems of human society. St. Thomas Aquinas said that
it was possible to make the world cohere as a logical system. The
imagery of the "body politic" conveyed this coherence, uniting biol-
ogy and politics. Yet economics could not be easily assimilated into
the scientific humanism of the time.

We recall that, in the *Policraticus,* John of Salisbury imagined the
merchants in his body politic to be the stomach of society. It was the
greedy organ of the body, as of the body politic. He wrote that "if
[these men of private wealth] have been stuffed through excessive
greed and if they hold in their contents too obstinately, [they] give
rise to countless and incurable illnesses and, through their vices, can
bring about the ruin of the body as a whole."[4] More than simple
greed, though, created the affront; the fact that they had earned their
rights challenged the very concept of hierarchy which placed kings
and bishops in the head of the body politic. For John of Salisbury, in
the words of the historian Walter Ullmann, wanted "the individual's
standing within society . . . based upon his office or his official function," not upon individual capacities; in John of Salisbury's view, the
greater a person's formal position, "the more scope it had, the
weightier it was, the more rights the individual had."[5]

The greedy man of affairs existed immemorially before John of
Salisbury wrote about him. But a more distinctive puzzlement pervades the *Policraticus:* this most obsessively geographical of all medieval writers had trouble describing the stomach of society. Of course
merchants trade in fairs and markets, but go month after month to a
particular market, he observed, and you will not see the same faces
trading, and the goods will be different. Go to the quays lining the
Seine year after year and again you will see merchants and goods
vanishing and appearing. The stomach of the body politic seemed
continually to change its diet. John of Salisbury, not econometrically
adept, searched but could not find a way to explain why economic
freedom should erode durable routine.

Looking backward to the cities of the Middle Ages, Max Weber
asserted that "the medieval urban community enjoyed political
autonomy" because of the market, trade giving the city an economic
power to rule its own affairs.[6] John of Salisbury, on the contrary,
thought the "commonwealth" had no secure governance in the hands
of men of wealth. John of Salisbury's conviction made sense to the
French urban historian Henri Pirenne, writing a generation after
Max Weber. Pirenne sought painstakingly to explain how trade

between cities brought them individually back to life; medieval cities were interdependent rather than autonomous and medieval traders had to act flexibly. Pirenne wrote,

> Under the influence of trade the old Roman cities took on new life and were repopulated, or mercantile groups formed round about the military burgs and established themselves along the sea coasts, on river banks, at confluences, at the junction points of the natural routes of communication. Each of them constituted a market which exercised an attraction, proportionate to its importance, on the surrounding country or made itself felt afar.[7]

The Hanseatic League formed such a trading chain spreading goods throughout Northern Europe. The Hanseatic League, begun in 1161, was based on the sea—goods moving from Genoa and Venice in Italy, from London and the Low Countries along the way, ending in northern German ports from which they filtered inland. Paris had its own trade chain by the twelfth century, which stretched east and west along the Seine River, north and south from Flanders to Marseilles. The modern historian was less cataclysmic in his views than the medieval theologian. Medieval city dwellers had strong attachments to their own cities, Pirenne argued, but these frequently conflicted with their economic interests, which made them more mobile and minded to a larger geography. Profit lay on the horizon of the possible, in the land of perhaps, toward which one travelled as often as one could, from which one often failed to return. Risk and chance took economics outside the tight, logical circle of scientific humanism.

The Christian religion was global in its theology, but it fostered intensely local attachments. A believer's bonds to Paris consummated the great reversal which began when early Roman Christians made peace with Rome. As medieval towns and cities revived under the Christian aegis, the stones of the churches and cathedrals were the materials with which Christians expressed their life-long and passionate attachment to the places in which they lived. Just as the soaring, gigantic churches put up even in small towns expressed commitment to a place, so did the Christian's need for community. This need for community took form through a new understanding of the Christian body. The "alien body of Christ" modulated in the

High Middle Ages into a body whose sufferings ordinary people could understand and with whom they could identify; the union of human and divine suffering took form in those medieval movements founded on the "Imitation of Christ." These movements renewed the Christian experience of compassion for one's neighbors, based on imagining the sufferings of others as one's own. Medieval doctors thought they had found a medical explanation for compassion, by observing how organs within the body responded when one of their number was cut or removed during surgery, a response they called "syncope." In a way, this new understanding of the body fit the larger science of the time, for phenomena like syncope seemed to show concretely the human organism as a connected, mutually responsive system of organs. But the Imitation of Christ was far more than an intellectual movement.

As Christ's bodily suffering became more comprehensible to the ordinary man and woman, a vast outpouring of popular religious fervor took form. Georges Duby may claim too much in asserting that, until the time of Jehan de Chelles, "Europe had displayed the externals of Christendom; Christianity was *truly* experienced only by rare elites. After . . . it was to have *every appearance of being a people's religion*."[8] But the great religious revival which took form in the Imitation of Christ altered relations between men and women in the Church, changed the experience of confession, and the practices of charity. These changes transformed convents and monasteries, hospitals and almshouses, parish churches and cathedrals. They had a particular meaning to Christians in the city.

In ordinary usage, "community" denotes the place in which people care about people they know well or immediate neighbors. When religious communities first took form in the darkest days of the Dark Ages, they worked in this way, but the conjunction of fervent religious impulses and urban growth gave "community" in medieval Paris a somewhat different meaning. The almshouses, the hospitals, and the convents in the city opened their doors more freely to strangers than in the countryside, taking in travellers, homeless people, and abandoned babies, the unknown sick and the insane. The religious community did not comprehend the whole city, but served rather as a place of moral reference; the almshouse, the parish church, the hospital, and the episcopal garden set standards against which to measure behavior in other parts of the city, particularly the aggressive economic competition which ruled the street markets and the loading docks along the Seine.

Thus, though Paris had filled with large crowds of strangers, its streets were rampant with gratuitous violence, its economy shuffled human beings from town to town as well as goods, the city could nonetheless be shaped into a moral geography. For those under the sway of the new religious values, sanctuary was the point of community—a place where compassion bonded strangers. In Jehan de Chelles' Paris, the sense of Christian community also rejuvenated local parish life; both the parish church and the site of de Chelles' work, the great episcopal community clustered around Notre-Dame, were urban sanctuaries.

Medieval economic and religious developments pushed the sense of place in opposite directions, a dissonance which echoes down in our own times. The economy of the city gave people a freedom of individual action they could not have in other places; the religion of the city made places where people cared about each other. *"Stadt Luft macht frei"* opposed "the Imitation of Christ." This great tension between economy and religion produced the first signs of the duality which marks the modern city: on one side, the desire to cut free of communal bonds in the name of individual liberty; on the other side, the desire to find a place in which people care about each other.

Aquinas sought to reconcile these contraries, in the *Summa Theologica,* in a master image of Christ, a Being which contains everything that exists in the world. For his contemporaries that unity did not hold—any more than today we have found a way to combine economic individualism and communal bonds.

This chapter examines the convictions that underlay the formation of Christian communities in medieval Paris, and the way these communities functioned. The next chapter analyzes the economic spaces in the city which challenged the Christian sense of place. One consequence of this conflict appeared in a dark episode in the history of Venice, the greatest international trading city of the Renaissance; Christian culture sought to reconcile the money of individuals and the morals of community by repression of those who did not fit the master image of the Christian. Venetian culture used repression as a tool to salve its own inner conflicts by imprisoning its Jews in ghettos.

2. THE COMPASSIONATE BODY

Framing the front doors of Notre-Dame, the visitor sees today sculptures of human beings constructed at a little more than human scale;

View of the west door, Notre-Dame, Paris, built 1250. *Foto Marburg/Art Resource, N.Y.*

though they seem somewhat dwarfed by the immense size of the cathedral building, their size is an act of faith. Beginning in the eleventh century, church builders sought to carve figures at human scale to show, in the words of a modern art historian, the "relationship between human values and those values immanent in the world."[9] The carved figures made a direct appeal to the viewer to see him- or herself as part of the church, an act of inclusion which began in an earlier age through the preaching of St. Francis of Assisi, who spoke directly to the ordinary Christian in simple language. By the year Jehan de Chelles began to complete Notre-Dame, such a union of flesh and stone had grown ever stronger as Christians began to connect their own bodily suffering to the suffering of Jesus.

Christ "was, as it were, roasted and slowly baked to save us," Jean Barthélemy wrote consolingly in *Le Livre de Crainte Amoureuse.*[10] Such an earthy, homey image made the Crucifixion a comprehensible experience in terms of daily life. Rather than Christ the King, people identified with "the suffering Christ, the Christ of the Passion. The Crucifixion was increasingly portrayed, and increasingly realistic."[11] This movement of passionate identification with Christ's bodily suffering was known as the "Imitation of Christ," just because Christ's sorrows seemed imitated by the human body's sufferings. This was no casual figure of speech. The image of imitation stood directly opposed to Origen's conviction that Christ's body is alien to our own. St. Francis of Assisi told his parishioners that if they thought about their everyday experience, their own sensations, the world around them, they would realize what God is. Theologically, St. Francis recovered Nature for Christianity: God is in the world, God is Flesh as well as Light.

By caring about the sufferings of other people, we imitate our religious feelings about Jesus on the Cross: St. Francis reaffirmed that identification with the poor and outcast which marked the earliest Christianity. Sociologically, he exploded a bomb. He taught that in our bodies we contain the ethical yardstick for judging rules, rights, and privileges in society: the more these cause pain, the more our bodies know they are unjust. If the Imitation of Christ recovered the flesh for religion, it thus made the flesh the judge of social hierarchy. More, this religious view contrasted the bonds among those who care about one another to societal structures like commercial dealings where love for others may be entirely absent.

To be sure, the Middle Ages practiced tortures and other bodily cruelties with an abandon that would have done credit to the Romans who slaughtered Christians in the Colosseum. But this new ethos of compassion introduced at least rudimentary ideas of respecting the pain of others during torture. The public torture in Paris of persons afflicted by devils, for instance, was not quite the casual affair from about 1250 onward that it had earlier been; the torturers sought ecclesiastical assurances that they were causing pain to the devils inside, not to the person in whose body they lodged.

By its very nature, the Imitation of Christ affirmed the life of the masses against the privileges of the elite. But it drew support, and indeed was articulated, by certain elements of medieval science because it accorded with what educated men and women believed about their own bodies.

Galen's Ars medica

"The medical and scientific assumptions of the ancient world," the medical historian Vern Bullough argues, "were incorporated into medieval thinking with but little challenge."[12] Ancient ideas of body heat, sperm, menstrual blood, and the architecture of the body did indeed pass into the medieval world with the authority of received wisdom—yet these beliefs were modified, often unwittingly, by the needs of a Christian society that received them a thousand years later.

One of the principal means by which ancient medicine passed into the medieval era was the publication of the Roman physician Galen's *Ars medica,* an edition that first appeared in Salerno before 1200, was later retranslated in Cremona, and by 1280 was taught in Paris as in other European centers of learning. Galen was born in Hadrian's era, probably in A.D. 130, and died sometime around 200. His own medical education derived from the ideas of Aristotle and Hippocrates, and his medical writings attracted Christian attention because he had shown himself friendly to Christians, though not a believer, and because he was reputed in the High Middle Ages never to have charged his patients for his services.

Galen had originally written in Greek. The edition of the *Ars medica* which medieval people read was translated from Arabic into Latin, since the early Islamic world had preserved many ancient texts and Islamic medicine had enriched the European knowledge it had received. The great Islamic doctor Ali ibn Ridwan added commentaries to the *Ars medica,* as did various European translators who worked on the manuscript. The *Ars medica* thus reads more as a compendium of received ideas than as the work of one man.

In this text Galen defines medicine as "knowledge of what is healthy, morbid, and neutral," a knowledge which depends on understanding how body heats and fluids interact in the principal organs of the body, the brain, heart, liver, and testes (the female genitalia, we recall, were treated by the ancients as reversed testes).[13] Body heat, Galen thought, ascended gradually along a sliding scale; body fluids, however, were of four types or "humors," blood, phlegm, yellow bile, and black bile. The combination of heat and fluid produced in turn four different psychological states in the body. Galen, following Hippocrates, called them the four "temperaments": sanguine, phlegmatic, choleric, and melancholic. Unlike a modern psychologist, Galen argued that a person's temperament depended on how hot or cold, dry or juicy, his or her body was at a given moment, and which juices were flowing hot and full, which trickled through the body cold.

In Galen's view, ethical behavior such as aggression or compassion derived from the temperaments created by the heat and fluids in the body. Here, for instance, is how Galen describes the choleric temperament of someone whose heart is warm and dry:

> The pulse is hard, big, rapid, and frequent, and breathing is deep, rapid, and frequent. . . . Of all people, these have the hairiest chest . . . they are ready for action, courageous, quick, wild, savage, rash, and impudent. They have a tyrannical character, for they are quick-tempered and hard to appease.[14]

We may balk at correlating a hairy chest to a tyrannical character, but this totalizing was the very essence of Galenism, and formed part of its appeal to medieval readers under the sway of scientific humanism. It tied the body to the soul.

Galen's Islamic preserver and commentator Ali ibn Ridwan had linked the four temperaments to four social types: the choleric temperament described above characterizes the soldier; the sanguine temperament marks the statesman; the phlegmatic temperament is typical of the scientist; and the melancholic temperament pervades a man or woman full of religious feeling.[15] The merchant was missing in this typology, and indeed from Western commentary on the *Ars medica*—a significant absence; the aggressive behavior necessary for economic success could be slotted neither under the heroic exploits of a soldier nor the equable impulses to rule of a statesman. The person sorrowing for others is in a melancholic state; compassion makes the black bile in particular run hot in the heart; this was the physiology of a body experiencing the Imitation of Christ.

Health appeared to Galen as a well-tempered body, that is, a body whose heats and humors were in equilibrium in the four major organs. Was religious compassion therefore a state of ill health, even a bodily disease? We might reason so, but Galen's medieval readers approached the question another way. They observed the operations of compassionate melancholy at work when human bodies fell under the surgeon's knife.

Henri de Mondeville's discovery of syncope

A surgeon working in fourteenth-century Paris, Henri de Mondeville, thought he had discovered through surgical experiment the mechanics of compassion within the human body, that is, the way the body distributes heat and fluid during times of crisis. De Mondeville began to publish his medical opinions in 1314.[16] These bear the imprint of Galen, yet de Mondeville organized the body's architecture in a distinctive way.[17] De Mondeville divided the body into two general regions, the noble region of head and heart and the productive region of the stomach; each region has its own physiological "oven." Illnesses occur when these two zones heat at different temperatures, unbalancing the body's fluid humors.

De Mondeville noted that during and after the performance of an operation, one organ of the body tended to compensate for the weakness of another; as a result of surgery, he wrote, "the other members pity [the wounded member's] sufferings, and to succour it send all their spirits and warmth." Another doctor, Barthelmey l'Anglais, also explained this compassionate mechanism in terms of the flow of heated blood toward the wounded organ: "There is such a great love among the [members of the body] that one takes pity on the other, that is to say the one which suffers less takes pity on the one which suffers more; hence when a member is injured, the blood of the other [members] immediately comes to succour it."[18] De Mondeville called this compassionate reaction "syncope." (In modern medicine, it has taken on quite another meaning.)

De Mondeville sought further to describe the syncopes of people who witness a surgical operation (done at the time without anesthesia and with scalpels as blunt as modern bread knives), in order to show

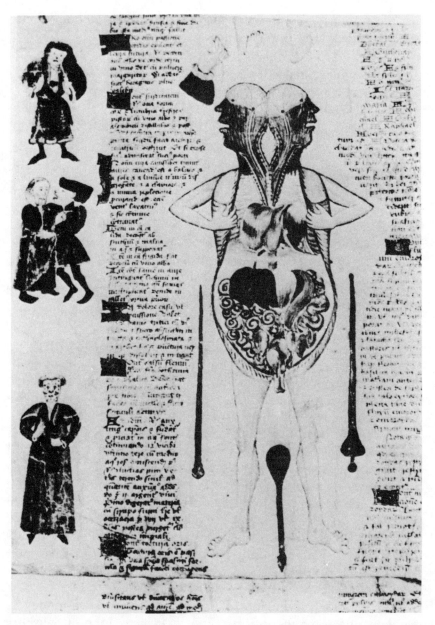

The dual body. Illustration from *Art de la médecine et de la chirurgie*, edition of 1412.

that the response to suffering which occurs within the body occurs between bodies as well. He wrote:

> Syncope occurs in the following way in healthy men witnessing terrible surgical operations: the fear they feel pains their heart; there is a sort of meeting of the general *chapter* of the spirits, so that, they being gathered together and stimulated, the vital force of the heart is succoured.[19]

De Mondeville carefully used, and underlined, the word "chapter" to describe people gathered together to watch an operation. A chapter was a religious body, and also referred to members of a guild. To him, the origins of community could thus be explained by the physical responses people have to another's suffering during surgery. The author of the thirteenth-century *Ménagier de Paris* had similarly declared that a person feels "the same friendship towards your neighbor who is a member [using the same French word for a bodily 'member'] of you, for we are all members of God, who is the body."[20] Surgery revealed the physical reality of Christ's Passion and Crucifixion, teaching the lesson of moral arousal through suffering.

If "medieval piety had always sought to fortify the inclinations of the soul by the adhesion of the body," yet the discovery of syncope suggested social relations as well, a melancholic social scene.[21] In the *Policraticus,* John of Salisbury argued that "The sovereign [*potestas*], when he cannot with benevolent hand save the lives of his subjects . . . by a *virtuous cruelty,* attacks the evil until the safety of the good is assured."[22] If people rebel against their place in the hierarchy, a ruler knows what to do: expel or kill the unruly, just as a surgeon cuts out diseased organs. Christian compassion played little role in the *Policraticus.* De Mondeville thought it overkill to follow John of Salisbury's advice. In surgery, organs come to the aid of the body's diseased parts, helping it recover. So, in society, crises have their positive side; it is during social crises that people respond most vividly to each other.

The century separating John of Salisbury and Henri de Mondeville may have made for the difference in their view. John of Salisbury lived in a Europe just beginning to make itself secure; his grandparents knew a time when small villages easily fell prey to marauders and internal anarchy. The walled city seemed to guarantee physical safety; within the walls medical knowledge, codified in an hierarchical image of the body, revealed the principles of social order. De

John of Salisbury's "body politic," showing social hierarchy. Manuscript illustration, thirteenth century.

Mondeville lived in a more secure time, and imagined the meaning of walls, for instance, in a different way. In syncope, the organs seek to send their own fluids and heat across zones, crossing the tissue walls of the body. In a social crisis, the walls between people are breached, leading them to perform unusual acts of generosity.

Like John of Salisbury, Henri de Mondeville thought there was a direct analogy between the structure of the body and the structure of the city, yet his image of the body showed him a different city, a city of continually unequal heats and stresses.[23] For instance, de Mondeville's colleagues likened to a knife wound the appearance in a city of foreign exiles driven from their own homes; these doctors imagined a more humane outcome than the other organs in the body politic recoiling. The natural impulse would be to extend mercy to the exiles. There is, they maintained, a medical foundation for the impulse to aid others during a crisis; as we would say in modern jargon, there is a biological foundation for altruism.

Between John of Salisbury and Henri de Mondeville there lay a great divide in imagery of the body politic. One asked: Where do you belong? The other asked: How will you respond to others? One envisioned the city as a space which ranks bodies living together; the other envisioned the city as a space which connects bodies living together.

The medicine allied to the Imitation of Christ would challenge certain social barriers in the ordinary dealing of Christians in a city, most notably the great human boundary conceived by ancient medicine and carried into the medieval world, the boundary of gender.

Medieval women, even those as forceful as Heloise of Paris, the abbess of the powerful Convent of the Paraclete, seemed to accept without question their supposed biological weakness in relation to men. In John of Salisbury's concept of the body politic, its heart was a place in the body politic filled by men, by state counselors. Yet, as the historian Caroline Bynum has shown, those inspired by the Imitation of Christ began to think of the heart, its blood, and its placement under the breasts as an androgynous, if not female, zone of the body, linked to the powers of the Virgin Mary.[24] Jesus also appeared to cross the lines of gender, many medieval clerics and thinkers conceiving of him as a mother.[25] St. Anselm asked, "But you, Jesus, good lord, are you not also a mother? Are you not that mother who, like a hen, collects her chickens under her wings? Truly, master, you are a mother."[26]

The blurring of Christ's gender, like the celebration of Mary's powers in the body and the growth of Marian cults, all put an emphasis on *nurturing,* that is, on compassion expressed through maternal images. Bernard of Clairvaux in particular sharpened this compassionate, maternal imagery of Christ; "To Bernard, the maternal image [appears] . . . not as giving birth or even as conceiving or sheltering in a womb, but as nurturing, particularly suckling."[27] The dignity now accorded women's bodies helped women acquire a stronger voice in religious affairs in the twelfth century, evinced in the flowering of many convents like the Paraclete with educated leaders and serious spiritual purposes.

Yet the impulse to nurture did not neatly accord with the melancholic temperament of the body. Melancholy, as the historian Raymond Klibansky observes, was the most inward-turning of the four temperaments. Under its sway a person tried to fathom a soul-secret which seemed contained within, rather than mull over a problem in the world as did the more scientific, phlegmatic temperament.[28] Melancholy provoked meditation on the evils that caused people to suffer and on the secrets of God's grace. The traditional spaces of melancholy were thus enclosures, cells and walled gardens.

Modern medicine often confuses melancholy with clinical depression. The comportment of the medieval melancholic little resembled the heavy movements, sluggish response to others, and pained dullness of the clinically depressed. The way a melancholic could more actively show compassion and nurturance appeared in the medieval orchestration of death. In front of the Cathedral Church of Notre-Dame, Parisians saw in the Passion plays the death of Jesus depicted with stark realism, the actor playing Jesus often flagellated until he bled. This intensely physical scene served to draw them close to Jesus' suffering as a fellow human being. Within the Cathedral the new, popular piety on Easter sought to eliminate "all forms of enclosure . . . all partitions. Everyone everywhere had to be able to hear the sermon, to see the body of Christ being raised."[29] This same open and vivid experience of bearing witness to another's suffering orchestrated the last moments before an ordinary human died. In Perikles' Athens, as we have seen, "the Ancients feared being near the dead and kept them at a distance."[30] In the Middle Ages the death chamber had become the space of "a public ceremony. . . . It was essential that parents, friends, and neighbors be present," the historian Philippe Ariès writes.[31] Deathbed scenes show crowds of people chatting, drinking and eating as well as praying; they kept the dying company.

How was the person supported in this way to respond? The dying, Ariès observes, were meant to depart "in a ceremonial manner . . . but with no theatrics, with no great show of emotion."[32] In a study of gestures of despair in the visual arts, Moshe Barasch observes that "the artists of the late Middle Ages expressed the grief of the Virgin Mary holding the dead Christ on her lap in a variety of ways, but they usually renounced frantic gesticulation as a means of conveying her sorrow."[33] Through this restraint in gesture, the body expressed a dignified melancholy. The proper way to die was to say a word, if possible, to each person in the room, or make a movement of the hand or eyes to recognize them, but to go no further. In life, as in art, the moment of death is to be a moment of meditation rather than depression.

To serve the Christian duality of compassion and inwardness in the city, among the living, required more than such bodily comportment. The ideal of nurturing spaces first appeared in the writings of Pierre Abelard, the twelfth-century Parisian philosopher. He asserted that "cities are 'convents' for married people. . . . Cities are . . . bound together by charity. Every city is a fraternity."[34] It required new conceptions and uses of convents, monasteries, and sacred gardens—the traditional spaces of melancholy.

3. THE CHRISTIAN COMMUNITY

At this point, we might look at how medieval Paris was divided between Church and State. There was anything but a neat geographic division, because state and religion were deeply intertwined. When a king was crowned in a cathedral, "the coronation rite transformed him sacramentally into a *Christus Domini,* that is, not only into a person of episcopal rank, but into an image of Christ himself," Otto von Simson writes.[35] The medieval King, as a Christus Domini, echoed the Roman emperor's image as a living god. Similarly, the Bishop of Paris stood on the same level "as that of counts, dukes, and of the king," in the words of another historian; "he was served by the same high and petty officers. He had his seneschal or steward, his cupbearer, his marshal, his chamberlain or treasurer, his equerry,

his master of the pantry, secretaries, chaplains. . . ."[36] The eleventh
century saw the bishop loosen his feudal bond to the King; the
bishop took an oath of loyalty but no longer an oath of homage—the
sort of distinction which seemed to that age of privileges to mark an
enormous gulf.

Palace, cathedral, and abbey

For centuries Paris had been a royal city, but by the time of Jehan
de Chelles the meaning of a royal seat had changed. Before the spurt
of urban growth in the twelfth century, the King and his circle spent
time constantly on the roads of the kingdom, staying at the castles of
principal nobles. By making such "progresses," the King put the
stamp of personal dominion on his lands; the physical presence of
the King helped define what the kingdom was. As his cities revived,
the French King travelled somewhat less. His palace on the Ile de la
Cité became imbued with the symbolism of his office; kingship
became a construction in stone as well as a set of geographical possessions, again like a Roman emperor.

Philip II, known as Philip Augustus (1165–1223), lived in a palace
on the Ile de la Cité hard by the religious complex of buildings surrounding the Cathedral of Notre-Dame, at the eastern end of the
Ile. The great nobles of his court built palaces for themselves to the
south of the Ile, on the Left Bank of Paris, on lands owned by
abbeys. Charles V later removed the space of kingship from this con-
finement. He built the first of the palaces of the Louvre, just beyond
the protection of Philip Augustus' wall. This first Louvre was a great
square tower, its center a *donjon,* an immense open ceremonial hall,
with arms and prisoners kept beneath its floor, and the offices of the
court on rooms around the sides. The Louvre of Charles V was one
of the first buildings in which military protection became more an
architectural symbol than a matter of practical defense. The four
great turrets on the corners of the Louvre donjon were a declaration
of kingly might to the inhabitants of Paris; actual physical protection
came from new city walls beyond the grounds of the palace.

During the time of Philip Augustus the estates of the nobles
within the city echoed the country; their gardens, for instance, were
used to grow grapes, other fruits and vegetables. Now these gardens
began to be more decorative than agricultural. And whereas Philip
Augustus lived in his palace amid orphans, students, and clerics, the
new palace of the Louvre soon became crowded, around what is now

the rue de Rivoli, with palaces of the principal nobles of his court, each with its own ceremonial halls, turrets, and gardens. From these urban turrets, a noble might look to the outside, not to see if enemy troops were approaching, but who his neighbor had invited to dinner. The court thus became a community within the city; but it was not a community of the sort Abelard would have approved. The buildings of the great nobles pressed ever closer to the Louvre and to each other, forming a great honeycombed structure of intrigue.

Paris was also an episcopal city, a seat of religious wealth, power, and culture in the city balancing the powers lodged in the palace. The Bishop of Paris rivalled the King in urban possessions; he owned the entire Ile St.-Louis, the land around his own Cathedral of Notre-Dame, and land elsewhere in the city. When Maurice de Sully began to build the Cathedral of Notre-Dame in 1160, the "Cathedral" included not just the great church building, but a religious cluster of buildings where monks lived, a hospital, storehouses, and extensive gardens. Boats came to the private landings of the Cathedral complex to supply the physical needs of the members of the chapters and Cathedral, boats often sent from Saint-Germain and other abbeys which had their own gardens and storehouses. The Left Bank of the city remained in 1200 more agricultural than the Right Bank, an extensive vineyard surrounding Saint-Germain.

By 1250, when Jehan de Chelles launched the final phase of constructing Notre-Dame, this religious enclave within the city contained conflicting interests. "The episcopal community was not quite rationally divided," the historian Allan Temko writes with admirable restraint; "within and without the Cathedral, the territory of the Church was marked by curious feudal boundaries."[37] The bishop controlled the chapel sanctuaries and some aisles within the church, while the chapter of canons, nominally the subjects of the bishop, controlled the rest of the building. "The chapter's jurisdiction wandered south of the Cathedral, through the Bishop's gate to the entrance of his palace," while "the Bishop's traveled north, following certain streets to little isles of authority within the cloister."[38] Control of these spaces in Notre-Dame defined particular groups' power within the Church hierarchy. Moreover, the seductions of city life pressed in on the forty houses of the chapter clustered around Notre-Dame; King, Pope, and Bishop sought, usually in vain, to tame the roughhousing and whoring of many of the canons. Again, it was not quite what Abelard had in mind.

An abbey had both a precise meaning, as a place controlled by specific Church functionaries—abbots and abbesses—and also a looser meaning, to include a complex of buildings which created a "church home." An abbey might incorporate monastic or convent living quarters, a hospital, almshouse, and garden as well as a church. One of the earliest and best known today is the abbey-monastery of St. Gall in Switzerland, since detailed plans for it have survived. In Carolingian times there were few large seignorial castles, so it fell to the abbeys to provide for the general public during wars or famines as well as for the members of their own orders. Yet these early religious settlements, too, would not have suited Abelard's image of the community a city should become, for they were hardly places of free and generous charity. The keepers of the gates rigorously screened who was to be admitted; the almshouse served only the local poor in a parish, those eligible being entered in an official poor list called the *matricula*.

In Paris, the Dominicans and Franciscans settled near the city's Left Bank walls early in the thirteenth century. The space behind these walls was the least populated on the Left Bank, so that these orders had least contact with urban problems. The Servites had more, because they made a church home on the Right Bank near the central market. The mendicant orders were the most urbanized of all religious orders, relative latecomers on the scene who nevertheless actively sought to aid the sick on the streets and to root out heresy. The Benedictines controlled the Abbey of Saint-Germain-des-Prés, a large religious "home" as well as vineyard. New orders, like the Knights of the Temple, which participated in the Crusades, sent an army of pilgrims back and forth across Europe in need of local aid. As trade revived in Paris, travellers from place to place sought temporary shelter and food in the church homes, first in the Cathedral complex and Saint-Germain-des-Prés, then in the Servite quarters, later in the homes of the mendicant orders.

The most important religious place was the parish. "If the cathedral was the pride of the bourgeois [the urban dwellers]," the urbanist Howard Saalman writes, "his birth, life, and death—his very identity—were inextricably bound up in [the parish]."[39] All legal documents depended on parish records; markets formed around parish churches; the parish was the first source of help for people in need. Yet as Paris swelled with people, the parishes could no longer cope with these local needs, and the canons of larger religious institutions took charge of many of the charitable functions previously performed by parish church wardens. Hospitals for the poor and their almshouses expanded; many of the new hospitals in the city were founded by higher Church authorities, "at the instigation of bishops. Built near the bishop's or canons' residence, the descendants of these institutions are still found today near the old cathedrals: for example, the modern religious hospitals of Paris. . . ."[40] By 1328, there were about sixty hospitals in the city, concentrated in the center on the Ile de la Cité and the Right Bank; the largest was near Notre-Dame, the hospital of the Hôtel-Dieu. The central Church authorities also increased the houses which gave out alms, the almonries, spreading these widely throughout the city.

Yet as the scale of these activities increased, becoming citywide rather than local, the sense of what the Church did became more personal rather than bureaucratically cold, thanks to the religious revival. To see how this occurred, let us look at the work of the confessor, the almoner, and the gardener in Jehan de Chelles' Paris.

Confessor, almoner, and gardener

In the early Middle Ages, confession was a relatively passionless affair. The confessee gave a circumstantial account of his or her actions, the confessor prescribed a penance or directed his charge to change behavior. During the twelfth century, confession became a much more personal, emotionally charged exchange between two individuals, due to the tide of religious renewal. The space of the confessional remained physically what it had been earlier, a closed box divided by a screen so that priest and parishioner could not see each other. In the confessional space, now "the friars came forward with a new approach to confession and penance"; in place of the older practice of simply issuing orders according to an abstract calendar of sins, priests "willingly entered into negotiation with the confessee to determine, through a series of questions and responses, the relative seriousness of the fault and hence the appropriate harshness of the penance."[41] By exchanging questions and confidences, confession drew priest and parishioner into a more personal relationship.

The priest, for his part, could no longer simply speak a formal language of duties and obligations; he had to listen harder to the parishioner to make sense of what he heard. Confession became a narrative, a story neither the teller nor the listener at first understood. The priest was expected to express feelings of compassion toward his parishioner's sins at the moment when the story began to make sense. The act of confession was a melancholic occasion, in the medieval sense of melancholia: it required openness between confessor and confessee, and it required inwardness, as the one who confessed sought to make sense of his or her sins. Since the parishioner sought not merely to follow an abstract formula in speaking of his or her own sins, but to interpret his own case with the aid of the priest, these melancholic exchanges empowered the parishioner. He or she was seen as capable of participating actively in the faith.

The Imitation of Christ pervaded Catholic practice, in rural convents as much as urban cathedrals. The idea of an urban Middle Ages in northern Europe can be misleading, for the sheer numbers of people living in cities at the time was very small; within what we now call France, the population of Paris formed about 1 percent of the whole. But there was an urban dimension to the *practice* of confession in the new way. The condition of confession is strict anonymity. In a small village, however, the priest would likely recognize the confessee's voice, know the situations to which the confessee referred, and make judgments and suggestions based on that external knowledge. In a city, the fiction of the confession would become a social fact. The actual words spoken in the urban confessional mattered more than in a small town or parish. The confessor had to attend to them as significant, a stranger's story he could not manage simply by formula. In Jehan de Chelles' Paris, this would have been particularly so in the confessional booths of Notre-Dame and Saint-Germain-des-Prés, since these two churches drew communicants from beyond their local parishes. For the mendicant orders, who ministered to the poor and sick not otherwise assisted, the importance of listening seriously to strangers was even greater, since the "parishioners" had no parish. The religious revival disposed the cleric to listen; the city obliged him to do so when confronted with the unknown.

The almoner's tale resembled the confessor's. Although Christianity emphasized identification with the poor, early medieval charity was not based on feeling compassion for them. In doing the work of charity, the almoner obeyed a higher power; he was obliged to perform acts of charity no matter what his own inclinations. The twelfth-century Parisian scholar Humbert de Romans evoked this traditional view of charity in a sermon he delivered to those who ran a charity hospital for the poor: charity is an act in "service of the Creator," in which the Christian's own emotions do not enter into discharging his obligations.[42] No more did compassion need to motivate those who donated wealth to the early monasteries for the care of the poor and the sick. These gifts brought honor to the benefactors; moreover, the benefactors sought the goodwill of monks, for "the best available means of assuring eternal salvation was to have the monks intercede for the living and to [bury and] commemorate the dead."[43]

The religious revival altered both the spirit and the practice of urban charity. The Franciscans and the Dominicans urged engagement in the world, not spiritual isolation. By serving others, the Christian purified his or her own soul. The Imitation of Christ strengthened this engagement. In medieval Paris, one historian argues, charity administered in a spirit of compassion for those who suffered "included an ethical justification for urban society itself as well as for the characteristic activities of its more influential members."[44] To be sure, the city concentrated people in need, but a more specific change marked this justification. The Servite community near the central market on the Right Bank began to make extensive use of lay members as almoners in the mid-1200s. The fact that lay persons now frequently engaged in giving alms, formerly a privilege of clergy (and a significant source of graft), meant that the urban citizen now played a significant role in the power structure of the Church.

The medieval urban almoner worked quite differently from a modern welfare bureaucrat, who deals with human needs as just so many forms to be filled out. As charitable institutions spread throughout the city, and drew upon the Servite example, the almoner frequently took to the streets, acting on priests' reports or popular rumor; like the mendicant friars, the lay almoner sought to round up lepers, to discover where the dying had been abandoned, or to bring the sick into hospital. Work on the streets required an active engagement in the lives of people beyond parish boundaries, and was unlike the passive local charity of earlier eras, regulated by entry or refusal of entry at the church's gates. The advent of lay almoners and then mendicants on the streets in turn encouraged ordinary people in need to come *to* churches, churches they felt to be responsive beyond the letter of duty.

This charitable bonding altered somewhat the physical forms of Notre-Dame's immediate surroundings. The cloister walls Jehan de Chelles made surrounding the great Cathedral garden on the south side of Notre-Dame were low—one estimate puts them at only three feet high. Because the cloister walls were low, and also ungated, any-

Christian charity in the city, *Good Deeds*, miniature, ca. 1500.

An urban garden.
Pierre de Crescens, *Le Livre des prouffitz champestres,* fifteenth century.

one could enter easily. Prompted by the greater responsiveness of
the Church to the people, the garden filled with abandoned babies,
homeless people, lepers, and the dying; they spent the day waiting
for the monks to come out among them and the night sleeping on
straw pallets strewn on the ground. Yet the gardens of cloisters were
also meant to encourage people to consider the state of their souls.
The cloister gardens of Notre-Dame exemplified melancholy in
space, open, filled with suffering, and also contemplative.

A long tradition had established, by 1250, how to plant a garden to arouse the impulses of melancholic contemplation. Unfortunately, almost all information about the specific plantings in the medieval garden of Notre-Dame is lost, but we know at least the rules which Jehan de Chelles' gardeners possessed to set about this task.

Urban French castles with ornamented gardens began to appear in the late ninth century. In Paris, traces of large ornamented gardens outside monasteries, attached to secular houses or standing alone, appeared in the tenth century, on the Ile de la Cité on its southern side. Originally, urban gardens produced herbs, fruits, and vegetables for the city. By the 1250s, it was more profitable to build than to farm in the city and, correspondingly, it was cheaper to buy food shipped to Paris. The working gardens surrounding Notre-Dame in 1160 had shrunk by 1250.

Parisians used the gardens of Notre-Dame instead as a place to relieve the sheer pressure of population in the city's houses and streets. Within the house, as on the street, people lived packed tightly together. The rooms of urban houses functioned like streets, people coming and going at will at all hours, "crowded together cheek by jowl, living in promiscuity, sometimes in the midst of a mob. In feudal residences there was no room for individual solitude."[45] The medieval Parisian did not know the notion of a private room reserved for an individual. The gardens of Notre-Dame also were crowded with people, but gardening practice meant that here one could find calm and tranquility, if not solitude.

Three elements of garden design were thought in the medieval era to create a place that encouraged introspection: the bower, the labyrinth, and the garden pool. A bower was simply a place to sit sheltered from the sun. Ancient gardeners made bowers by constructing wooden roofs or bare trellises over benches. The medieval gardener began to grow plants, most often roses and honeysuckle, on the trellises to create a thick enclosure of leaves and flowers within which a person could sit, hidden from others.

Medieval gardeners adapted the labyrinth—another ancient form—to their own quest for respite. The Greeks made labyrinths by using low bushes; they set lavender, myrtle, and santolina in a circle with a well-defined center and many, if confusing, lines out to the circumference. A stroller could simply step over the bushes if he or she couldn't find the right path out, whereas in the medieval labyrinth "there were paths between hedges taller than a man, so that

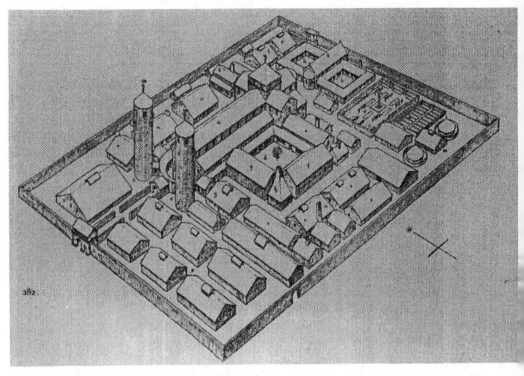

Bird's-eye view of the monastery at St. Gall, based on the Master Plan of 816 and 817. Modern rendering by Karl Gruber. *Horn and Born, from* The Plan of St. Gall *(University of California Press). All rights reserved.*

anyone wandering about and taking a wrong turn could not see over and set himself right."[46] The plants used for such a maze were mostly box, or box mixed with yew, as in a famous medieval maze of box planted in the garden of the Hôtel des Tournelles in Paris. Fragmentary evidence suggests Jehan de Chelles planted a tall labyrinth in the cloister garden of Notre-Dame shaped, for reasons now not understood, like the Jewish Star of David. In the early Middle Ages, labyrinths symbolized the soul's struggle to find God at the soul's own center; in the city, the labyrinth served a more secular purpose. Once a person had worked out the pattern of the maze, he or she could retreat to its center without fear of being found easily by others.

The garden pool served as a mirror of the person looking into it, a reflective surface. Wells could be found on every Parisian street; to protect them from the urine, faeces, and garbage running in the streets, builders raised the well walls several feet high. In the time of Jehan de Chelles, ornamental fountains graced a few street wells, but not many. The relative protection of the cloister gardens meant a builder could lower the well walls; moreover, the maker of a pool in a cloister thought twice about putting a fountain in it, for the stream of water would disturb the pool's surface. The cloister pool was meant to be a liquid mirror one stood over, a mirror in which to contemplate oneself.

The plants a garden contained also were used to create a sense of tranquility. The sacristan set cut roses within the church to indicate the shrines near which people must be silent, and placed lilac bows beneath statues of the Virgin during time of plague, their scent seeming a tranquilizer. On the streets of Paris, people carried little bunches of herbs which they frequently pressed to their noses to ward off noxious smells; these same herbs in the cloister took on both an introspective and a medicinal value. At Christmas, smelling dried myrrh was thought to arouse memories of one's own, as well as Christ's birth. During Lent, the sacristan made incense from dried bergamot; the smell was thought to calm the anger that marked this time of year.

We can only guess what a person thought, sitting in a rose bower outside Notre-Dame, when suddenly aware of a leper whose body was covered in running sores. Not sheer surprise, for now the tradi-

The Hôtel de Cluny in Paris, built between 1485 and 1498. It consummates military architecture as urban ornament.

The garden as earthly paradise from which the world and its dangers are excluded. Anonymous artist, *The Cloister Garden*, 1519. *All rights reserved. The Metropolitan Museum of Art, Harris Brisbane Dick Fund, 1925.*

tional space of melancholy had opened to the city: if the hopes of Henri de Mondeville were realized, the jolt might have induced an altruistic response. We can be more certain what the gardener felt about the labor of creating this place. It was labor which diverged in its very dignity from the effort required of people who engaged in trade.

Christian labor

The dream of finding sanctuary is age-old; in the *Eclogues,* the Roman poet Virgil wrote,

> For them, far from the strife of arms, the earth, ever just, pours an easy living on the land of its own accord. . . . By their own will the trees and the fields bear produce, and he picks it. His peace is secure and his living cannot fail.[47]

Early Christian ascetics, particularly in the East, had sought spiritual sanctuary by living as hermits. Later Western European ideas of sanctuary on the contrary were "coenobitic," commanding people to live together in a monastery. St. Benedict, who gave sanctuary this communal, place-bound form, also decreed how monks should live together: *"laborare et orare,"* work and pray. That labor focused on the garden.[48]

Christian labor had always been tied to providing a refuge from a sinful world. By the time monasteries began to flourish in the French countryside, in the late ninth century and the tenth, the provisioning of sanctuary occurred in two locations in the religious house. One was in small chapels along the sides of a church; the other was in the cloisters attached to church buildings. Chapel sanctuaries were oriented to the veneration of a saint. Cloister sanctuaries were tied symbolically and practically to the veneration of Nature, specifically to creating and maintaining the garden contained within the cloister's walls. Christian meditation set in the cloister garden drew upon the imagery of the Garden of Eden, which set the scene for thinking about the human self-destructiveness that led to Adam and Eve's expulsion from the Garden. For the monks who first dwelt in rural sanctuaries, tending a garden was meant to be a restorative act, a Christian's restitution of Adam and Eve's exile. Nicolas of Clairvaux "divided all creation into five regions: the world, purgatory, hell, heaven, and the *paradisus claustralis.*"[49] The last of the five, the cloister garden, aimed to be a paradise regained on earth. To labor here was to regain one's dignity.

The *paradisus claustralis* of the monastery contrasted in this to the Islamic "paradise gardens," as described in the Koran, and planted in cities like Cordoba. The Islamic gardens sought to provide relief from labor; when William of Malmesbury wrote about the gardens of Thorney Abbey, by contrast, he declared that "not a particle of the soil is left to lie fallow . . . in this place cultivation rivals nature; what the latter has forgotten the former brings forth."[50]

Christian monastic reformers thought that work in the garden not only restored the worker to the original Garden, but also created spiritual discipline; the harder the work, the greater its moral value. This was specially emphasized by the Cistercians, who sought to recall monks through labor from the sloth and corruption into which many religious orders had sunk. And for this reason, also, the monk's labors in the garden came to be silent labor—a rule of silence observed in the garden by Franciscans and Cistercians, as well as many Benedictines. *Laborare et orare* indicated how early medieval Christians thought labor dignified the body in making a place.

The connection in the High Middle Ages between human pain and God's pain intensified the dignity of work, as the person making a physical effort considered in a new light the relations between flesh and soul. To be sure, as Caroline Bynum remarks, the personal awareness gained by labor "was not what we mean by 'the individual' "; the monk labored for the community.[51]

The monks of St. Gall or Clairvaux worked in a guarded space. The city made the dignity of labor stand forth in a less controlled world, dignity and indignity mixed in the fabric of urban space. The stones of Notre-Dame were hard by the stone quays of the Seine. The spires of the Cathedral told those in need where to come in the city for help, these spires which reached up to Heaven, offering sanctuary from the quays, the streets, and the urban hovels. Still, the celebrations in 1250 of the workers who made Notre-Dame testified to the spread of *laborare et orare* beyond the garden into the city: the gardener was now joined by the mason, the glassblower, and the carpenter.

If the merchants who helped fund these sanctuaries were also celebrated in 1250, their honor was less certain, their dignity more questioned. Trade was no melancholic labor in the medieval sense, no introspective effort. Indeed, trading puzzled the traders as much as it did Bernard of Clairvaux in his cloister or John of Salisbury in his

study. The adage *"Stadt Luft macht frei"* seemed to cut traders free
of the emotional attachments which they sought as Christians. If the
urban Christian garden of medieval Paris meant to renew humanity
in its state of grace before the Fall, if this new garden harbored laborers who had learned lessons of suffering unknown to Adam and Eve,
those who worked outside the sanctuary seemed to wander in an
urban wilderness.

CHAPTER SIX

"Each Man Is
a Devil to Himself"

The Paris of
Humbert de Romans

The member of the Athenian polis was a citizen. The member of a medieval town called himself a *bourgeois* in French, a *Burgher* in German. These words named more than middle-class people; the carvers who worked on Notre-Dame were bourgeois, yet in medieval Paris few bourgeois had voting rights like Greek citizens. The historian Maurice Lombard describes the bourgeois instead as a cosmopolitan, thanks to commerce and trade in the city. "[The medieval bourgeois] is a man at a crossroads, the crossroads at which different urban centers overlap," Lombard writes; "he is a man open to the outside, receptive to influences which end in his city and which come from other cities."[1] This cosmopolitan outlook influenced the sense of one's own city. The non-charitable labor of medi-

Map of medieval Paris, ca. 1300.

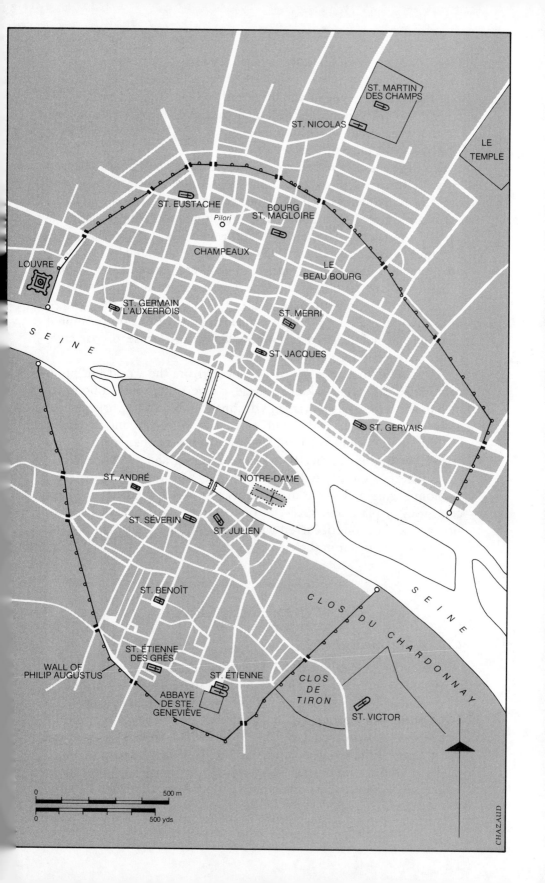

ST. MARTIN
DES CHAMPS

ST. NICOLAS

LE
TEMPLE

ST. EUSTACHE

BOURG
ST. MAGLOIRE

Pilori

CHAMPEAUX

LE
BEAU BOURG

LOUVRE

ST. GERMAIN
L'AUXERROIS

ST. MERRI

ST. JACQUES

S E I N E

ST. GERVAIS

ST. ANDRÉ

NOTRE-DAME

ST. SÉVERIN

ST. JULIEN

S E I N E

ST. BENOÎT

C L O S   D U   C H A R D O N N A Y

ST. ÉTIENNE
DES GRÈS

ST. ÉTIENNE

*CLOS
DE
TIRON*

WALL OF
PHILIP AUGUSTUS

ABBAYE
DE STE.
GENEVIÈVE

ST. VICTOR

0   500 m

0   500 yds.

CHAZAUD

eval Paris occurred in urban space rather than places: spaces to be bought and sold, altered in form by buying and selling, space becoming the territory in which, rather than for which, a person worked. The bourgeois made use of urban space.

The distinction between space and place is a basic one in urban form. It turns on more than emotional attachment to where one lives, for it involves as well the experience of time. In medieval Paris, the flexible use of space appeared in conjunction with the appearance of the corporation, an institution with the right to change its activities in the course of time. Economic time unfolded by following up opportunities, taking advantage of unforeseen events. Economics prompted a conjunction of functional use of space and opportunistic use of time. Christian time, by contrast, was founded on the story of Jesus' own life, a history people knew by heart. Religion prompted emotional attachment to place coupled with a sense of narrative time, a narrative fixed and certain.

The early Christian who "turned away" from the world felt pregnant with change but lacking in place; conversion provided no roadmap to show the early Christian's destination. Now the Christian had a place in the world and a path to follow, yet economic endeavor seemed to push him off both. People's sense of their own bodies entered into this conflict between economics and religion. While Christian time and place drew on the body's powers of compassion, economic time and space drew on its powers of aggression. These contraries of place and space, of opportunity and fixity, of compassion and aggression, occurred within every bourgeois trying both to believe and to profit in the city.

1. ECONOMIC SPACE

Cité, bourg, commune

The geography of medieval Paris, like other cities of the time, consisted of three kinds of property. First there was land fortified by a permanent wall, and owned within the wall by defined powers. In Paris, stone walls protected the Ile de la Cité, for instance, and the island was also protected by the Seine, which served as a natural moat; most of the island belonged to the King and the Church. Such land the French called a *cité*.

The second kind of land had no walls but was still owned by large

Farming outside a cité in medieval Paris. The Limbourg Brothers, *Les Très Riches Heures du duc de Berry,* Calendar, fragment for month of June, ca. 1416.

and defined powers. This kind of territory the French called a *bourg.* The oldest bourg in Paris lay on the Left Bank, the bourg of Saint-Germain. It was like a dense village, save that all the land was owned by the four churches which composed Saint-Germain parish, the largest where the modern Church of Saint-Sulpice stands today. A bourg need not have been controlled by a single power. On the Right Bank across from Notre-Dame a new quarter had grown up along the river by 1250, serving both as a port and a market; one minor noble controlled the port, another the market.

The third kind of densely peopled land was neither protected by permanent walls nor controlled by a well-defined power. The French called it a *commune.* Communes dotted the periphery of Paris and were usually small landholdings, villages without a master.

The rebirth of Paris in the Middle Ages transformed the status of the communes and bourgs by enclosing ever more land within walls. The walls expanded in two stages. King Philip Augustus walled in both the north and south banks of Paris in the early thirteenth century, protecting an area which had grown steadily in the previous century; Charles V enlarged the walls of Paris again by the 1350s, entirely on the right bank. These changes forged what we would call a city out of the original small, isolated cité, its bourgs, and its communes; the King accorded and guaranteed economic privileges to the bourgs and the communes within the walls.

Parisians measured urban improvement by the amount of stone in the city. As Jacques Le Goff points out, "From the eleventh century the great boom in building, a phenomenon which was essential in the development of the medieval economy, very often consisted of replacing a wooden construction with one in stone—whether churches, bridges, or houses," a desire to invest in stone that marked private investment as well as public works.[2] The use of stone in turn encouraged the development of other craft industries. Jehan de Chelles' final stages in building the Cathedral of Notre-Dame, for instance, radically expanded the trade in glass, precious jewels, and tapestries in the city.

The process of joining the old bourgs, cités, and communes together did not, however, make the map of Paris any clearer.

The street

We would expect a large trading city like medieval Paris to have well-made roads to move goods through the city. Along the banks of the Seine River they existed; from 1000 to 1200, these banks were lined with stone walls so that trade on the river could be moved more efficiently. But inland, the growth of the city did not create a system of roads easily accommodating transport. "Roads were in a poor state," Le Goff notes; "there was a limited number of carts and waggons, which were expensive, and useful vehicles were absent"; even the lowly wheelbarrow did not appear on Parisian streets until the end of the Middle Ages.[3] The Roman city, with its beautifully engineered roads bedded deep into the earth, was a construction miracle of the past.

The messy form as well as sorry physical condition of the medieval street resulted from the very processes of growth. The roads of one commune had seldom been laid out to join those of a neighboring commune, since its boundaries were originally the end of a smaller, villagelike settlement turning inward. Nor were the bourgs laid out to connect to other bourgs. The chaotic shape of the streets also arose from the use the owners made of the land they controlled.

Most pieces of land in a cité or bourg were leased, or the building rights on them sold, to individuals. These diverse builders had the right to construct as they saw fit on the land owned by a large institution like the Crown or the Church; moreover, the various parts of a single building, on different floors or the same floor, might be owned and developed by different persons. "There was," says the urbanist Jacques Heers, "a veritable colonization of building land within the city or in its immediate environs."[4] Rarely did the landholder attempt to influence the builder in terms of urban design; indeed, on a purely economic level only in exceptional cases could the King or Bishop seize a building or force its owner to sell to someone else. In Paris, King or Bishop invoked "eminent domain" mostly to add to a palace or a church.

Only medieval cities which had been founded in Roman times were likely to have a street plan or an overall design, and the Roman grids had, save in a very few cities like Trier and Milan, been cracked by the growth process into disconnected bits and pieces. Neither King nor Bishop nor bourgeois had an image of how the city as a whole should look. "The cramped, fragmented nature of the public sphere reflected, in the very topography of the city, the weakness, lack of resources, and limited ambitions of the state," claims one historian.[5] Builders put up whatever they could get away with; neighbors fought each other's constructions with lawsuits, and often more brutally with hired gangs of thugs who ripped down a neighbor's work. From this aggression came the Parisian urban fabric, "mazes of twisting, tiny streets, impasses, and courts; squares were small, and there were few broad vistas or buildings set back from the street; traffic was always clogged."[6]

Medieval Cairo and medieval Paris formed a telling contrast, though to the modern eye they might have seemed equally jumbled. The Koran lays down precise instructions for the placement of doors

A surviving medieval street in Paris.

and the spatial relationship of doors to windows. In medieval Cairo, land owned by a Muslim had to be built according to these instructions, which were enforced by charitable foundations in the city. Such buildings, moreover, had to relate in form to one another, had to be aware of one another; one could not, for instance, block a neighbor's door. Religion decreed contextual architecture, though the context was not one of linear streets. The buildings of medieval Paris were under no such divine—or royal, or noble—command to take account of one another. Each was fenestrated and floored according the single owner's will; it was common for builders to block access to other buildings with impunity.

The space of the Parisian medieval street was no more and no less than the space which remained after buildings had been constructed. Before the great Renaissance palaces arose in the Marais, for instance, this swampy settlement on the Right Bank had streets which suddenly narrowed so that a single person could barely pass between buildings that different owners had built out to the edge of the lot lines. The abbeys and the King's quarter had more serviceable streets, since the owner was also the builder, though even in the episcopal district around Notre-Dame different orders pushed into the street according to their own desires, and to test the limits of their privileges.

The street bore the imprint of aggressive assertion, then, it was the space left over after people asserted their rights and powers. The street was no garden, no coenobitic place created by common labor. If the street lacked those qualities of place, however, it did possess certain visual features which made it function well as an economic space. These features could be read on its walls.

In the non-ceremonial and poorer districts of ancient Greece and Rome, the wall related to the street as a solid barrier. The medieval urban economy made the street wall permeable. In the Parisian district of leather workers on the Right Bank, for example, the windows of each shop displayed goods to people walking in the streets through an innovation in window architecture: the windows had wooden shutters that folded down to serve as counters. The first building with windows known to be designed in this fashion dates from the early 1100s. Using the walls in this way, the merchants focused on the display of their goods, to make people on the street aware a shop contained something worth looking at inside as well. The buyer walking the street looked to the walls, their surfaces now active economic zones.

The workshop of an urban artisan. Late fifteenth-century miniature by Jean Bourdichon.

The medieval courtyard became tied in the same way to the economic activity of the street. The courtyard served as a showroom as well as a workroom, its entrance gradually enlarged so that people passing by could see what was happening within. Even in very grand palaces in the Marais district, as late as the sixteenth century, the

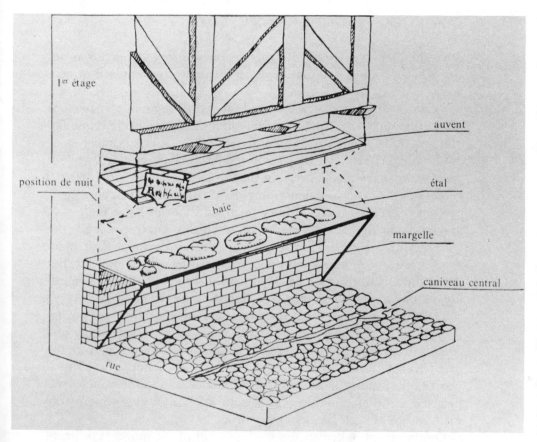

1er étage

auvent

position de nuit

étal

baie

margelle

caniveau central

rue

Schematic plan of a medieval street-wall shop in Paris.

ground-floor courtyard was planned as a beehive of shops producing and selling to the general public, as well as provisioning the noble household above.

The development of this porous economic street space encouraged a change in street time. The ancient city depended on daylight; trade in medieval Paris extended the hours of the street. People went into the streets to shop before or after they had finished their own labors; the dusk as well as dawn became hours of consumption, the bakery at dawn, for instance, and the butcher shop late at night, after the butcher had purchased, prepared, and roasted his meats during the day. The counter stayed down and the courtyard stayed unlocked as long as there were people in the street.

These streets whose buildings arose from the aggressive assertion of rights, whose porous surfaces and volumes encouraged economic competition, were also famously violent. Modern experiences of urban street crime give us no way to imagine the viciousness which ruled the medieval street. But this medieval street violence was not also what we might logically deduce, a simple consequence of economics.

Violence in the street was aimed far more frequently at persons rather than property. In 1405–06 (when the first reliable crime figures are available for Paris), 54 percent of the cases that came before the criminal courts of Paris concerned "passionate crimes," while 6 percent arose from robberies; in the decade from 1411 to 1420, 76 percent of the cases were about impulsive violence against persons, 7 percent concerned thefts.[7] One explanation for this lay in the nearly universal practice among merchants of hiring guards; indeed, the very wealthy maintained little private armies to protect their mansions. There were municipal police in Paris from 1160 onward, but their numbers were small, and their duties consisted mostly in guarding public officials when they travelled through the city.

The crime statistics from the High and late Middle Ages are far too crude for us to know who was attacked, whether family and friends or strangers on the street. It is a plausible inference, from the existence of so many hired guards and soldiers among the affluent classes, that most of the violence practiced by poor people was directed at other poor people. We do know, however, one of the main causes of such attacks; it was drink.

Drinking was linked to about 35 percent of the murders or grave violent attacks in the Touraine, largely a rural region of France. In Paris the correlation was even higher, for drinking occurred not only at home, where a drunk could go to sleep, but in the public cellars and wine shops which lined the streets of the city.[8] Groups of people got drunk together and then late at night erupted into the street, picking fights.

The need to drink had a compelling origin: it came from the need for bodily heat. In this northern city, wine warmed people's bodies in buildings that lacked effective heating; the fireplace set against a reflecting wall, with a flue leading to an external chimney, made its appearance only in the fifteenth century. Prior to this, open braziers or fires built directly on the floor provided a building's heat, and the smoke of these fires kept people from settling too close. Moreover, the heat was quickly dissipated, as few ordinary urban buildings had windows sheathed with glass. Wine served also as a narcotic that dulled pain. Like heroin or cocaine in modern cities, fortified wine created a drug culture in the Middle Ages, particularly in the public cellars and wine shops.

To be sure, street violence could take a political turn, in Paris as in other medieval cities. "Urban revolts were born, were propagated, and were aggravated in the street."[9] These revolts had impersonal causes, such as corrupt officials charged with distributing grain. But in Paris the constables of both King and Bishop suppressed these uprisings quickly; most lasted for only a few hours, at most a few days. The usual physical violence people experienced on the streets was unpredictable—an unprovoked knife thrust, a fist in one's stomach by a man who lurched by, blind drunk. We need to imagine, then, a street marked by different but discontinuous forms of aggression: purposeful economic competition and impulsive non-economic violence.

Verbal violence did play an important role in economic competition, if it rarely translated into violent action. People came to houses to threaten, without restraint and in the most gory detail, the person or the families of debtors. Some historians believe the very violence of this language served as a kind of emotional discharge, permitting competitors to act aggressively without in fact coming to blows. Be that as it may, the political and ecclesiastical powers ruling the city made little effort to punish sellers who threatened to punch or stab buyers who resisted concluding a sale, or who harassed other sellers in the street.

The low levels of property crime signalled that an effective but peculiar order reigned in urban space. It might have been invisible to the contemporary resident of Cairo, whose trading followed the overt dictates of religion. Beyond injunctions against usury and stealing, neither the Old nor the New Testament offered much guidance about how to behave economically. And perhaps this was why John of Salisbury also could not make sense of economic behavior. Competition was not choleric, in the sense the *Ars medica* described choler, the violent choler of the fighting soldier. It bore little resemblance to the sanguine civic command of the ruler, none to the phlegmatic considerations of the scholar. Competition certainly was not melancholic, nor nurturing. Just who was this economic creature became a little more evident in the organization of fairs and markets, spaces subject to more overt civic control than the streets.

Fairs and markets

The medieval city was an example of what we would today call a mixed economy of government and market on the Japanese model.

The use of the Seine in medieval Paris gives an idea of how the two mixed.[10]

Imagine that one had travelled on a ship loaded with cargo from elsewhere on the river. When the boat arrived in Paris, it was subject to a toll at the Grand Pont and its goods registered by a local corporation called the *marchands de l'eau*. If the shipment contained wine, one of the city's major imports, only Parisians were allowed to unload it at the quays, and a boat could rest at anchor filled with wine for only three days. This regulation ensured a good volume of traffic, but it put the merchant-seaman under immense pressure to sell. The quays thus were scenes of frantic activity, where every minute counted.

Only two major bridges crossed the Seine in 1200, the Grand Pont and the Petit Pont. Each of them was lined with houses and shops, and each bridge was the site of particular trades, apothecaries on the Petit Pont, for example, taking the spices delivered at the docks below and converting them into medicines. The city regulated the purity of the ingredients and the strength of the medicines. Even fishing in the river "was regulated by the king, the canons of Notre-Dame, and the abbey of Saint-Germain-des-Prés. Three year contracts were granted to fishermen who had to swear on the Bible that they wouldn't take carp, pike, or eels under a certain size."[11]

Once merchants bought goods on the bridges and the quays, they transported their wares to the fairgrounds of the city, spaces meant for trade in higher volumes than the streets. Some goods would return from the fairs to the quays after they had been sold, to be redistributed along the trade route to other cities; some would filter down into the more local economy of the streets. The most important fair in medieval Paris was the Lendit Fair, convened annually on a fairground established near the city, a fair begun in the darkest of the Dark Ages, in the seventh century. During the era of urban collapse in Europe, trading at fairs like the Lendit meant small, local deals, and barter of goods rather than the use of money; only rarely did a professional middleman enter the picture. The fairs developed, however, the first tissues between cities, connecting market to market.

By the High Middle Ages, these panoramas of goods had become vast and elaborate pageants. The great fairs were no longer conducted physically in open-air stalls or tents. Instead they occurred, as the economic historian Robert Lopez writes, in "stately halls for sectional or specialized trade, covered plazas and arcaded alleys."[12]

Flags and pendants hung over the booths; long tables spread out in the aisles where people ate, drank, and dealt. The pageantry was redoubled by the display of statues and painted images of saints, for the timing of fairs coincided with religious holidays and feasts; this meant the traders had the opportunity to deal with potential customers at leisure. Because fairs were tied to religious rituals, the desire to prolong trading often encouraged the adoration of ever more saints. Though the religious festivals seemed to sanctify trade, many clerics railed against the coupling, as the saints were enlisted to bless deals in perfumes, spices, and wine.

The great splendor of these medieval fairs perhaps misleads the modern eye, for their color concealed a fatal irony. As the urban economy promoted by the fairs grew, the fairs themselves weakened. For instance, by the twelfth century the Lendit Fair provided metalworkers and textile workers in Paris a chance to sell their own manufactures. The Parisians found that they had ever more customers for these products, coming from ever farther away from the city, and the parties quite naturally wanted to continue trading with the customers they found at the fair throughout the year, not just seasonally. Thus, "if the absolute volume of transactions . . . kept increasing as the Commercial Revolution progressed, [the fairs'] share of total trade inevitably diminished."[13] Economic growth weakened, that is, the location of trade in a single, controllable place. The metalworkers and textile makers began to deal with the customers found first in seasonal fairs throughout the year in the streets where they worked.

"Though markets and fairs are terms often used indiscriminately, there is a difference between them," declared the cleric Humbert de Romans, writing in the mid-thirteenth century. He referred particularly to the markets set up weekly in the city's streets, markets which often spilled out of that porous space into courtyards, or even into the numerous small graveyards dotting the city. During the twelfth century these street markets continued on a weekly basis the trade inaugurated at the annual fairs, displaying leather and metal goods, and selling financial services and capital in open-air offices with walls of cloth, the firms' gold hidden far from the street.

These market spaces quite effectively frustrated the state's power to regulate trade. Dealers in goods hounded by regulations at one street market simply moved to another. More, these markets broke the religious restraints, such they were, on the fairs; buying and selling took place on holy days, usury flourished. Perhaps because it was unrestrained, to both contemporary and later writers the market seemed a far more aggressive economic space than the fair or the non-market days on the street. "Markets are usually morally worse than fairs," Humbert de Romans noted, developing the contrast between the two as follows:

> They are held on feast days, and men miss thereby the divine office. . . . Sometimes, too, they are held in graveyards and other holy places. Frequently you will hear men swearing there: "By God I will not give you so much for it" . . . "By God it is not worth so much as that." Sometimes again the lord is defrauded of market dues, which is perfidy and disloyalty . . . quarrels happen. . . . Drinking occurs.[14]

To explain what made markets morally worse than fairs, Humbert de Romans told a story. It concerned a man who,

> entering an abbey, found many devils in the cloister but in the market-place found but one, alone on a high pillar. This filled him with wonder. But it was told him that in the cloister all is arranged to help souls to God, so many devils are required there to induce monks to be led astray, but in the market-place, since each man is a devil to himself, only one other devil suffices.[15]

The phrase "each man is a devil to himself" in the market makes the story curious. We can understand that economics would make a man a devil to others, but why to himself? A religious interpretation of course comes to mind: the devil of aggressive competition makes a man insensitive to what is best in himself, his compassion. But a more profane explanation was equally pervasive: unbridled economic competition could prove self-destructive. By laying waste established institutions like the fair, the economic animal who hoped to gain in fact could lose. It was all a matter of time.

2. ECONOMIC TIME

Guild and corporation

The medieval guild began as an institution to protect against economic self-destruction. A craft guild integrated all workers in an industry into a single body, where duties, promotions, and profits were defined by master workers for journeymen workers and apprentices in a contract meant to govern the worker's entire career; each guild was also a community which provided for the health of the workers as for their widows and orphans. Lopez describes the urban guild as "a federation of autonomous workshops, whose owners (the masters) normally made all decisions and established the requirements for promotion from the lower ranks (journeymen or hired helpers, and apprentices). Inner conflicts were usually minimized by a common interest in the welfare of the craft."[16] The French called craft guilds *corps de métiers;* the *Livre des Métiers,* compiled in 1268, "enumerates about a hundred organized crafts at Paris, divided into seven groups: foods, jewelry and fine arts, metals, textiles and clothes, furs, and building."[17] Though the guilds were in principle independent bodies, in fact the King's ministers determined their functioning through royal charters written and revised by ministers who, at best, took counsel from the guild masters.

Many of the charters for the metiers of Paris contained elaborate rules for how competitors in the same commodity were to behave; the charters laid down strict instructions, for instance, forbidding one butcher to insult another, or on how two hawkers of clothes were to shout at the same time to a potential group of customers in the street. More consequently, early guild charters sought to standardize products, in an effort to create collective control over the craft; the charters specified the amount of material to be used in a given product, its weight, and most importantly, its price. By 1300, for example, Parisian guilds had defined a "standard loaf" of bread, which meant that the weight and the kinds of grain used in making the bread determined its price, rather than market forces.

The guilds were highly aware of the destructive economic effects of unbridled competition. As well as controlling price, they sought to control the quantity of goods a shop manufactured, so that competition would focus on the quality of the workmanship. Thus, "a guild would normally forbid overtime work after dark and sometimes limit the number of dependents a master could employ."[18] The guilds' effort to regulate competition appeared in their dealings with the fairs, through their control of sale prices as well as the volume of goods on offer. Yet the control of competition did not make the guilds strong.

For one thing, different guilds had competing interests. In towns where food crafts were powerful, the economic historian Gerald Hodgett writes, "attempts to keep down prices were less effective than in those towns where merchant guilds wished to minimize food prices"; the merchants had a greater interest in low food prices, since this meant lower wages, and so cheaper goods to trade.[19] And, though they grew ever more stringent in their formal rules, the guilds could not cope in practice with the changes and shifts attending economic growth over the course of time.

Guilds that handled goods shipped long distance had constantly to deal with foreigners, and individuals within the guilds often tried to do their own business with these strangers who weren't part of the local fabric; when a few got away with violating the rules, others in the guild broke ranks. In the twelfth century, the standardization of products also began to break down, as individuals sought market niches when faced with stiff competition; in Paris, for instance, the way in which meat was cut began to vary from butcher to butcher. In some business dealings it was still possible to evade the destructive pressures of the market; non-competitive trading occurred especially in luxury goods like jewels, where credit arrangements between buyer and seller were as much at issue as the goods themselves. Yet more generally within medieval urban guilds, though in principle a worker might be bound to observing a fixed set of rules during the course of his lifetime, this observance became ever more a ceremonial show rather than a compelling practice.

As their hold over their members weakened, the guilds sought to underline their importance as venerable institutions, firming up the rituals and displaying the goods which marked their earlier days of glory. At a fair in the mid-1250s, for example, metalworkers put on display armor of an ancient, heavy, clumsy sort quite unlike what they were selling daily throughout Europe. Still later, guild membership meant little more than appearing resplendently dressed at dinners in the great guild halls, displaying the guild's chains and seals among people one now treated mostly as threats to one's own survival.

The guilds were corporations, and while the guild form began to weaken, other kinds of corporations, more adept at managing change, started to flourish. The medieval corporation was no more and no less than a university. The word "university" had no narrow connection to education in the Middle Ages; rather, "it connoted any corporate body or group with an independent juridical status."[20] A university became a corporation because it possessed a charter. And a charter defined the rights and privileges of a particular group to act; it was not a constitution in the modern sense, not even a general social charter such as the Magna Carta in England. The medieval era conceived of "charters of liberties [rather] than of charters of liberty," in the words of one legal historian.[21] A group had collective rights which might be written down, and more important, rewritten. In this, the university differed from the rural medieval *feudum,* a contract which, even if written out, was meant to be permanent, or if issued from the guild was meant to last a lifetime. Universities could easily be—and often were—renegotiated about what they did and where they did it, as changing circumstances dictated; they were economic instruments set in time.

Feudalism "gave the masses a certain security, from which a relative well-being was born."[22] The university might seem unstable, but the right to rewrite its charter and reorganize actually made it more durable. The historian Ernst Kantorowicz cites the medieval doctrine *rex qui nunquam moritur*—the King that never dies—to explain how, in the state, though a particular King dies, the office does not die with him: the doctrine of the "King's two bodies" supposed that there were an enduring King, a kingship, which passes in and out of the body of each flesh-and-blood King.[23] The rights of charter paralleled in certain ways this medieval doctrine of the "King's two bodies." The university continued to do business, no matter that the individuals who started it died, or that the nature of the business changed, or that the business changed locale.

Thus, medieval corporations in fact dedicated to education consisted of teachers rather than buildings. A university began when masters gave lessons to students in rented rooms or churches; the educational university at first held no property of its own. Scholars abandoned Bologna in order to found a university in 1222 in Padua, as did scholars who left Oxford to create Cambridge in 1209. "This lack of possessions paradoxically gave the universities their greatest power; for it meant their complete freedom of movement."[24] The autonomy of a corporation freed it from bondage to place, and to the past.

The charter's powers joined the worlds of education and commerce in practice, for to revise charters required people skilled in playing with language. Those language arts developed in the educational corporations. Early in the twelfth century, Peter Abelard taught theology at the University of Paris by staging debates with his students; this process of intellectual competition *(disputatio)* contrasted to the older way of teaching *(lectio),* which consisted of a teacher reading aloud Scripture sentence by sentence, and explaining it, while the students wrote down the lesson. Disputatio took an initial proposition and worked changes on it, like a theme and variations in music, passed back and forth between teacher and student. Though disputatio was anathema to much of the Church hierarchy, seeming to threaten the very durability of the Word, it had a great appeal to students for practical reasons that are not hard to seek: disputatio taught a skill which would serve those students in adult competition.

In the medieval era the state did decide whether, when, and how a particular corporation could rewrite itself. For instance, sometime during the 1220s four Parisian nobles were persuaded to invest in shoring up the northern quays of the Seine opposite the Ile St.-Louis. The King told the nobles that if they invested in the land, he would guarantee to the tenants of the nobles elsewhere in the city that they were free of their old contractual obligations and could move to these more modern quarters. It may seem simple to us, but was an epochal event. Economic change had become a *right,* guaranteed by the state.

The power to make revisions in time thus first defined the modern concept of the corporation. If a charter can be revised, the corporation defined by it has a *structure* which transcends its *function* at any one time; if, for instance, the University of Paris dropped a subject from its curriculum, or the teachers moved elsewhere, it would not have to go out of existence—in the same way that a modern corporation named the Universal Glass Corporation might no longer make glass. The corporate structure which transcends fixed functions takes advantage of changing market conditions, new goods, and the accidents of chance. A firm can change yet be permanent.

The origins of the corporation suggest another meaning for us to the Weberian word "autonomy." Autonomy means the capacity to change; autonomy requires the right to change. This formula, which seems so self-evident to modern eyes, involved a great revolution in time.

Economic time and Christian time

In 1284 King Phillip the Fair found that interest rates in his kingdom were occasionally as high as 266 percent annually, but more nearly 12 to 33 percent. Such charges seemed to make a mockery of time. Guillaume d'Auxerre, in his *Summa aurea* written in 1210–20,

declared that the usurer "sells time."[25] The Dominican monk
Etienne de Bourbon similarly declared that "usurers only sell the
hope of money, that is, time; they sell the day and the night."[26] Guillaume d'Auxerre explained his meaning by invoking the powers of
compassion and communal feeling contained in the Imitation of
Christ. "Every creature is obliged to make a gift of himself," Guillaume said; "the sun is obliged to make a gift of itself to provide
light, the earth is obliged to make a gift of all it can produce"; but
the usurer blocks the power of a man or woman to give, robs the
person of the means to contribute to the community. The debtor
cannot participate in Christian history.[27] This explanation may be
more comprehensible to us if we reflect that many people in the
Middle Ages thought Christ's Second Coming imminent. Those who
had not participated in the community as Christians would be swept
away by the Day of Judgment only years, perhaps months, away.[28]
But one needn't have been waiting for the Millennium or thought
only of usurers to have perceived that a great gulf separated the
Christian sense of time from economic time.

The corporation could blot out the past with the stroke of a pen.
It was an arbitrary and, as Jacques Le Goff notes, a very urban time:
"the peasant submitted . . . to a meteorological time, to the cycle of
the seasons," while in the market, "minutes and seconds could make
and destroy fortunes," as on the quays of Paris.[29] This urban, economic time had another side. Time become a commodity, measured
in hours of labor for which fixed wages would be paid. In Humbert
de Romans' Paris, this measured time was just beginning to make its
appearance in the guilds: guild contracts, especially in the manufacturing trades, specified the hours of work and computed wages on
this basis, rather than on piecework, where a worker received money
for finishing a piece of goods.[30] Change time and clock time were the
Janus faces of the economy. This economic time possessed powers of
rupture and powers of definition, but lacked narrative—it unfolded
no story.

The theologian Hugues de Saint-Victor declared, on the contrary,
that Christian "history is a narrative body."[31] By this he meant that
all the significant signposts in a Christian's life history have been put
in place by the story of Christ's life. The closer one draws to Christ,
the clearer will the meaning of events become which otherwise seem
senseless or merely random. The belief that Christian history is a
narrative body derived form the impulses contained in the Imitation
of Christ: His body tells not an alien story, or a story of what once

happened, but an ever contemporary story; draw closer to Him and the direction in which time's arrow points will be clear.

This Christian time knew no idea of individual autonomy such as the corporation defined it. Imitation of Christ rather than autonomy should rule one's actions; the imitation should be strict, because nothing happened by chance in Christ's life. Moreover, Christian time had little in common with clock time. The length of a confession, for example, had little relation to its value; the old counting of sins had given way by the High Middle Ages to what the modern philosopher Henri Bergson calls *durée,* a "being in time" when confessor and sinner emotionally connect. Whether it lasts a second or an hour is of no consequence; the only thing that matters is that it occurs.

Homo economicus

Now we can better understand why Humbert de Romans said the man of the market "is a devil to himself." *Homo economicus* lived in space rather than for place. The corporation which began to flourish in the Commercial Revolution treated time like space. It was a structure with a flexible form; it endured because it could change. Its fixities lay in the quantities of time in which it dealt, work organized into daily or hourly wages. Neither its autonomy nor its quantities of labor-time accorded with the narrative time of Christian belief. As a trader driving his competitors to ruin, as a usurer, as a boss, as a gambler with other people's lives, *Homo economicus* might be their devil, but he was a devil to himself because he could self-destruct; the very institutions through which he hoped to prosper could leave him out at the Day of Judgment. *Commitment* was lacking in this economic time and space.

The destructive powers of early capitalism do not appear in the account the economic historian Albert Hirschmann gives of the origins of *Homo economicus.* For Hirschmann, economic activity was a calming pursuit, in contrast to the "striving for honor and glory . . . exalted by the medieval chivalric ethos."[32] Although Hirschmann sets his sights in *The Passions and the Interests* on a later period, he might have been thinking of the medieval writer William of Conches, who praised a quality lacking in the choleric temperament of the knight, the Crusader, or indeed the millenarian religious believer. This quality is *modestia,* which William of Conches defined as "the virtue which keeps manners, movements, and all our activity above insufficiency but below excess."[33] St. Louis himself "both observed and praised the *juste milieu* in everything, in clothing, in food, in worship, in war. For him, the ideal man was the *prudhomme*, the man of integrity, who could be distinguished from the brave knight because he linked wisdom and *measure* to prowess."[34] Yet *Homo economicus* was inherently imprudent.

The weight of economic individualism hangs so heavily on modern society that we cannot imagine altruism or compassion as necessities in the conduct of life. Because of their faith, medieval people could. It was imprudent, indeed sheer folly, to neglect the state of one's soul. To lose one's place in a Christian community meant living the degraded life of a beast. With reason, people looked upon economic individualism as a form of spiritual temptation. What then could hold the community together? The dilemma of resolving the tensions between space and place first made manifest in Paris during the High Middle Ages can perhaps be seen in three paintings executed else-where, at the end of the medieval era.

3. THE DEATH OF ICARUS

The first retells an ancient story. In 1564, Peter Brueghel the Elder made his largest painting, telling a dark story through a barely visible detail. *The Procession to Calvary* fills with a crowd of figures stretching across a rolling landscape which meets a dark blue and cloud-thickened sky. The painting has three zones from near to far: close up, a small group of grieving figures seated on the brow of the hill; in the middle distance, a crowd of hundreds moving across a field toward a hill; at the back of the scene the cloudy sky which meets this hill at the horizon.

The grieving figures close up are the family and disciples of Jesus; Mary forms the centerpoint in this group, her eyes closed, her head bent, her body sagging. Brueghel painted these figures with great clarity and detail, a precision contrasting strongly to the obscure action occurring in the middle distance. There we see a procession of people painted in daubs and flecks of paint, the only visual order created by a line of red color which denotes the uniforms of mounted horsemen strung out in the procession. At the center of this procession, and dead center on the canvas, is a man in gray who has fallen in crossing a stream; he has dropped something, which the viewer can just barely make out, since this object is painted almost the same light yellow as the bare earth. It is a cross.

Pieter Brueghel the Elder, *The Procession to Calvary*, 1564. *Kunsthistorisches Museum, Vienna. Foto Marburg/Art Resource N.Y.*

Brueghel buried Christ among the crowd, which seems to trample over this speck of gray and yellow in blind movement along the red line. Miniaturizing the Christian drama reduced the tragedy to a minor visual detail. By so doing, Brueghel conveys in the most traditional way the divide between the sacred and the profane. In the words of Brueghel's modern biographer, "The less we see of Christ . . . the more room there is for a display of the indifference of the common man. . . ."[35] In this rendering of the ancient Christian story, the human landscape is a wasteland, sere and cold. But in depicting this scene, Brueghel invoked a traditional Christian theme, the need to respond to suffering, to draw together. The sharply etched tableau in the foreground shows us people who have done so, united by the sufferings of Christ. But they are in a wilderness.

Piero della Francesca's *Flagellation,* painted between 1458 and 1466 for a chapel in the Ducal Palace in Urbino, creates a sense of Christian place in explicitly urban terms. Within this small painting (58 by 81 cm), Piero depicts a scene divided into two complex parts. One side of the painting looks into an open room in which Christ has been tied to a column; a tormentor whips Him while two others stand by, a further seated figure in the background also watching the flagellation. The other half of the painting seems an unrelated scene, taking place out of doors in an urban square. Here three figures, two older men and a boy between them, stand in front of a group of buildings. The only immediate connection between the two parts of the painting consists of white lines drawn on the ground, appearing as inlaid floor tiles in the room; these continue outside as street paving.

Thanks to the researches of modern art historians, we know that in Piero's time the two parts would have appeared as one, though depending on the historian the connection varies. In the view of Marilyn Lavin, the explanation is that two older men in the city had each lost sons, one to the plague, the other to tuberculosis. These events "brought the two fathers together and caused the commission of Piero's painting"; the young man between them "personifies the 'beloved son.' "[36] The contemporary viewer thus saw a connection between the suffering Son of Man within the building and the shared loss of a son outside it.

The two parts are also connected in purely visual terms. Piero was a theorist of perspective, and the whipping in the inner recesses of the building and the three men in front fit precisely into a single perspective. The two parts of the *Flagellation* join together as if Piero had created a single work of architecture, which he painted by standing directly in front. The modern painter Philip Guston writes of this enigmatic scene that "the picture is sliced almost in half, yet both parts act on each other, repel and attract, absorb and enlarge one another."[37] The viewer standing, like Piero, in front feels the complex unity of place evoked by Guston's words, but these visual values are tied to the religious story being told. By addressing himself to the theme of solace for the grieving fathers—their pain reflected, transfigured, and redeemed by Christ's own pain—Piero made a cohering urban place. This scene conveys the Imitation of Christ in an urban landscape.

Brueghel's *Landscape with the Fall of Icarus,* painted six years before *The Procession to Calvary,* depicts a pagan story which suggests a third possibility. Again, the painting turns on suffering represented in a detail. Brueghel doesn't show the young man flying up toward the sun on his wings of wax, nor the moment when the wings melt and Icarus begins to fall out of the sky. The painter shows only two small legs splashing into water amidst a tranquil scene by the sea, the

Piero della Francesca, *The Flagellation*, 1444. *Galleria Nazionale delle Marche, Palazzo Ducale, Urbino. Scala/Art Resource, N.Y.*

death but a small detail in the landscape. Even the colors hide the event; Brueghel painted the flesh of the boy's legs in a bluish-white tone that blends in with the blue-green of the sea. By contrast, he boldly designed and painted in vivid colors a farmer ploughing his fields, a shepherd tending his sheep, a fisherman casting his line. Rather than to the legs in the water, the painter drew the viewer's eye to a ship sailing toward a Dutch city in the far distance along the seashore.

A proverb of the time said that "no plough is stopped for the sake of a dying man."[38] The people in Brueghel's landscape pay no attention to the strange and terrible death happening in the sea. In this, the poet W. H. Auden has said, Brueghel painted again man's lack of compassion to man. The poem Auden wrote about the painting, "Musée des Beaux Arts," runs in part:

> In Brueghel's Icarus, *for instance: how everything turns away*
> *Quite leisurely from the disaster; the ploughman may*

Pieter Brueghel, *Landscape with the Fall of Icarus,* 1558(?). *Musées Royaux des Beaux-Arts, Brussels. Giraudon/Art Resource, N.Y.*

Have heard the splash, the forsaken cry,
But for him it was not an important failure . . .[39]

Yet the painting is one of the gentlest landscapes Brueghel ever made; it radiates peace. The rural scene is so beautiful that our eyes are diverted from the story; we care more about the colors than the death; the beauty of the painting is repressive. The sere wasteland of Brueghel's *Procession to Calvary* is gone, the unity of place and suffering marking Piero's *Flagellation* absent. The sense of place has become an end in itself; the beautiful Garden is restored.

This third painting suggests a resolution of the tensions arising from the attachment to place generated by the medieval world. Not programmatically of course; *Landscape with the Fall of Icarus* throws us into contraries of beauty and horror which know no time. It is no more and no less than an image of place in which strange events and alien presences have been denied. That denial came to be ever more seductive, as Christian communities sought to survive in an ever more alien world.

CHAPTER SEVEN

Fear of Touching

The Jewish Ghetto in Renaissance Venice

The plot of Shakespeare's *Merchant of Venice* (1596–97) turns on a circumstance which seems odd the moment we think about it. Shylock, the rich Jewish moneylender of Venice, has lent Bassanio 3,000 ducats for three months, and Bassanio's friend Antonio has pledged to repay the loan to Shylock. If Antonio fails, Shylock, who hates the aristocratic Christian Antonio and all he stands for, wants a pound of Antonio's flesh as a forfeit. As things tend to happen in plays, fortune goes against Antonio; ships carrying all his wealth are ruined in a storm. The odd thing is that Antonio and the Christian authorities who enter the play should feel obliged to keep their word to a Jew.

Outside the theatre, Shakespeare's audience treated Jews as half-human animals due little respect at law. Just a few years before Shakespeare wrote *The Merchant of Venice*, the most prominent Jew in England had been denied legal protection. Elizabeth I's physician

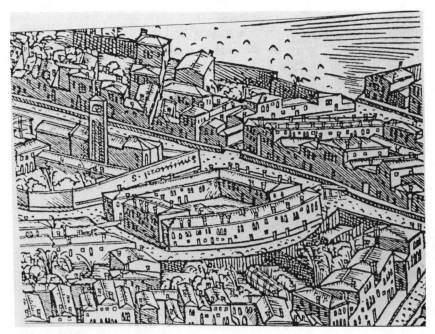

Jacopo dei Barbari's woodcut drawing of the Venetian Ghetto, 1500.

Dr. Lopez was accused of having been in a plot to poison her; even though the Queen insisted Dr. Lopez should be tried, the public needed no other proof than his Jewish race, and Dr. Lopez was lynched. In his play, Shakespeare compounds these prejudices by making the Jewish moneylender into a cannibal.

Thus one might expect the Duke *(Doge)* of Venice to enter, a powerful *deus ex machina,* and throw the cannibal into prison, or at least declare the contract immoral and therefore void. Yet when one of the minor characters in *The Merchant of Venice* says he is sure the Duke is going to solve things exactly in this way, Antonio responds that "The Duke cannot deny the course of law."[1] The power Shylock holds over Antonio is the right of contract; once both parties have "freely entered into it," nothing else matters. The Duke acknowledges this when he meets Shylock, for all the Duke can do is plead with Shylock, who, safe in his rights, turns a deaf ear to the supreme power in the city. Portia, the woman who will eventually cut this Gordian knot, declares, "There is no power in Venice can alter a decree established."[2]

The plot of *The Merchant of Venice* seems to display the power of the economic forces first formed in the medieval university and other corporations. Shylock's money rights rule, the state cannot resist them. The play shows indeed a new extension of economic might as well in the binding power of a contract once, like Antonio and Shylock, the parties have agreed to it.

The Jew's economic force attacks, moreover, Christian community among Shakespeare's beleaguered Venetians. Antonio has generously agreed to help his friend Bassanio. Unlike Shylock, Antonio asks for nothing in return; he feels compassion for Bassanio's plight. Shakespeare's Venetians are English gentlemen in business. These dream Venetians reappear in many guises in other plays of Shakespeare, in *A Midsummer Night's Dream* for instance, when Christian compassion sets things right in the end. But Venice had a special significance for Shakespeare and his contemporaries.

Venice was undoubtedly the most international city of the Renaissance, thanks to its trade, the gatepost between Europe and the East and between Europe and Africa. Englishmen and continental Europeans hoped they could develop navies like the great Venetian fleet, and thus profit from this international trade. Although by the 1590s, when Shakespeare wrote *The Merchant of Venice,* the wealth of Venice was in fact beginning to fade, its image in Europe was of a golden and luxuriant port. This image of the city Shakespeare could have gleaned from books like the expatriate Italian John Florio's *A World of Words,* or through the music of another expatriate, Alfonso Ferrabosco; a little later Shakespeare's audience would have seen the influences of the great Venetian architect Palladio on the architecture of Inigo Jones.

Venetian society appeared as a city of strangers, vast numbers of foreigners who came and went. The Venice which Elizabethans saw in their imagination was a place of enormous riches earned by contact with these heathens and infidels, wealth flowing from dealings with the Other. But unlike ancient Rome, Venice was not a territorial power; the foreigners who came and went in Venice were not members of a common empire or nation-state. Resident foreigners in the city—Germans, Greeks, Turks, Dalmatians, as well as Jews— were barred from official citizenship and lived as permanent immigrants. Contract was the key to opening the doors of wealth in this city of strangers. As Antonio declared,

> *For the commodity that strangers have*
> *With us in Venice, if it be denied,*

Will much impeach the justice of the state,
Since that the trade and profit of the city
Consisteth of all nations.[3]

In the real Venice where Shakespeare set his play, much of the action of the story would have been impossible. At one point Antonio invites Shylock to dinner. In the play, the Jew declines; in the real Venice, he would have had no choice. A real Jewish moneylender lived in the Ghetto the Venetians built for Jews in the course of the sixteenth century. A real moneylender was let out of the Ghetto, situated at the edge of the city, at dawn, where he made his way to the financial district around the Rialto wooden drawbridge near the city's center. By dusk the Jew was obliged to return to the cramped Ghetto; at nightfall its gates were locked, the shutters of its houses that looked outward closed; police patrolled the exterior. The medieval adage *"Stadt Luft macht frei"* would leave a bitter taste in the Jew's mouth, for the right to do business in the city did not bring a more general freedom. The Jew who contracted as an equal lived as a segregated man.

In that real Venice, the desire for Christian community lay somewhere between a dream and an anxiety. The impurities of difference haunted the Venetians: Albanians, Turks, and Greeks, Western Christians like the Germans, all were segregated in guarded buildings or clusters of buildings. Difference haunted the Venetians, yet exerted a seductive power.

When they shut the Jews inside the Ghetto, the Venetians claimed and believed they were isolating a disease that had infected the Christian community, for they identified the Jews in particular with corrupting bodily vices. Christians were afraid of touching Jews: Jewish bodies were thought to carry venereal diseases as well as to contain more mysterious polluting powers. The Jewish body was unclean. A little detail of ritual in business illuminated this unease of touch; whereas among Christians a contract was sealed with a kiss or with a handshake, contracts with Jews were sealed with a bow, so that the bodies of the parties need not touch. The very contract Shylock draws with Antonio, the payment in flesh, conveyed the fear the Jew would defile a Christian's body by using his power of money.

In the medieval era, the Imitation of Christ made people more sympathetically aware of the body, especially the suffering body. The fear of touching Jews represents the frontier of that conception of a common body; beyond the frontier lay a threat—a threat redoubled because the impurity of the alien body was associated with sensuality, with the lure of the Oriental, a body cut free from Christian constraints. The touch of the Jew defiles, yet seduces. The segregated space of the Ghetto represented a compromise between the economic need of Jews and these aversions to them, between practical necessity and physical fear.

The making of the Ghetto occurred at a crucial moment for Venice. The city leaders had lost a great advantage in trade, and suffered a crushing military defeat, a few years before. They blamed these losses largely on the state of the city's morals, bodily vices provoked by the very wealth now slipping from its grasp; from this moral campaign to reform the city came the plan for the Ghetto. By segregating those who were different, by no longer having to touch and see them, the city fathers hoped peace and dignity would return to their city. This was the Venetian version of Brueghel's tranquil dreamscape in *Landscape with the Fall of Icarus.*

It is easy to imagine today that Jews had always lived in Europe isolated in ghetto space. Indeed, from the Lateran Council of 1179 forward, Christian Europe had sought to prevent Jews living in the midst of Christians. In all European cities which harbored colonies of Jews, such as London, Frankfurt, and Rome, they were forced to live apart. Rome typified the problem of enforcing the edict of the Lateran Council. Rome had what is now called its Ghetto from early medieval times; a few streets in the Jewish quarter of medieval Rome were gated, but the urban fabric was too disordered for the Jews to be totally sealed in. In Venice, the physical character of the city made it possible finally to realize the rule prescribed by the Lateran Council—Venice a city built on water, water the city's roads which separated clusters of buildings into a vast archipelago of islands. In the making of the Jewish Ghetto, the city fathers put the water to use to create segregation: the Ghetto was a group of islands around which the canals became like a moat.

If the Venetian Jews suffered from the struggle to impose a Christian community on the economic mosaic, they did not suffer as passive victims. The formation of the Jewish Ghetto tells the story of a people who were segregated but who then made new forms of community life out of their very segregation; indeed, the Jews of Renaissance Venice gained a certain degree of self-determination in the Ghettos. Moreover, the city protected a Jew or a Turk against Christian mobs at Lent or at other times of high religious passion, so long as the non-Christian was in the space reserved for the outsider.

Segregation increased the Jew's daily Otherness, non-Christian lives ever more enigmatic to the dominant powers beyond Ghetto walls. For the Jews themselves, the Ghetto raised the stakes of contact with the outside world: their own Jewishness seemed at risk when they ventured outside the Ghetto. For over three thousand years the Jews had survived in small cells mixed among their oppressors, a people sustained in their faith no matter where they lived. Now the bonds of faith among these People of the Word began to depend more upon having a place of their own, where they could be Jewish.

Community and repression: Venetian Christians sought to create a Christian community by segregating those who were different, drawing on the fear of touching alien, seductive bodies. Jewish identity became entangled in that same geography of repression.

1. VENICE AS A MAGNET

Henri Pirenne criticized Max Weber for discounting medieval cities as porous places of trade, with all the ambiguity and mixture which long-distance trade brings to the life of a city. Pirenne's great example of the city as a magnet could have been Venice. The spice trade showed the kind of commerce which made Venice wealthy at the price of attracting Jews and other foreigners to the city.

The earliest spice that Venice controlled was salt, the most elemental means of preserving food. In early medieval times, Venetians dried salt on the coastal marshes and then sold it locally; this required control of land. Venetians became richer from trading in spices like saffron which, like the trade in cloth and gold, came from long distances. The immediate local market for saffron was small, the European-wide market immense. This kind of trade depended more on control of the seas rather than on possession of land. Saffron, cumin, and juniper were grown in India and other countries of the East, and Venice served, in William McNeill's phrase, as the "hinge of Europe" by bringing them to the West.[4]

As early as the year 1000, Venice had established itself as the dominant power all around the Adriatic Sea, which served as one route to Jerusalem; Venice thus also became a city of passage in the European Crusades to the Holy Lands. After the Third Crusade, the city had acquired trading rights with the East, and these it used to import its spices: pepper, some of which came from India, some from the east coast of Africa, via the Egyptian port of Alexandria; saffron and nutmeg from India, cinnamon from Ceylon. The Crusaders had returned from the East with the taste of these spices in their memories, and the advent of spices changed the European diet. The trade in spices became so great a part of the Venetian economy that special bureaucracies, such as the Office of Saffron, were set up to regulate it. In 1277, Venice's rival Genoa began to send annual convoys of goods to Bruges and other Channel ports in Northern Europe; the Venetians controlled many of these goods as the first European port of entry. Soon Venice itself began its own Northern European trade via England.

Venice organized trade through joint venture partnerships between individual merchant families and the Venetian state. "The joint ventures lacked the permanence of the modern corporation and they had quite limited objectives," the modern historian Frederick Lane observes; "they lasted only for the duration of a voyage or until a cargo had been sold."[5] Only a few great families directed these joint ventures; the Grimani family, for instance, took 20 percent of the profits from that year, about 40,000 ducats.[6] The principal manufacture of Venice was the boats for these seagoing voyages.

Spices and other goods were carried by a special kind of merchant galley ship, rowed by two hundred men near to land, powered by sail only on the high seas. Longer and wider than military galleys, these ships travelled in convoys called *muda;* the city owned the galleys and rented them to merchants like the Grimani, who in turn rented out space in the mammoth vessels to smaller spice merchants. The convoy of galleys would sometimes set out from Venice to pick up cargo around the south coast of the Mediterranean, but the costs and structure of the giant galleys made them more profitable to operate on longer voyages, through the Straits of the Bosphorus into the Black Sea. At the eastern edges of the Black Sea, the convoy received spices brought overland from India and Ceylon. Then the flotilla of ships returned, a fat target. In the fourteenth century, before the growth of Turkish power, the principal danger to the returning vessels was pirates; in later years, the ships filled with their precious cargoes had to blast their way back through Turkish attackers as well. Shakespeare's drama thus drew on a real threat.

If a ship managed to survive at sea, it sailed up the Adriatic, passed through the sandbars at the edge of the Venetian lagoon, and made its way into the city. The water of the lagoon and the sandbars served as the most effective walls Venice could have against foreign inva-

The Customs House of Venice.

sion, since they rigidly controlled access by ships. The Cathedral in the Piazza of San Marco served as the steering point for a returning vessel; as the convoy approached, vessels from the customs service came out to meet it, and customs officers boarded the ship. The size of these merchant galleys made it difficult for them to navigate very far into the principal water road of Venice, the Grand Canal; the cargo was unloaded into smaller boats, which proceeded to landings all along the Grand Canal and its tributaries.

The moment ships returned safe to harbor, officials swarmed over them, and their goods were reckoned and taxed. Surveillance was the very lifeblood of the Venetian port, and the physical form of the city made surveillance possible in many ways. The narrow entry straits of the lagoon, the promontory of the customs house, the great mouth of the Grand Canal permitted government surveillance by the eye as well as in law. The government supervised and taxed anew the loading of ships with spices which then travelled through the Mediterranean, the larger ships quitting the Straits of Gibraltar to sail to Portugal, France, England, and the northern countries.

The middlemen in this system were the traders, financiers, and bankers clustered around the Rialto Bridge spanning the Grand

A Jewish moneylender. *From G. Grevembroch,* Customs of the Venetians; *Museo Civico Correr, Venice.*

Canal a mile up from the great public square of San Marco. Here Shakespeare had Shylock do business: "the banker . . . sat behind a bench under the portico of a church at the Rialto, with his big journal spread out in front. The payor orally instructed the banker to make a transfer to the account of the person being paid."[7] The banker's funds were sacks of gold or silver coins; written scrip or printed money was less used, since the traders came from places which would be highly dubious about the worth of a piece of paper printed in a foreign language. The buildings around the Rialto were filled with strongrooms where the banker kept his gold or jewels. By necessity, the Rialto also filled every day with gossip and rumor, since the middlemen plied their trade without much information about what passed far away on the seas.

"His word is his bond": Like the way business later developed in the City of London, the brokers clustered around the Rialto Bridge depended on informal, verbal agreement. Verbal trust was tied to the use of untaxed or unregistered capital—which the brokers wished to keep from the eyes of the state. They did so by putting as little as possible on paper, and so could fiddle as well with the strict regulations which controlled the entry and exit of boats from the city. Illegal business, then, but not dishonorable. "His word is his bond" developed in little rituals played out around the Rialto Bridge, the rituals of coffee, the group of professional witnesses lingering around the bridge whose stocks-in-trade were probity and silence. Though the Doge was willing to oblige Antonio, Antonio's problem with Shylock was "I have given him my word."

The fortunes of the spice trade also epitomized the forces which came into play when the Venetians began to create the Ghetto. In 1501 the Venetians learned that the Portuguese had opened up a sea route to India, by sailing around the southern tip of Africa, a route that would cut out Venice as the point of delivery of spices to Northern and Western Europe. It was, in the words of one contemporary, Girolamo Priuli, "the worst news the Venetian Republic could ever have had, excepting only the loss of our freedom."[8] This safer if longer route between East and West came at a time when the Venetians realized the Turks could hem them in on their own sea, the Adriatic. Now began a decade of disaster.

Throughout the fifteenth century the Venetians had sought to provision themselves against the uncertainties of international trade by creating a land empire in northern Italy; traditionally, the town of Mestre on the Venetian lagoon had been their principal link to solid land, to terra firma. The Venetians had taken over towns like Verona, Vicenza, and Padua. Now, in the spring of 1509, they were to lose them all in the space of a few weeks. The French and other powers moved against them, and defeated the Venetians at Agnadello, near Lodi, on May 14, 1509; three weeks later Venetians could hear the sounds of foreign armies three miles off on the terra firma of the lagoon. Eclipsed at sea, threatened by infidels, confined to their island-city, the result of these blows was a city feeling "a sudden loss of equilibrium in the assessment of its own energies," in the words of the modern historian Alberto Tenenti, "with a consequent unsteadying of the subjective sense of time and space."[9]

It was at this moment that Jews began to flee into Venice. As a result of the wars of the League of Cambrai in 1509, about five hundred Jews fled from Padua and Mestre. The magnet city seemed to offer them safety. Jews had come into northern Italy from Germany after 1300, when severe pogroms in Germany had sent waves of refuges to Padua and Verona, and a small number to Venice itself. Ashkenazic Jews had lived in Venice from 1090, their numbers increased after the Sephardic Jews were expelled from Spain in 1492. These medieval Jews were mostly poor: peddlers and dealers in second-hand goods. The sole liberal profession open to them was medicine; only a few of these pre-disaster Jews worked as moneylenders, the banking in the city done mostly by Venetians and Christian foreigners. A sizable number of the Jews who fled to Venice after the disaster of Agnadello had become rich through moneylending, however, and brought their diamonds, gold, and silver with them. Moreover, a small but eminent group of Jewish doctors also fled. These high-status Jewish moneylenders and doctors became highly visible refugees, since their lives intersected more with Christians in the Venetian community.

2. THE WALLS OF THE GHETTO

Corrupt bodies

In the seven years from the disaster of Agnadello to the making of the first Jewish Ghetto in Venice, hatred against the increased presence of Jews combined with a campaign for the moral reform of Venice itself, as though the city's defeats in the world came from moral rot. Attacks against the Jews were led, among others, by Friar Lovato of Padua. His oratorical energies in 1511 aroused the Venetians to destroy the homes of Jews living near the Campo San Paolo; two years earlier he had advocated seizing all the money of the moneylenders, "and leave them nothing to live on."[10] At the same time, the historian Felix Gilbert writes, "the view that moral corruption was the decisive reason for the decline of Venetian power was expressed not only by private citizens but was an officially held and recognized thesis."[11]

Sensuality was a crucial element in the image of Venice in Europe, and in the Venetians' sense of themselves. The facades of the great palaces along the Grand Canal were richly ornamented, light reflecting their colors onto the rippling water; the buildings were diverse facades but roughly uniform in height so that they composed an unbroken street wall of ornamented color. The canal itself was filled with gondolas which in the Renaissance were often painted in vivid reds, yellows, and blues, rather than the later obligatory black, and hung with tapestries and flags woven of gold and silver threads.

Christian strictures on bodily pleasure had relaxed in the days of Venetian affluence. There was a flourishing homosexual subculture devoted to cross-dressing, young men lounging in gondolas on the canals wearing nothing but women's jewels. The spice trade also contributed to the image of a sensual city, since spices like saffron and tumeric were thought to be aphrodisiacs for the human body as well as seasonings reviving wilted, stale, or rotted food. Most of all, prostitution flourished in the port.

The work of the prostitutes spread a new and terrible disease, syphilis, which appeared in Italy in 1494. Almost from the moment it appeared, syphilis destroyed large numbers of people, both men and women. It had no certain name, diagnosis, or treatment—syphilis was recognized to be sexually transmitted, but the physiology of the transfer seemed mysterious. By the 1530s, as the historian Anna Foa points out, Europeans had decided that the appearance of syphilis in the Old World had something to do with the conquest of the New World, and blamed the origins of the disease on the American Indians, using Columbus's voyages as an historical touchstone.[12] But in the generation before, the more prevalent explanation held that Jews spread syphilis throughout Europe when they were driven from Spain in the crucial year 1494.

The bodies of Jews appeared to harbor a myriad of diseases due to their religious practices. Sigismondo de'Contida Foligno connected syphilis to Judaism via the proneness of Jews to leprosy, a link he made sometime before 1512 as follows: first, "the Jews, because they abstain from pork, are subject to leprosy more than other peoples"; second, "Sacred Scripture . . . makes clear that leprosy was a sign that revealed an even more vile incontinence: in fact, it began to manifest itself in the genitals"; ergo, "this illness [syphilis] derived

... from the *Marrani*," the Jews expelled from Spain.[13] The confla-
tion of syphilis with leprosy in such explanations had an importance
to this first generation of victims not apparent to us. Since it was
thought that leprosy spread when a person touched the sores of a
leper, contracting syphilis could occur not only by sleeping with a
prostitute: you might also get it by touching the body of a Jew.

On March 13, 1512, the Venetian Senate, at the behest of Giovanni
Sanuto, voted in a decree whose aim was "to placate the anger of our
Lord" by preventing "immoderate and excessive expenditure." The
decree defined moral reform in terms of a new bodily discipline. The
decree of 1512 sought to put an end to the overt display of sensuality: jewelry was regulated for both men and women; "transparent
materials were forbidden and lace could not be used [by women].
Men were forbidden attire which would increase physical attrac-
tiveness. Shirts should cover the entire upper part of the body and
close neatly around the neck."[14]

Fifteen years before the Venetians enacted their laws against sensuality, the monk Girolamo Savonarola had led a similar campaign
against "vanities" in Florence, after that city had also been defeated
by a foreign power in 1494. In Florence, as later in Venice, "inglori-
ous defeat and inexplicable reversal were necessarily seen as signs of
God's displeasure."[15] Like Sanuto, Savonarola had also called for a
stricter code of sexual behavior and a renunciation of jewels, perfumes, and silk clothes in order to restore the city's fortunes. However, Savonarola's attack on the sensuous body was meant as a
recovery of the supposedly severe virtues of the early Florentine
Republic; the Venetian revulsion against the sensual body could not
be framed in the same terms. It was a city whose fortunes were too
bound to pleasure; moreover, many of the diseased bodies in Venice
were heathens and infidels who could never have a place in a Christian community.

The Venetian attack against the Jews intertwined with this revulsion against bodily sensuality. Syphilis was one focus of the attack,
but the ways Jews made money also focused discussion and decision.
Jews made money through usury, and usury had a direct connection
to bodily vice.

As practiced in Venice from the twelfth century on, usury consisted in lending money at rates from 15 to 20 percent, which was
less on the whole than rates charged in late medieval Paris. Usury

contrasted to an honorable loan, which had a lower and also a variable rate of interest. More, an honorable loan was one in which the lender would not collect on the security offered for the loan, if it would destroy the borrower; instead, as in modern bankruptcies, collecting on a bad loan meant renegotiating the relations between creditor and debtor in future dealings.

Usury appeared to medieval Christians as a "theft of time." An even more ancient charge was made against usury: its connection to sex. In the *Politics,* Aristotle had condemned usury as a "gain out of money itself," as though money could breed like an animal.[16] "During the thirteenth and fourteenth centuries," the sociologist Benjamin Nelson writes, the definition of usury "took its shape from the analogy of the prostitute in the brothel."[17] A contemporary of Shakespeare's declared, in *The Seven Deadly Sins of London,* that "The usurer lives by the lechery of money, and is bawd to his own bags."[18] The Jews who lent money were all thought to engage in usury, and therefore to be like prostitutes; another Christian critic of the Jews wrote that the usurer "puts his money to the unnatural act of generation."[19] Moreover, the sinful practice of usury among Jews could not be cleansed through confession. In Venice, this economic stereotype now co-existed with the official effort to purify the bodies of Venetians and so recover the fortunes of the city-state.

The refugee doctors in Venice provoked Christians in the city in an even more direct way. Touch is a bodily experience deeply encoded in Christian culture. "The image of touch, from Eve touching Adam . . . through the seduction of Bathsheba or the healing touch of Christ's ministry that cleanses Mary Magdalene," asserts the historian Sander Gilman, "haunts all of the representations of biblical images of sexuality."[20] For St. Thomas, the sense of touch was the most base of all the body's sensations.[21] If the touch of Jews seemed like a physical, sexual infection, as Jews became associated in the public mind with the spread of syphilis, Jewish doctors were also called on to treat the disease. The race of the doctor became in the public mind inseparable from the taint of the disease itself. In 1520 Paracelsus railed against these Jews who "purge [syphilitics], smear them, wash them, and perform all manner of impious deceptions"; again in their impurity Jews were associated with the leper's touch: "The Jews were more subject to [leprosy] than any other people . . . because they had neither linen, nor domestic baths. These people were so negligent of cleanliness and the decencies of life that their legislators were obliged to make a law to compel them even to wash

A Jewish doctor outfitted to treat victims of plague. The costume protects him from plague vapors, protects other people from his breath, and emphasizes his inhuman qualities. *From Grevembroch,* Customs of the Venetians; *Museo Civico Correr, Venice.*

their hands."[22] Such were the risks of being treated by a Jewish doctor, a man constantly exposed to sexual diseases, a doctor who did not wash his hands except when ordered.

The study of religious prejudice is not an exercise in rationality. The desire for purity, the anthropologist Mary Douglas has written, expresses a society's fears; in particular, the self-loathing a group may feel can "migrate" to become attached to a group which represents the impure.[23] Such a migration occurred in Venice after Agnadello. The Venetians believed they were threatened by sensual decline, and displaced their self-loathing onto the Jews.

This displacement also had a class character—as Renaissance Venice defined the classes. The city was divided into three groups: aristocrats *(nobili);* rich bourgeois *(cittadini);* and common people *(populani).* The war on sensuality aimed at the nobili, who accounted for about 5 percent of the population, and some of the children of the cittadini, who accounted for another 5 percent in 1500, out of a total population of about 120,000. Resentment of luxury and resentment of aristocracy were inseparable: the immorality of the idle rich had brought God's wrath down upon the industrious city. The Jews of Venice at this time numbered between 1,500 and 2,000 at most. Thus the purge focused on small groups of people at the top and an ambiguous small element at the bottom; though the Jewish usurers and doctors were economically and practically significant, culturally they lay beneath the mass of the Christian populani. As often happens in purges, minorities became symbolically more populous and more visible than their actual numbers.

This symbolic visibility caused an explosion on Good Friday, April 6, 1515. The Lenten season was usually a time when Jews kept out of sight. This Good Friday, a doubly mournful occasion because of Venetian defeats, a few Jews among the small minority in the city did venture out. It seemed to one Venetian that "since yesterday they are everywhere, and it's a terrible thing; and no one says anything because, due to the war, [the Jews] are needed, and so they do as they please."[24] There were immediate calls for confiscation of Jewish property, to pay for a new military campaign, or for the expulsion of the Jews from the city. Yet the Jews could not be driven away. Economic self-interest could not permit it. In the words of a leading citizen, "Jews are even more necessary to a city than bankers are, and especially to this one."[25] Even poor Jews were necessary to the city, for instance, the Jews who dealt in second-hand goods. (In 1515 the government officially licensed nine such Jewish shops.) All Jews paid high taxes.

Given the practical necessity, Venice sought a spatial solution to deal with its impure but necessary Jewish bodies. It opted, in the words of the historian Brian Pullan, for "the segregation, though not the expulsion, of the Jewish community."[26] Purity of the mass would be guaranteed by isolation of the minority. One of the great themes of modern urban society thus first appeared. The "city" would stand for a legal, economic, and social entity too large and various to bind people together. "Community" of an emotionally intense sort would require division of the city. The Venetians acted on this divisive desire for community by availing themselves of their own watery geography.

The urban condom

The Jews were not the first group of outsiders that the Venetians shut away in a prophylactic space; Greeks, Turks, and other ethnic groups were also segregated. Perhaps the least controversial of the outsiders segregated before were the Germans, who were, after all, fellow Christians. The link between Germany and Venice was apparent to Shakespeare in England, who has Shylock burst out at one point in *The Merchant of Venice,* "A diamond gone [that] cost me two thousand ducats in Frankfurt."[27]

By Shakespeare's time, trade with Germans had become of great importance to Venice. The Germans came to Venice to sell, as well as to buy. In 1314, the Venetians decided they would make sure that the Germans paid their taxes by concentrating them all in one building; here the Germans registered themselves and their goods, and were meant both to live and work. This building was the *Fondaco dei Tedeschi*—the "Factory of the Germans." The original Fondaco dei Tedeschi was a medieval house writ large, with the further condition that all its inhabitants be German. As a building, it provided the model for later, more repressive spatial forms of segregation.

In its early form, the Fondaco served as a reception center for distinguished foreigners in addition to resident Germans. But in principle no one was supposed to leave it after dark; in fact nighttime proved the busiest part of the day for the Germans, who smuggled goods in and out under cover of darkness to avoid paying customs. In 1479, the government therefore took steps to ensure that this place of segregation became a building of isolation; it was decreed that at dusk the windows were to be shut and the doors to the Fondaco locked—from the outside.

Within, the building also became a repressive space, the Germans constantly under the watchful eyes of the Venetians. "Everything was

The location of foreigners in Venice, ca. 1600.

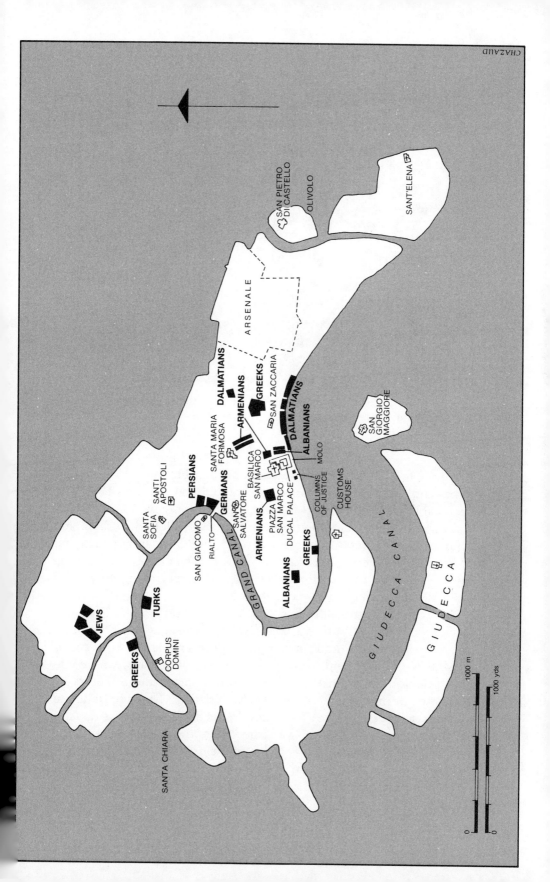

CHAZAUD

SANTA CHIARA

SANTA SOFIA

SANTI APOSTOLI

JEWS

TURKS

GREEKS

CORPUS DOMINI

SAN GIACOMO

RIALTO

PERSIANS

SANTA MARIA FORMOSA

GERMANS

SAN SALVATORE

ARMENIANS

BASILICA SAN MARCO

PIAZZA SAN MARCO

GRAND CANAL

ALBANIANS

GREEKS

DUCAL PALACE

COLUMNS OF JUSTICE

CUSTOMS HOUSE

ARMENIANS

GREEKS

SAN ZACCARIA

DALMATIANS

MOLO

ALBANIANS

DALMATIANS

SAN GIORGIO MAGGIORE

GIUDECCA CANAL

GIUDECCA

GIUDECCA

ARSENALE

SAN PIETRO DI CASTELLO

OLIVOLO

SANT'ELENA

0   1000 m

0   1000 yds

The area around the Rialto Bridge in Venice; the large square building was the Fondaco dei Tedeschi in the Renaissance.

arranged for them," says the historian Hugh Honour. "All the servants and higher functionaries were appointed by the State. The merchants were allowed to transact business only with born Venetians and only through the brokers who were allotted to them and who took a percentage on every deal."[28] The German Fondaco that exists today in Venice was built in 1505. It is an enormous building, and testified to the wealth of the Germans, yet in its very form refined the principles of concentration and isolation which had shaped the use of the older Fondaco. The new Fondaco dei Tedeschi, which today serves Venice as a post office, is a squat, uniform building built around a central court; open galleries ran around this courtyard at each story, and were policed by the Venetians, who could thus practice surveillance day and night of their northern "guests."

These Germans, of course, were Christian. Their surveillance began as a matter of pure economics. In the decades after the disaster of the League of Cambrai wars, however, the Venetians as good Catholics were first becoming aware of the great tide of Reformation taking place in Germany and in other lands to the north; and so the city's control over its German merchants began to shift from a purely commercial basis to a cultural one as well. At this point, images of the body intruded. The authorities wanted to halt the "infection" of the Reformation, its heresies perceived as forms of self-indulgence, free of the priests, leading to sins like sloth and luxury. The Reformed German moved closer in the Catholic imagination to the Jew.[29] Until 1531 some few Germans, usually the very wealthiest, could buy their way out of the Fondaco dei Tedeschi. In 1531 the city ordered all Germans to live together in the Fondaco, once and for all, and added spies to the guards in their midst to detect signs of religious heresy.

As a consequence of segregation, herded together, isolated, these foreigners began to feel a bond amongst themselves. They acted cohesively in their dealings with the Italians, even though in fact there were sharp divisions between the Protestants and the Catholics in the building. The space of repression became incorporated into their own sense of community. This was the future which awaited the Jews.

In 1515 the Venetians started to explore the possibility of using the Ghetto Nuovo as a site for segregating Jews. *Ghetto* originally meant "foundry" in Italian (from *gettare*, "to pour"). The Ghetto Vecchio and Ghetto Nuovo served as the old foundry districts of Venice, far from the ceremonial center of the city; their manufacturing functions had shifted by 1500 to the Arsenal. The Ghetto Nuovo was a rhomboid piece of land surrounded on all sides by water; buildings created a wall all around its edges with an open space in the center. Only two bridges connected it to the rest of the urban fabric. With these bridges closed, the Ghetto Nuovo could be sealed up.

At the time the Ghetto Nuovo was transformed, the city's "streets, squares, and courtyards were not covered, as they are now, with the uniform paving of rectangular blocks of volcanic trachyte. Many streets and courtyards had no hard surface at all. . . . Often only the parts of squares adjoining particular buildings were paved."[30] During the century before the Ghetto Nuovo enclosed the Jews, the city began to form steep banks to line the sides of the canals. These banks encouraged the rapid flow of water, and so kept the canals from silting up. The built-up banks then made it possible to place paths alongside the canals, a water-and-land form called a *fondamente*. The Cannaregio area of Venice was regularized in such a way, and it was near this area that the Ghetto Nuovo and Ghetto Vecchio were

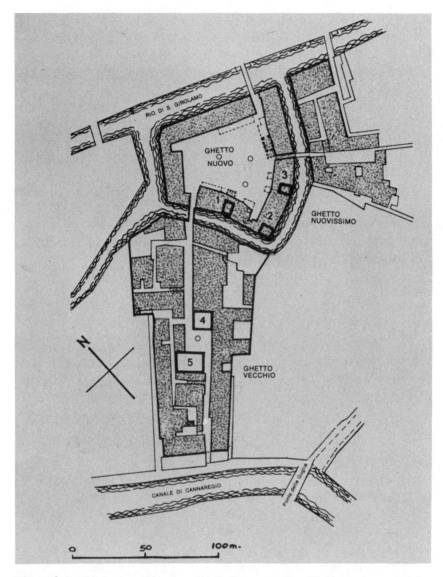

Plan of the Venetian Ghettos: (1) Italian temple, (2) Cantonese temple, (3) German temple, (4) Levantine temple, (5) Spanish or Pnentina temple.

located. The two Ghettos, abandoned for industry and lightly populated, were not part of this renovation; they were both physical and
economic islands within the city. The few bridges that connected
these inner islands to other landmasses debouched in an ancient
Venetian urban form, the *sottoportegho*. The sottoportegho was a pas-

Entrance to the Ghetto Nuovo in Venice. *Copyright Graziano Arici. All rights reserved.*

sageway made under a building, low and dank, since the passageway lay at the same level as the pilings and foundation stones which supported the buildings above. At the end of the *sottoporti* were locked doors. It was a scene far, far removed from rich boys dressed only in jewels gliding past the Ca D'Oro on the Grand Canal.

The proposal to make use of the Ghetto Nuovo came from Zacaria Dolfin in 1515. His plan for the segregation of the Jews was to

> Send all of them to live in the Ghetto Nuovo which is like a castle, and to make drawbridges and close it with a wall; they should have

only one gate, which would enclose them there and they would stay
there, and two boats of the Council of Ten would go and stay there at
night, at their expense, for their greater security.[31]

This proposal contains one key difference from the conception of
segregation built into the Fondaco dei Tedeschi: in the Jewish
Ghetto there was to be no *internal* surveillance. External surveillance
would take place from the boats, circling the Ghetto throughout the
night. Imprisoned inside, the Jews were to be left to themselves, an
abandoned people.

Dolfin's proposal was put into practice beginning in 1516. Jews
were moved into the Ghetto Nuovo from all sections of the city, but
particularly from the Giudecca, where Jews had congregated since
1090. Not all Jews, however. When the Sephardic Jews were
expelled from Spain in 1492, a group came to live in a little colony
in Venice near a burial ground for executed criminals. There they
remained, as did Levantine Jews in other parts of the city, who
passed in and out of Venice from the Adriatic coast and the Middle
East. Moreover, an important part of the story of the Ghetto is that
many Venetian Jews, when faced with the prospect of living in the
Ghetto, left the city instead.

About seven hundred Jews, mostly Ashkenazim, were first sent
into the Ghetto in 1516. The original annexation in the Ghetto was
twenty houses only. These were owned by Christians, since Jews in
Venice, as elsewhere, were denied the right to own land or buildings;
they could only rent from year to year. As more houses were reno-
vated, rents sky-rocketed; Brian Pullan says that rent on "the narrow
houses in the Ghetto was three times as high as it would have been
on similar cramped accommodation in the Christian city."[32] The
buildings were gradually added to, reaching six or seven stories in
height, listing to the sides since their weight was not well supported
by piles in the substrate.

The drawbridges opened in the morning and some Jews fanned
out into the city, mostly around the area of the Rialto where they
circulated with the ordinary crowd. Christians came into the Ghetto
to borrow money or to sell food and do business. At dusk, all the
Jews were obliged to be back in the Ghetto, the Christians to be out;
the drawbridges were raised. Moreover, the windows fronting the
exterior were shut every evening and all balconies removed from
them, so that the buildings facing the canals outside became like the
sheer walls of a castle.

The Ghetto Nuovo in Venice. *Copyright Graziano Arici. All rights reserved.*

This was the first stage of segregating the Jews. The second stage involved expanding the Jewish quarter to the Ghetto Vecchio, the old foundry district. This occurred in 1541. By this time, the Venetians were hurting even more financially; their customs tariffs had become higher than other cities and they were losing trade. The long twilight of the Venetian Republic, so feared since the discovery of another route to the Far East, had begun. The Venetian authorities decided in the 1520s to lower their customs barriers, and one result was that Levantine Jews, mostly from what is now Romania and Syria, stayed longer in the city. They were slightly more than travelling peddlers and slightly less than bourgeois businessmen; they hawked whatever they could lay their hands on. Sanuto put crisply the attitude of his fellow Venetians toward such Jewish dealers: "Our countrymen have never wanted Jews to keep shops and to trade in this city, but to buy and sell and go away again."[33] But now these Jews did not go away; they wanted to stay and were willing to pay a price for it.

To house them, the old Ghetto was transformed into a Jewish space, its outer walls sealed, its balconies removed. Unlike the first, this second Ghetto had a small open square and many small streets, a squalid turf entirely unpaved, the piles so carelessly driven into the substrate that the buildings of the Old Ghetto began to sink the moment they were constructed. A century later, a third Ghetto space, the Ghetto Nuovissimo, was opened in 1633, a smaller plot of land with somewhat better housing stock, which was again treated to the castle-and-moat process of walling in. When the third Ghetto was filled with people, the population densities were about triple those of Venice as a whole. Because of these physical conditions, plague found a welcome home in the Ghetto. The Jews sought to protect themselves by recourse to their own doctors, but medical knowledge could not combat the condition of soil and buildings, as well as the ever-mounting density of population. When plague struck in the Ghetto, the gates of the Ghetto were instead locked for most of the day as well as night.

No attempt was made to alter the behavior of Jews after forcing them into the Venetian Ghettos, for there was no desire to reclaim the Jew for the city. In this, the Ghetto of Venice embodied a different ethos of isolation from the ethos practiced shortly afterward in Renaissance Rome, in the Roman Ghetto Pope Paul IV began to build in 1555. The Roman Ghetto was indeed meant to be a space to transform the Jews. Paul IV proposed closing up all the Jews together in one place in order that Christian priests could systematically convert them, house by house, forcing the Jews to listen to Christ's word. The Roman Ghetto was a miserable failure in this, only twenty or so Jews a year out of a population of four thousand inhabitants succumbing to conversion.

Moreover, the Roman Ghetto differed from the Venetian in that it occupied a highly visible place in the center of the city. Its walls cut into two a commercial zone previously controlled by prominent Roman commercial families, who in turn traded with the resident community of Jews. In taking over the space of the Roman Ghetto for conversion, the Pope sought to weaken the spatial grip of this old Christian merchant class on Roman affairs. To be sure, Rome at this time was more insular than Venice, despite the presence of the papacy; it contained many fewer foreigners, and the strangers who came to the Papal Court were clerics, ambassadors, or other diplomats. Venice was a different kind of international city, suffused with dubious foreigners.

A moralizing force sure of itself will challenge and transform moral "filth," as did the Roman papacy. A society profoundly uncertain of itself, as at this moment Venice was, fears that it lacks powers of *resistance*. It fears it may succumb when it mixes physically with the Other. Infection and seduction are inseparable. The Venetian moralists after Agnadello feared that a city of many thousand would succumb by contact with a few hundred; the moralists spoke of the Jews with their bags of money and the boys gliding naked on the canals in the same breath, or of usury as tinged with the allures of prostitution. The Venetian language in which touch seems fatal resonates with some of the same moral undertow as modern rhetoric about AIDS, in which seduction and infection also seem inseparable. In turn, the Ghetto represented something like an urban condom.

The discourse on usury connected whores and Jews. What the fear of touching Jews meant for the Jews themselves appeared in the differences, however, between these two groups of despised bodies in Venice.

Jews and courtesans

On October 31, 1501, the Duke of Valentino threw a notorious sex party in the Vatican, which Pope Alexander VI attended:

> In the evening a supper was given in the Duke of Valentino's apartment in the Apostolic palace, with fifty respectable prostitutes, called courtesans, in attendance. After supper they danced with the servants and others present, at first in their clothes and then naked. Later candelabra with lighted candles were taken from the tables and put on the floor and chestnuts were scattered around them. The prostitutes crawled naked on their hands and knees between the candelabra, picking up the chestnuts. The Pope, the Duke, and his sister Donna Lucrezia, were all present to watch. Finally prizes of silk doublets, shoes, hats and other clothes were offered to the men who copulated with the greatest number of prostitutes. According to those who were present, this performance duly took place in the public hall [that is, the Sala Regia, used for public consistories].[34]

The Pope's presence at such a lascivious affair may surprise the modern reader, but the papacy was a worldly society, staffed by many high officials who had not taken holy vows. In this world, what did it mean for a courtesan to be a "respectable prostitute"?

The word "courtesan" came into use in the late 1400s as the feminine form of "courtier"—in Italian usage, these women were the *cortigiane* who provided pleasure for the *cortigaiani,* the men who were the nobles, soldiers, administrators, and hangers-on populating the

A Venetian courtesan. *From Grevembroch,* Customs of the Venetians; *Museo Civico Correr, Venice.*

Renaissance courts. The court was a political scene, its dinners, receptions of ambassadors, and meetings serious occasions. The courtesan provided men relief from this official world.

Girls who entered into prostitution of any sort did so at about the age of fourteen. Aretino wrote of a young girl saying, "I learned in a month all that there is to know about prostitution: how to rouse passion, to attract men, to lead them on, and how to plant a lover. How to cry when I wanted to laugh, and how to laugh when I felt like weeping. And how to sell my virginity over and over again."[35] Becoming a courtesan took longer. It meant establishing a network of high-class clients, learning the gossip of the city and the court with which to amuse them, the acquisition of a house and clothes which would be pleasing to them.

Unlike the geisha system in Japan, where the sociable arts were codified into strict rituals taught and passed down from generation to generation, as a lawyer might receive training, the Renaissance prostitute who hoped to become a courtesan had to create herself. In this her problem was a bit like that of the male courtier, who had need of such books of behavior as Castiglione's *Book of the Courtier* which showed a man how to navigate in a cosmopolitan setting. Many scurrilous books purported to give the courtesan similar instruction, but her real education came through learning by observation to imitate upper-class women, to dress, talk, and write like them.

In learning "to pass," the courtesan posed a peculiar problem: if successful, she had donned a disguise and could go anywhere. It was not so much that she could pass among virtuous women as that she could replace them, looking and sounding like them yet also serving as sensual companion to their men. It was for this reason that the courtesan was seen as a special threat, the threat of a lewd woman who seemed just like any other. In a proclamation issued in 1543, the Venetian government declared that prostitutes appear "in the streets and churches, and elsewhere, so much bejewelled and well-dressed, that very often noble ladies and women citizens, because there is no difference in their attire from that of the above-said women, are confused with them, not only by foreigners, but by the inhabitants of Venice, who are unable to tell the good from the bad. . . ."[36]

By Shakespeare's time, Venice had for centuries contained a large cadre of prostitutes who lived off the trade of visiting sailors and traders. Indeed, the sheer volume of money trading hands in the Venetian "sex industry" during the Renaissance gradually meant that it became "a legitimate source of profit for noble entrepreneurs of good family."[37] Because Venice was a port city, power and sex were differently related than in Rome. Given a morally minded Pope, courtesans could be instantly and effectively banished from court functions. As much of the population of Venice was constantly coming and going, foreign men far from their licit beds, the port tolerated prostitutes as part of its economy, just as it tolerated Jews who loaned money. Trade furnished a steady, flush clientele; the possibility glittered before any young prostitute of becoming a courtesan.

Faced with this possibility, the city attempted to treat prostitutes the same way it treated other alien bodies: by segregating them. Moreover, the city sought to draw a special connection between prostitutes and Jews, by making them both wear yellow clothing or badges. Wearing special clothes as such did not set the two groups apart, for everyone in the city wore a uniform of some sort to indicate their standing or their profession; but only prostitutes and Jews wore this particular color. Jews in Venice were first required to wear a yellow badge in 1397; prostitutes and pimps in 1416 were ordered to wear yellow scarves. Jewish women seldom left the Ghetto wearing any of their ornaments or jewels, and so were remarkable in the city for being plainly dressed as well as dressed with something yellow. The authorities sought to mark out prostitutes in the same way. A decree of 1543 defined those aspects of a virtuous woman's appearance which a prostitute could not adopt: "Therefore it is proclaimed that no prostitute may wear, nor have on any part of her person, gold, silver, or silk, nor wear necklaces, pearls or jewelled or plain rings, either in their ears or on their hands."[38]

The part of this decree prohibiting earrings was more significant than it might first seem. "Only one group of women regularly encountered on the streets of northern Italian cities adorned their ears with rings," Diane Owen Hughes writes; "these were Jews."[39] In the time before Jews were segregated into Ghettos, the earring was a way to mark the presence of a Jewish woman on the street, her pierced ears like a circumcision mark. Some places legally treated Jewish women as whores, but other cities simply obliged the wearing of earrings, for "although it was a . . . less obviously degrading sign, the earring might also convey notions of sexual impurity. . . . Earrings tempted."[40] They marked a lascivious body. In forbidding the earring, the Venetians chose to repress the sexual body, but paid the price of not knowing who were the impure women on their streets.

To confine prostitutes in place, the Venetians had first thought to introduce something like state-run brothels, and purchased two houses for this purpose. But the prostitutes found it more lucrative to work privately through pimps who recruited clients throughout the city and provided rooms or created anonymous brothels that escaped the state's vigilance; these illegal places for illicit sex could evade the state's proposed taxes, to be carefully calculated on each sexual transaction. The plan for the state-run brothels came to nothing, but the desire to confine prostitutes continued. A law was passed to forbid prostitutes from establishing themselves along the Grand Canal, a position in the city they could afford thanks to their lucrative earnings; this only meant they spent their money to infiltrate other respectable areas. In the same way, the dress codes failed. Edicts forbade prostitutes to dress using white silk, a fabric meant only for unmarried young ladies and certain kinds of nuns, or again adorning their hands with the rings of married women. However, just as the courtesans overran their geographic legal boundaries, their bodies continued to "pass."

For all these reasons, the courtesans had nothing to gain by being isolated or marked, and so resisted segregation with every means at their disposal. The Jews, on the other hand, faced a more complicated reality.

3. A SHIELD BUT NOT A SWORD

Qadosh

Dolfin's concluding words when he first proposed making the Ghetto into a Jewish space were, "two boats of the Council of Ten would go and stay there at night, at their expense, for their greater security."[41] The last phrase indicates one interest the Jews had in submitting to this form of isolation. In exchange for segregated isolation the Jews gained their bodily security, within the walls of the Ghetto. The police boats protected them on occasions when mobs came shouting to the Ghettos, occasions which arose annually at Lent when the Christian populace was reminded of the old myth that Jews had killed Christ. In its dealings with all the foreign communities, the city-state was willing to prosecute violent Venetians so long as the foreigners were in their own quarters. Geography also gave a guarantee to the Jews. The isolated space protected them in 1534, for example, when the Jews were subject to one such wave of attacks during Lent; the bridges were drawn up, the windows closed, and the crowds of Christian zealots couldn't get at them.

While the state had nothing to offer the courtesan in exchange for wearing the yellow scarf, it offered something more precious than security to the Jew for entering the Ghetto. In the Ghetto, the city allowed Jews to build synagogues. For much of Jewish history, those who followed the faith met in homes, somewhat as did early Christians. The Jews never truly possessed their synagogues, since they could not own the land; they occupied and made holy the places secured for them by favor of a city's local ruler. The Venice Ghetto offered the Jews the chance to make synagogues binding institutions within a closed community, protected by a Christian city-state. Fraternal organizations used the synagogue for supervision of the daily lives of people within the closed community. The Ghetto soon became the site for synagogues representing the different confessional groups of Sephardim and Ashkenazim. By the Middle Ages, synagogues were in two ways more like Islamic mosques than Christian churches. First, "most synagogues and all mosques since about the late eighth century . . . prohibited human imagery."[42] Second, like the mosque, synagogues separated male and female bodies. In the synagogue of the Scuola Grande Tedesca, for instance, women sat in an oval gallery running around the entire second-story level, an arrangement that brought them visually close to all the male activity happening on the floor. This religious space became also a space of licit sensuality for the female body. An English visitor of Shakespeare's time, Thomas Coryat, wrote of the scene in the gallery:

> I saw many Jewish women, whereof some were as beautiful as ever I saw, and so gorgeous in their apparel, chaines of gold, and rings adorned with precious stones, that some of our English Countesses do scarce exceed them, having marvailous long traines like Princesses that are borne up by waiting women serving for the same purpose.[43]

Such a display of wealth would have been a gross provocation outside the Ghetto, activating all the Christian stereotypes about Jewish greed. In Renaissance Venice this would have been particularly an affront, as so much official energy was bent toward repressing sensual display by alien bodies, whether among ethnic groups or courtesans. But here, in the protected space of the Ghetto, a class of despised women could take pride in their appearance.

Qadosh is a fundamental word in Hebrew. As Kenneth Stow remarks, *Qadosh* "literally means separate, or separated. This is its original, biblical sense." In a way, this indicated that Jewish tradition seldom aimed at conversion of other peoples to Judaism. The more consequent meaning of the word encompasses holiness. "The link with godliness is in Leviticus: 'You shall be *Qedoshim*, for I, the Lord, your God, am *Qadosh*.' "[44] The meanings of *Qadosh* can also combine something like the Church Latin meanings of *sanctus* and *sacer*, "holy"

The interior of the Scuola Grande Tedesca in Venice. *Copyright Graziano Arici. All rights reserved.*

and "accursed." One way to understand what the presence of synagogues in the Venetian Ghetto meant to Jews was an accursed space became a holy place.[45]

For Venetian Jews, this meant a more complex religious environment than they had known as cells of Jews dispersed in the city. The strands of Renaissance Judaism were woven of very different social materials; Ashkenazic Jews and Sephardic Jews came from different cultural backgrounds. Hebrew constituted a shared formal language, but in daily life the Sephardim spoke Ladino, a language combining Spanish and some Arabic with Hebrew. In the Ghetto diverse Jews were constrained in the same dense, bounded space; this reinforced the single characteristic they shared, that of "being Jewish," just as in the Fondaco dei Tedeschi, religious differences were replaced by being all "German."

The spatial forging of this identity appeared in quite concrete ways, large and small. The different kinds of Jews cooperated to protect their interests, and evolved forms of collective representation so that they spoke as "Jews" to the outside world; in the Venetian Ghetto, as shortly afterward in the Roman Ghetto, the Jews formed fraternal organizations, which met in the synagogues but dealt with purely secular matters concerning the Ghetto. In Venice, the spice economy of the city at large refracted to produced a distinctive culture of the Ghetto. Traditionally, ordinary Jewish prayers and religious study in the late Middle Ages occurred in the morning. The advent of coffee, readily available in the city, was greeted by the Jews as a way to make particular use of their spatial segregation. They drank it as a stimulus to stay up at night, during the hours they were incarcerated in the Ghetto; these now became the ordinary hours of prayer and study.[46]

Separation protected, separation welded an oppressed community together; separation also turned the oppressed inward in new ways. In the words of one historian, "the Jew whose work took him out of the ghetto and among Gentiles for the day or the week felt as if he were leaving his natural environment and entering a strange world."[47] By the end of the sixteenth century, rabbinic courts began to forbid dancing between Jewish women and Christian men; the fear of voluntary conversion grew to almost obsessive proportions in these courts, though the incidence of voluntary conversion remained very low, on the scale first indicated in Rome fifty years before. In this, the growth of ghettoized communities coincided with an exhaustion of everyday Jewish thinking about the relation of the religion to the world around it. Old medieval distinctions about the absolute separation of Judaism from all other "nations" were revived in the age of the ghetto, whereas in the early Renaissance there had been an exploration of the doctrinal margins between Judaism and Christianity. The Christian became simply an alien Other. The modern scholar Jacob Katz argues that this everyday "indifference of Judaism to Christianity is all the more astonishing, in that profound changes had occurred in Western Christendom with the Reformation, which presented an opportunity for a restatement of the Jewish position vis-à-vis the Christianity so transformed."[48]

This is a harsh judgment, however, and not entirely accurate. It would be more fair to say that isolation in space now became part of the problem defining what it meant to "be Jewish." The geography of identity puzzled one of the most famous Jews of the Renaissance. Leon (Judah Aryeh) Modena, who lived from 1571 to 1648, was a scribe, a poet, a rabbi, a musician, a political leader, a scholar of Latin, Greek, French, English, and, surprisingly, a compulsive gambler; his autobiography's title *The Life of Judah* is a play on words, since gambling was supposed to be the sin of Judah. Born outside the city, Modena came to Venice in 1590, when he was nineteen years old; three years later, and now married, he decided to become a rabbi. It took him nearly twenty years to achieve this aim. His life during those twenty years was unsettled; he wrote a great deal, travelling from place to place, but felt uncomfortable. The quintessential Wandering Jew, it was only when he entered the closed world of the Venetian Ghetto, surrounded by Jews of every sort leading an active public life, that Modena began to feel at peace with himself. When in 1609 he was finally ordained in Venice, his life took on an intensely local character. As a rabbi, he attended the synagogue three times a day "to lead the service, to recite prayers for the sick and the dead, to preach every Sabbath morning before the Torah was removed from the ark to be read, and to teach two or three laws after it was read and returned to the ark Mondays and Thursdays."[49]

In the early seventeenth century, educated opinion among some Christians did reach out to the Jews not only in Italy but in Northern Europe as well; the anti-Semitism of Martin Luther would be balanced by Calvin's greater openness, or in England by open-minded scholars like Lord Herbert of Cherbury. Leon Modena represented, in turn, the disposition among educated Jews to participate in cultural life beyond the boundaries of the Jewish community while retaining their religious faith and practices.[50]

Because of his intellectual gifts and his ceaseless writing, Modena's sermons had become internationally famous, and he began to attract Christians into the Ghetto to hear him speak. Modena's personal gifts constituted a kind of test case as to how far an illustrious man could break the isolation of the Ghetto. Throughout the 1620s his reputation rose, to a summit in 1628 when he took control of the Jewish musical academy *(L'Accademia degl'Impediti)* and gave performances of Jewish choral music and Psalms in the Sephardic synagogue. "The Christian nobility of Venice flocked to this spectacular event," in the words of his most recent biographer, "and the authorities had to intervene to control the crowds."[51] However, those Venetian Christians who did visit the Ghetto were rather like modern European tourists going to Harlem in New York, the visit a matter of voyeurism, the voyage to a forbidden culture. And Christians like Paulo Scarpi who listened seriously to Jews like Leon Modena paid a penalty; for Scarpi, it meant being denied a bisphoric because, so he was accused, he had "consorted with Jews."

During the years of his fame, Modena appreciated the protections of the Ghetto, approved the concentration of Jewish activities within its walls, and thought through efforts like his own, the repressions imposed on Jews could be eased. He was not alone in this last hope. In the economic realm, Daniel Roderiga, a financial leader, struggled against the restrictions confining Jews to the Venetian Ghetto. Roderiga argued that the declining fortunes of Venice could be rescued only by giving Jewish merchants more geographic freedom. In 1589, he sought to establish a charter of Jewish rights whose first provision was that Jewish merchants and their families could live anywhere in the Venetian state, and whose second provision was that synagogues could be built anywhere in Venice. The authorities denied the first outright, and dealt with the second by bureaucratic evasion.

Roderiga's charter of economic rights of 1589 succeeded in other provisions which brought Shylock's assertion of his rights at least partially to life. The most important feature of the charter was the granting of the right of free trade to all non-Turkish Venetians, and the guarantee of the sanctity of contract to almost all Venetians. In the words of the modern historian Benjamin Ravid, "the right to engage in overseas trade with the Levant on the same terms as native Venetians was a concession unprecedented in the commercial history of Venice."[52] That was Shylock's claim; foreign but equal, his condition as a Venetian. But it was an economic right, not a cultural right.

The careers of famous men like Modena or Roderiga give a misleading impression of the ordinary cultural relations between the Ghetto and the outside world. Even Leon Modena, who, as the modern historian Natalie Davis points out, "is discrepant from Shylock on almost every page: a Jew who chances his money with thriftless abandon, who cries for revenge against Jewish slayers of his son, who basks in Christian admiration," found the Ghetto to weigh ever more heavily upon him as his life drew to its end.[53]

The weight of place

In 1637, after the publication of a magnum opus on Jewish rites, Modena found the limits of his own value in the eyes of Christians. He was hauled before the Venetian Inquisition in 1637, and only his personal relations with the Grand Inquisitor saved him and his book, which continued to be excoriated by lesser dignitaries of the Church. Modena's book on Jewish ritual was a threat because it placed in the overt, public realm of anthropology the Jewish religious and communal culture which had before been confined to the shadows of Christian fantasy. The attacks on his great book culminated a series of events which had made clear to him, as his life drew to a close, the terrible truth revealed by Brueghel's *Landscape with the Fall of Icarus.* The culture of Christian community, that compassion and fine feeling which Antonio and Bassanio exemplify in Shakespeare's play, was inseparable from indifference to those who were different.

That dark knowledge forced itself upon Modena when a great plague swept through Venice from 1629 to 1631. Despite Jewish appeals during a crisis which affected all those who resided in the city, the law of the Ghetto held firm: Jews could not move, even temporarily, to a more hygienic place, and so those under Modena's pastoral care suffered particularly from the ravages of the disease. Five years later he had to reckon not merely with the indifference of the Christians to sufferings of Jews, but with a more positive disposition to hurt the Jews, promoted by the very effects of segregating his people.

By the mid-1630s, save for fragmented contacts among the elite, the Jews in the Ghetto became enigmas to their Christian contemporaries, who no longer saw Jews routinely in their midst. The Ghetto promoted fantasy about what the Jews were doing and how they lived; rumor flourished unchecked. The Jewish body itself had from the earliest times been thought of as a body of concealment. Circumcision, as we have seen in Chapter Four, was originally renounced by early Christians in order to make all bodies equally susceptible to conversion; by the Renaissance, circumcision was said to be a secret practice of self-mutilation allied to other sexual sadistic practices the Jews keep hidden from outsiders. Circumcision was associated "with castration, the making of the Jew by unmanning him, by feminizing him."[54] From this, late medieval writers like Thomas de Cantimpre deduced that Jewish men menstruated, a "scientific fact" confirmed by Franco da Piacenza in a catalogue of "Jewish maladies" which appeared in 1630. The space of the Ghetto reinforced such beliefs about the Jewish body: behind the Ghetto's drawn bridges and closed windows, its life shut off from the sun and the water, crime and idolatry were thought to fester.

The fantasies surrounding concealment came to a head in March 1636, when goods stolen elsewhere in Venice were received and hidden by a group of Jews in the Ghetto. The fantasy that all Jews were engaged in a stolen-goods ring became in the course of two or three days an unshakable conviction in the minds of the Venetian public. From the stealing, other crimes were devised in the minds of those beyond the Ghetto's walls, such as the imprisonment of Christian children in the Ghetto, and an orgy of circumcision. Modena described the police search for the hidden silk, silk clothing, and gold. "On Purim the ghetto compound was closed off in order to conduct a house-to-house search for them in great haste"; this could be done simply by drawing up a few bridges and locking a few doors.[55] Modena railed against it, saying that "when one individual committed a crime, they [Christians] would grow angry at the entire community"; the reason the Christians blamed all the Jews was that they thought "every kind of crime is concealed in the ghetto."[56] As rumor mounted over the course of the next few days, Jews suffered one of the worst pogroms they had ever known in Europe. Christian mobs entered the Ghetto, burned or stole sacred books and objects in the synagogues, set fire to buildings. Because they were concentrated in a single mass, the Jews could be attacked like animals penned up for slaughter.

In the wake of the pogrom of 1636, Modena the Wandering Jew, the cosmopolite par excellence, began to rue the life he had settled into. His son-in-law Jacob, with whom he was very close, had been banished to Ferrara as part of the general punishment inflicted on the Jews in the persecution of 1636. In 1643, old and ill, Leon Modena asked the authorities to let Jacob return. They refused, still reeling under the hatreds which had caused the great persecution. Modena's memoir of his life near its end bursts out with a terrible confession of helplessness: "Who will give me learned words of lamentations, moaning, and woe so that I may speak and write of how much worse my luck has been than that of any other person? I shall suffer and bear what began to make me desolate on the day I was born and has continued without respite for seventy-six whole years."[57]

In this lament, we hear a larger echo than one man's tragedy. A group identity forged by oppression remains in the hands of the oppressor. The geography of identity means the outsider always appears as an unreal human being in the landscape—like the Icarus who fell unremarked and unmourned to his death. And yet Jews had taken root in this oppressive landscape; it had become part of themselves. It can be no reproach to say that they had internalized the oppressor in making a community out of a space of oppression. But this communal life proved to be, at best, a shield rather than a sword.

4. THE MIRACULOUS LIGHTNESS OF FREEDOM

The Merchant of Venice marks a sharp contrast to Christopher Marlowe's play *The Jew of Malta* (1633). Marlowe forms Barabas, the Maltese Jew, into a figure of fun, made merely contemptible because of his greed. Shylock is a more complex human being, for his greed is intermixed with justified rage. Perhaps the greatest speech in *The Merchant of Venice* is Shylock's speech on the universal dignity of the human body. It runs:

> Hath not a Jew eyes? Hath not a Jew hands, organs, dimensions, senses, affections, passions? Fed with the same food, hurt with the same weapons, subject to the same diseases, healed by the same means, warmed and cooled by the same winter and summer as a Christian is? If you prick us, do we not bleed? If you tickle us, do we not laugh? If you poison us, do we not die? And if you wrong us, shall we not revenge? If we are like you in the rest, we will resemble you in that.[58]

This dignity had been denied by the Christians who condescended to take Shylock's money. But this speech is not just a writer's work of rounding all his characters, even his villains; it is too consequent.

Shylock's charge against the Christians reverberates in *The Mer-*

chant of Venice in the plot, and in an unexpected way. By Act IV, Shakespeare has built up a great dramatic tension between the honor of Christian gentlemen like Antonio and Bassanio, and the contractual rights of Shylock. The Christians entreat Shylock, the Duke makes a moving speech, but Shylock is implacable. All seems lost. Suddenly in Act IV Shakespeare throws it all away.

Portia enters in disguise as a lawyer and mediator, to assure Shylock his claim is just, but that he must absolutely adhere to its terms, taking a pound of flesh but not a drop of blood, which was not specified in the contract, and he can only carve a pound of flesh, not an ounce more or less. Since Shylock cannot be so scientific a cannibal, the game is up. Like a pricked balloon, Shylock deflates. The way Portia cuts the Gordian knot of contract is hardly a moral resolution of events; the larger issues are evaded by her lawyerly trickiness, and many critics have found the denouement lame. The only way to deal with the devil, it seems, is to beat the devil at his own game.

This denouement underlines an ambiguity that marks the play as a whole: does *The Merchant of Venice* lean to the side of comedy or tragedy? The Christian characters, admirable as they are, are lighter in weight than Shylock; they suit the frame of comedy, and *The Merchant of Venice* is often performed in this way. Trivializing the denouement prepares us for the various comic intrigues resolved in Act V. The Christians triumph, Portia sets Antonio free, and *The Merchant of Venice* becomes a comedy of manners.

Something odd, though, has happened. Even before the denouement, we experience it in the subplot turning on Shylock's daughter Jessica. The moment she falls in love with a Christian, Jessica flees her father, her house, and her faith. She evinces remarkably little grief at leaving the world of her father—nor at robbing him, which she does when she takes jewels from Frankfurt to pay for her own pleasures on her honeymoon. Recounted thus, she seems a vile creature, yet in the play she is made wholly charming. For this daughter who lives in no Ghetto, "being Jewish" is a little like wearing a set of clothes, which you shed if you happen, for instance, to fall in love. The action displays the inconsequence of experience again in another subplot which involves a game of love, as in its final act when the male lovers in the play are manipulated by the women who love them in a kind of erotic business deal. Neither bodily pain nor bodily desire matters in the end; dealing does. Who has triumphed?

The Merchant of Venice can be read without straining as a premonition. Shakespeare puts on display a world in which the community of Christian gentlefolk has become either ineffective or inconsequential. Their freedom lightens culture's burden, unlike the bodies weighed down by culture in the Ghetto. Freedom which transcends life's burdensome weight and obligations: at the end of the play, we have entered the modern world.

PART THREE

ARTERIES
AND VEINS

CHAPTER EIGHT

Moving Bodies

Harvey's Revolution

1. CIRCULATION AND RESPIRATION

For more than two thousand years medical science accepted the ancient principles of body heat which governed Perikles' Athens. Sanctified by the weight of long tradition, it seemed certain that innate heat of the body explained the differences between men and women, as well as between human beings and animals. With the appearance of William Harvey's *De motu cordis* in 1628, this certainty began to change. Through discoveries he made about the circulation of the blood, Harvey launched a scientific revolution in the understanding of the body: its structure, its healthy state, and its relation to the soul. A new master image of the body took form.

The new understandings of the body coincided with the birth of modern capitalism, and helped bring into being the great social transformation we call individualism. The modern individual is, above all else, a mobile human being. Adam Smith's *Wealth of Nations* first reckoned what Harvey's discoveries would lead to in this regard, for Adam Smith imagined the free market of labor and goods operating much like freely circulating blood within the body and with similar life-giving consequences. Smith, in observing the frantic business behavior of his contemporaries, recognized a design. Circulation of goods and money proved more profitable than fixed and stable possession. Ownership served as the prelude to exchange, at least for those who improved their lot in life. Yet for people to benefit from the virtues of a circulating economy, Smith knew, they would be obliged to cut themselves free from old allegiances. This mobile economic actor would moreover have to learn specialized, individualized tasks, in order to have something distinctive to offer. Cut loose, specialized *Homo economicus* could move around in society, exploit possessions and skills as the market offered, but all at a price.

Moving around freely diminishes sensory awareness, arousal by places or the people in those places. Any strong visceral connection to the environment threatens to tie the individual down. This was the premonition expressed at the end of *The Merchant of Venice:* to move freely, you can't feel too much. Today, as the desire to move freely has triumphed over the sensory claims of the space through which the body moves, the modern mobile individual has suffered a kind of tactile crisis: motion has helped desensitize the body. This general principle we now see realized in cities given over to the claims of traffic and rapid individual movement, cities filled with neutral spaces, cities which have succumbed to the dominant value of circulation.

Harvey's revolution helped change the expectations and plans people made for the urban environment. Harvey's findings about the circulation of blood and respiration led to new ideas about public health, and in the eighteenth century Enlightened planners applied these ideas to the city. Planners sought to make the city a place in which people could move and breathe freely, a city of flowing arteries and veins through which people streamed like healthy blood corpuscles. The medical revolution seemed to have substituted health for morality as a standard of human happiness among these social engineers, health defined by motion and circulation.

The route from Harvey's discoveries about healthy circulation within the body, coupled to new capitalistic beliefs about individual movement in society, has thus only posed anew an enduring problem in Western civilization: How to find a sensate home for responsive bodies in society, particularly in the city, bodies now restless yet alone. Circulation as a value in medicine and in economics has created an ethics of indifference. The wandering Christian body, exiled from the Garden, was at least promised by God it would become more aware of its environment and of other displaced human beings. Harvey's contemporary John Milton told the story of the Fall this way, for instance, in *Paradise Lost*. The secular body in endless motion risks not knowing this story, instead losing its connections to other people and to the places through which it moves.

This chapter traces the path from Harvey's discoveries about circulation in the body to the urban planning of the eighteenth century, and what circulation meant for individuals and groups in the Enlightenment city. The next chapter focuses on the challenge circulation posed to the sense of place in revolutionary Paris. Out of this conflict there arose in the nineteenth century urban spaces made for individuals in motion, rather than for crowds in motion. The penultimate chapter traces this evolution, and its psychological consequences, as expressed in Edwardian London by E. M. Forster in his novel *Howards End*. The final chapter focuses on modern New York, today a multi-cultural city filled with uprooted people from around the globe. The word "uprooted" suggests an unhappy condition, but I do not wish to conclude this history in the negative. *Flesh and Stone* ends by asking if there is any chance in a multi-cultural city, against all the odds of history, that the differences between people racially, ethnically, sexually might become points of contact rather than grounds for withdrawal. Can we avoid the fate of Venetian Christians and Jews? Can urban diversity curb the forces of individualism?

These questions begin in the flesh.

Blood pulses

Harvey made what seems in retrospect a simple discovery: the heart pumps blood through the arteries of the body, and receives blood to be pumped from the veins. This discovery challenged the ancient idea that the blood flowed through the body because of its heat, and that different bodies contained different degrees of "innate heat *(calor innatus)*"—male bodies, for instance, being hotter than female bodies. Harvey believed circulation heated the blood, whereas the ancient theory supposed heat in the blood caused it to circulate. Harvey discovered that such circulation occurs mechanically: "it is by the heart's vigorous beat," he declared, "that the blood is moved, perfected, activated, and protected from injury and decay."[1] He pictured the body as a great machine pumping life.

Harvey first studied the venous valves in the heart in 1614–15, and then the differences between the functioning of arteries and veins; his students in the 1620s removed hearts from fresh corpses to observe how the heart muscle continued to contract and expand, even though the heart had no blood to pump. One of his students discovered that the blood of birds is actually hotter than human blood, due to the more rapid pumping of the bird's heart. By observing the machinery of circulation, these scientists became increasingly convinced that the same mechanics operated in all animal life.

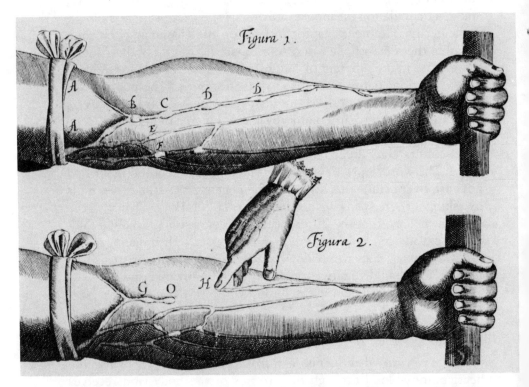

Harvey's image of the blood system of the arm, from *De motu cordis*, 1628.

Up to the eighteenth century, Christian doctors hotly debated where the soul lurked in the body, whether the soul made contact with the body via the brain or the heart, or if the brain and heart were "double organs," containing both corporeal matter and spiritual essence. While in his writings Harvey clung to the medieval Christian notion of the heart as an organ of compassion, by the time he published his findings he knew that it was also a machine. He insisted on scientific knowledge gained through personal observation and experiment rather than on reasoning from abstract principles. Some of Harvey's adversaries, such as Descartes, were prepared to believe that the body is a machine, just as the Deity itself might operate by a kind of celestial mechanics. God is the principle of the machine. To the question, "Does the rational (immaterial) soul have physiological functions?" Descartes answered yes.[2] Harvey's science led to answering no. In Harvey's own view, though the human animal has an immaterial soul, God's presence in the world does not explain how the heart makes the blood move.

Harvey's researches into the blood prompted other researchers to look at other body systems in similar ways. The English doctor Thomas Willis, who lived from 1621 to 1675, sought to understand how the nervous system in the body operates in some fashion through mechanical circulation. Though he could not see the visible movement of "nerve energy" along the nerve fibers as Harvey could watch blood pulsing, Willis could study the tissues of the brain. Like Harvey's pupils he found, by comparing the brains of human beings and animals, that there was "little or no difference . . . as to the Figures and Exterior Conformations of the Parts, the Bulk only excepted . . . from hence we concluded, the Soul Common to Man with the Brutes, to be only Corporeal, and immediately to use these Organs."[3] Willis's successors in late seventeenth- and eighteenth-century neurology discovered, by experimenting on living frogs, that throughout a living body the ganglia of nerve fibers responded equally to sensory stimulation; by experimenting on fresh human corpses, the doctors found that the ganglia in human beings continued to respond as did frog nerve fibers, even after the soul had presumably departed the body to meet its Maker. In terms of the neural system, the body had no need of "spirit" in order to sense. Since all the nerve ganglia seemed to operate in the same fashion, the soul might hover everywhere, but existed nowhere in particular. Empirical observation could not locate the soul in the body.[4]

Thus mechanical movement in the body, nervous movements as well as the movements of the blood, created a more secular understanding of the body in contesting the ancient notion that the soul (the *anima*) is the source of life's energy.

This shift led researchers to challenge the hierarchical imagery of the body which governed medieval thinkers like John of Salisbury. Long before the discovery of the electrical nature of the movements between nerve fibers, for instance, it had become evident to eighteenth-century doctors that the nervous system was more than a sim-

The blood vessels as twigs growing out of the human body. From Case's *Compendium anatomicum*, 1696.

ple extension of the brain. The physiologist Albrecht von Haller argued in his *Demonstrations of Physiology* of 1757 that the nervous system worked by involuntary sensations which in part circumvented the brain—and certainly conscious control; nerves somehow transmitted sensations of pain from the foot to the wrist when a person stubbed a toe, so that these two members twitched together. Like blood, pain seemed to circulate through the body. Doctors indulged in a veritable orgy of cruel animal experiments to show that nerve tissues had life "distinct from the conscious mind or higher soul," in the words of the historian Barbara Stafford; "hearts were ripped out while still beating, bowels eviscerated, tracheas sliced open to stifle the yelping of frightened and suffering animals as they twitched or writhed."[5]

The heart was similarly dethroned from the place Henri de Mondeville assigned it. Though Harvey asserted that the heart is "the starting point of life," he believed that "blood is life itself."[6] The heart is but a machine for circulation. The science of circulation thus emphasized the individual independence of parts of the body.

In place of the puzzles of body and soul, this new science focused on the body's health, as determined by its mechanics. Galen had defined health as balance in body heat and fluids; the new medicine defined it as free flow and movement of blood and nerve energies. The free flow of blood seemed to promote the healthy growth of individual tissues and organs. The neurological experimenters believed similarly that free-flowing nerve energy promoted individual tissue and organ growth. It was this paradigm of flow, health, and individuality within the body which eventually transformed the relationship between the body and society. As a medical historian observes, "In an increasingly secular society . . . health was viewed more and more as one of the responsibilities allotted to the individual, rather than a gift from God."[7] The city taking form in the eighteenth century helped translate that internal paradigm into a picture of the healthy body in a healthy society.

The city breathes

The links between the city and the new science of the body began when the heirs of Harvey and Willis applied their discoveries to the skin. We owe to the eighteenth-century doctor Ernst Platner the first clear analogy of circulation within the body to the body's environmental experience. Air, Platner said, is like blood: it must circulate through the body, and the skin is the membrane which allows the body to breathe air in and out. Dirt seemed to Platner the prime enemy of the skin's work; Platner maintained, in the words of the historian Alain Corbin, that dirt clogging the pores "held back the excremental humors, favored the fermentation and putrefaction of substances; worse, it facilitated the 'pumping back of the rubbish' that loaded the skin."[8] The movement of air through the skin gave a new, secular meaning for the word "impure." Impurity meant dirty skin rather than a stain on the soul. Skin became impure due to people's social experience rather than as a result of moral failure.

In the country, among peasants, dirt crusted on the skin appeared natural and seemed indeed health-giving. Human urine and faeces helped nourish the earth; left on the body they also seemed to form a nourishing film, especially around infants. Therefore country people believed that "one should not wash too often . . . because the crust of dried faeces and urine formed part of the body, and played a protective role, especially in [swaddling] babies. . . ."[9]

Scrupulously cleaning excrement off the body became a specifically urban and middle-class practice. In the 1750s, middle-class people began to use disposable paper to wipe the anus after excretion; chamber pots were by that date emptied daily. The very fear of handling excrement was an urban fear, born of the new medical beliefs about impurities clogging the skin. More, purveyors of that medical knowledge lived in the city. "Peasants and physicians were literally unable to communicate within an agreed world of representations of the body and its fortunes," the historian Dorinda Outram writes; the peasants knew men of science only in the persons of barbers who also served as surgeons in villages, and these barber-surgeons numbered only about one in a thousand by 1789 in France, while licensed doctors numbered one in ten thousand and lived mostly in cities.[10]

Such beliefs in the importance of letting the skin "breathe" helped to change the way people dressed, a change which became evident as early as the 1730s. Women lightened the weight of their clothes by using fabrics like muslin and cotton-silk; they cut gowns to drape more loosely on the human frame. Though men kept the artifice of wigs, which in fact grew more complicated during the eighteenth century, below the hairline men too sought to lighten and unbind the clothing around their bodies. The body free to breathe was healthier because its noxious vapors were easily dispelled.

More, for the skin to breathe, people had to wash more frequently than they had before. The Roman's daily bath had disappeared by medieval times; bathing was considered by some medieval doctors to be, in fact, dangerous, since it radically unbalanced the temperature of the body. Now people who dressed lightly and bathed often no longer had to disguise with heavy perfumes the smell of sweat; the perfumes used by women, and the tonic waters used by men, had been compounded in the sixteenth and seventeenth centuries with oils which frequently caused skin rashes, so that men and women gained sweet-smelling bodies at the price of blotchy skins.

The desire to put into practice the healthy virtues of respiration and circulation transformed the look of cities as well as the bodily practices in them. From the 1740s on, European cities began cleaning dirt off the streets, draining holes and swampy depressions filled with urine and faeces, pushing dirt into sewers below the street. The very street surface changed in this effort. Medieval paving consisted of rounded cobblestones, between which pieces of animal and human excrement clung. In the middle of the eighteenth century the English began to repave London using flat, squared granite flagstones which fitted closely together; Paris first laid these stones down in the early 1780s around the streets of the modern Odéon theatre. The streets could then be cleaned more thoroughly; below them, urban "veins" replaced shallow cesspools, the sewers in Paris carrying dirty water and excrement to new sewage canals.

These changes can be charted in a series of municipal health laws in Paris. In 1750, the city of Paris obliged people to sweep away the dung and debris in front of their houses; in this same year it began to sluice down major public walkways and bridges; in 1764, it took steps to clear overflowing or blocked gutters throughout the city; in 1780, it forbade Parisians to throw the contents of their chamber pots into the streets. Within houses, Parisian architects used smooth plaster on walls for the same purpose; the plaster sealed the wall surface, making it easy to clean.

Enlightened planners wanted the city in its very design to function like a healthy body, freely flowing as well as possessed of clean skin. Since the beginnings of the Baroque era, urban planners had thought about making cities in terms of efficient circulation of people on the city's main streets. In the remaking of Rome, for instance, Pope Sixtus V connected the principal Christian shrines of the city by a series of great, straight roads on which pilgrims could travel. The medical imagery of life-giving circulation gave a new meaning to the Baroque

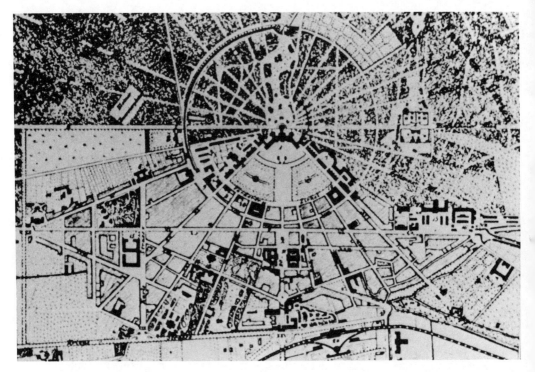

Karlsruhe in the eighteenth century. An early design for a circulatory city.

emphasis on motion. Instead of planning streets for the sake of ceremonies of movement toward an object, as did the Baroque planner,
the Enlightenment planner made motion an end in itself. The
Baroque planner emphasized progress toward a monumental destination, the Enlightened planner emphasized the journey itself. The
street was an important urban space, in this Enlightened conception,
whether it ran through a residential neighborhood or through the
city's ceremonial center.

Thus were the words "artery" and "veins" applied to city streets in
the eighteenth century by designers who sought to model traffic systems on the blood system of the body. French urbanists like Christian Patte used the imagery of arteries and veins to justify the
principle of one-way streets. In both German and French urban maps
based on the blood system, the prince's castle forms the heart of the
design, but the streets often bypassed connection to the urban heart,
and instead were directly connected to each other. Though bad anat-
omy, the planners practiced sanguine mechanics: they though that if
motion through the city becomes blocked anywhere, the collective
body suffers a crisis of circulation like that an individual body suffers
during a stroke when an artery becomes blocked. As one historian

has remarked, "Harvey's discovery and his model of the circulation of the blood created the requirement that air, water, and [waste] products also be kept in a state of movement," a state of movement in a human settlement that required careful planning; haphazard growth would only make worse the clogged, closed, unhealthy urban fabric of the past.[11]

We can see these principles of circulation put into practice in the planning of Washington, D.C., just after the American Revolution. Because of the interplay of various power interests in the young Republic, the designers of Washington had to transform a near-tropical swamp into a national capital, rather than locate power in an established city or building on a more hospitable open site a hundred miles north. The plan for Washington, and its partial realization in the Washington we know today, is a vindication of Enlightenment beliefs in the power to create a healthy environment in a highly organized, comprehensive urban design. This urban design reveals as well a certain social and political vision contained in the image of a "healthy" city in which people can breathe freely.

Washington's planners sought to echo the ancient virtues of the Roman Republic on the site they had chosen for the new capital, in part by using Roman urban designs, in part by labelling the geography of the new city in Roman terms. The American "Tiber River" was, for instance, a mosquito-infested creek running through swampland; the hills of Rome could only be conjured in imagination. Closer in time, the three principal figures in this plan—Thomas Jefferson, George Washington, and Pierre Charles L'Enfant—seemed to summon the great vistas of Versailles, Karlsruhe, and Potsdam in thinking about a new capital; these contained magnificent open spaces authorized by the stroke of monarchical pens. "It was a supreme irony," an historian remarks, "that the plan forms originally conceived to magnify the glories of despotic kings and emperors came to be applied as a national symbol of a country whose philosophical basis was so firmly rooted in democratic equality."[12]

Yet the result would prove not quite so because of the American dialogue with ancient Rome. Thomas Jefferson had envisaged in the late 1780s a street plan for a national capital based on the rural land divisions into which he wished to divide the entire continent; the shape of both city and country derived in his mind from the ancient Roman grid plan used for making geometric cities. Like the ancient

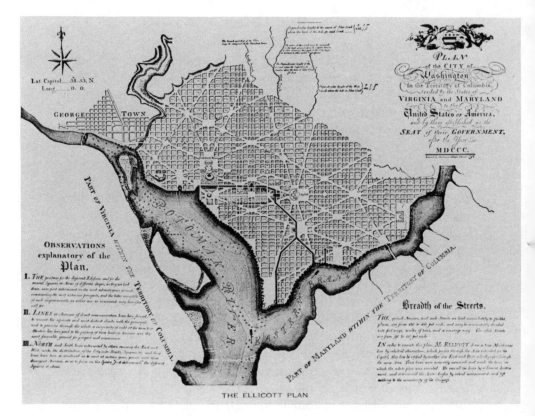

Washington, D.C.: L'Enfant's Plan, as drawn by Andrew Ellicott in 1792.

Roman city, Jefferson's Washington—so far as we know his intentions—would have seated the government squarely in the center of the city. Pierre Charles L'Enfant demurred; he read a different Roman lesson.

Like several other young idealistic Frenchmen, the young engineer L'Enfant had joined the American cause during the Revolution, and seen service at Valley Forge, remaining in America after the victory. In a note to President Washington probably in 1791, L'Enfant derided grid planning as "tiresome and insipid . . . [coming from a] cool imagination wanting a sense of the real grand and the truly beautiful."[13] In place of this he proposed a more democratic space; his "Map of Dotted Lines" of 1791, reproduced as a more formal Plan of Washington by Andrew Ellicott in 1792, shows a city with several traffic nodes and centers reached by a complex system of radial streets cutting through the rectangular divisions of the grid. For instance, L'Enfant drew a great intersection of two major streets, Virginia and Maryland Avenues, which had little to do with the seats of national power nearby, the President's House and the Congressional Capitol. Not all the nodes of the city were nodes of power.

Moreover, L'Enfant sought to mix the social and the political, as these two elements had been in the early Roman Republican forum. The Congress, L'Enfant wrote in his near-perfect English to President Washington in 1791, would form part of a "place of general resort and all along side of which may be placed play houses, room of assembly, accademies [sic] and all such sort of places as may be attractive to the learned and afford diversion to the idle."[14] L'Enfant's was a truly republican concept of a national capital: a place in which great power is absorbed into the tapestry of a multi-centered, mixed-use city. This political imagery Jefferson immediately recognized and applauded, giving way to the young Frenchman.

L'Enfant's republican plan for a multi-centered, multi-use capital reflected also Enlightened rather than Baroque beliefs about the meaning of circulation in a city. The swampy site and disgusting summer climate of Washington obliged L'Enfant to think about creating urban "lungs." For this he drew upon his native experience, specifically the great Place Louis XV in the center of Paris; the Place Louis XV was the European capital's floral lung, edging the Seine at the

View of Place Louis XV in Paris. Painting attributed to J.-B. Leprince, ca. 1750.

end of the formal Tuileries Gardens which fronted the palace of the Louvre.

As in L'Enfant's work, the lung was as important a reference as the heart to Enlightenment planners. For instance, nothing was more striking in eighteenth-century Paris than the vast Place Louis XV: though exactly in the center of Paris, it was laid out as a place of free garden growth. L'Enfant's contemporaries knew little about photosynthesis but they could feel the results when breathing. The Place Louis XV was left to grow into an urban jungle, into which people wandered when they wanted to clear their own lungs. The central garden thus came to seem far from urban street life. "The place Louis XV was then felt, even by those who were fond of its architecture, to be outside Paris."[15]

More, this central lung contravened the power relations which shaped open space in a royal garden outside a city, like Louis XIV's Versailles or Frederick the Great's Sans Souci. The Versailles gardens built in the mid-seventeenth century disciplined regular lines of trees, paths, and pools into endless vistas receding to the vanishing point: the King commanded Nature. Another kind of open space appeared in the influential English landscaping of the early eigh-

Site plan for Place Louis XV in Paris, from the Bretez plan, called "Turgot," 1734–39.

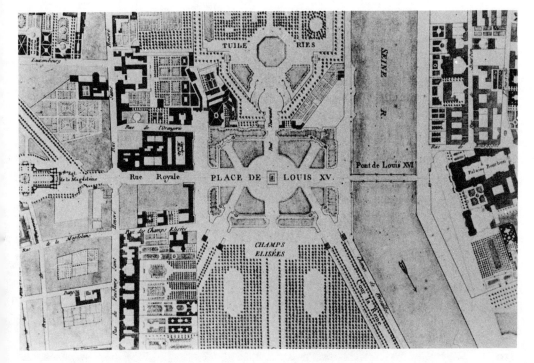

Place Louis XV in Paris. Context plan showing proposed new bridge.
Engraving by Perrier after Le Sage.

teenth century, "the boundless garden" which, in the words of Robert Harbison, lacked an "obvious beginning or end . . . the bounds are confused on all sides."[16] The English gardens seized the imagination in irregular space full of surprises as the eye wandered or the body moved, a place of lush and free growth.

L'Enfant's generation sought, however, to give the urban lung a more defined visual form. In Paris, in 1765, the authorities sought out various schemes to make this great garden more accessible to the people of the city, either on foot or in carriages, a lung through which the Parisians could stream and refresh themselves. These streets and footpaths marked a great break with the older fabric of the city; no commerce would be permitted on them, or rather, only commerce with the air and the leaves, and one another. Movement through the urban lung was still to be a sociable experience.

Curiously, the plan L'Enfant made for Washington is not quite so at ease with nature in the city as was the Parisian park. The great Mall, as Ellicott drew it according to L'Enfant's design, retains some of the formal linear elements of Versailles in the axis it establishes between the Potomac River and the President's House, and in the

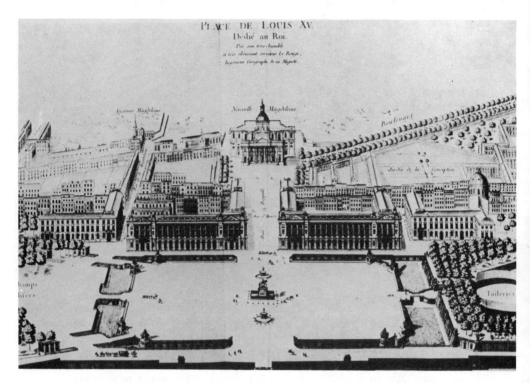

Place Louis XV in Paris. Engraving by G. L. Le Rouge, ca. 1791.

axis between the Potomac and the Capitol. But L'Enfant emphasized that in this great Mall the citizens would move and congregate, as they began to do in Paris in 1765. The Mall was not meant to provide vistas down which George Washington could oversee his domains, as Louis XIV looked out over the park of Versailles, seemingly to an infinity all his. L'Enfant declared to the first President that he wished both to "afford a great variety of pleasant seats and prospects" and to "connect each part of the city."[17] Open spaces freely available to all citizens would serve both these ends.

By being out in the open air, a citizen, Jefferson said, breathes free: Jefferson applied this metaphor to the countryside, which he loved; L'Enfant applied it to the city.[18] The medical origins of the metaphor suggested that, thanks to circulating blood, the individual members of the body equally enjoyed life, the most minor tissue as endowed with sanguine life force as the heart or brain. Though the urban lungs excluded commerce, the master image of the circulating body invited it.

2. THE MOBILE INDIVIDUAL

Smith's pin factory

In his *Great Transformation,* the modern historian Karl Polanyi sought to trace the transformation of European society he thought occurred when all social life became modelled on market exchange. Polanyi of course did not deny the importance of the market in medieval or Renaissance Europe, yet he saw in the seventeenth and eighteenth centuries the principle of "I can only gain by hurting you" taking hold of cultural and social relations as well as economics, gradually crowding out Christian beliefs in the necessity of charity and the impulses of altruism. In a way, *The Great Transformation* reads as though Shylock had in the end triumphed, that social life had everywhere become a matter of reckoning and extracting pounds of flesh.[19]

In fact, the eighteenth-century writers who preached the virtues of the free market were extremely touchy on the subject of human greed. One of the ways they sought to defend themselves against this charge drew on the new science of the body and its spatial environment. The proponents of free marketeering in the eighteenth century directly likened the flow of labor and capital in society to the flow of blood and nervous energy in the body. Adam Smith's colleagues spoke about economic health in the same terms doctors used for bodily health, using images of the "respiration of goods," "the exercise of capital," and "the stimulation of laboring energy" via the market. It seemed to them that, just as the free flow of blood nourished all the tissues of the body, so economic circulation nourished all the members of society.

Some of this was of course self-serving nonsense; no buyer suddenly faced with the prospect of paying double for bread or coal was likely to accept the price as "stimulating." Yet the economist Adam Smith added to commonplace convictions about the free market an insight which his contemporaries had not grasped with equal clarity, and which did rescue this biological-economic language from serving as a mere cloak of greed. Smith sought to show how people involved in market movements become ever more distinct individual actors in the economy; they do so, he said, through the division of labor inspired by the market.

Smith demonstrated this with severe elegance at the very opening of *The Wealth of Nations.* He gave the example of ten workers in a pin factory. Were each man to perform all the actions required to manufacture a pin, each could make perhaps twenty pins a day, two hundred in all; by dividing the tasks up, the ten men can make forty-eight thousand.[20] What will cause them to divide their labor in this way? The market for their products will: "When the market is very small, no person can have any encouragement to dedicate himself entirely to one employment, for want of the power to exchange all that surplus part of the produce of his own labor," Smith declares.[21] When the market is large and active, the laborer will be encouraged to produce a surplus. Thus the division of labor arises from "the propensity to truck, barter, and exchange one thing for another."[22] The more circulation, the more specialized people's labors, the more they become individual actors.

Smith's pin factory was a significant site for his argument. First of all, Smith sought to advance the most general principles of political economy on the most humdrum sort of work, the making of pins. In the ancient world, as we have seen, ordinary human labor seemed animal and bestial, lacking dignity. The dignity of the medieval monk's labor lay in its spiritual discipline and in its charitable use. Smith extended the dignity of labor to all workers who could freely exchange the fruits of their labor, and so would become ever more skilled at a specific task. *Skill* dignified labor, and the free market promoted the development of skills. In this, Smith's economics echoed Diderot's great *Encyclopedia* of the mid-eighteenth century. The *Encyclopedia* showed in beautifully detailed plates and exact descriptions the skills required to cane a chair or to roast a duck; the artisan or servant so skilled appeared in Diderot's pages as a more worthwhile member of society than the master who knew only how to consume.

Smith's pin factory was an urban place. Indeed, *The Wealth of Nations* was unusual in its time for the way it portrayed relations between the city and the country. From medieval thinkers like Humbert de Romans onward, writers tended to view the wealth of towns as coming at the expense of the countryside. Adam Smith instead argued that the development of cities stimulates the economy of the countryside, by creating market demand for agricultural goods. He believed that farmers should become like pinmakers, specializing in crops for market rather than self-sufficiently doing everything by themselves for themselves.[23] The virtues of circulation, that is, bind town and country, in the process of creating specialized labor in each.

This view of town and country showed what was most Enlightened and hopeful in Smith's thought, his sense of the economic individual as a social being, rather than as aloof or greedy. Each individual in the division of labor, as Smith imagined it, needed all the others to do his or her own work. If, to modern critics like Polanyi, Smith stands as an apologist for the zero-sum game, to his contemporaries he appeared both scientific and humane. He found in the circulation of labor and capital a force which dignified the most mundane labor, and which reconciled independence and interdependence.

This, then, was one contemporary answer to the question of how the sort of cities designed by L'Enfant, Patte, and Emmanuel Laugier might work. When urbanists of the eighteenth century drew plans for cities meant to operate on circulatory principles, Smith made both legible and credible the economic activities which fitted those cities. This in turn promised a more emotional possibility of individual freedom.

Goethe flees south

The freedom promised to an individual in motion appears in one of the most remarkable documents of the eighteenth century, published just before the French Revolution. This was the *Italian Journey* of Goethe, recording his flight in 1786 from an idyllic small Ger-German court to the fetid cities of Italy, a flight which brought the poet's body, so he thought, back to life.

Goethe had served Carl August, the ruler of the small duchy, as an accountant, overseer, and general administrator for over ten years. As the drudgery of sorting out Carl August's finances and supervising the draining of the prince's fields wore on, year after year, Goethe had written less and less; the extraordinary achievements of his youth—his poems, the novel *The Sorrows of Young Werther,* the play *Götz von Berlichingen*—threatened to become mere memories, his star burnt out. At last he fled south.

Goethe's *Italian Journey* describes Italian cities filled with ruined, cracked, and pillaged stones, runny excrement flowing down the streets, but the poet in flight wandered in joyous awe through this wreckage. He wrote from Rome on November 10, 1786: "I have never been so sensitive to the things of this world as I am here."[24] Six weeks earlier he had written to a friend, "I am living frugally and keeping calm so that objects do not find a heightened mind, but themselves heighten it."[25] Goethe found that circulating among masses of foreigners roused him sensually, as an individual. In Venice, among the crowd in San Marco, "at last I can really enjoy the solitude I have been longing for, because nowhere can one be more alone than in a large crowd through which one pushes one's way."[26] One of the most beautiful passages in the *Italian Journey,* written in Naples on March 17, 1787, expresses the inner peace that came to the poet in the midst of a noisy, disorderly mob:

> To thread one's way through an immense and ever-moving crowd is a peculiar and salutary experience. All merge into one great stream, yet each manages to find his way to his own goal. In the midst of so many people and all their commotion, I feel peaceful and alone for the first time. The louder the uproar of the streets, the quieter I become.[27]

Why should he feel more roused as an individual in the midst of a crowd? On November 10, Goethe writes that "anyone who looks about him seriously here and has eyes to see, must become *solid;* he must get a conception of solidity such as was never so vivid to him before."[28] The seemingly ungainly phrase "become *solid*" (in German, *solid werden*) comes oddly from Goethe's reaction to the "uproar of the streets"; the circulation in a crowd made Goethe particularize his impressions.[29] Goethe admonishes himself in Rome to "let me seize things one by one as they come; they will sort themselves out later."[30]

It may seem strange to compare Adam Smith's *The Wealth of Nations,* first published in 1776, to Goethe's *Italian Journey* of a decade later, yet the two works resonate; in both, movement articulates, specifies, individualizes experience. The results of this process began to show in Goethe's poetry at this time as well as in the *Italian Journey.* In Rome, at age thirty-eight, Goethe began an affair with a younger woman, and the love of concrete things fused with this erotic love; he wrote the last of his *Roman Elegies* as a love poem to his mistress by describing the metamorphosis of plants, the unfolding of love as specific as the growth of a vegetable. Goethe was conscious that in the course of his travels he was becoming ever more minded to specific aesthetic experience.

The poet's journey was unique, and yet the belief that movement, travel, exploration would heighten one's sensate life informed the eighteenth-century desire to journey. Some forms of travel of course continued to promise the European the possessive stimulation of capturing foreign, strange climes. Goethe's journey did not involve that kind of tourism; he didn't go to Italy in search of the unknown or the primitive, but rather felt the urge to displace himself, to move off center; his journey was closer to the *Wanderjahre* which took form in the same era, the year in which both young men and women were encouraged by their elders to travel and float before settling down. In the culture of the Enlightenment, people sought to move for the sake of physical stimulation and mental clarification. These hopes derived from science, extended into the design of the environment, the reform of the economy, even into the formation of poetic sensibility.

Yet Goethe's *Italian Journey* also shows the limits of this Enlightened mentality. Seldom does he describe the Italian crowds through which he moves with the same particularity he describes himself. Similarly, faced with the crowds of the city, Adam Smith's impulse is to describe them as divided into separate characters and categories, rather than as a human whole. In the public health discourse of the urban reformers, the urban crowd appeared as a cesspit of disease, to be purified by dispersing the crowd individually throughout the city. Jefferson famously feared the urban mob, and L'Enfant showed ambivalence toward it; he hoped his plans would prevent the "clotting" of crowds on Washington's streets. The reforms proposed for the Place Louis XV in Paris sought to make them suitable roads for individuals walking or riding singly, rather than in post carriages or other large conveyances.

The inability to reckon the urban crowd, or accept it whole, has of course to do with the people the crowd contained—people who were mostly poor. The poor, however, experienced movement in the city in ways which lay beyond the scope of these prejudices. That experience crystallized in the meaning of market movements to the poor: the difference between survival and starvation they measured in the fluctuations of pennies or sous in the price of bread. The city's crowds wanted less market movement, more government regulation, fixity, and security. Physical movement in the city only sharpened their hunger pains. The insecurity inspired by movement became most evident in the most provocative of European capitals, Paris on the eve of the Great Revolution.

3. THE CROWD MOVES

At the accession of Louis XVI, the historian Léon Cahen has reckoned, there were perhaps 10,000 clergy in Paris, 5,000 nobility, a bourgeoisie of manufacturers, wealthy merchants, doctors, and law-yers numbering about 40,000; the rest of the city's 600,000 or more inhabitants lived at the edge of poverty.[31] In retrospect, an upper class and middle class of 50,000 or so in a city of 600,000 seems small; historically, however, it was large, larger as a proportion of the city than in the time of Louis XIV, when the King held the reins of finance as well as government outside the city at the Palace of Ver-sailles. Indeed, the King's realm at Versailles had grown ever poorer while Paris prospered during the eighteenth century; royal finances became serious after the French adventures in North America in the middle of the century, and catastrophic after the French investment in the American Revolution. Louis XIV's Versailles also atrophied because the clergy and the nobility themselves began to generate new wealth in Paris, by the same means the commercial bourgeoisie generated wealth: the sale of land, investment in enterprises, and other forms of market activity.

Paris became not simply a site to generate wealth, but a place to practice conspicuous consumption. Its signs in stone were the vast new houses built in the Faubourg Saint-Honoré. George Rudé, drawing on the records of the chronicler of eighteenth-century Paris, Sebastien Mercier, estimates that ten thousand houses and one third of Paris had been built by the last decade of the Ancien Régime, and Mercier himself gives us stunning glimpses of the sweetness of life in the new Paris, of an ever more leisurely society passing long after-noons drinking tea, reading, and eating hothouse fruits in homes warm enough that people could wear their simple, healthy clothes, of evenings spent in one theatre after another, easily reached by coaches drawn along the increasingly well-paved streets.

To make this sweetness possible required ever greater numbers of craftsmen, servants, clerks, and construction workers; it did not require that they be well paid, and they were not. In service indus-tries like the garment trade, a free marketeer would expect wages to rise as luxury demand rose; instead, real wages fell from 1712 to 1789, because the labor supply grew even more rapidly than demand, making for lower wages in an expanding economic sector. In general, goods and services circulated freely as Paris grew steadily more prosperous throughout the century; this wealth which per-vaded the physical city did not permeate the lives of the mass of the people.

Inequality became a sensory provocation when people moved around the city. It is a social truism that feeling poor diminishes when people live only among those like themselves. And by looking at a map of mid-eighteenth-century Paris, the modern viewer might be tempted to draw two erroneous conclusions in this regard. One is that the knotted tangle of streets meant Parisians lived only in local little knots; the other is that the city consisted of clearly defined rich and poor *quartiers*. On the eve of the French Revolution, a walker through the city did traverse purely working-class quartiers, like the Faubourg Saint-Antoine on the eastern edge of the city; strolling through streets like the rue de Varenne on the Left Bank, however, which had filled with new private palaces *(hôtels particuliers)*, the urban traveller saw smears of miserable lodging houses in between the palaces, huts built on the edge of their gardens. These contained the mass of service workers and craftsmen supporting the mansions. Similar ramshackle buildings surrounded the King's Louvre Palace, all crevices of poverty in the cracks between wealth.

Perhaps the most striking place in Paris mixing rich and poor was the Palais-Royal, next to the Louvre. This home of the Orléans family had been developed as a great rectangular building enclosing a park. Open colonnades lined the building at ground level and the

Galeries du Palais-Royal, L. L. Boilly, 1809. *Musée de la Ville de Paris, Musée Carnavalet, Paris. Giraudon/Art Resource, N.Y.*

park was cut in half by a long wooden shed, the *galerie de bois*. Instead of sealing the park as a garden, the dukes of Orléans put the land to more economic use. Here was the Times Square of Ancien Régime Paris; the Palais-Royal housed innumerable cafés, brothels, and open-air gaming tables, as well as used-clothes shops, pawnshops, and shady stockbrokerages. A young man who had just lost his week's wages at the tables, or his health in the arms of a venereal lady of the night, had only to look up beyond the galerie de bois to the west wing of the Palais-Royal, where on the upper floor he might catch a glimpse of the Duke of Orléans at the tall windows, surveying the profitable squalor below.

Rather than isolated amongst themselves, many of the poor circulated in the physical, spatial presence of inaccessible wealth. The medieval markets of the city had depended, as we have seen, on inter-city trade. The local street became a focus of distribution in this trade, taking goods from outside the city and sending them outside. By 1776, when Smith published his economic theory, the markets of the city looked like neither those of the past nor those Smith described. The city now traded as part of a nation; its ports at Bordeaux or Le Havre lay at the geographic edge of the nation. Economic exchange in Paris derived its importance from being at the center of government power, an urban economy ever more dependent on serving an urban bureaucracy and the cultural trappings of that bureaucracy. Thus, when people felt the pangs of inequality in the city, they turned for relief not to the market, not to the circulation of labor and capital, but to the government as a source of stability. These desires surfaced around the issue of the price of bread.

In Paris, unskilled laborers earned around 30 sous a day, skilled laborers upward of 50. Half of this income went for bread, the basic food staple, which cost 8 or 9 sous for a four-pound loaf; a working-class family ate two or three loaves a day. Another fifth of the worker's income went for vegetables, scraps of meat and fat, and wine. Having used most of his or her money for food, the worker would then apportion the rest, calculated down to the last centime, for clothing, fuel, candles, and other necessities. George Rudé remarked that should the market price of bread, "as all too frequently happened, rise sharply to 12 or 15 (or even to 20) *sous* . . . the bulk of the wage-earners faced sudden disaster."[32]

Before and during the Revolution, riots occurred far more often over the cost of food than over wages. In the Flour War of 1775, for instance, near-starving people in Paris sought to make the price of flour correspond to their ability to pay, rather than to market value; as the historian Charles Tilly observes of an incident where the Parisians broke into the shop of a grain merchant, the poor, who were "mainly women and children . . . took care to leave untouched merchandise other than bread [and] at least some of them insisted on paying for their bread at two sous per pound, about three-fifths of the current market price."[33]

Because the market lay largely beyond the people's ability to control, their attention focused on the state, particularly in the case of bread. In principle, the state fixed the price of bread; in practice, this was then undone or ignored by the movements of the market. When people struck over the cost of food, they addressed a single, clear power—the government—and measured the success or failure of their actions by the rise and fall of a single number. Let us look at one important instance of how the actual movements of a crowd in search of bread led them to the doors of the state.

The great bread riot of October 1789 began in Paris on the morning of the 5th in two places, in the eastern working-class district of Saint-Antoine and in the food stalls at the city's center. The riot started when women refused to pay the price of bread for sale on that day, an elevated price of 16 sous because grain was in short supply. Other women then swelled the crowd in revolt, masses of Parisian women who had to calculate finely what they could afford to eat.

In the Saint-Antoine quarter the women forced the sacristan of the Church of Sainte-Marguerite to ring the church bell constantly, the "tocsin" peeling to signal an emergency which required the presence of the people in the streets. Word of mouth spread news of the food riot from Saint-Antoine to neighboring quarters, the crowds moving toward the town hall, the Hôtel de Ville, in the center of the city. Armed with pikes and bludgeons, the crowd of some six thousand stormed the Hôtel de Ville—but there was no one there who would answer their pleas. Only the King and his administrators, it was said, could respond, because the city was bankrupt. In the afternoon the crowd of women, now joined by men, swept through the city center, down the arterial route of the rue de Vaugirard toward Versailles, some ten thousand strong. "The momentous march of women to Versailles," the historian Joan Landes writes, came from "a long tradition of women's participation in popular protest, especially during subsistence crises."[34] They arrived at dusk, and made first for the Assembly hall, where their leader Maillard "quoted liberally from the new popular pamphlet *When Will We Have Bread?* ["Quand aurons-nous du pain?"], in which the authorities rather than the bakers were held responsible for the shortage."[35]

At dawn the crowd, which had camped out during the night, faced the guards of the Versailles Palace, killing two of the guards, cutting off their heads, and parading the heads on pikes. But the gates of the palace held fast; the crowd milled about, swelling in size as more people poured out to the royal suburb from Paris. At last, in the early afternoon of the 6th, the King and Queen appeared on a balcony in front of the crowd, greeted by the roar of people shouting, "To Paris!", and that evening the mob, now some sixty thousand, escorted the acquiescent monarchs back to the city in triumph. On the 7th, the King was shown barrels of flour putrid with lice, which were then dumped by the still active mob into the Seine.

The result of the riot begun on October 5 was two-fold; the authorities sought to strengthen their military might in the city, in order to curb future outbursts, and the price of bread was fixed at 12 sous. Moreover, the government guaranteed wheat supplies to the city from its own granaries, which contained wheat of good quality. An ethereal peace then descended over the city; Marie-Antoinette wrote to Mercy d'Argenteau, the Austrian ambassador,

> I talk to the people; to militiamen and to the market women, all of whom hold out their hands to me and I give them mine. Within the city I have been very well received. This morning the people asked us to stay. I told them that as far as the King and I were concerned, it depended on them whether we stayed, for we asked nothing better than that all hatred should stop. . . .[36]

At this moment, the Queen was not deceived in the sudden outburst in her favor. A popular market song expressed the women's belief that their desire for authority had been gratified:

> *To Versailles like bragging lads*
> *We brought with us all our guns*
> *We had to show though we were but women*
> *A courage that no one can reproach us for*
>
> *{Now} we won't have to go so far*
> *When we want to see our King*
> *We love him with a love without equal*
> *Since he's come to live in our Capital.*[37]

Thus the urban crowd moved toward a different destination than Adam Smith envisioned. The historian Lynn Hunt sees events such as this food riot demonstrating the very essence of a paternal relationship between the monarch and his "children," a relationship of trust, stability, and fixity.[38] Harvey's paradigm sought to equalize the importance of the individual parts within the body, to make these parts appear more interdependent through the motions of the blood. Adam Smith's vision of the market similarly focused on the equal importance and interdependence of all the actors in the market's movements, actors becoming ever more distinct through the division of labor. But the crowd moving forward in this bread riot was more than a collection of individuals exchanging among themselves. Just as it had group economic needs, its identity could not be compared to the identity of individuals. The very word "movement" took on a collective meaning, one which would be tested in the fire and the bloodshed of the Revolution.

CHAPTER NINE

The Body
Set Free

Boullée's Paris

At the height of the French Revolution, the most radical newspaper in Paris declared that there could be no real revolution if people did not feel it in their bodies. "Something which we must never tire of saying to the people," the paper maintained, "is that liberty, reason, truth are . . . not gods . . . they are parts of ourselves."[1] Yet when the French Revolution sought to bring the body to life on the streets of Paris, something quite unexpected happened. Often the crowds of citizens became apathetic. In part, the spectacles of violence numbed their senses; in part the revolutionary spaces created in the city often failed to arouse people. During a time of upheaval when we should least expect it, the moving crowds of the city frequently thus halted, fell silent, and dispersed.

These moments of crowd passivity failed to interest Gustave Le Bon, the most influential modern writer on crowds. Le Bon was cer-

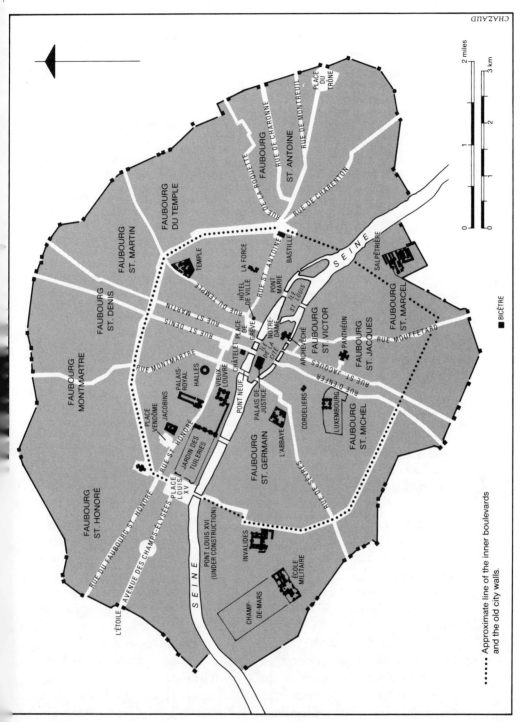

Map of Revolutionary Paris, ca. 1794.

···· Approximate line of the inner boulevards
and the old city walls.

■ BICÊTRE

2 miles

3 km

tain that movement on the streets of Paris brought revolutionary sensations vividly to life in the crowd. He believed the great bread riot described at the end of the last chapter continued as crowd behavior for the next four years. It is to Le Bon that we owe the concept of crowd psychology and behavior, as distinct from individual behavior, based on that vision of a collective body constantly alert, angry, and active. Le Bon believed that in the movement of such a crowd, people do things together they would never dream of doing alone. The sheer strength of numbers, he argued, makes people feel grandiose; each person succumbs to "a sentiment of invincible power which allows him to yield to instincts which, had he been alone, he would perforce have kept under restraint."[2] In isolation, a person "may be a cultivated individual; in a crowd, he is a barbarian—that is a creature acting by instinct."[3]

If, Le Bon said, this transformation occurs in any moving, densely packed group of human beings, the French Revolution marked a watershed in history; the Revolution legitimated the random violence of crowds as a political end in itself. Of the leaders of the Revolution, Le Bon declared:

> Taken separately, the men of the French Revolutionary Convention were enlightened citizens of peaceful habits. United in a crowd, they did not hesitate to give their adhesion to the most savage proposals, to guillotine individuals most clearly innocent, and . . . to decimate themselves.[4]

Le Bon's beliefs about crowds had great appeal to Freud, who drew heavily on them later in his own writings on the "primal horde" and other crowds throwing off the restraints of individuality. Le Bon's writings have proved more largely persuasive to modern readers, for they seem to explain how otherwise decent and humane individuals could actively participate in violent crimes, as in Nazi or Fascist mobs.

The other face of the Parisian crowd foreshadowed a different kind of modern experience. Modern forms of individual passivity and of insensitivity in urban space made their first, more collective, appearance on the streets of revolutionary Paris. The bread riots declared a need for collective crowd life which the Revolution did not fulfill.

1. FREEDOM IN BODY AND SPACE

The historian François Furet has observed that the Revolution "sought to restructure, by an act of imagination, wholeness to a society which lay in pieces."[5] The Revolution had to invent what "a citizen" looked like. But that imaginative invention of a new human being was a difficult act; the "citizen" had somehow to look like everyone, in a society which had etched social differences deeply into the way people dressed, gestured, smelled, and moved. Moreover, the "citizen" had somehow to convince all these people who gazed at the image that they recognized themselves but saw themselves reborn. The need to invent a universal figure, one historian has argued, meant that ideally the "citizen" would be a man, given the prejudices at the time about women's irrationality; the revolutionaries would search for a "neutral . . . subject; one capable of subjecting . . . individual passions and interests to the rule of reason. Only men's bodies fulfilled the ideal requirements of this contained form of subjectivity."[6] Even so ardent a feminist at the time as Olympe de Gouges viewed the emotional physiology of women as disposing them toward the emotion-charged, paternal order of the past, rather than toward the new machinery of the future.[7] Certainly the Revolution played out these prejudices in its imagination, just as it crushed by 1792 the organized activities of women who had, as in the food riot of 1789, helped fire up the society.

Yet among all the revolutionary emblems, the busts of Hercules, Cicero, Ajax, and Cato which littered the revolutionary landscape, the people were most drawn to the image of an ideal citizen called "Marianne." Marianne's image appeared everywhere—in newspaper engravings, on coins, in public statues set up to replace the busts of kings, popes, and aristocrats. Her image compelled the popular imagination because she gave a new, *collective* meaning to motion, flow, and change within the human body, flowing and freeing movement now nurturing a new kind of life.

Marianne's breasts

The Revolution modelled Marianne's face as that of a young Greek goddess, with a straight nose, a high brow, and well-formed chin; her body tended to the fuller domestic form of a young mother. Sometimes Marianne appeared dressed in ancient flowing robes

La Jolie sans Culotte armée en Guerre.

An armed female *sans-culotte* in Paris. Anonymous etching with hand coloring, ca. 1792.

which clung to her breasts and thighs; sometimes the Revolution dressed her in contemporary clothes, but with her breasts bared. The revolutionary painter Clement depicted the goddess this latter way in 1792, Marianne's breasts firm and full, her nipples articulate; he titled this version of Marianne "Republican France, opening her

Marianne. Etching of painting by Clement, 1792. *Musée Carnavalet, Paris, photo Edimedia.*

bosom to all the French." Whether in sheer robes or with her body exposed, Marianne stood forth giving not the slightest hint of a lascivious woman revealing herself, in part because the breast appeared by the late Enlightenment as much a virtuous as an erogenous zone of the body.

The exposed breast revealed the nurturing powers of women when breast feeding. In Clement's painting, Marianne's full breasts were meant for all the French to nurse at, an image of revolutionary nourishment underlined in the painting by an odd ornament: a loop of ribbon around her neck falls between her breasts and holds below them a level, to signify that all French people have equal access to her bosom. Clement's painting shows the most basic appeal made by the symbol of Marianne: equal care for all.

The veneration of a maternal figure recalled the cult and adoration of the Virgin Mary; several commentators have remarked on the very similarity of the revolutionary and religious names. Yet if Marianne drew on the weight of popular emotion and understanding contained in the love of Mary, breast feeding meant something quite historically specific to her viewers.

By the Revolution, breast feeding had become a complicated experience for women. Until the eighteenth century all but the poorest women put their infants out to wet nurses, many of whom were indifferent to their charges. People earlier in the Ancien Régime often neglected infants and young children; even in wealthy households children dressed in rags and ate scraps left over from the servants' meals. Rather than willful cruelty, this neglect of the young partly reflected the harsh biological realities of an age in which infant mortality was very high; an affectionate mother would likely be in a constant state of mourning.

Haltingly and unevenly, though, the family became focused on its children. Changes in public health meant by the 1730s that rates of infant mortality began to fall, particularly in cities. And by the 1730s mothers, particularly the broad spectrum of mothers in the middle ranks of society, marked a new affectionate relation to their infants by breast-feeding them. Rousseau's *Emile* (1762) helped define this maternal ideal through Sophie, central moral character in his story. Sophie's flowing breasts, Rousseau wrote, were proof of her virtue. Yet, Rousseau declared, "We men could subsist more easily without women than they could without us . . . they are dependant on our feelings, on the price we place on their merit, and on the opinion we have of their charms and of their virtues."[8] The maternal revolution confined women within the domestic sphere, as Mary Wollstonecraft and other admirers of Rousseau were soon to note; at liberty to love her children, Sophie yet lacked the freedom of a citizen. "The Republic of Virtue," the critic Peter Brooks observes, "did not conceive of women occupying public space; female virtue was domestic, private, unassuming."[9] And Marianne's task was not quite to set Sophie free.

When Marianne's life-giving virtues became a political icon, her body seemed open to adults as well as children, a maternal body open to men. In principle, her body served as a political metaphor uniting society's vast variety of unlike human beings within her frame. Yet the Revolution used her in fact as a metonymic device: by looking at her image the Revolution saw, as in a magic mirror, changing reflections of itself rather than a single image.

Marianne's generous, flowing, and productive female body first of all served to mark off the virtuous present from the evils of the Ancien Régime. Her image served as a contrast to the pleasure-seeking, supposedly sexually insatiable bodies of the Revolution's enemies. Even in the 1780s, popular pornography chose Louis XVI's queen as a subject for scandal, imputing to Marie-Antoinette lesbian desires and liaisons to her ladies-in-waiting, and popular doggerel attacked her for lacking maternal feeling. In the Revolution, these attacks grew sharper. Shortly before her condemnation to death, reports swept Paris that Marie-Antoinette and one of her ladies-in-waiting, in the course of a lesbian affair, kept the Queen's eight-year-old son with them in bed at night and taught the young prince to masturbate while the women made love. In the mid-eighteenth century, doctors like Tissot had published, in the name of medical science, explicit accounts of the supposedly degenerative effects of masturbation on the body, such as loss of sight and weakness of the bones.[10] For the sake of illicit pleasure, Marie-Antoinette—so the accusations ran—sacrificed her own son's health. Marie-Antoinette appeared in revolutionary engravings as nearly flat-chested in contrast to Marianne's breasts which were bursting with milk. The difference in their breasts underlined popular accusations that the pleasure-seeking Queen was immature and puerile, a spoiled adolescent, while Marianne appeared as an adult giving pleasure which did not cause pain to others.

Another reflection of Marianne softened the Revolution's sorrows. In this guise the Revolution endowed her with no speech; her nurturance was a silent, unconditional love. She replaced a King whose paternal care for his subjects supposed command and obedience. The revolutionary state which sent citizens to death abroad and condemned them to death at home had need of her thus, to represent the state as a mother. As the French fought foreign wars while fighting one another, the numbers of orphaned and abandoned babies rose rapidly in the nation. Traditionally, convents had cared for such infants, but the Revolution had closed the convents. Mari-

Marie-Antoinette, her female lover, and her son, in an engraving from the 1795 edition of the marquis de Sade's *La Philosophie dans le boudoir*.

anne's image symbolized the revolutionary state's guarantee that it would care for these infants as a matter of patriotic duty. Children in need of breast feeding were rebaptized, as the historian Olwen Hufton observes, "under the generic heading *'enfants de la patrie'* ['children of the nation'] and regarded as a precious human resource of potential soldiers and mothers."[11] The Revolution in turn elevated wet nurses to the title *citoyennes précieuses* ("precious citizens").

Revolutions are not notably amusing events, but the figure of Marianne permitted the release of a certain Gallic wit. A remarkable anonymous engraving of Marianne shows her equipped with angel's wings, flying over the rue de Panthéon; with one hand she holds a trumpet to her lips, with the other she holds a trumpet stuck into her anus, at once blowing and farting clarion calls to liberty.[12] (Could one imagine George Washington so fully engaged?) Humor aided citizens when, in looking around themselves, at one another, they asked, "What does fraternity look like?"

The lactating breast of Marianne most of all suggested that fraternity was a sensate bodily experience rather than an abstraction. A contemporary pamphlet declared: the "nipple does not flow freely until it feels the lips of a baby in need; in just the same way, those who are the guardians of the nation can give nothing without the kiss of the people; the incorruptible milk of the Revolution then gives the people life."[13] The act of breast feeding became in the revolutionary broadsheet an image of *mutual* arousal—between mother and child, government and the people, citizens among themselves. And the image of the "incorruptible milk" of the people tinged fraternity with a family feeling stronger than the associations of rational mutual interest supposed by Whigs or Physiocrats, who saw at best in the first months of the Revolution an opportunity to strengthen the workings of the free market.

Underlying all these reflections is the image of a body full of inner fluid which overflows. In this collective image of a new citizen, milk has replaced the blood of older Harveyean imagery, lactation has replaced respiration—but free movement and circulation remain the principles of life. The image conveyed the sheer surfeit of circulation. And just as the Harveyean individual needed a space in which to move, so did Marianne. One of the great dramas of the French Revolution lay there: if the Revolution could see Marianne, it could not succeed in placing her. The Revolution searched for spaces in which citizens could express their freedom, spaces in the city which would bring Marianne's virtues of liberty, equality, and fraternity to life; yet freedom as conceived in space conflicted with freedom conceived in the body.

The volume of liberty

Sheer volume defined the revolutionary imagination of freedom in space, volume without obstruction, without limits, a space in which everything was "transparent," in the words of the critic Jean Starobinski, nothing hidden.[14] The revolutionaries put their imagination of free space into practice in 1791, when the town council of Paris began to chop down trees and pave over the gardens of the Place Louis XV, hollowing out the land to make it an open, emptying volume. Competing designs for the center of the city all kept it empty of vegetation and other obstructions, a vast, hard-surfaced plaza. In a plan by Wailly for the remaking of the old Place Louis XV in the center of Paris (rebaptized the Place de la Révolution during the period when it served as the home of the guillotine), the town square was to be regularized by buildings on four sides to form an enormous empty central space, without roads or paths through it. In another plan, Bernard Poyet stripped away from the bridges spanning the Seine River and leading to the square all the encrusted little shacks which had obstructed entrance and exit to the square.[15] Elsewhere in the city, as on the Champ de Mars, revolutionary planners sought to create open volumes denuded of all natural hindrances to movement and sight.

These empty volumes were meant to provide a home for Marianne's freely giving body. In civic festivals she became a monumental figure in the open air, no longer hidden in church naves as were statues of the Virgin; the rituals devised to take place around statues of Marianne spoke of mutual openness and transparence, the fraternity of those who have nothing to hide. Moreover, the volume of liberty consummated Enlightened beliefs in the freedom of movement; sheer open space was a logical next step from streets freed of obstructions to movement, central squares conceived as unclogged, freely breathing lungs.

And yet, logical as is the connection in the abstract between a giving, freely moving body and empty space, it would be strange more concretely to imagine a woman nursing an infant in the midst of emptiness, surrounded by no other signs of life. That strangeness the Parisians during the Revolution began to see in fact on the streets of the city.

Power as well as idealism explains the volumes of liberty, for they were spaces permitting maximum police surveillance of a crowd. Yet revolutionary vision, as François Furet speaks of it, also sought for this dissonance, the dissonance of articulating a new human order in emptiness. No one more exemplified the faith in the liberating powers of open space than the architect Etienne-Louis Boullée, who was born in Paris in 1728 and lived there to his death to 1799. Personally modest, comfortable with the honors accorded him by the Ancien Régime (he was made a member of the Académie in 1780), reform-minded but not bloody-minded during the Revolution, Boullée epitomized the civilized, Enlightened adult. Boullée's was mostly a paper architecture, an architecture tied closely to his work as a critic and thinker. His writings connected the body to the design of space as explicitly as did Vitruvius, and Boullée's architectural projects harkened back to classical Roman works like the Pantheon.

Yet for all his awareness of the past, Boullée was truly a man of his time, truly a revolutionary of space. In an odd way, the furies of power paid tribute to him for this vision: on April 8, 1794, indeed, he was near arrest, threatened by the self-contradictory accusations which mobilized the Terror, charged in a notice posted all over Paris with being one of the "madmen of architecture," who "hates artists" and is a social parasite, yet who also makes "seductive proposals."[16] His seductive proposals in particular rendered great volumes enclosed by severely disciplined walls and windows as emblems of liberty.

Boullée's most famous project before the Revolution was a monument to be dedicated to Isaac Newton, a vast building shaped around a spherical chamber; the chamber meant to serve, like a modern planetarium, as an image of the heavens. In imagining this great spherical chamber, Boullée wrote, he wished to evoke the majestic emptiness of nature which he believed Newton had discovered. Boullée's planetarium would do so by making use of a novel system of lighting: "The lighting of this monument, which should resemble that on a clear night, is provided by the planets and the stars that decorate the vault of the sky." To accomplish this effect, he proposed that the planetarium's dome would be pierced by "funnel-like openings. . . . The daylight outside filters through these apertures into the gloom of the interior and outlines all the objects in the vault with bright, sparkling light."[17] The viewer enters the building from an outside passage far below the sphere, then walks up steps to enter at the very bottom of the chamber; having glimpsed the heavens, the

Etienne-Louis Boullée, Newton's Cenotaph, interior view, by night, 1784.

viewer descends steps and files out at the other side of the building. "We see only a continuous surface which has neither beginning nor end," he wrote "and the more we look at it, the larger it appears."[18]

Hadrian's Pantheon, which the French architect took as the model for his planetarium, almost compulsively oriented the viewer within it. Looking up into the artificial heavens, the viewer in Boullée's planetarium would have no sense of his or her own place on earth. There are no internal designs to orient the body; more, in Boullée's sectional drawings for Newton's Tomb, the human beings are nearly invisible within the immensity of the sphere: the interior sphere is thirty-six times higher than the mere human specks drawn at the base. As in the heavens outside, unbounded space inside is to become an experience in itself.

In 1793, Boullée designed—again on paper—perhaps his most radical project, a "Temple to Nature and Reason." Once more he made use of the sphere, scooping out raw ground to form the bottom half of the sphere, the half of "Nature," answered by the top half, an architectural dome perfectly smooth and crisp, the half of "Reason." People who enter this temple walk round a colonnade in the middle where earth and architecture, Nature and Reason, meet. As one looks up into the dome of Reason, all one sees is a smooth, feature-less surface free of any particularity. As one looks below, one sees

Etienne-Louis Boullée, Temple to Nature and Reason, ca. 1793.

the answering but rocky crater of earth. It is impossible to climb down to this Nature from the colonnade, and no worshipper at this shrine of Nature would wish to touch the earth: Boullée drew the rocky crater as rough and slashed in the center by a fissure, extending down into blackness, the fissure like a knife slash. There is no foothold here, on the ground, for man or woman. Human beings have no place in this terrifying temple devoted to the union of concepts.

In Boullée's own writings on urban design, he argued that streets should have the same properties of space as his planetarium and temple, with neither beginning nor end. "By extending the sweep of an avenue so that its end is out of sight," he argued, "the laws of optics and the effects of perspective give an impression of immensity."[19] Sheer volume: space free of the twisted streets and irrational accretions to buildings which had accumulated over the centuries, space free of tangible signs of human damage in the past. As Boullée declared, "The architect should study the theory of volumes and analyze them, at the same time seeking to understand their properties, the powers they have on our senses, their similarities to the human organism."[20]

The historian Anthony Vidler calls designs such as these the "architectural uncanny," by which he means designs which arouse feelings of sublime grandeur along with a sense of personal unease and disturbance. The term derives from Hegel's writings on architecture, and the word Hegel uses in German is *unheimlich,* which can also mean "undomestic."[21] And this is why the monuments to Newton or to Reason and Nature seem so ill-suited as homes for Marianne, whose place is the home, who symbolizes a comforting unity between family and state. Against the desire for connection, for maternity-fraternity embodied in Marianne, here was another revolutionary desire, for a chance to start over with a fresh, blank slate, which means uprooting the past, leaving home. The vision of fraternity in human relations expressed itself as flesh touching flesh; the vision of freedom in space and time expressed itself as empty volume.

Perhaps the dream of freely connecting to other people may always conflict with the dream of starting over again fresh and unencumbered. But the French Revolution showed something more particular about the result of these conflicting principles of liberty, something more unexpected. Rather than the nightmare of a mass of bodies running wild together in a space without boundaries, as Le Bon feared, the Revolution showed how crowds of citizens became increasingly pacified in the great open volumes where the Revolution staged its most important public events. The space of liberty pacified the revolutionary body.

2. DEAD SPACE

"The French Revolution was caught in the throes of destroying one civilization before creating a new one."[22] That act of destruction most infamously engaged the human body in the operations of the guillotine. The grim business of killing people with the guillotine formed part of what the art critic Linda Nochlin has called "revolutionary dismemberment," which meant the belief that figures of the past had to be killed in a certain way, the enemies of the Revolution literally taken apart, so that their deaths became a lesson. Rather than arouse the kind of blood lust depicted by Le Bon, the space in which this lesson was taught numbed the crowds who witnessed the killings.

The guillotine is a simple machine. It consists of a large, heavy blade which moves up and down between two wooden channels; the executioner raises the blade up three yards or so by a rope attached to a winch, and when the executioner lets go of the rope, the blade hurtles between the channels, slicing through the neck of the victim

Robespierre Guillotining the Executioner After Having Guillotined All the French, anonymous etching, ca. 1793.

strapped to a bench at the base of the blade. Although the guillotine became known as the "national razor" {*rasoir national*} in the French Revolution, it kills as much by the force of the blade snapping the neck in two as by the sharpness of the blade.

Dr. Joseph-Ignace Guillotin, who was born in 1738 and lived until 1814, did not in fact invent the guillotine. Machines to chop off people's heads by the fall of a heavy blade existed in the Renaissance; "the Maiden" was one such device, built in Scotland in 1564. Lucas Cranach's *The Martyrdom of St. Matthew* shows the saint beheaded by a device almost identical to the "national razor." But the Ancien Régime rarely used decapitation devices, since they killed too quickly; they were thought to deprive a public execution of the rituals required for punishment. The public gathered in large crowds to witness spectacles of pain in all towns and cities of the Ancien Régime; indeed, public executions often took a festive spirit, as they were one of the few holidays off the religious calendar. Madame de Sévigné describes such a jaunt into Paris from Versailles, in order to see three criminals gutted, then hung; the outing offered a breathing space from her court duties.

Like Roman crucifixions, Christian executions sought to dramatize the powers of the state to inflict pain. Killing machines like the wheel or the rack delayed death as long as possible in order that the public could see the victim's muscles ripping apart and hear the victim's screams. Unlike crucifixions, the Christian authorities prolonging pain sought to force the victim to confess the enormity of his or her sins before he or she was little more than a piece of meat; torture had a religious and in a certain way charitable purpose, affording the criminal a last chance in the rite of confessing sin to be spared the depths of Hell.

Dr. Guillotin rejected these claims. He pointed out that most criminals became unconscious or deranged after only one or two turns of the wheel, and so were incapable of choosing to repent. Moreover, he thought that even the most abject criminal had certain natural bodily rights that the law could not violate. Based on a great Enlightenment treatise on prisons, Beccaria's *Of Crimes and Punishments,* Dr. Guillotin argued that when the state inflicts the death penalty, it must show the maximum respect for the body it is about to destroy; it must contrive a swift death, free of useless pain. By doing so, the state will show itself superior to a common murderer.

Guillotin's aims, then, were entirely humanitarian. Moreover, he

thought he had freed death from the irrationalities of Christian rituals like the confession of sin. Dr. Guillotin put forward his proposal
for an Enlightened ritual-free death early in the Revolution, in
December 1789, but the National Assembly did not authorize the
use of his machine until March 1792. A month later a common-law
criminal died under the blade, and on August 21, 1792, the machine
was first put to political use, decapitating the royalist Collenot
d'Augrement.

Because the guillotine aimed to free punishment from religious
ritual, the first enthusiasts for the guillotine thought it should be
used in neutral space, outside the city. An engraving of early 1792
showed this neutral event occurring in an anonymous, wooded place,
and the explanation which accompanies it emphasizes that "the
machine will be surrounded by barriers to prevent the people
approaching."[23] In the guillotine's first applications, the authorities
sought to render punishment invisible. When the guillotine moved
back into the city, however, the display of death feared by Dr. Guillotin returned with a vengeance.

The long procession from jail to the place of execution exposed a
condemned person to the gaze of the city at large. The procession
usually moved slowly from the city jail down a main street, a procession lasting some two hours, the crowds lined ten or twelve deep
along the street. Such a parade of condemned prisoners formed a
traditional element of executions in the Ancien Régime; the spectators participated in the procession, as they had in earlier execution
rites or religious processions through the city. People lining the
street often shouted out abuse or words of encouragement, and
those in the carts responded. As the tumbrels slowly inched forward,
the condemned might in turn harangue the crowds. The character of
the crowds also might alter along the route, a hostile crowd modulating into a friendly one as the tumbrel passed down the street, often
the same people following the cart of the condemned changing their
views. The procession to the guillotine comes the closest in the Revolution to exemplifying that vivid and spontaneous crowd life which
the French call the "carnavalesque."

Once arrived at the place of execution, this active crowd life suddenly ceased. The traditional form of ritualized punishment ended
at the foot of the guillotine. Now the condemned body entered a
space cleared of obstacles, an empty volume.

Dr. Guillotin's machine was first located in the Place de Grève, a medium-sized square on the Right Bank which could accommodate crowds of two to three thousand curious to see common criminals die the new kind of death. In August 1792, soon after the political executions began, the town authorities moved the guillotine to a larger open space, more centrally located and politically significant in the city, the Place du Carrousel; enclosed by the outer wings of the palace of the Louvre, this site accommodated between twelve and twenty thousand people at important executions. For the execution of Louis XVI himself, the guillotine was moved once again to a larger space at the other end of the Tuileries Gardens and in the very center of the city. This plaza, the old Place Louis XV, was renamed the Place de la Révolution—and we know it today as the Place de la Concorde. The guillotine thus moved to larger urban volumes as it struck deeper into the heart of the old state.

None of the three public spaces for the guillotine was sloped like the ancient Pnyx in order to increase visibility through raked sightlines. The scaffold platform was not high enough in any of the three town squares to make the events occurring on it visible at more than 100 feet away; this barely sufficed in the Place de Grève, but not in the two larger spaces. In political executions, moreover, rows of troops filled the space immediately surrounding the scaffold; in important executions, as many as five thousand guarded the guillotine. In these ways the larger open spaces broke both visceral and visual contact between the condemned and the crowd.

The machine itself also made the act of dying no longer a visible event. The blade of the guillotine descended so fast that one moment one saw a living human strapped beneath the blade, the next moment an inert corpse. Only the gush of blood out of the victim's neck stem intervened, but this gush of blood lasted but a moment, and then the blood began to drain slowly, like a leaking pipe, out of the body through the wound. Here is how Madame Roland's body looked the moment after the blade fell:

> When the blade had cut off her head, two huge jets of blood shot forth from the mutilated trunk, a thing not often seen: usually the head that fell was pale, and the blood, which the emotion of that terrible instant had driven back towards the heart, came forth rather feebly, drop by drop.[24]

Because the technology of death changed, the actors in the spectacle of death no longer played the roles they had assumed in earlier executions. Newspaper accounts "refer to neither the personality of the condemned man nor to the person of the executioner; the emphasis was now on the machine itself."[25] The torturer-executioner in the Ancien Régime had been like a master of ceremonies, revealing to the crowd new tricks and responding to its pleas for a hot iron or a turn of the wheel. Now the executioner had only one small, physically insignificant act to perform, that of letting go of the rope which held the blade. Only a few executions in the Revolution gave the executioner, and the crowd watching, more active roles. Hébert's execution was such an exceptional death. The people demanded that the blade be lowered just above the traitor's neck, so that he could feel the blood dripping off the iron from a previous execution; while he screamed out in terror, the massive crowd in the Place du Carrousel waved their hats and chanted "Long live the Republic!" Such deaths in which executioner and crowd actively participated were considered indecent lapses of revolutionary discipline, and rarely repeated.

The victim was seldom allowed to make a speech to the crowd before being strapped to the bench beneath the blade; the authorities lived in fear of just the dramatic scenes of noble death conjured by Charles Dickens in *A Tale of Two Cities* and countless royalist pamphlets, noble last words which could turn the crowd against the authorities. In fact, the authorities had less to fear than they imagined, the volume of space serving the neutrality of death by machine. When a victim burst out, the mass of citizens might see a gesture, but the only people who usually could hear were guards. Strapped immobile onto the guillotine, face down, neck shaved so that the blade could cleave cleanly through the skin, the victim did not move, did not see death coming, and felt no pain; Guillotin's "humane death" created passive bodies at this supreme moment. Just as the executioner did nothing more than slightly release the pressure of his hand to kill, the condemned had simply to lie still to die.

Louis XVI was guillotined on January 21, 1793, in the Place de la Révolution. Bishop Bossuet had preached before the King's grandfather a sermon in 1662 in which Bossuet declared, "even if you [the King] die, your authority never dies. . . . The man dies, it is true, but the King, we say, never dies."[26] Now the authorities, by killing the King, sought to change this; with his death would come their own sovereignty. Despite the immense complexities which surrounded this fatal step, certain facts about the manner of his death are clear. For one, the procession to the guillotine, though the King was taken in a tumbrel, was quite unlike the carnavalesque events preceding other executions. An immense military guard surrounded the cart; moreover along his route through the city, Louis XVI faced an eerily silent crowd. This silence has been taken by revolutionary interpreters as a mark of the respect of the people for the change of sovereignty; royalist interpreters thought the crowd's silence was the first sign of popular remorse. The historian Lynn Hunt believes the crowd experienced both: "As revolutionaries cut themselves adrift from the moorings of patriarchal conceptions of authority, they faced a dichotomous, highly charged set of feelings: on the one hand, there was the exhilaration of a new era; on the other, a dark sense of foreboding about the future."[27] There was a third element as well. To watch a king on his way to death yet make no response of one's own avoids a sentiment of responsibility; one was present but could not be held accountable.

To mark the fact that Louis Capet was no longer King of the French, the instruments used to kill him in the Place de la Révolution were the same as the instruments used for other executions—

The execution of Louis XVI, 21 January 1793. Contemporary etching. *Musée Carnavalet, Paris. Photo Edimedia.*

the same machine, the same blade, a blade which had not even been wiped clean since its last use. Mechanical repetition equalizes; Louis Capet would die like anyone else. However, those who had condemned the King to death were not so naive as to believe that this mechanical symbol alone would carry the crowd. Many of the organizers of the execution feared that the King's severed head might talk, that indeed perhaps the King never dies. They feared more rationally that he might speak too movingly on the scaffold before he died. Thus they sought to neutralize as completely as possible the circumstances of his dying. An immense phalanx of soldiers surrounded the crowd, facing inward toward the scaffold rather than outward toward the crowd; there were at least fifteen thousand soldiers arrayed in this way. The soldiers served as insulation; more than 300 yards thick, this lining of soldiers made it impossible for the crowd beyond to hear anything Louis XVI said, and impossible to see any details of his face or body. "Contemporary engravings all make it clear that the crowd would indeed have had grave difficulties in seeing anything of the execution."[28]

The lack of ceremony in the actual event, which seems otherwise so curious, comes from the same desire for neutrality. Not one of the King's killers appeared on the scaffold with him, or spoke to the crowd; no one stood forth as a master of ceremonies. Like most other political prisoners, the King was denied the use of the scaffold as a stage; whatever last words he uttered were audible only to the guards around him at the scaffold's base. Sanson performed the ultimate gesture, showing Louis Capet's head to the crowd, but the thick insulating band of soldiers meant few people could see the head. Thus did the King's destroyers protect themselves during the execution by seeming only passively involved, part of the machinery of circumstance.

Eyewitness records of the Revolution's violent events, Dorinda Outram observes, "often emphasize crowd apathy"; in the Terror, an "image of the ghoulish execution crowd" misses the mark while "depictions of passive crowds are more likely to approach the truth."[29] Death as a non-event, death which comes to a passive body, the industrial production of death, death in emptiness: these are the physical and spatial associations which surrounded the killing of the King and of thousands of others.

The working of the guillotine will make sense to anyone who has dealt with a state bureaucracy. Neutrality allows power to operate without responsibility. Empty volume was a fitting space for the evasive operation of power. To the extent revolutionary crowds suffered from the mixed feelings which Lynn Hunt evokes, the empty spaces conceived by Boullée and his colleagues also served a purpose. In them, the crowd was freed from responsibility; the space lifted the visceral burden of engagement. The crowd became a collective voyeur.

But the Revolution was not just another machine of power; it sought to create a new citizen. The dilemma faced by those fired by revolutionary passion was how to fill an empty volume with human value. In creating new revolutionary rituals and festivals, the organizers of the Revolution attempted to fill this void in the city.

3. FESTIVAL BODIES

The Parisian streets swelled continually with popular demonstrations in the early years of the Revolution. In "masquerades," for instance, groups of people dressed up as priests or aristocrats, using stolen clothing, parading around on donkeys and making fun of their previous rulers. The street also served as the public space of the *sans-culottes,* poor, thin men without breeches, women dressed in tattered muslin shifts—revolutionary bodies without artifice. As the Revolution progressed, masquerades became threatening to those at the top of the revolutionary heap; the regime sought to discipline the street. The sans-culottes, too, wanted more than reflections of themselves in revolt; they who had known only suffering and denial in the past needed to see what a revolutionary looked like when the Revolution was consummated.

Successive revolutionary regimes thus sought to create formal festivals which choreographed the proper dress, gesture, and behavior of a crowd of citizens, enacting abstract ideas in the human body. Yet the French festivals of citizenship came to be caught in the same trap as the purges of enemies; the rituals often ended by pacifying and neutralizing the bodies of the citizens.

Resistance banished

It was in the second year of the Revolution that the organizers of revolutionary festivals began systematically to explore open sites in

Anti-religious parade during the Revolution. Watercolor by Béricourt, ca. 1790.

the city for these activities. The historian Mona Ozouf ties this impulse with the wave of feeling sweeping the city in 1790 that the Revolution needed "emancipation from religious influence."[30] While the Revolution from its second year took aim at the machinery of established religion, artists like David and Quatremère de Quincy rather than priests took charge of civic ritual. Many older religious rituals nevertheless continued under new guises and names; for instance, scenarios of the Passion plays were replaced by the street theatre in which a representative of the people took the role of the risen Jesus, and members of the new ruling elite substituted for the Apostles.

Two massive crowd festivals organized at the height of the Revolution in the spring of 1792 show how these spectacles made use of the geography of Paris. The Festival of Châteauvieux occurred on April 15, 1792; the Festival of Simonneau, meant as a response, took place on June 3, 1792. The Festival of Châteauvieux in Paris "was intended to honor . . . the Swiss of Châteauvieux, who mutinied in

August 1790 and were rescued from the galleys," Mona Ozouf
writes; it was "a rehabilitation of rioters, if not a glorification of
riots," whereas the Festival of Simonneau "was intended to honor
the mayor of Etampes, killed in a people's riot while upholding the
law on foodstuffs: a glorification, this time, of the victim of riot."[31]
Châteauvieux was produced by the revolutionary artist Jacques-
Louis David, Simonneau by the architectural designer and writer
Quatremère de Quincy. The volume of liberty in both played a deadening role.

David's festival began at 10:00 A.M. in the same quarter, Saint-
Antoine, where the great food riot of 1790 had started. The route
chosen moved from the working-class district on the eastern edge of
the city westward across Paris to the destination of the festival, the
great open space of the Champ de Mars. As in a religious festival,
David marked out "stations," or symbolic pausing points: the first
major station was the Bastille, where the crowd dedicated a statue of
Liberty; the second station was the Hôtel de Ville, where leading
politicians like Danton and Robespierre joined the people; the third
station was the Place de la Révolution in the center of the city. Here
the stage designer blindfolded the statue of Louis XV which dominated the square, and gave it a red Phrygian cap to wear; this symbol-

The Festival of Châteauvieux, 15 April 1792. Contemporary engraving
by Berthault.

ized that royal justice ought to be impartial and that the King wore the new garment of French citizenship. The crowd of twenty to thirty thousand made its final station in the Champ de Mars at dusk, twelve hours after it had set out.

To encourage participation, David hit upon an inspired symbol: "it was a noteworthy fact that marshals of the festival, poetically armed with sheaves of wheat instead of riot sticks, took the place of the public police."[32] The symbolism of grain reversed the symbolism of the foot riots: here grain was ceremonially present, a symbol of plenty rather than scarcity. The unthreatening, life-giving sheaves of wheat encouraged people along the route to think there was no disciplinary barrier among themselves; the newspaper *Révolutions de Paris* observed that while "the chain of the procession broke many times . . . the onlookers soon filled up the gaps: everybody wanted to take part in the festival. . . ."[33]

The crowd moved amiably but without much sense of what it was doing; this walking mass could see few of the costumes and ceremonial floats David had created. This confusion in the streets David foresaw and tried to rectify at the climactic station of the festival in the Champ de Mars. In the wide-open field of sixteen acres, he ranged people in massive semicircular bands, six to seven thousand to a band, now imposing form on the crowd by keeping bands of empty space between each half-ring of people. A ceremony consisting of a few simple acts was meant to consummate an entire day. A politician lit a bonfire on the Altar of the Fatherland, to cleanse by fire the impurity of unjust imprisonment in the galleys; the crowd sang a hymn to Liberty, composed for the event by the musician Gossec and the lyricist M.-J. Chenier. Finally, according to another contemporary journal, *Les Annales Patriotiques,* the people danced around the altar to celebrate "patriotic happiness, perfect equality, and civic fraternity."[34]

The scenario did not work out as planned. Out in the open air of the Champ de Mars, the words and tunes of the revolutionary song composed for that day did not carry very far. David intended the massive bands of people to dance around the altar, but only those close up heard the command to dance and knew what to do. Participants spoke of their great confusion in trying to behave as citizens. "I cannot say how dancing on the Champ de Mars made me a better citizen," one declared; "we were bewildered," said another, "and so soon made our way to a tavern."[35] To be sure, the very peacefulness of the demonstration affirmed the solidarity of the people. But the substance of this festival mattered to David and other revolutionary designers. They wanted to train the crowd of bodies, knowing spontaneous eruptions of the people could threaten the revolutionary order as much as the Ancien Régime, and its scenario failed at the end.

The streets bore, in such ceremonies, the most evident echoes of the past: the procession of the damned, the stations of the saints-day parades and the like. More, the street was a place whose very diversities posed obstacles to union, its economic purposes not wiped away, its decayed houses not disappearing from sight, by the parade of a new order. In an empty space, by contrast, it seemed possible to start over; the ceremonies conducted in emptiness had nothing intervening, in the historian Joan Scott's view, between the bodily gesture and its political referent, nothing in the way between sign and symbol.[36]

And yet that very erasure of the street seemed to pacify the body. A young boy at a similar event on the Champ de Mars a few months later put David's problem simply and starkly:

> he saw many people up on the altar of the fatherland; that he heard the words "King" and "National Assembly" spoken, but he didn't understand what was said about them . . . that, in the evening, he heard it said that the red flag would arrive, that he looked around to flee; that he noticed that on the altar of the fatherland they were saying that good citizens had to remain there. . . .[37]

Nothing stood in David's way: the great festival reached its consummation out in the open, in unobstructed space, in a pure volume. At that denouement, confusion and apathy reigned.

Quatremère de Quincy designed his counterfestival of Simonneau as a display of legal authority and stability which would cow people into more disciplined behavior. Instead of crowd marshals armed with sheaves of wheat, Quatremère de Quincy armed his marshals with rifles and bayonets. Like David, he was anything but indifferent to the crowd; the whole point of staging this spectacle was to make an impression on the people of Paris. The organizers wanted people to feel that a new regime was in charge, that the doors of the state had closed on anarchy. Quatremère de Quincy drew upon the same scenario David had used: the festival followed the same route, begin-

The Festival of Simonneau, 3 June 1792. Contemporary engraving by Berthault.

ning in the eastern parts of the city, with stations at the Bastille, then the Hôtel de Ville, the Place de la Révolution, a consummation on the Champ de Mars with a simple piece of stage business meant to bind the participants together, the crowd crowning Simonneau's bust with a wreath of laurel. Nature did help out at this moment, when the heavens suddenly parted, dramatic flashes of lightning illuminated the crowd as they presented arms to the statue, and artillery boomed amidst the thunder. Yet this event too fell apart. The participating group almost immediately disintegrated, not knowing what to do or to say next to one another. Quatremère de Quincy had thought the sheer volume of the open space would arouse the public's sense of the majesty of the law. And the public had watched listlessly this show of unity and strength on the field.

These festivals made clear a disturbing lesson about freedom. Freedom which seeks to overcome resistance, to abolish obstacles, to start afresh with a blank slate—freedom conceived like a pure, transparent volume—dulls the body. It is an anesthetic. Freedom which arouses the body does so by accepting impurity, difficulty, and obstruction as part of the very experience of liberty. The festivals of the French Revolution mark a point in Western civilization where this visceral experience of freedom was dispelled in the name of a mechanics of movement—the ability to move anywhere, to move without obstruction, to circulate freely, a freedom greatest in an empty volume. That mechanics of movement has invaded a wide swath of modern experience—experience which treats social, environmental, or personal resistance, with its concomitant frustrations, as somehow unfair and unjust. Ease, comfort, "user-friendliness" in human relations come to appear as guarantees of individual freedom of action. However, resistance is a fundamental and necessary experience for the human body: through feeling resistance, the body is roused to take note of the world in which it lives. This is the secular version of the lesson of exile from the Garden. The body comes to life when coping with difficulty.

Social touching

When modern society began to treat unobstructed movement as freedom, it fell into a quandary about what to do with the desires represented by Marianne's body; these are fraternal desires for connection to other people, a social rather than merely sexual touch. Hogarth's engraving of *Beer Street* had forty years before the advent of Marianne shown an imaginary city of people touching each other in a sociable way. As the volume of liberty began to pacify the body, such sociability became an ideal to which people paid correct but abstract obeisance, as one might pass public monuments on the way to work.

Marianne herself appeared as such a monument in a festival staged on August 10, 1793. The "Festival of the Unity and Indivisibility of the Republic" featured a high-pressure water fountain fitted up in the breasts of an enormous, nude female sculpture, the woman sitting on a dais, her hair braided around her head in Egyptian fashion. Dubbed "the Fountain of Regeneration," this revolutionary goddess poured forth white-colored water in two streams from her lactating breasts, the water scooped up and drunk in bowls by revolutionary celebrants at the bottom of the plinth, symbolizing their nourishment by the "incorruptible milk" of the Revolution.

When the festival began, the president of the political Convention gave "a speech explaining how nature had made all men free and

The Fountain of Regeneration, from the Festival of the Unity and Indivisibility of the Republic, 10 August 1793.

equal (presumably in their access to the breast), and the fountain bore the inscription, 'Nous sommes tous ses enfants' ['We are all her children']."[38] Yet only the political leaders of the moment were permitted to drink her incorruptible milk. The organizers of the festival justified this unequal access to her breasts as a matter of making the spectacle simple and visible to all. The extant drawings of this event show few people paying this self-serving art, in any event, much attention. A contemporary drawing by Monnet of the crowd gathered round the Fountain of Regeneration shows people arrayed in great confusion on the Champ de Mars just as they were in the festivals of Châteauvieux and Simonneau.[39]

The historian Marie-Hélène Huet has observed that "to make a spectator of the people ... is to maintain an alienation that is the real form of power."[40] As if to emphasize that truth, contact with Marianne's body during this festival served as a prelude to a further "station" for the day; the crowd moved from Marianne to a statue of Hercules—a Hercules sculpted with an enormous muscled chest, his right arm carrying a sword—to swear fealty in front of him to the Revolution. In answer to his body, the crowd was to close ranks in the shape of a military phalanx. The script thus called for a movement from female to male, from the domestic to the military, from the sociable to the obedient.

As the Revolution hardened, Herakles (or his Roman version, Hercules), the male warrior par excellence, took Marianne's place. The modern historian Maurice Agulhon has traced the ways in which Marianne become depicted as ever more a passive Goddess of Liberty; during the years from 1790 to 1794 her facial features softened, her body lost its muscles, her poses became more tranquil and passive, from a warrior striding into battle to a seated woman. These changes in the symbol of Marianne paralleled the experience of women in the course of the Revolution, women who were the Revolution's driving force in the beginning, who organized their own political clubs and mass movements, only to be suppressed by groups of male radicals as the Revolution slid into the Terror in 1793. In comparing the space Marianne and Hercules occupied in this festival, modern historians like Mary Jacobus and Lynn Hunt have thus concluded that "the edging out of Liberty, or 'Marianne,' by this decisively masculine figure of popular strength ... was in part a response to the threat of women's increasing political participation."[41]

Yet Marianne's presence was not so easily to be banished: As a living symbol, she represents the desire to touch and be touched. Another name for this desire is "trust." As the modern reflection of an older religious symbol, the Virgin mother, Marianne represents an emblem of compassion, of nurturing those who suffer. But, in the kind of revolutionary space imagined by Boullée and implemented by David, Marianne became inaccessible. She could neither touch nor be touched.

A curious and moving reflection of these themes came at the time from one of the Revolution's designers of the festival body, Jacques-Louis David. Lynn Hunt points out that "the heroes of the French Revolution were dead martyrs, not living leaders."[42] How could the Revolution honor their suffering? David sought to do so in famous portraits of two revolutionary martyrs, one of Jean-Paul Marat, assassinated in his bath on July 13, 1793, the other of the thirteen-year-old Joseph Bara, who had died earlier that year fighting off counter-revolutionaries in the countryside. In both portraits, empty space takes on a tragic value.

David's rendering of that tragic value in Marat's death has perhaps been lost in the course of time, for David transformed the scene in which Marat was forced to live. Marat suffered from a painful skin disease which could only be alleviated by immersion in cool water, so he spent much of his working day in a tub receiving people or writing on a board laid over the top. A wealthy man, Marat had made his bathroom a comfortable chamber, decorating it with white wallpaper on which antique columns were painted; there was a large map placed on the wall behind the tub. Some contemporary painters who sought to represent Marat's death depicted in detail the room in which Charlotte Corday stabbed the revolutionary journalist. Others decorated the dying Marat's body with symbols of virtue: in one of these etchings, for instance, Marat is wearing a crown of laurel in his bath; in another, he is somehow bathing while dressed in a toga.

David has scraped away the crown of laurel, the toga, the decor. He fills the upper half of his painting with an empty space made from a neutral background painted in green-brown tones. The bottom half he fills with the dying Marat in his bath, holding in one hand stretched out on the writing board the letter Marat received from Charlotte Corday which gained her entry to his chamber; the other hand falls over the side of the tub, clutching a pen. Marat's naked body is exposed, but here too David has stripped the surface; there are no boils or scabs on the skin, which is white, hairless, and smooth, colored only by dribbles of blood from the small slit Corday made in Marat's chest when she stabbed him. In front of the tub are

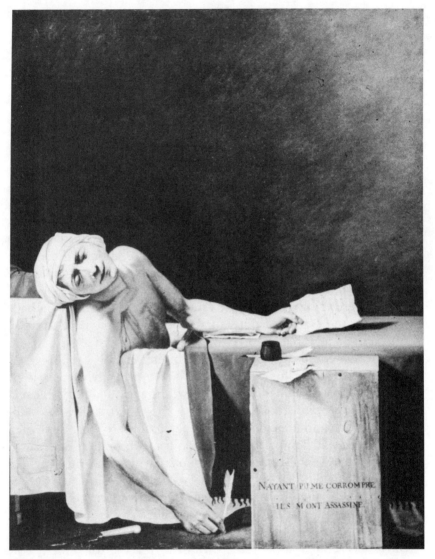

Jacques-Louis David, *The Death of Marat*, 1793. *Musées Royeaux des Beaux-Arts, Brussels.*

a writing pedestal, an inkpot, and a piece of paper; David renders these objects as a little still life of their own, "in the manner of Chardin," one historian of the painting observes.[43] Stillness and emptiness mark this scene of a violent assassination; in looking at the painting a half century later, Baudelaire evoked that emptiness: "in the cold air of this room, on these cold walls, around this cold and funereal bathtub" one becomes aware of Marat's heroism.[44] But the painting struck Baudelaire, as it has others, as impersonal. Filled with a heroic story, it does not acknowledge Marat's human pain. Compassion is absent in this neutral and empty space.

The portrait of Joseph Bara evokes martyrdom in a similarly empty space, but this memorial is filled with compassion. David left this canvas unfinished, and his painterly intentions made it perhaps unfinishable. The young boy, killed in the Vendée as he sought to defend a revolutionary outpost, is stripped naked and the dead body is set against the same neutral background as in *Marat,* an even more extreme emptiness since there is no decor which tells his story. Left in this barren state, the painting focuses all attention on the body itself. Death, erasure, emptiness—these are the marks the Revolution has made upon the body.

The painter has however made the young Joseph Bara into a sexually ambiguous figure. The boy's hips are wide, his feet small and delicately formed. David twists the torso toward the viewer so that the figure's genitals are shown frontally; the boy has little pubic hair and his penis is folded away between his legs. Young Bara's hair curls

Jacques-Louis David, *The Death of Bara,* 1794. *Musée du Louvre, Paris.*

down around his neck like a girl's loosened coiffure. To say, as the art historian Warren Roberts does, that David has created an androgynous figure does not quite hit the mark.[45] Nor is this portrait of a martyr a "revalorization of femininity." This revolutionary hero looks as different as one could imagine from the virile, heroic youths David painted before the Revolution in such canvasses as *The Oath of the Horatii,* for death has emptied Bara's body of sex. His childlike innocence, his unselfishness, place him within the circle of all the hopes contained in the figure of Marianne. Joseph Bara, the last hero of the Revolution, has returned to Marianne; he is her child and perhaps her vindication.

The Death of Bara forms a stark contrast to Piero's *Flagellation.* Piero created a great icon of place, of compassion made legible as an urban scene. David depicts compassion in an empty space. Compassion in the Revolution could be conveyed through a body but not as a place. This moral divide between flesh and stone has become one of the marks of the secularization of society.

CHAPTER TEN

Urban Individualism

E. M. Forster's London

1. THE NEW ROME

An American businessman walking through London on the eve of the First World War might be pardoned the conviction that his country should never have rebelled. Edwardian London displayed its imperial magnificence in ribbons of magnificent buildings running mile after mile, vast government offices in the center flanked by the dense economic cells of the banker's and trader's City to the east, the imposing mansions of Mayfair, Knightsbridge, and Hyde Park stretching west giving way to more middle-class but still imposing residences, all slathered block after block in ornate stucco. American cities like Boston and New York had wealthy swatches, to be sure—the band of mansions running up Fifth Avenue in New York, the new Back Bay in Boston—but London displayed the spoils of a global reach unknown since the Roman Empire.

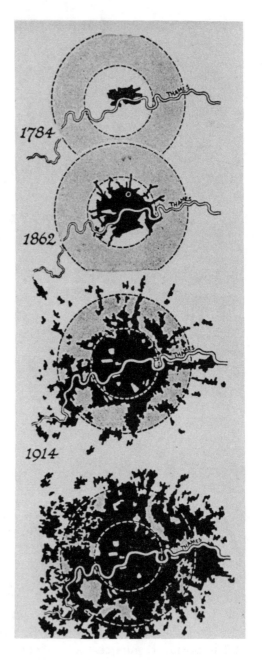

The growth of London. A map of its population in four eras: 1784, 1862, 1914, and 1980

Henry James had called Edwardian London "the modern Rome," and in size and wealth the comparison seemed apt. In the modern imperial capital the relentless continuity of its ceremonial fabric seemed insulated from equally vast scenes elsewhere in London of poverty and social distress as the ancient city or the islands of wealth in modern New York and Boston were not.

A French politician might envy the city for other reasons. Though English cooking rendered London unthinkable as a permanent habitation, the Frenchman risking a visit might be struck by the city's political orderliness, class envy seeming among the English stronger than class warfare, the upper classes expecting and exacting deference in everyday life from the lower classes. Many continental visitors indeed noticed the great courtesy which prevailed among the English working classes toward strangers and foreigners, a courtesy far at odds with the stereotype of John Bull who detested "abroad." The visiting Parisian might contrast London, which had never known a revolution, to the explosions which had occurred in Paris since 1789, in 1830, in 1848, and in 1871. The young Georges Clemenceau, for instance—who, though a gastric martyr, wandered the streets of London in a state of sociological awe—connected the internal order of the city to its imperial fortunes. This unimaginably wealthy place had placated, Clemenceau thought, its poor with the spoils of conquest.

Of course first impressions mislead us about the felicity of places as about people, and are often preferable precisely for that reason; these false impressions are, however, instructive. Take the comparison between London and Rome.

Hadrian's Rome lay at the center of an Empire which the emperors and their engineers knitted together, physically and socially, through a great road network; the fortunes of capital and provinces depended on each other. Edwardian London had a different relation to the land beyond it. As London and other British cities grew in the later nineteenth century, the English countryside rapidly emptied, the victim of a crisis prompted by international trade; the English cities were increasingly fed by grain grown in America, clothed with wool from Australia, cotton from Egypt and India. This discontinuity occurred rapidly, within the lifetime of an Edwardian adult. "Even as late as 1871 more than half the population lived in villages or in towns of less than twenty thousand people," an observer notes; "only just over a quarter lived in cities, and the mark for the city, in that computation, is a hundred thousand people."[1] By the time forty years later

E. M. Forster wrote *Howards End,* his great novel contrasting city and country, three quarters of the English population lived in cities, a quarter of this within the greater London orbit, leaving a swath of desolate fields and distressed villages in its wake. The Rome of Hadrian's time, though an enormous city about the same size as King Edward VII's London, required six hundred years to grow to that size.

The modern geographic transformation swept over all the Western nations during the latter half of the nineteenth century. In 1850, France, Germany, and the United States, like Britain, were dominantly rural societies; a century later they were dominantly urban, highly concentrated at their cores. Berlin and New York grew at the same headlong rate, roughly, as did London, and both cities grew as the national countryside submitted to the flux of international trade. For good reason the hundred years spanning 1848 to 1945 are called the age of "urban revolution."

The growth of manufacturing and free markets, however, as envisaged by Adam Smith, cannot alone explain such rapid urban change. London, like New York or Paris or Berlin, was not dominantly a city of big manufacturing enterprises—urban land was too expensive. Nor were these cities free market centers; they were the places where government, big banks, and corporate trusts sought to control markets for goods and services nationally and internationally. Again, the cities did not grow simply because they attracted victims—victims of rural disasters, or of political or religious persecution, though there were plenty of all three. Large numbers of unattached young people came voluntarily as well, entrepreneurs of their own lives not deterred by lack of capital or of work. The "urban revolution," like most sudden social changes, was an overdetermined event—and experienced first hand as nearly senseless growth. London seemed on the one hand to exemplify the sudden, vast urban swelling occurring throughout the Western world, and yet to promise that it need not be a disaster.

A second contrast between Imperial Rome and Imperial London lay in the fact that Rome served as the model for cities throughout the Roman Empire; during the great spurt of urbanization at the end of the nineteenth century, London increasingly diverged from other English cities, particularly those in the North and Midlands like Manchester and Birmingham. Clemenceau imagined the English city to be a place of stability, of people fixed in their place in the pecking order, because of the progress of manufacturing; his illusion would have been better served in these industrial cities filled with mills, factories, and shipyards than in London. Here the economy mixed shipping, craftwork, heavy industrial, financial, and imperial management, and an enormous trade in luxuries and luxury goods. The critic Raymond Williams therefore says that its "social relations . . . were more complex, more mystified" than in the North.[2] In *Howards End*, Forster writes about London similarly that "money had been spent and renewed, reputations won and lost, and the city herself, emblematic of their lives, rose and fell in a continual flux."[3]

The illusory comparison to Rome might have suggested to the visitor impressed by London's grandeur that a firm government had the populace in hand. It was such central control which the visitor's own cities sought for themselves: after the upheavals of the Commune in 1871, the authorities in Paris had perfected the instruments of an efficient centralized government of the city; after the breaking of the Boss Tweed organization in New York, reformers were similarly trying to forge these tools of rational civic control.

Unlike New York or Paris, though, London lacked a central government structure. Until 1888, London "had no city government other than a Metropolitan Board of Works, dozens of little vestries and parishes, and forty-eight boards of guardians."[4] Its central government after the reforms of 1888 remained comparatively weak. Yet the absence of central political authority did not mean the absence of central power. That central power lay in the hands of the great landowners who privately controlled large tracts of land in the city.

From the building of the first Bloomsbury squares in the eighteenth century, urban development in London consistently razed housing and shops inhabited by the very poor to create homes for the middle class or the rich. The fact that hereditary landowners controlled large tracts of land made these sudden transformations possible, with little public intervention or restraint. The aristocratic landowners were free to build, and their urban "renewal" schemes resulted in further concentrating poverty in London, the displaced poor crowding ever more closely together; as a Royal Commission on the Housing of the Working Classes observed in 1885,

Rookeries [dilapidated slums] are destroyed, greatly to the sanitary and social benefit of the neighbourhood, but no kind of habitation for the poor has been substituted. . . . The consequence of such a proceeding is that the unhoused population crowd into the neighbouring streets and courts when the demolitions commence, and when the new dwellings are completed little is done to relieve this increased pressure.[5]

During the course of the nineteenth century, urban development schemes pushed poverty to the east of the financial City of London, to the south of the Thames, and to the north of Regent's Park. Where poverty existed in the center, it remained in concentrated pockets, hidden from public view by the stucco. Earlier than Paris, more comprehensively than New York, London created a city of class-homogenous, disconnected spaces.

In its fortunes London mirrored the great differences in wealth which marked England, Wales, and Scotland as a whole. In 1910, the richest 10 percent of the families in Great Britain owned about 90 percent of the national wealth; the richest 1 percent alone owned 70 percent. The urbanized society maintained pre-industrial divisions between poverty and wealth, if on new terms; in 1806, 85 percent of the nation's wealth was owned by the richest 10 percent, 65 percent by the top 1 percent. Over the course of the century, some landed magnates became poorer while more manufacturers and imperial businessmen took their place in that upper crust. By contrast, fully half of the population of the nation lived off incomes that comprised only 3 percent of the national wealth, and very few Londoners broke free from such deprivation.[6] In this way, Clemenceau had it dead wrong: the spoils of conquest had not reached the mass of people.

Given these facts of the modern imperial city, how then to account for a visitor's sense of fullness and of public order? Though social unrest certainly made itself felt, many Londoners were themselves impressed that their capital had managed to reap the benefits of capitalism without the challenges of revolution. This stability could not conceivably be explained by English indifference to the class system. Though "the class war is hardly an English prerogative," as the critic Alfred Kazin says, the English have been far more sensitive to class than their American and German counterparts. Kazin thinks, for instance, of the remark George Orwell made in 1937, "Whichever way you turn, this curse of class differences confronts you like a wall of stone. Or rather it is not so much like a wall of stone as the plate glass pane of an aquarium."[7]

Other forces at work seemed to keep this great, unequal city from open revolution. The urbanist Walter Benjamin called Paris "The capital of the nineteenth century," based on its exemplary culture. London can also be taken as the capital of the nineteenth century, based on its exemplary individualism. The nineteenth century was indeed often spoken of as the Age of Individualism, a phrase Alexis de Tocqueville coined in the second volume of *Democracy in America.* The brave side of individualism may be self-reliance, but Tocqueville saw its more melancholic side, which he conceived as a kind of civic solitude. "Each person," he wrote, "behaves as though he is a stranger to the destiny of all the others. . . . As for his transactions with his fellow citizens, he may mix among them, but he sees them not; he touches them, but does not feel them; he exists only in himself and for himself alone. And if on these terms there remains in his mind a sense of family, there no longer remains a sense of society."[8]

Individualism of this sort, he thought, might bring a certain order to society—the co-existence of people inward-turned, tolerating one another out of mutual indifference. Such individualism had a particular meaning in urban space. The planning of nineteenth-century cities aimed to create a crowd of freely moving individuals, and to discourage the movement of organized groups through the city. Individual bodies moving through urban space gradually became detached from the space in which they moved, and from the people the space contained. As space became devalued through motion, individuals gradually lost a sense of sharing a fate with others.

The triumph of Tocquevillian individualism in London was very much on the mind of the novelist E. M. Forster in 1910 when he wrote *Howards End.* His book opens famously with the epigraph, "Only connect . . .", a social as much as a psychological command. Forster's novel shows us a city that seems to hold together socially precisely because people don't connect personally; they live isolated, mutually indifferent lives which establish an unhappy equilibrium in society.

The novel reflects upon London's extraordinarily rapid transformation during the larger urban revolution; as to many others of his time, *speed* seemed to Forster the central fact of modern life. The pace of change seems epitomized to the novelist by the appearance of automobiles, and *Howards End* is full of anathemas against the new machine. The Tocquevillian strain appears as Forster depicts Edwardian London as a dead city though pulsing with frenetic changes—if London is a place of "anger and telegrams," he says, it is also full of scenes of "stupid sensate dullness." Forster seeks to evoke a pervasive, if hidden, sensate apathy as a result in the conduct of everyday life in the city—something invisible to the walking tourist—an apathy among the wealthy and fashionable as among the masses of the poor amidst the sheer flux of life. Individualism and the facts of speed together deaden the modern body; it does not connect.

Howards End drew all this from a rather lurid tale of an illegitimate child, a crossed inheritance, and a murder. As Virginia Woolf—no great enthusiast for the novel—commented, Forster invites us to read him as a social critic rather than as an artistic craftsman. "We are tapped on the shoulder," she observed; "we are to notice this, to take heed of that."[9] Indeed, *Howards End* frequently hustles the reader in a few paragraphs through cataclysmic events altering people's fortunes so that the author can return to pondering their significance at leisure. If the novelist of ideas often paid an artistic price for thinking too much, this novel ended with a surprising insight which remains provocative: the individual body can come back to sensate life by experiencing displacement and difficulty. The command "Only connect . . ." can be obeyed only by people who acknowledge that there exist real impediments to their individual, rapid, free movement. A living culture treats resistance as a positive experience.

In this chapter we shall look more closely at the developments in modern society which led to the novelist's indictment of urban individualism—the experiences of bodily movement and bodily passivity on which he bases his tale. His surprising denouement suggests a new way to think about urban culture.

2. MODERN ARTERIES AND VEINS

Nineteenth-century urban design enabled the movement of large numbers of individuals in the city, and disabled the movement of groups, groups of the threatening sort which appeared in the French Revolution. The nineteenth-century urban designers drew upon their predecessors in the Enlightenment who conceived of the city as arteries and veins of movement, but put that imagery to a new use. The Enlightened urbanist had imagined individuals stimulated by movement through the city's crowds; the nineteenth-century urbanist imagined individuals protected by movement from the crowd. Three great construction projects during the century mark this change: the building of Regent's Park and Regent Street in London, a project directed early in the nineteenth century; the rebuilding of the Parisian streets during the time of Baron Haussmann in the middle of the century; and the making of the London Underground at the end of the century. All three were enormous undertakings; we shall explore only how these projects taught people to move.

Regent's Park

In both eighteenth-century Paris and London, planners had created parks as the lungs of the city, rather than as sanctuaries like the urban gardens of the Middle Ages. The eighteenth-century park-as-lung required policing of its plants. In Paris, the authorities enclosed the King's park in the Tuileries, once open to the public at large, with railings in the mid-1750s, in order to protect the plants which provided the salubrious air for the city. The great London urban squares begun during the eighteenth century were by the early nineteenth century similarly fenced in. The analogy of park to lung was, as the modern urbanist Bruno Fortier observes, simple and direct: the people flowing through the city's street-arteries were meant to circulate round these enclosed parks, breathing their fresh air just as the blood is refreshed by the lungs. The planners of the eighteenth century drew on the contemporary medical premise that, in Fortier's words, "nothing can actually become corrupted that is mobile and forms a mass."[10] The greatest work of urban planning in London, the creation of Regent Street and Regent's Park early in the nineteenth century, undertaken by the future King George IV working with the architect John Nash, was based on the principle of park-as-lung, but adapted to a city where greater speed was possible.

Created out of the old Marylebone Park, the sheer landmass of Regent's Park is enormous. Nash wanted this great landmass graded level, and decided to make the lung in Regent's Park largely out of grass, rather than trees; many of the tree plantings we now see in the park, such as those around Queen Mary's Rose Garden, are of later origin. A great, flat, grassy open space might seem the perfect invitation to organized groups, and at times during the Victorian era that invitation was accepted. Yet Nash's plan worked against such use of open space by creating a wall of rapidly moving traffic around the park. The road ringing Regent's Park outside its railings served as the belt carrying this heavy volume of traffic; many natural outcroppings and stray buildings along the belt were removed in order

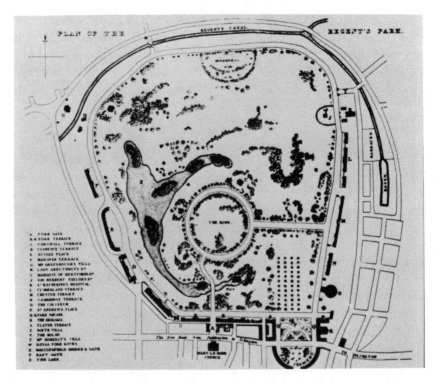

Site plan for John Nash's design of Regent's Park in London, 1812.

to make sure the carriages could move without interruption, and eventually the bed of a canal running through Regent's Park was also altered so that it did not disturb traffic. Dickens thought the belt road around the park resembled a racetrack. Some interior roads were similarly built for a heavy volume of carriage traffic, and laid out so that these carriages could move fast.

If Nash's London was a site for speed, it seemed an unlikely space for individuals. The urban squares which appeared in London in the eighteenth century belie, to the eye, the fact that London is dominantly a city of individual houses. The grand houses facing the squares were constructed in large blocks of fifteen to twenty to give the impression of a severe unity; London building codes in the eighteenth century, especially a law passed in 1774, forbade signs or other individual markers. In Bloomsbury, the plain building blocks contrasted to the floral profusion planted in the squares; they also made a sharp demarcation between outside and inside, public and private.

Although Regent's Park is bigger than these earlier squares, Nash designed the buildings facing it across the traffic stream as though it were similar in kind, lining it with individual houses. These Nash bound together by making liberal use of stucco. Stucco is the architect's medium for creating illusion; when wet, it can be shaped to resemble the great squat stones supporting Renaissance palaces or poured into molds to create elaborate, finely detailed columns. In the terrace houses on Regent's Park Nash slathered stucco across the housing fronts in such a way as to bind these immense blocks together, the detailed stucco crusts creating a kind of rhythm from block to block.

Yet this building material could also signify social disconnection. The blocks ringing Regent's Park were almost self-consciously magnificent. By their very elaborateness they helped draw a line between the space of the park and the urban fabric outside it. That nether fabric was patchy, poor, and disordered. In the areas surrounding Regent's Park, Nash's plan pushed the poor who had formerly lived on some of its landmass to the north, toward the Chalk Farm and Camden Town districts. The immense space lined by grand houses, walled together in stucco, like the stream of traffic, made the park difficult to penetrate. As a result, Regent's Park in its early years was a largely empty space. The design coupled rapid movement to "dedensification," a useful piece of planning jargon. This rapid motion, moreover, was individualized transport—it occurred in hansoms and carriages.

Nash's plan envisaged traffic coming to the park not from the immediate environs—for behind the magnificent walls few people could have afforded a carriage—but from the center of the city. At its southern edge, Regent's Park gives way through a connector to the great boulevard which Nash created, Regent Street. To create this boulevard Nash had to deal with a number of immovable obstacles, such as a church which could not be torn down, obstacles they overcame by designing a street that curved around whatever it could not destroy. Again the street was designed for high-volume traffic, here on foot as well as by carriage; again there were immense blocks of uniform buildings. In Regent Street these served a new commercial purpose, for Nash designed continuous shop space at the ground-floor level—whereas the shops in older London houses had been more erratically adapted from their original domestic intentions. Nash had moved the principle of the shopping arcades of London, which were glass-roofed basilicas with shops along the spine, into the street.

Regent Street was an epochal event in urban design. It coupled a continuous, heavy traffic stream to single-function use at ground level. This organization of the street created a division between the street and the territory behind the street lining, as in the park Nash built to the north. Commerce did not overflow into the side streets; the carriage trade could not penetrate far into the ancient tangle, and the orientation of the pedestrian flow of the street, as in a basilica, lay along the spine rather than at right angles to it. The single-function street created a spatial division akin to the division of labor, the street line serving only the purposes of up-market trade while spaces nearby served craft or business functions which had no necessary relation to the street.

The ensemble of Regent's Park and Regent Street gave a new social meaning to motion. The use of traffic to insulate and thin out space, as occurred in Regent's Park, diffused the gathering of a purposeful crowd. The pressure of linear pedestrian movement on Regent Street made, and still makes, it difficult for a stationary crowd to form, to listen to a speech, for instance. Instead, both street and park privileged the individual moving body. To be sure, Regent Street was itself, and remains, anything but lifeless. More, Nash left

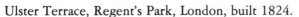

Ulster Terrace, Regent's Park, London, built 1824.

little in the way of writing to indicate that he intended these social consequences to come from his design. Like many English urbanists, he abhorred the kind of theorizing in which Boullée engaged. Yet mass movement on a single-function street was the necessary first step in privileging individuals pursuing their own concerns in a crowd.

Haussmann's Three Networks

The work Nash did in London prefigured the plans the Emperor Napoleon III and his chief urban planner, Baron Haussmann, laid two generations later in Paris. The motions of the masses were on the minds of these officials, who had lived through the Revolutions of 1848 and 1830, and who preserved vivid memories of the Great Revolution in the time of their grandfathers. Much more than we know was true of Nash, they consciously sought to privilege the motions of individuals in order to repress the movements of the urban masses.

The plan for the remaking of Paris in the 1850s and 1860s was Napoleon III's own. In 1853, "on the day when Haussmann took the oath of office as the Prefect of the Seine," the historian David Pinckney writes,

> Napoleon handed to him a map of Paris on which he had drawn in four contrasting colors (the colors indicating the relative urgency he attached to each project) the streets that he proposed to build. This map, the work of Louis Napoleon alone, became the basic plan for the transformation of the city in the two following decades.[11]

Haussmann using this guide carried out the greatest urban redevelopment scheme of modern times, gutting much of the medieval and Renaissance urban fabric, building new, uniform street walls of enveloping, straight streets that carried high volumes of carriage traffic, the plan of the streets connecting the center of the city to its outlying districts. He rebuilt the central market of Paris using a new building material, cast iron—shouting to his architect Baltard, "Iron! Iron! Nothing but iron!"[12] He built great monuments like the Paris Opéra, redesigned the city's parks, and created a new underground network of giant sewer canals.

In his streetmaking, Haussmann put Roman principles of linear form to work in new ways. Napoleon III had handed his prefect little

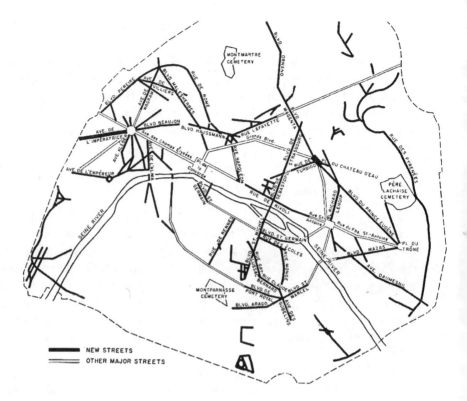

Principal new streets in Paris built between 1850 and 1870.

more than a neat sketch. To make the actual streets of the plan, Haussmann constructed tall wooden towers up which his assistants—whom he called "urban geometers"—ascended, measuring out straight streets with compass and ruler to the old walls of the city. The directions the urban geometers looked, especially to the north and northeast, covered terrain largely built over with workers' houses, craftworks, and small factories. In cutting through these territories, Haussmann separated and divided communities of the poor with boulevards flowing with traffic.

As in Nash's belt around Regent's Park, traffic flow now created a wall of moving vehicles, behind which the poor districts lay in fragments. The width of these streets was finely calculated moreover in terms of Haussmann's fears of the movement of crowds in revolt. The street width permitted two army wagons to travel abreast, enabling the militia, if necessary, to fire into the communities lying beyond the sides of the street wall. Again, as around Regent's Park, the street wall composed a continuous block of buildings, with shops on the ground floor and apartments above, the richest inhabitants nearest the street, the poorest nearest the sky. Haussmann's efforts in the poorest districts focused almost exclusively on the facades of buildings; "builders had to conform to certain standards of height and to erect prescribed facades, but behind those facades they were free to build crowded and airless tenements, and many of them did."[13]

The urban map produced by Haussmann and his geometers divided the city into three "networks." The First Network dealt with the tangle of streets originally formed by the medieval city; Haussmann's effort here was to cut through buildings and straighten streets on the territory close to the Seine, in order to make the old city usable by carriage traffic. The Second Network consisted of streets which connected the city to the periphery, beyond its walls called the *octroi;* as the streets extended out to the periphery, the city administration took power over the localities now connected to the center. The Third Network was more amorphous, consisting of connector streets between the major routes out of the city, and linking streets between the First and Second Networks.

In Haussmann's scheme, the streets of the First Network served as urban arteries of the kind L'Enfant had already built in Washington. The relation of built form to the moving body mattered, monuments, churches, or other structures marking the progress of a vehicle or a walking body. The street linking the Palais-Royal, just north of the Louvre, to the new opera house was such a First Network artery, as was the rue de Rivoli linking the city hall to the Church of Saint-Antoine.

The Second Network streets served as the city's veins. Movement in them was to be largely out from the city, oriented to commerce and light industry, since Haussmann hardly desired to draw more poor people in toward the center. Here the precise nature of the built form lining the street mattered less. The Boulevard du Centre, which we know today as the Boulevard de Sébastopol, was such an urban vein, stretching from the Place du Châtelet out to the northern city gate of Saint-Denis. This great street exemplified the social control contained in linear form. Almost a hundred feet wide and a mile long, the Boulevard de Sébastopol cut in two a dense, irregular, and poor territory. The old street and building fabric did not feed into or relate to this vein, streets often joining the boulevard at awkward or even impassable angles. Nor was the Boulevard de Sébastopol meant to bring nourishment to these fragmented spaces behind its street wall; instead, it was meant to provide a way to feed goods to the north. Haussmann indeed conceived it as a one-way street flowing in that direction. Above all, a Second Network road of this sort was to be a space where vehicles could move fast.

The map of the Third Network, as befitted its purposes, consisted of both arteries and veins. Haussmann's aborted proposal for the rue Caulaincourt is typical of this type; it confronted the problem of how to move wagons loaded with goods around the Montmartre cemetery at the north end of the city, connecting traffic between the Second Network veins to the east and to the west. Here Haussmann was forced to disturb the dead rather than the living, running part of the road over the cemetery; this plunged him, in inimitably French fashion, into extensive lawsuits with the families of the departed, haggling about the price of air rights over the dead. But the rue Caulaincourt project aroused more serious opposition, because it dramatized just how much the new geography of mobility in Paris violated all aspects of the city's life.

In his great study of nineteenth-century Parisian culture, Walter Benjamin described the glass-roofed arcades of the city as "urban capillaries," all the movements which gave pulsing life to the city concentrated in these small, covered passages with their special shops, little cafés, and surging clots of people. The Boulevard de Sébastopol was the scene of another motion, a thrust which divided, a directional motion too rapid, too pressed, to attach itself to such eddies of life. Again, like Regent Street, the Boulevard de Sébastopol was in its nineteenth-century form a vivid space. If it broke apart the urban crowd as a political group, it plunged individuals in wagons, carriages, and on foot into an almost frenzied whirl. Yet, as a design, it too proved ominous. For two new steps had been taken in privileging motion over the claims of the people: the design of street traffic become divorced from the design of building mass along the street, only the facade mattering; and the urban vein made the street into a means to escape the urban center, rather than dwell in it.

The London Underground

The social revolution inaugurated by the London Underground is usually described as one of getting people into the city. But the developers of the Underground system learned from Haussmann's network system; they sought to get people out of the city, as well as into it. That outward movement had a class character, and one with which even the most resolute *flâneur* of the streets must sympathize.

The London Underground Railway, from *Universal Illustrated*, 1867.

Domestic servants were the single largest group of poor workers in Mayfair, Knightsbridge, Bayswater, and other wealthy districts of London at the end of the nineteenth century, as in affluent Paris, Berlin, and New York. Allied to house servants was a secondary army of service workers—menders of domestic appliances, purveyors of domestic necessities, handlers of coaches, horses, and the like. The live-in house servants mixed with their employers in the most intimate scenes of family life; during the London social season, which lasted from late May to August each year, a third army of some twenty thousand young girls swarmed up from the country to assist young ladies with the arrangement of their clothes and hair when the ladies were presented to fashionable society. Edwardian London represents the last age in European history when rich and poor would live in such domestic intimacy; after the Great War machines would increasingly take the place of servants.

Most of the secondary army of workers servicing rich homes, however, as well as the massive numbers of clerks and low-level service workers required by the imperial bureaucracy and the city, lived packed together in the dense pockets of old London untouched by the projects of the big landowners; by the middle of the nineteenth century, many of these poor but employed laborers crowded as well into sections of the East End and the South Bank formerly inhabited only by derelicts or by temporary lodgers like seamen.

The pockets of poor housing in the center and the housing in the East End and on the South Bank displayed a far different city than the monuments of imperial stucco. Here, one might think, one had come at last to a city truly resembling ancient Rome, the Rome of mass squalor. Yet in contrast to the apartment blocks, or *insulae*, of ancient Rome, and indeed in contrast to the vast slums which had arisen in other European cities, London built misery on a smaller architectural scale. In England, as the urbanist Donald Olsen writes, "typically the unit of dwelling and the unit of building are the same; on the continent the former is but a portion of the latter," consisting of ribbons of individual houses spread along a street wall.[14] In the really wretched sections of the East End, families lived in single rooms of small houses. The Underground helped transform their condition.

Among the upper half of that 50 percent which had access to 3 percent of the national wealth, the cheap transport furnished by the Underground made it possible to explore living somewhere better. The growth of cooperative building societies furnished the capital for realizing that dream. By the 1880s, the urban tide which had flooded into London began to flow out. Thanks to improved public transportation, the working poor who could scrape together the money could now move away from the city center to individual homes of their own, south of the Thames and north of the center in districts like Camden Town, in new row housing. As in housing for the privileged, these modest row houses consisted of uniform blocks, with individual small yards and outhouses in the back. To Forster and his middle-class contemporaries, the architectural quality seemed appalling; the housing was depressing, badly built, damp, the outdoor privies stinking. By working-class standards, however, the housing was an immense achievement. People slept on a different floor than they ate; the smell of urine and faeces no longer pervaded the interior.

The Underground, it is true, served both as an artery and a vein. It helped open up London's center, especially for mass consumption in the new department stores which took form in the 1880s and 1890s. Until then it had been possible to live in the wealthy West End of London in isolation from the non-servant poverty of the East End. Beginning in the 1880s, however, as the historian Judith Wal-

Golders Green, London. Advertisement, ca. 1900. *Photo: Richard Tobias.*

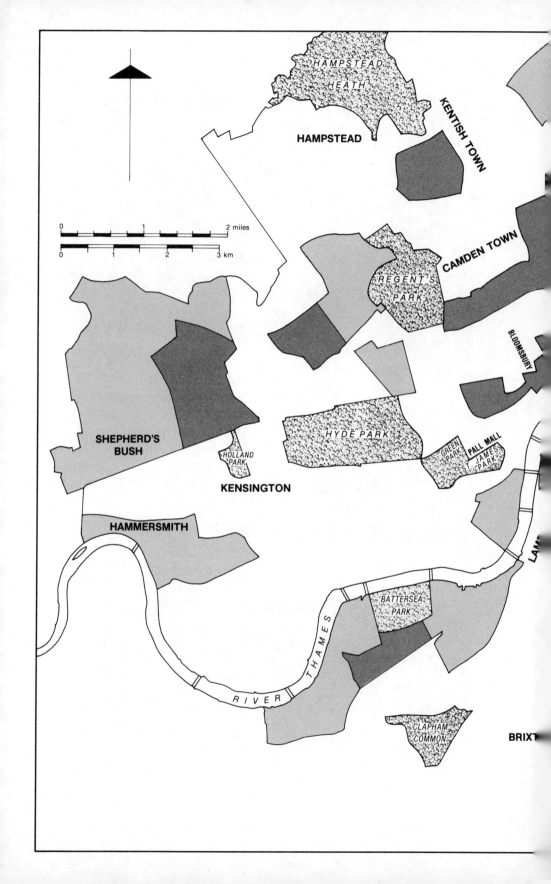

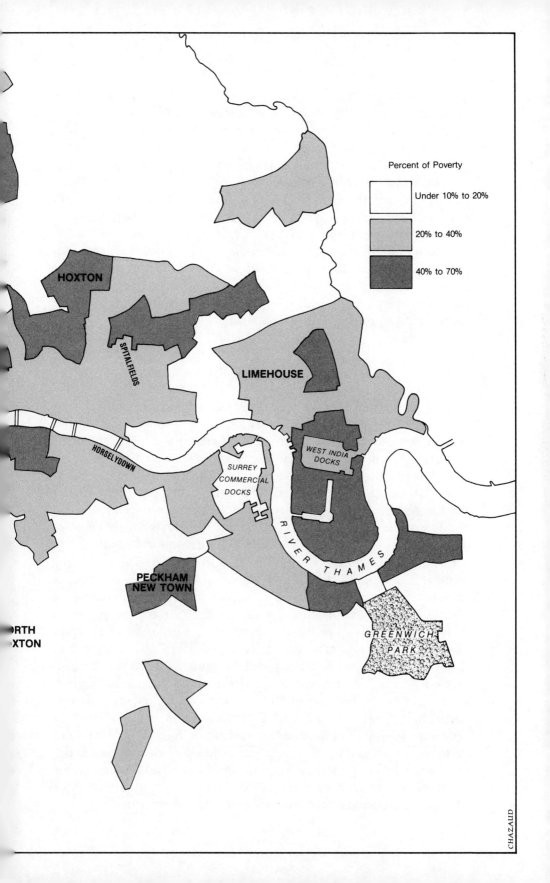

Percent of Poverty

Under 10% to 20%

20% to 40%

40% to 70%

HOXTON

SPITALFIELDS

LIMEHOUSE

HORSELYDOWN

SURREY
COMMERCIAL
DOCKS

WEST INDIA
DOCKS

RIVER THAMES

PECKHAM
NEW TOWN

GREENWICH
PARK

ORTH
XTON

CHAZAUD

kowitz observes, "the prevailing imaginary landscape of London [shifted] from one that was geographically bounded to one whose boundaries were indiscriminately and dangerously transgressed."[15] The transgressors were far more likely to be shoppers than thieves.

Yet if the Underground system of arteries and veins in London created a more mixed city, this mixture had sharp limits in time. During the day, the human blood of the city flowed below ground into the heart; at night, these subterranean channels became veins emptying the mass out of the center, as people took the Underground home. With mass transit on the model of the Underground, the time geography of the modern urban center had now taken form: density and diversity by day, sparsity and homogeneity by night. And that mixture by day implicated no strong human contact between the classes. People worked and shopped and then left for home.

3. COMFORT

In the poetry of Baudelaire, speed was depicted as a frenetic experience, and the speeding urbanite as a man or woman living on the edge of hysteria. In point of fact, speed took on a different character in the nineteenth century, thanks to technical innovations in transport. These made the travelling body comfortable. Comfort is a condition we associate with rest and passivity. The technology of the nineteenth century gradually made movement into such a passive bodily experience. The more comfortable the moving body became, the more also it withdrew socially, travelling alone and silent.

Comfort is of course a sensation easy to despise. The desire for comfort has a dignified origin, however, as an effort to rest bodies fatigued by labor. During the first decades of factory and industrial labor in the nineteenth century, workers were forced to continue at their tasks without a break throughout the day as long as they could stand or move their limbs. By late in the century, it became evident that the productivity of such forced labor diminished as the day progressed. Industrial analysts noticed the contrast between English workers, who by the end of the century worked mostly ten-hour labor shifts, and German and French workers, who labored in twelve, or sometimes fourteen-hour shifts: the English workers were far more productive by the hour. The same difference in productivity appeared among manual laborers who worked on Sunday versus manual laborers who were given the Sabbath to rest; the workers who rested on Sunday worked harder the rest of the week.

Market logic suggested to crude capitalists like Henry Clay Frick that the "better sort of worker" was a laborer who wanted to work all the time, a worker whose energies were aroused by the chance to push his body to the limits in order to make money. But fatigue spoke practically of a different economy. In 1891, the Italian physiologist Angelo Masso was able to explain the relation between fatigue and productivity. He showed, in his book *La Fatica,* that people feel fatigued long before they are incapable of further effort; the sensation of fatigue is a protective mechanism by which the body controls its own energies, protecting it from injuries which "lesser sensibility" would cause to the organism.[16] The onset of this protective sensation of fatigue defines the moment when productivity begins sharply to drop.

The pursuit of comfort in the nineteenth century has to be understood within this sympathetic context. Comfortable ways to travel, like comfortable furniture and places to rest, began as aids for recovery from the bodily abuses marked by sensations of fatigue. From its very origins, though, comfort had another trajectory, as comfort became synonymous with *individual* comfort. If comfort lowered a person's level of stimulation and receptivity, it could serve the person at rest in withdrawing from other people.

The chair and the carriage

The ancient Greek in his andron, or the Roman couple in their triclinium, lay sociably on their sides or stood sociably. This sociable posture of the body at rest contrasted to the "pathetic" or vulnerable posture of sitting, as in the ancient theatre. In medieval times, sitting in a near squat became a sociable position, though dependent upon the rank of the sitter. The most common piece of furniture made for rest was the low stool without a back, or low chests; chairs with backs were reserved for people of rank. By the seventeenth century an elaborate etiquette determined how and when and with whom people sat, as in Louis XIV's Versailles. A countess had to stand in the presence of a princess of the blood, but could sit on a stool in the presence of a princess not collaterally related to the King; the princesses of both sorts sat in chairs with arms, except in the presence of the King or Queen, when a non-collateral princess then stood up, and a princess of the blood could remain seated but only in a chair without arms. Standing became a deferential position; everyone from princesses to servants stood in the presence of their social superiors who enjoyed the comfort of sitting.

In the Age of Reason, chairs became vessels for more relaxed sitting positions, reflecting a gradual relaxation of manners from the court patterns of Versailles. The back of the chair became as important as the seat, and the back sloped, so that the sitter could lean into it; the arms were lowered so that the sitter could move freely from side to side. This change became marked around 1725, appearing in informal chairs with names invoking Nature like the *bergère,* the "shepherd's chair," upon which no real shepherd was ever likely to sit. The furniture maker Roubo remarked that in such chairs a person can rest his or her shoulder against the chairback, "while leaving the head entirely free to avoid disarranging the hair either of the ladies or the gentlemen."[17] Eighteenth-century comfort thus meant freedom of movement even while sitting, the sitter leaning to one side or another, talking easily to people all around. This freedom to twist and move while sitting marks the simplest chairs of the eighteenth century as well as the most expensive; the beautiful wooden "Windsor" chairs which graced poor English and American houses at the time supported the back, as did the aristocrat's bergere, while opening wide to free the rest of the body.

Nineteenth-century chairs subtly but powerfully changed this experience of sitting sociably; they did so thanks to innovations in upholstery. By 1830, manufacturers of chairs used springs beneath the seats and on the backs; over the springs the manufacturers set heavy cushions, using for stuffing either pleated horsehair or the wool combings which were by-products of the new mechanized spinning machines. The chairs, divans, and sofas thus became enormous in size, overstuffed by design. The French upholsterer Dervilliers began to manufacture such chairs in 1838, calling them "confortables." He followed with various models such as the *confortable senateur* of 1863 and the *confortable gondole* of 1869, which was like a boat into which the sitter lowered him- or herself at the side. In all these "confortables" the body sank into the enveloping structure, engulfed and no longer easily moving. As the processes of mass manufacturing advanced, particularly in the mechanical weaving of cushions, the chairs came within the reach of a large public. The "comfortable chair" in a worker or clerk's home served as a point of pride and a place of respite from the cares of the world. Comfort in these chairs came to imply a particular kind of human posture, the historian Sigfried Giedion believes, "based on relaxation . . . in a free, unposed attitude that can be called neither sitting nor lying" by comparison to earlier ages.[18]

Formal chair. Late eighteenth century.

The comfortable chair. Mid-nineteenth century.

The nineteenth-century sitter engaged in a ritual of relaxation by sinking into the uphostered chair, his or her body immobilized. This same surrender marked the nineteenth-century rocking chair. In its eighteenth-century form, as in the Windsor rocking chair, the soothing motion comes directly from the push of the sitter's feet; when nineteenth-century manufacturers added springs to these chairs, more complicated mechanical motions resulted. In 1853 the first American patent was issued for what we now call the tilting office chair, at the time known simply as a sitting chair. Its rocking action via springs and coils meant that "relaxation" is derived from small and often "unconscious shifts of position."[19] Leaning back in a spring-held, tilting office chair is a different physical experience from leaning back in a wooden rocking chair; to experience comfort, the body moves less; the springs do the work of the feet.

The junction of comfort and passive bodily surrender appeared in the most private of seated acts. The development of flush toilets in the middle of the nineteenth century continued the eighteenth-century drive toward hygiene. But the vitreous-glass toilet bowls and wooden seats of the Victorian era far surpassed utilitarian concerns. Their bowls cast in fanciful shapes and their porcelain painted, the more exuberant of these toilets were meant to be furniture; their manufacturers anticipated that people would rest when sitting on them, just as people rested in other chairs. Some were outfitted with magazine racks, others with holders for glasses and plates; an ingenious "rocking Crapper"—named after its inventor—was even launched upon the seas of Victorian commerce.

Defecation became a private activity in the nineteenth century— entirely unlike the habit people had a century earlier of talking to friends while sitting on a *chaise-percé* beneath which lay a chamber pot. In the chamber which now contained bath, sink, and toilet, one sat quietly, thinking, perhaps reading or taking a drink, and literally let go, completely undisturbed. This same withdrawal occurred in easy chairs in more public parts of the house, chairs in which a person exhausted after work had the right not to be disturbed.

Sitting while travelling came to follow the same trajectory of individualized comfort. Dervilliers' techniques of upholstery spread to the design of carriage interiors; the springs underneath carriages became ever more cushioning against jolts. The comfort of the carriage made its increase in speed bearable to passengers, who in older vehicles had suffered most when the carriages went fast.

These changes altered the social conditions of travel. The nineteenth-century European railway carriage placed its six to eight passengers in a compartment where they faced one another, a seating plan derived from the large horse-drawn coaches of an earlier era. When it first appeared as train seating, the historian Wolfgang Schivelbusch argues, this arrangement provoked a sense of "the embarrassment of people facing each other in silence," for now the cover of noise in the horse-drawn carriages was gone.[20] The comfortable smoothness of the railroad carriage, however, permitted people to read by themselves.

The railway carriage filled with close-packed bodies who read or silently looked out the window marked a great social change which occurred in the nineteenth century: silence used as a protection of individual privacy. On the streets, as in the railway carriage, people began to treat as their right not to be spoken to by strangers, to treat the speech of strangers as a violation. In Hogarth's London or David's Paris speaking to a stranger carried no connotation of vio-

Men's compartment of an American railroad coach, 1847.

lating his or her privacy; in public people expected to talk and be talked to.

The American railroad carriage, as developed in the 1840s, put its passengers in a position which virtually assured the desire to be left alone in silence. Without compartments, the American railroad carriage turned all passengers looking forward, staring at one another's backs rather than faces. American trains frequently travelled immense distances—by European standards—yet it struck Old World visitors that one could cross the North American continent without having to address a word to anyone else, even though there were no physical barriers between people in the carriage. Before the advent of mass transport, the sociologist Georg Simmel remarked, people had rarely been obliged to sit together in silence for a long time, just staring. This "American" way of sitting in public transport now also appeared in Europe in the ways people sat in cafés and pubs.

The café and the pub

Cafés on the European continent owe their origins to the English coffeehouse of the early eighteenth century. Some coffeehouses began as mere appendages to coaching stations, others as self-contained enterprises. The insurance company Lloyd's of London began as a coffeehouse, and its rules marked the sociability of most other urban places; the price of a mug of coffee earned a person the right to speak to anyone in Lloyd's room.[21]

More than sheer chattiness prompted strangers to talk to one another in the coffeehouse. Talk was the most important means of gaining information about conditions on the road, in the city, or about business. Though differences in social rank were evident in how people looked and in their diction, the need to talk freely dictated that people not notice, so long as they were drinking together. The advent of the modern newspaper in the later eighteenth century sharpened, if anything, the impulse to talk; displayed on racks in the room, the newspapers offered topics for discussion—the written word seeming no more certain than speech.

The French café of the Ancien Régime took its name from and operated much like the English coffeehouse, strangers freely arguing, gossiping, and informing one another. In the years before the Revolution, political groups often arose from these café encounters. At first many different groups met in the same café, as in the original Café Procope on the Left Bank; by the outbreak of the Revolution, contending political groups in Paris each had their own place. During and after the Revolution the greatest concentration of cafés was in the Palais-Royal; here, early in the nineteenth century an experiment began which was to transform the café as a social institution. The experiment was simply to put a few tables outside the wooden galerie du bois running through the center of the Palais-Royal. These outside tables deprived political groups of their cover; the tables served customers watching the passing scene, rather than conspiring with one another.

The development of the great boulevards of Paris by Baron Haussmann, particularly in the Second Network streets, encouraged such use of outdoor space; the wide streets provided much more space for the café to sprawl. Apart from the cafés of the Second Network, there were two centers of café life in Haussmann's Paris, one clustered around the Opéra, where the Grand Café, the Café de la Paix, and the Café Anglais were to be found, the other in the Latin Quarter, whose most famous cafés were the Voltaire, the Soleil d'Or, and François Premier. The clients of the great cafés were in the nineteenth century drawn from the middle and upper classes, the price of drinks discouraging poorer customers. Moreover, in these vast cafés, Parisians acted like Americans in their trains; the café-goer expected that he or she had a right to be left alone. The silence of people in these large establishments proved uncongenial to the working classes, who clung to the sociability of the *cafés intimes* in the side streets.

At an outdoor table in the big café one was expected to remain seated in one place; those who wanted to hop from scene to scene stood at the bar. The speed of service for these fixed bodies became slower than for the standing patrons. In the 1870s, for instance, it became a common practice for the oldest waiters to be relegated to the outer tables of cafés, their slowness no failure in the minds of these patrons. On the terrace, the denizens of the café sat silently watching the crowd go by—they sat as individuals, each lost in his or her own thoughts.

By Forster's time there were a few big French-style cafés in London near Piccadilly Circus, but the more universal drinking place in the city was, of course, the pub. For all their coziness, Edwardian pubs in London had assimilated some of the public manners of their continental café-cousins; if people talked freely standing at the bar, elsewhere they could sit, silent and alone. Cafés for the most part in Paris were as much neighborhood affairs as were London pubs; "in the boulevard, Opéra and Latin Quarter café, the backbone of trade was the habitué rather than the tourist or the elegant out with a demi-mondaine."[22] Of course the pub did not relate spatially to the street as did the café; it appeared as a refuge space, fragrant inside with the comforting mixed smells of urine, beer, and sausage. Yet the Parisian dawdling on a café terrace also was disconnected from the street; he or she inhabited a realm rather like that of the American travelling across a continent in silence, the people on the street now appearing as scenery, as spectacle. "Half an hour spent on the boulevards or on one of the chairs in the Tuileries gardens has the effect of an infinitely diverting theatrical performance," the traveller Augustus Hare wrote.[23] Or, in both pub and café, this spectacle could take place in the theatre of one's private thoughts while one sat.

The exterior crowd composing itself into a spectacle no longer carried the menace of a revolutionary mob—nor did people on the street make demands on the person nursing a beer or a *fine*. In 1808, police spies looking for dangerous political elements in Paris spent a great deal of time infiltrating cafés; in 1891, the police disbanded the bureau dedicated to café surveillance. A public realm filled with moving and spectating individuals—in Paris as much as in London— no longer represented a political domain.

Like the chair, the café thus provided a space of comfort which joined the passive and the individual. Yet for all this the café was, and remains, intensely urban and urbane. One was and is surrounded by life, even if detached from it. The space of comfort took another turn inward when urban architecture began to be mechanically sealed.

Sealed space

The designers of the eighteenth century had sought to create a healthy city on the model of a healthy body. As the urbanist Reyner Banham has observed, the building technology of that time hardly served this purpose; buildings were both drafty and stuffy, the movement of air in them irrational, the loss of heat, when heating existed at all, extravagant.[24] In the late nineteenth century, these difficulties of respiration within stone began to be addressed.

The advent of central heating may not seem a great event in the history of Western civilization, any more than the invention of the overstuffed chair. Yet central heating, like later advances in interior lighting, air conditioning, and the management of waste, did create buildings that fulfilled the Enlightenment dream of a healthy environment—at a social price. For these inventions isolated buildings from the urban environment.

We owe to Benjamin Franklin the concept of heating a room with radiating hot air, rather than an open fire. Franklin created the first "Franklin stove" in 1742. The inventor of the steam engine, James Watt, heated his own offices by steam in 1784; large buildings began to be steam-heated early in the nineteenth century. The boiler which produced the steam could also produce hot water, distributed by pipes to each room where needed, rather than carried there by servants who heated water in the kitchen. In 1877, Birdsill Holly conducted experiments in New York aimed at providing several buildings with steam heat and hot water from a single boiler.

The problem with these inventions was two-fold: the buildings were so poorly insulated that the hot air seeped outside; they were so poorly ventilated that hot air did not move inside. The ventilation problem could be, and was in part, solved through the development of forced-air heating in the 1860s by the Sturtevant Company, but this new technology still suffered from the evils of leakage. When architects began to seal buildings, they could also address the problem of efficient circulation of air, directing its flow within the building and sucking stale air outside. The development of effective, flexible insulating materials came late, in the 1910s and 1920s; nineteenth-century efforts focused on effective sealing through design. One way of doing so was to use new materials like continuous sheets of plate glass to clad window openings, a development that first occurred in department stores in the 1870s; the other was to make ventilating ducts do the work formerly done by windows. The giant Royal Victorian Hospital, completed in 1903 in Belfast, Northern Ireland, made ducts work in this way.

Sealing buildings also succeeded thanks to advances in lighting. The gaslights of nineteenth-century buildings usually leaked, often dangerously so. Thomas Edison's assembly of materials to make electric light became by 1882 a reference point for British builders in new construction, as it became in France and Germany a few years later. In 1882, electric lights for street lighting also began to replace gaslights. The development of electric light for large urban buildings meant that interior spaces could become even more usable, and more independent from the windows giving onto the street; eventually the window could be done away with, in buildings entirely filled with uniform electric light. The new technology broke the necessary lighting tie in earlier construction between inside and outside.

All of these technologies could be installed in existing urban buildings. The electric lights, for instance, could be fitted into the older gas sockets; heating pipes and ventilator ducts could be cut into floors or put in stairwells. The greatest source of physical discomfort in large buildings, however, generated a new urban form. This was the effort of walking up many flights of stairs; overcoming the rigors of vertical ascent through the technology of the elevator gave birth to the skyscraper. The elevator began to be used in buildings in 1846, at first powered by men pulling on counterweights, later by steam engines; the Dakota Apartment House in New York and the Connaught Hotel in London used water hydraulics to move the platform up and down. The fortune of the elevator depended on its safety, and Elisha Graves Otis in 1857 made it a safe machine by inventing automatic locking brakes in case power failed.

We take elevators so much for granted that we do not readily perceive the changes they have wrought in our bodies; the aerobic strain of climbing has been largely replaced by standing still in order to ascend. The elevator, moreover, has permitted buildings to become sealed spaces in an entirely new way; one can in a few seconds rise far from the street and all it contains. In modern buildings which couple their elevators to underground garages, it is possible for a passively moving body to lose all physical contact with the outside.

In all these ways, the geography of speed and the search for comfort led people into the isolated condition which Tocqueville called "individualism." Yet in an age whose architectural emblem is the airport waiting lounge, few people today are likely to walk through the ornate streets of Edwardian London thinking, "How dull!" Moreover, the spaces and technology of comfort have produced real pleasures in the modern city. A New Yorker would think, for instance, of a much-loved building constructed within fifteen years of the writing of *Howards End,* the Ritz Tower at the northeast corner of 57th Street and Park Avenue. Centrally heated and ducted, forty-one stories tall, when the Ritz Tower opened in 1925, it was the first skyscraper composed entirely of residences and the tallest building of this kind in the Western world. Its setbacks, making use of a 1916 zoning ordinance, meant there were Babylonian terraces high in the sky, the noises of the street muffled, the views at the time giving out to empty space. "It looked like sheer verticality as it narrowed," writes the architectural historian Elizabeth Hawes, "like a telescope, up through its setbacks, to tower in the clouds."[25]

The Ritz Tower was efficient as well as dramatic; the internal engineering of heat and fresh air by the builder Emery Roth was impeccable in design and in execution, so that the Ritz apartment dwellers were no longer tied to the window as a lifeline. Even today, when the Ritz Tower is surrounded by other skyscrapers and Park Avenue is a hideous scene of traffic congestion at this corner, inside the building one has a great sense of calm, of peace, in the heart of the world's most neurotic city. Why resist? *Howards End* gave one answer.

4. THE VIRTUE OF DISPLACEMENT

Against the social organization of speed, comfort, and efficiency, E. M. Forster invoked the virtue of a more psychological kind of movement, one which dislodges people from feeling secure. The author may seem rather unsuited for this task; the man who commanded, "Only connect . . ." also declared, in *Two Cheers for Democracy,* "I hate the idea of causes, and if I had to choose between betraying my country and betraying my friend, I hope I should have the guts to betray my country."[26] In *Howards End* the heroine reflects, "Doing good to humanity was useless, the many-coloured efforts thereto spreading over the vast area like films and resulting in a universal grey"; she believed instead that "to do good to one, or . . . to a few, was the utmost she dare hope for."[27] The artist's world seems particular and small. And yet within this intimate compass, monumental challenges to comfort occur. The novelist convinces us that they must occur.

Howards End charts the fortunes of three families which cross at the modest English country house of Howards End. The Wilcox family lives mostly for money and prestige, but possesses also enormous energy and resolve; they are part of the new Edwardian urban elite. The Schlegel family consists of two orphaned and modestly wealthy sisters, Margaret and Helen, and their younger brother, who live for high art and elevated personal relationships. The third family comes from much lower in society, consisting of the young clerk Leonard Bast, whose mistress eventually becomes his wife.

Because Forster was not a good contriver of plots, his stories read like abstract crossword puzzles, everything tidily worked out. Helen Schlegel has a brief but messy romance with the younger Wilcox son. Mrs. Wilcox dies; her husband marries the older Schlegel sister, Margaret; both Helen and the other Wilcox children hate the marriage. Helen befriends and sleeps with the working-class clerk Leonard Bast; his sluttish wife turns out to be the mistress of the elder Mr. Wilcox during his first marriage. The denouement of these histories occurs at Howards End when the elder Wilcox son attacks Leonard Bast, who has come to the country to find his beloved Helen. Leonard dies; the Wilcox son is charged with manslaughter and goes to jail; the disaster reconciles the elder Wilcox and his wife; the unmarried sister and her child install themselves at Howards End as their home.

The novel is saved by the human displacements its action requires, and these displacements Forster describes in almost surgical prose. To understand them, it helps to see *Howards End* as half of a larger project, for this novel is linked to another—*Maurice*—which Forster began to write immediately after publishing *Howards End* in 1910. The second novel told the story of a homosexual love between an upper-middle-class stockbroker and an uneducated gamekeeper. A story which transgresses the bounds of both sex and class should, according to the standards of Forster's time, end in disaster; instead, *Maurice* ends with the ultimate happiness of the otherwise conventional and classbound gentleman in the arms of a servant. Forster said, "a happy ending was imperative . . . I was determined that in fiction, anyway, two men should fall in love and remain in it for the ever and ever that fiction allows."[28]

Howards End also tells a tale of illicit sex among people of different classes, in Helen Schlegel's one-night affair with Leonard Bast. *Howards End* does not end in the enduring "for ever and ever" of fictional love which concludes *Maurice.* Instead, there is murder: the most conformist and respectable character in the novel murders Leonard Bast and goes to jail. There is betrayal discovered: Margaret Schlegel learns her husband has lied to her about sex and about money. There is indeed happiness achieved: the intrepid sexual outlaw Helen Schlegel moves with her bastard son to the country house of Howards End. All of the characters in *Howards End* come to feel uncertain about themselves by the end—they do not find the confirmation of an identity such as Maurice finds in his homosexuality. Yet even as the people in *Howards End* lose certainty about themselves, they become physically aroused by the world in which they live and they gain more awareness of one another. Forster conceived of displacement somewhat as Milton thought of exile from the Garden in *Paradise Lost.* In Forster's novel, personal displacements have a specific social dimension.

Forster's readers might have thought at first, for instance, to understand only too well the Schlegel sisters, who conformed to the image of the "Glorified Spinster," a stereotype of the liberated young woman which first appeared in the pages of *Macmillan's Magazine* in 1888. *Macmillan's* described the Glorified Spinster both admiringly and with condescension; she was unwilling to live "in a position of dependence and subjection," she wanted to extract "the greatest possible amount of pleasure out of every shilling," she sought "to find happiness and intellectual pleasures and to care comparatively little about social environment."[29] The Glorified Spinster paid for her freedom with the loss of her sexuality and of motherhood.

In the course of *Howards End,* Margaret and Helen Schlegel subverted the Glorified Spinster in separate ways, Margaret by finding sexual fulfillment with the elder Wilcox even as she remains critical and independent of him, Helen even more radically by becoming a happily unmarried mother. Yet the sisters do not quite understand what they have done, and by the end of the novel they have stopped trying to explain themselves or analyze each other.

Howards End is an unusual novel because the characters do insistently try to reckon who they are through the look, smell, and touch of their surroundings. Like sex, stereotypes of place gradually crack apart. When Margaret Schlegel first sees the beamed, low rooms of Howards End, for instance, she thinks she has found Innocence and Peace: "Drawing-room, dining-room, and hall . . . here were simply three rooms where children could play and friends shelter from the rain."[30] Against this she contrasted "the phantom of bigness, which London encourages," and which "was laid [to rest] for ever when she paced from the hall at Howards End to its kitchen and heard the rains run this way and that where the watershed of the roof divided them."[31] By the end of the novel, these stereotypes no longer work.

Forster prepares for this change when Henry Wilcox declares to Margaret, as the weight of his son's and his own misfortunes falls upon him, "I don't know what to do—what to do. I'm broken—I'm ended." The novel could at this moment collapse into sentimental bathos. Forster saves it through Margaret's response: "No sudden warmth arose in her . . . she did not enfold the sufferer in her arms . . . he shambled up to Margaret . . . and asked her to do what she could with him. She did what seemed easiest—she took him down to recruit [i.e., recover] at Howards End."[32] Though her husband is shattered, her own full and independent life now begins there. For him to recover, he must live without the clichéd pieties which have ruled his past—he must accept her "ruined" sister and accept Margaret's own independent power. It will be a place which tests and alters him. Perhaps the subtlest declaration in this book is when Margaret tells her sister that at Howards End they must do "battle against sameness. Differences—eternal differences, planted by God in a single family, so that there may always be colour; sorrow perhaps, but colour in the daily grey."[33] The country house has filled with the uncertainties and provocations of vivid life.

This shifting sense of place matters as much to the author as to any one of his characters. Forster modelled the house in the novel on the home he lived in as a child from the ages of four to fourteen, when he and his mother were forced to leave. Yet he looked upon being turned out of this childhood home as providential: "if the land had welcomed me then, the Tory side of my character would have developed and my liberalisms been atrophied"; or, as he put it even more strongly at the end of his life, "The impressions received there . . . still glow . . . and have given me a slant upon society and history. It is a middle-class slant . . . and it has been corrected by contacts with those who have never had a home in [this] sense, and do not want one."[34]

Displacement thus becomes something quite different in this novel from sheer movement, the detestable, meaningless movement epitomized for Forster by the automobile. Human displacements ought to jolt people into caring about one another, and where they are. Thus the possibility of the good sort of displacement appears even in descriptions of London, as when the Schlegel sisters in London, like the young author in the country, lose their own home. At this moment, Forster remarks more generally, "the Londoner seldom understands his city until its sweeps him . . . away from his moorings; Margaret's eyes were not opened until the lease of Wickham Place [her home in the city] expired."[35]

Forster once said to his friend Forrest Reid about his own life, "I was trying to connect up and use all the fragments I was born with."[36] The characters in his novels try to do that as well. Yet the places

Rooksnest, the model for Howards End.

where people connect in Forster's novels lack the *"simple oneness* of things" the philosopher Martin Heidegger imagined in a farmhouse in the Black Forest of Germany, an enduring dwelling "designed for the different generations under one roof, showing the character of their journey through time."[37] Howards End is a place where discontinuity becomes a positive value.

Alfred Kazin writes of Forster's hope in *Howards End* that "a grievously class-proud, class-protecting, class-embittered society may yet come to think of some deeper, more ancient 'comradeship' as one of its distinguishing marks."[38] In both *Maurice* and *Howards End* Forster wants to show that by breaking through sexual and class boundaries. But in *Howards End* he also reflects on a possible modern meaning of place. His sense of place is not that of a sanctuary; instead, it is a scene in which people come alive, where they expose, acknowledge, and address the discordant parts of themselves and one another.

What can this critique mean for us who live today in discordant cities filled with differences, different races, ethnicities, sexualities, classes, ages? How could a multi-cultural society be in need of displacement, rather than security and comfort?

CONCLUSION

Civic Bodies

Multi-Cultural New York

1. DIFFERENCE AND INDIFFERENCE

Greenwich Village

Like so many others, I had read my way into Greenwich Village, before arriving there twenty years ago, in the pages of Jane Jacobs's *The Death and Life of Great American Cities*—the Village appearing in her famous book as the quintessential urban center, mixing groups and stimulating individuals through its diversity. Unlike Harlem or the South Bronx, she painted a picture of the races living in fair harmony here, as did the ethnic mixture of Italians, Jews, and Greeks. The Village appeared to her a modern agora in the heart of New York.[1]

The place I found did not belie her words. Though by 1970 the Village had lost many of the children of these immigrants to the suburbs, the community was indeed diverse and tolerant. Teenagers

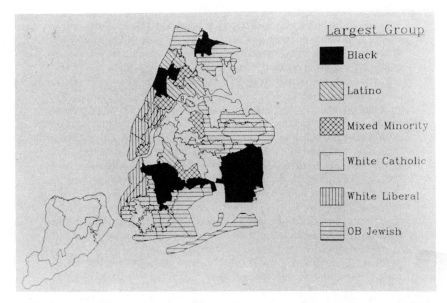

Ethnic and political makeup of New York Assembly Districts, ca. 1980. *Reproduced with permission from John Hull Mollenkopf,* A Phoenix in the Ashes: The Rise and Fall of the Koch Coalition in New York City Politics *(Princeton University Press, 1992).*

with clean sheets and warm beds elsewhere slept on the ground in the open air of Washington Square, lulled to sleep by competing nocturnal folk singers, unmolested by thieves, untroubled by the presence of people who had nowhere else to sleep. The well-kept houses and streets in the Village contributed to the impression that this place differed from the rest of New York, possessing a strong sense of community among strangers who lived in relative safety.

The village continues to be a space of differences today. There are still knots of Italian families surviving along MacDougal Street, mixed in with tourists. The community's charming houses and apartment buildings still contain elderly people who have guarded their cheap housing and live intermixed with newcomers who are richer and younger. Since Jacobs's time, a large homosexual community has flourished on the western edge of the Village, harassed by some of the tourists but living in relative harmony with immediate neighbors. The writers and artists who remain are, like myself, people who came when rents were cheap; we are ageing, bourgeois bohemians upon whom this variegated scene works like a charm.

Yet one's eye often provides misleading social information about diversity. Jane Jacobs saw people in the Village so tightly packed together they seemed to have fused. On MacDougal Street, though, the tourist action consists mostly of people looking at one another; the Italians occupy the space above the street-level shops, talking to their neighbors in opposite buildings as though there were nobody below. Hispanics, Jews, and Koreans interweave along Second Avenue, but to walk down Second Avenue is to pass through an ethnic palimpsest in which each group keeps neatly to its own turf.

Difference and indifference co-exist in the life of the Village; the sheer fact of diversity does not prompt people to interact. In part this is because, over the last two decades, the diversities of the Village have grown more cruel, in ways *The Death and Life of Great American Cities* did not envision. Washington Square has become a kind of drug supermarket; the swings of the children's north sandlot serve as a stand-up boutique for heroin, the benches under the statue of a Polish patriot serve as display counters for various pills, while all four corners of the square deal wholesale in cocaine. No young people sleep in the park now, and though the various dealers and their outriders are familiar figures to the mothers watching infants on the swings or to students at the university next to the square, these criminals seem all but invisible to the police.

In his *History,* Thucydides reckoned the civic strength of Athens by pairing Perikles' Funeral Oration to the outbreak of plague in Athens a few months later. Nothing like the moral collapse Thucydides depicted occurred when the modern plague of AIDS appeared on the streets of the Village. In the western part of the community the spread of the disease made many homosexual residents more politically engaged; the health machinery of the city has positively if inadequately responded to them; much of the art, theatre, and dance made or performed in the West Village explores AIDS.

At the eastern edge of the Village where Greenwich Village shades into the great swatch of poverty on the Lower East Side, however, it is a different story. Here are concentrated drug addicts of both sexes who have become ill with AIDS from sharing needles, and women who have become ill through sexual encounters as prostitutes. AIDS and drugs mix most graphically along Rivington Street, a gap-toothed place of abandoned houses off the Bowery, the houses serving as "shooting galleries" for the addicted. Occasionally young social workers can be seen wandering Rivington Street, knocking at the locked doors or on the boarded-up windows of the shooting galleries, offering free, clean needles. But Villagers otherwise tend not to give the dying trouble; tolerated by citizens, perhaps profitable to the police, the crackhouses are flourishing.

If locals do not bother the police about drugs, having drawn the obvious conclusion, few of my neighbors are inclined to telephone about the homeless, new strangers to the Village. By one count, during the summer nearly one in every two hundred people in the center of New York is homeless, placing the city above Calcutta but below Cairo on this particular index of misery.[2] In the Village the homeless sleep in streets near Washington Square, but off the drug route; during the day, they stand outside the local banks, my own financial "doorman" claiming that while people in the Village give him less money than in more affluent parts of the city, we also give him less trouble. It is no more and no less than that; here people let one another alone.

In the course of the development of modern, urban individualism, the individual fell silent in the city. The street, the café, the department store, the railroad, bus, and underground became places of the gaze rather than scenes of discourse. When verbal connections between strangers in the modern city are difficult to sustain, the impulses of sympathy which individuals may feel in the city looking at the scene around them become in turn momentary—a second of response looking at snapshots of life.

Diversity in the Village works this way; ours is a purely visual agora. There is nowhere to discuss the stimulations of the eye on streets like Second Avenue, no place they can be collectively shaped into a civic narrative, nor, perhaps more consequently, a sanctuary which takes account of for the disease-ravaged scenes of the East Village. Of course the Village as elsewhere in the city offers myriad formal occasions in which our citizens voice civic complaint, outrage. But the political occasions do not translate into everyday social practice on the streets; they do little, moreover, to compound the multiple cultures of the city into common purposes.

It may be a sociological truism that people do not embrace difference, that differences create hostility, that the best to be hoped for is the daily practice of toleration. This truism would argue that the arousing personal experience conveyed in a novel like Howards End cannot be translated more largely into society. Yet New York has been for over a century a city filled with a diversity of cultures, many often as discriminated against as the Jews of Renaissance Venice. To say that difference inevitably provokes mutual withdrawal means saying that such a multi-cultural city cannot have a common civic culture; it means taking the side of the Venetian Christians, who imagined a civic culture possible only among people who are alike. More, the sociological truism means dismissing a deeper Judeo-Christian source of faith—compassion—as though that animating religious force had simply washed away into the multi-cultural sea.

If New York's history poses the general question of whether a civic culture can be forged out of human differences, the Village poses a more particular question: how that diverse civic culture might become something people feel in their bones.

Center and periphery

The dilemmas of visceral arousal in a multi-cultural society have been compounded by New York's history and geography.

New York is a grid city par excellence, an endless geometry of equal blocks, though not quite the grid which the Romans envisaged; New York's grid has no fixed edge or center. The Roman city builders studied the heavens to site the earthly city, and plotted the boundaries of a town in order to define its internal geometry. The designers of modern New York conceived of the urban grid as an expanding chessboard; in 1811 the city fathers bestowed the grid plan on city lands above Greenwich Village, and in 1855 this plan was extended beyond Manhattan into the northerly borough of the Bronx and the easterly borough of Queens.

Like the Roman town grid, the New York plan was laid down on largely empty land, a city designed in advance of being inhabited; if the Romans consulted the heavens for guidance in this effort, the city fathers of New York consulted the banks. Of the modern grid plan in general Lewis Mumford has said that "the resurgent capitalism of the seventeenth century treated the individual lot and the block, the street and the avenue as abstract units for buying and selling, without respect for historic uses, for topographic conditions or for social needs."[3] The absolute uniformity in the lots created by the New York grid meant that land could be treated just like money, each piece worth the same amount. In the happier, early days of the Republic, dollar bills were printed when bankers felt the need of money; so too the supply of land could be increased by extending this turf, so that more city came into being when speculators felt the urge to speculate.

This boundless grid city lacked a center. Neither the city plan of 1811 nor of 1855 contains indications of greater or lesser value on the maps, nor reckonings of where people would be likely to meet, as the Roman could reckon abroad by finding the intersection of the principal streets. A visitor to New York logically suspects that the center of the city lies around Central Park; when Calvert Vaux and Frederick Law Olmsted began planning the park in 1857, they imagined it as a refuge from the city. From the moment local politicians harried Olmsted out of his great project, the park began to decay, people avoiding the ill-kept, crime-ridden lawns as meeting grounds.

In theory, a city plan lacking both a fixed boundary and a fixed center makes possible many diverse points of social contact in the city; the original plan does not dictate to later generations of builders. In New York, for instance, the great office compound of Rockefeller Center begun in the 1930s could have been located a few blocks north or south or further west; the neutral grid did not dictate its placement. Though the flexibility of space in New York may seem to echo in spirit L'Enfant's plan for a diverse rather than centralized city, New York is in fact closer to realizing urban space such as the revolutionary French urbanists conceived it. The lack of directives in New York's plan means spaces can easily be swept clear of obstacles, those obstacles constituted by the accretion of stone, glass, and steel from the past.

Until quite recently, perfectly viable buildings in New York disappeared with the same regularity they appeared. Within the space of sixty years, for instance, the great mansions lining Fifth Avenue for miles, from Greenwich Village to the top of Central Park, were constructed, inhabited, and destroyed to make way for taller buildings. Even today, with historic controls, new New York skyscrapers are planned to last fifty years, and financed accordingly, though as engineered objects they could last much longer. Of all the world's cities, New York has the most destroyed itself in order to grow; in a hundred years people will have more tangible evidence about Hadrian's Rome than they will about fiber-optic New York.

This chameleon urban fabric has had great importance for the history of multi-culturalism in New York. During the era after the Civil War when New York first became an international city, its immigrants crowded into great dense grids of poverty, principally on the Lower East Side of the borough of Manhattan but also behind the docks all along on the West Side of Manhattan and on the eastern edge of the borough of Brooklyn. Diverse miseries met on these blocks in so-called New Law Tenements. These buildings had been designed to provide light and air to interior spaces, but the good intentions of their architects were overwhelmed by the sheer numbers of people stuffed into the structures.

At the beginning of this century, the children of the immigrants began to push outward as their circumstances permitted, like the achieving English working classes who made use of the Underground to move out to better housing in North London. Some immigrant children moved first into Harlem, others farther into sparsely populated territory in the outer boroughs, the most prosperous into private houses, the sufficiently prosperous into apartment buildings whose designs broke the mold of the cramped New York tenements in the center. Two forces stemmed that outward flow; the bulk of jobs remained in the urban core, and the New York region lacked an elaborate network of urban arteries and veins.

After the Second World War, a new push outward became possible in New York largely thanks to the work of one man, Robert Moses. Like Haussmann's works, the sheer scale of Moses's enterprises begun in the 1920s and 1930s staggers the imagination; he built bridges, parks, ports, beachfronts, and highways. Again like Haussmann, and before Haussmann, Boullée and Wailly, Robert Moses viewed the existing urban fabric of his city as arbitrary in form, entailing no obligation on his part to preserve or renovate what others before him had made.

The great transport Moses made for the New York region consummated the Enlightenment impulse to create a city based on the moving body. Though New York had developed the most extensive mass transit system in the world by the time Moses began to build, he favored travel by individuals in automobiles. To other planners, this huge network of roads seemed to threaten the viability of the established urban center, rather than extend the center's reach. So it appeared, for instance, to the urbanist Jean Gottmann, who imagined in his classic study, *Megalopolis,* that a vast urban region would take form along the Eastern Seaboard of the United States, stretching from Boston to Washington. This megalopolis would destroy, Gottmann said, the central city as "the 'center,' the 'heart' of a region."[4]

Moses defended his highways as amenities rather than destructive designs. His sense of the pleasures of movement appeared in the parkway system, which were roads that excluded trucks, laid out in curving ribbons of concrete passing through artfully constructed parks, screened from houses; these expensive, illusionistic parkways were meant to make the experience of driving an automobile a self-contained pleasure, free of resistance.

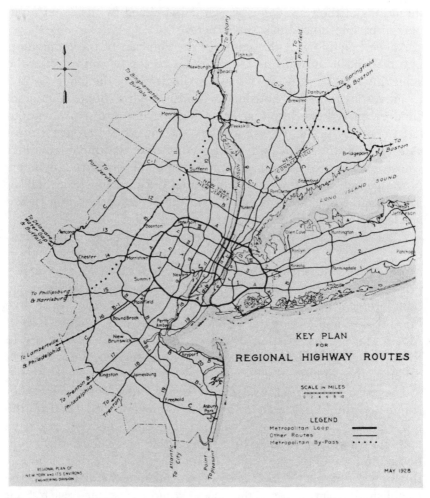

Key plan for New York regional highway routes, 1929. From *The Graphic
Regional Plan: Atlas and Description.* Courtesy of Columbia University,
Avery Architectural and Fine Arts Library, New York.

Thanks to this system of highways and parkways, he believed, people could put the stresses of the city out of mind. One of Moses's
great destinations in this regard was Jones Beach, the long stretch of
sand he organized into a public resort near the city. Of Moses's attitude toward the beach a colleague, Frances Perkins, remarked, "He'd
denounce the common people terribly. To him they were lousy,
dirty people, throwing bottles all over Jones Beach. 'I'll get them!

I'll teach them!' . . . He loves the public, but not as people."[5] In particular Moses tried to keep blacks out of Jones Beach, as in the public parks he created, considering them especially unclean.

The title Robert Caro chose for a biography of Robert Moses, *The Power Broker,* aptly characterizes the spirit in which Moses worked.[6] Moses was not himself a professional planner; instead he forged the governmental and financial instruments which designers used. Moses lacked in particular the visual imagination to see how map drawings and blueprints would actually look as three-dimensional forms. Often treated as a planning devil, he was in a way something else more frightening, a person of immense power who often did not understand what he was building. But, as in Jones Beach, his social aims were clear enough.

His planning sought to undo diversity. The impacted mass of the city seemed a rock to be chipped apart, and "the public good" was to be achieved by fragmenting the city. In this, Moses made a selective effort; only those who had succeeded—succeeded enough to own a car, to buy a house—were provided the means of escape, the bridges and highways offering them an exit from the noise of strikers, beg-

New York landscapes shaped by Robert Moses. From R. Caro, *The Power Broker: Robert Moses and the Fall of New York* (New York: Alfred A. Knopf, 1974), inside front cover.
Reprinted by permission.

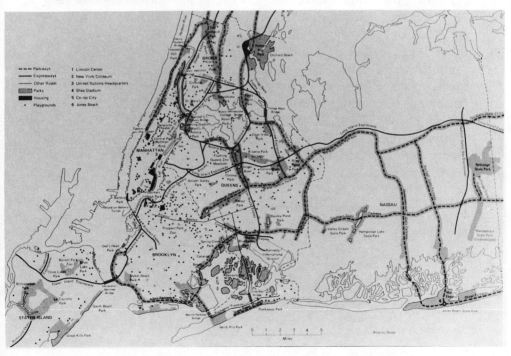

gars, and the distressed which had filled the streets of New York during the Great Depression.

It should be said that if Moses eroded the dense urban center, his interventions served a deeply felt communal need, the need for adequate family housing. When Moses spread out the New York urban region through fingers of highways out to the east, developers built housing tracts after the Second World War on the great estates and potato farms of Long Island; when he spread out other highway fingers to the north, more modest landholdings were transformed into suburbs. Herbert Gans studied a generation ago the new residential community of Levittown on Long Island made possible by the highways Moses built; he observed that the mass of single family houses provided "more family cohesion and a significant boost of morale" within each house.[7] Gans rightly derided those who snobbishly dismissed this housing; able to leave city apartments which were too cramped for families, people valued their new homes because of their "desire to own a free-standing house."[8]

Moses had difficulty understanding, though, that he had created a new economic territory. The growth of the New York periphery in fact coincided with the increase in office and service tasks which, thanks to electronic communications, no longer had to be located in the dense urban core where rents were high. The periphery also grew in concert with changes in manufacturing. Increasingly the periphery employed women workers in both services and small subfactories; the women were able to work in jobs close to where they live, but received wages inferior to those paid men.[9] As the periphery took on an economic life of its own, part of the dream of escape thus began to fade. Poverty and low-wage jobs reappeared in the suburbs. As did crime and drugs. The suburban hopes for a stable, secure family life recorded by Herbert Gans have also withered, insofar as they were premised on escape.

Yet the legacy of Robert Moses has endured in two ways. His restructuring of New York brought to a head the forces of individual movement which began to take form two centuries before in Europe. And he bequeathed to those who remained in the old, diverse urban core a sharpened, more difficult problem in dealing with their own perceptions and sensations of others.

Bodily movement first took on its modern importance as a new principle of biological activity. The medical analysis of circulation of the blood, of the respiration of the lungs, and of the electrical forces moving throughout the nerves created a new image of the healthy body, a body whose freedom of movement stimulated the organism. From this medical knowledge it followed that space should be designed to encourage bodily movement and the processes of respiration associated with it; this deduction about space was drawn by Enlightened urban planners in the eighteenth century. The person who moved freely felt more self-possessed and individual as a result of experiencing this physical freedom.

People now move rapidly, especially to and within peripheral territories whose fragments are linked together only by automobiles. The logistics of speed, however, detach the body from the spaces through which it moves; highway planners seek, for reasons of safety if nothing else, to neutralize and standardize the spaces through which a speeding vehicle travels. The act of driving, disciplining the sitting body into a fixed position, and requiring only micro-movements, pacifies the driver physically. Harvey's generation imagined movement as stimulating; in Robert Moses's New York we know it as monotonous.

In the nineteenth century designs for both movement and sitting became tied to technologies that made the individual body comfortable. Comfort lowers the amount, and relaxes the intensity, of stimulation; it, too, is an essay in monotony. The search for comfortable, lesser stimulation has a direct connection to how we are likely to deal with the disturbing sensations which potentially loom in a diverse multi-cultural community.

Roland Barthes first called attention to this connection in what he termed people's use of an "image repertoire" when they encounter strangers.[10] Scanning a complex or unfamiliar scene, the individual tries to sort it out rapidly in terms of images which fall into simple and general categories, drawing on social stereotypes. Encountering a black man or an Arab on the street, a white person registers threat, and does not look more searchingly. The judgment, Barthes observed, is instant and the result surprising; thanks to the classifying powers of the image repertoire, people shut out further stimulation. Confronted with difference, they quickly become passive.

The urbanist Kevin Lynch has shown how an image repertoire can be used to interpret urban geography in the same way. Every urbanite, he says, carries an image of "where I belong" in the mind's eye; in his research Lynch found that his subjects compared new places to this mental snapshot and, the less the two corresponded, the more indifferent the subjects felt about their new surroundings. Rapid movement, such as occurs in an automobile, encourages the use of an image repertoire, that disposition to classify and to judge immediately. Fragmented geography also strengthens the image repertoire, since on the periphery each fragment has its special function—home, shopping, office, school—separated by empty patches from other fragments. It is thus an easy and quick matter to judge if someone doesn't belong, or is behaving in an inappropriate way in a particular place.

Similarly, the sociologist Erving Goffmann sought to show how, where people do walk, "defensive de-stimulation" influences the ways people manage their bodies on the street; after that initial classifying glance at one another, people walk or position themselves so that they risk as little physical contact as possible.[11] By scanning one's surroundings through an image repertoire, subjecting the environment to simple categories of representation, comparing likeness to difference, a person diminishes the complexity of urban experience. By using an image repertoire to withdraw from others, the individual feels more at ease.

With such a tool for sensing reality, the puzzling and the ambiguous can be avoided. The fears of touching which gave rise to the Venetian Ghetto have been strengthened in modern society as individuals create something like ghettos in their own bodily experience when confronted with diversity. Speed, escape, passivity: this triad is what the new urban environment has made of Harvey's discoveries.

These perceptual walls around the self took a particular meaning in the lives of people left behind.

At the time Moses was finally driven from power in the late 1960s, it seemed likely that Jean Gottmann's prediction in *Megalopolis* would be fulfilled: the old, poor parts of the urban core would become as desolate and depopulated in New York as they were becoming in other American cities. And this was because immigration to the city seemed to have stopped by 1965, when a new national immigration law was written; the Puerto Ricans were often spoken of as the "last foreigners" in New York. The pushes and pulls of the global economy, however, defeated this expectation: new waves of immigrants came, first from the Caribbean and Central America, then from Korea, then from the collapsing Soviet Empire, the Middle East, and Mexico. These new immigrants are now half the city's population.

They have been joined by a reverse flow from the suburbs. The children of those who left a generation ago have sought to return to the center. In part this reverse flow has been dictated by the peculiarities of the housing market in the New York suburbs, in part because the sharpest increases in entry-level service and professional jobs have occurred in the national businesses located in Manhattan. But these local peculiarities also mesh with a larger desire among many young people to return to or come to the city; the largest single slice of humanity arriving into New York each year are white, young people between eighteen and thirty.

These new New Yorkers have had to deal with the complicated lives of those who never left the city. After the Second World War, a kind of social and familial triage took place in New York; successful Jews, Greeks, Italians, and Irish moved away from the core, their less successful compatriots did not. Many older people also chose to stay in the places where they had struggled to make a life. One of the great hidden dramas of New York in its last half century, for instance, has been that of inner-city Jewish poverty. The stereotyping of New York Jews as a particularly successful ethnic group has disguised the presence on the Lower East Side, on the Upper West Side, and in Flatbush of tens of thousands of poor Jews who remained behind, eking out a living in the craft and service trades in which most Jews began. In other communities which began by sharing the harshest of prospects, class mobility and the breaks between generations have created similar inner dramas of abandonment and betrayal, successful, middle-class blacks in the suburbs, for instance, leaving behind their brothers and sisters in poverty.

Purity in a ghetto requires a clear command to segregate—the sort of command issued in Venice to pack Jews into one place or in modern New York to avoid lending money to blacks. In their nineteenth-century origins, however, the New York ghettos were real estate zones rather than places larger authority sought to endow with a particular character or identity. New York's Lower East Side was purely poor, but highly mixed ethnically; Little Italy in the 1920s was home to Irish and Slavs, and today contains as many Asians as Italians; Harlem at the height of the "Harlem Renaissance" in the 1920s housed more Greeks and Jews than blacks.

As the core bled into the megalopolis in the wake of changes made by Robert Moses, the word "ghetto" took on the barely submerged meaning of "those who have been left behind." Harlem, for instance, depopulated; the Jews and the Greeks left it in the 1930s, the nascent black bourgeoisie left it forty years later. To belong to a ghetto came to be seen as a matter of sharing a common failure.

Many of the modern attempts to revive ghetto spaces have, in the manner of the Renaissance Jews, sought to transform segregated lives also into an honorable collective identity. This effort has occurred everywhere in New York, among new ethnic migrants as among the blacks, poor Jews, and other ethnics left behind. To revive the honor of the ghetto has meant turning inward both spatially and mentally. Most community-building efforts focus on defining a common identity and shoring up buildings or spaces which define a center of that common life, rather than making contact with those who are different. New York was never a melting pot, but its multi-cultural problems now are tinged with this history of abandonment, and the needs of the abandoned to restitute their honor. Yet the very forces which brought new people to the urban center after the heirs of Robert Moses left will not permit this inward turning, this honor forged in a space of separation on the model of the Venetian Jews.

In terms of population, New York has only been able to take in new ethnics by repopulating the old ghetto spaces. The zones of poverty to the northeast of Wall Street, for instance, are now filling with the night army who work as cleaners, printers, messengers, and service workers in the temples of fiber-optic finance. Dominicans, Salvadoreans, and Haitians are pressing into the still habitable housing at the northwest corner of Harlem. In Brooklyn, Russian Jews, Hasids, and Syrians have repopulated the places abandoned by the Jews who came in earlier generations. And throughout the urban core, the steady, inflowing stream of young native whites presses into the places vacated by an earlier middle class.

Moreover, the economy of the city will not permit this inward turning. National chain stores have replaced many local businesses; small businesses remain strong in New York engaged in those kinds of enterprises—from violin repair to copper restoration to specialist printing—which draw on a metropolitan rather than local clientele. These quirky, small, specialist businesses offer many immigrants now, as in the past, a first step up on the social ladder. The recent history of multi-culturalism in New York has moved in a separatist direction, but this ethnic separatism is a dead end, economically if nothing else.

From Perikles' Athens to David's Paris, the word "civic" has implied an intertwined fate, a crossing of fortunes. It was inconceivable to a Periklean Greek that his or her fortune could be separated from the fortunes of a city, or to a pagan Roman of Hadrian's time. Though early Christians believed their fate lay within themselves, this inner life was eventually reconnected to worldly fortunes they shared with others. The medieval corporation seemed to break with this notion of a common destiny, since it could will itself to change, and like the University of Bologna, break with its present circumstances. Yet the corporation was a collective body, literally an incorporation of particular people into a legal entity with a larger life of its own. And the Venetian Ghetto told a bitter story about a common destiny, for the Christian Venetians knew their fortunes could not be divorced from the Jews whom they kept in the city, while the fortunes of the Jews in the Ghetto could not be untied from the lives of their oppressors. The food riots launched by the Parisian women at the dawn of the French Revolution also sought to interlock their fortunes with powers beyond themselves.

In the modern world, belief in a common destiny suffered a curious division. Nationalist ideologies have asserted that people share a fate, as have revolutionary ideologies; the city, however, has falsified these assertions. During the course of the nineteenth century, urban development used the technologies of motion, of public health and of private comfort, the workings of the market, the planning of streets, parks, and squares to resist the demands of crowds and privilege the claims of individuals. Those individuals, as Tocqueville observes, feel "strangers to the destinies of each other"; in common with other observers of the progress of individualism, Tocqueville saw its profound connection to materialism, a "virtuous materialism," he wrote, "which would not corrupt, but enervate the soul, and noiselessly unbend its springs of action."[12] In withdrawing from common life, that individual would lose life.

The churning energies of destruction and rebuilding which have created and destroyed great office buildings, apartment houses, and homes in New York have denied time's claims on civic culture. The trajectories out of New York resemble socially the routes taken out of London and other cities—cities which have taken on their modern shapes through individually detaching movements. The denial of a common fate was crucial to all these movements.

Yet if the whites fleeing to Long Island after the Second World War flatly denied they shared a fate with the whites or blacks who remained, more subtle denials also occurred. Those who were left behind denied, for the sake of honor, that their fates intertwined with others. The privileged have protected themselves against the poor as they have protected themselves against stimulation; the needy have sought to wear a like armor, which only wards off those they need. Life in Greenwich Village exemplifies perhaps the most we have been able to achieve: a willingness to live with difference, though a denial this entails a shared fate.

2. CIVIC BODIES

At the beginning of this study, I said that I have written it as a religious believer, and now, at its end, I should like to explain why. In *Flesh and Stone* I have argued that urban spaces take form largely from the ways people experience their own bodies. For people in a multi-cultural city to care about one another, I believe we have to change the understanding we have of our own bodies. We will never experience the difference of others until we acknowledge the bodily insufficiencies in ourselves. Civic compassion issues from that physical awareness of lack in ourselves, not from sheer goodwill or political rectitude. If these assertions seem far from the practical realities of New York, perhaps it is a sign of how much urban experience has become divorced from religious understanding.

These lessons to be learned from the body are one of the foundations of the Judeo-Christian tradition. Central to that tradition are the transgressions of Adam and Eve, the shame of their nakedness, their exile from the Garden, which lead to a story of what the first humans became, as well as what they lost. In the Garden, they were innocent, unknowing, and obedient. Out in the world, they became aware; they knew they were flawed creatures, and so they explored, sought to understand what was strange and unlike; they were no longer God's children to whom all was given. The Old Testament recounts over and over stories of people who mirror this sorrowful awakening of the first humans, people who transgress in their bodily desires the commandments of God, are punished, and then, like

Adam and Eve in exile, awaken. The first Christians made from Christ's passage on earth such a story; crucified for man's sins, His gift to men and women is to rouse a sense of the insufficiency of the flesh; the less pleasure His followers take in their own bodies, the more they will love one another.

Pagan history told this ancient truth in another way, as the story of what bodies experience in cities. The Athenian agora and Pnyx were urban spaces in which citizens felt bodily insufficiency: the ancient agora stimulated people physically, at the price of depriving them of coherent speech with others; the Pnyx provided continuity in speech and so gave the community experiences of narrative logic, at the price of rendering people vulnerable to the rhetorical stimulation of words. The stones of the agora and the Pnyx put people in a state of flux, each of the two centers a source of dissatisfaction the other could resolve only by arousing dissatisfactions of its own. In the dual-centered city, people knew incompleteness in their bodily experiences. Yet no people more self-consciously valued civic culture than these same Athenians: "human" and "polis" were interchangeable words. Intense civic bonds arose from the very play of displacement, people cared strongly about one another in spaces which did not fully satisfy their bodily needs—indeed, a Jewish contemporary might have said, *because* these spaces did not satisfy bodily needs. Yet the ancient city was itself not like a monument to stability. Not even the most binding of human acts, ritual, could guarantee its cohesion.

It is a modern habit to think of social instability and personal insufficiency as pure negatives. The formation of modern individualism has in general aimed at making individuals self-sufficient, that is to say, complete rather than incomplete. Psychology speaks the language of people finding a center for themselves, of achieving integration and wholeness of the self. Modern social movements also speak this language, as though communities ought to become like individuals, coherent and whole. In New York, the pains of being left behind or left out have inflected this individual-communal language; racial, ethnic, and social groups turn inward in order to cohere, and so to heal. The psychological experience of displacement, of incoherence—the domain of what the psychoanalyst Robert Jay Lifton calls a "protean self"—would seem only a recipe for deepening those social wounds.[13]

However, without significant experiences of self-displacement, social differences gradually harden because interest in the Other

withers. Freud pointed to this sociological truth as a bodily truth in
Beyond the Pleasure Principle, the short essay he published in 1920.
He contrasts the bodily pleasure in wholeness and equilibrium to a
more reality-centered bodily experience which transcends that pleasure. Pleasure, Freud wrote, "is invariably set in motion by an
unpleasurable tension . . . [and] its final outcome coincides with a
lowering of that tension."[14] Pleasure, that is, is not like sexual excite-
ment, which involves an arousing disturbance of the senses; pleasure
instead seeks to return to a state which Freud imagined ultimately to
be like the comfort of a fetus in the womb, safe and unknowing of
the world. Under sway of the pleasure principle, people wish to dis-
engage.

Freud speaks to us as a worldly realist rather than as a religious
ascetic because he knows the desire for comfort expresses a profound biological need. *"Protection against* stimuli," he writes, "is an
almost more important function for the living organism than *reception
of* stimuli."[15] But if protection rules, if the body is not open to peri-
odic crises, eventually the organism sickens for lack of stimulation.
The modern urge for comfort, he said, is a highly dangerous impulse
for human beings; the difficulties we seek to avoid do not therefore
disappear.

What could defeat the urge to withdraw into pleasure? In *Beyond
the Pleasure Principle,* Freud envisaged two ways. One he called the
"reality principle": a person faces up to difficulties physical or emotional by force of sheer will. Under the sway of the reality principle,
a person resolves to know "unpleasure."[16] That "unpleasure"
requires courage in everyday life. But Freud is also a realist because
he knows the reality principle is not a very strong force, courage a
rarity. The other defeat of pleasure is more certain and more enduring. In the course of a person's experience, he writes, "it happens
again and again that individual instincts or parts of instincts turn out
to be incompatible in their aims or demands with the remaining
ones."[17] The body feels at war with itself; it becomes uncomfortably
aroused; but the incompatibilities of desire are too great to be
resolved, or to be pushed aside.

This is the work civilization does: it confronts us, in all our frailty,
with contradictory experiences which cannot be pushed away, and
which make us feel therefore incomplete. Yet precisely in that state
of "cognitive dissonance"—to use the term of a later critic—human
beings begin to focus upon, to attend to, to explore, and to become
engaged in the realm where the pleasure of wholeness is impossible.

The history of the Western city records a long struggle between this civilized possibility and the effort to create power as well as pleasure through master images of wholeness. Master images of "the body" have performed the work of power in urban space. The Athenians and pagan Romans made use of such master images; in the evolution of the Judeo-Christian tradition, the spiritual wanderer returned home to the urban center where his suffering body became a reason for submission and meekness, the spiritual body thereby becoming flesh and stone. At the dawn of the modern scientific era, the center served a new master image of "the body"—the body a circulating mechanism and the center its heart-pump and lungs—and this scientific body image evolved socially to justify the power of the individual over the claims of the polity.

Yet, as I have tried to show, this legacy contains deep internal contradictions and strains. In the Athenian city, the master image of male nakedness could not fully control or define the clothed bodies of women. The Roman center served as the mythic focus of a fiction of Rome's continuity and coherence; the visual images which expressed this coherence became the instruments of power. Yet, if in the democratic center, the Athenian citizen became a slave of the voice, in the imperial center the Roman citizen became a slave of the eye.

When early Christianity took root in the city, it reconciled its relation to this visual and geographic tyranny so antithetical to the spiritual condition of the wandering people of the Judeo-Christian Word and Light. Christianity reconciled itself to the powers of the urban center by dividing its own visual imagination in two, inner and outer, spirit and power; the realm of the outer city could not fully conquer the need for faith in the inner city of the soul. The Christian cities of the Middle Ages continued to experience this divided center, now built in stone as the differences between sanctuary and street. Yet not even Christ's body, meant through imitation to rule the Christian city, could rule the street.

Nor could the center hold by acts of purification. The impulse to atone and to cleanse the polluted Christian body which animated the segregation of the Jews and other impure bodies in Christian Venice could not restore its spiritual core. Nor could the ceremonies of revolution make the core cohere. The impulse to clear away obstacles, to create a transparent space of freedom at the urban center of revolutionary Paris, became mere emptiness and induced apathy, helping defeat the ceremonies aiming at a durable civic transformation. The modern master image of the individual, detached body has hardly ended in triumph. It has ended in passivity.

In the crevices and contradictions of master images of the body in space, there have appeared moments and occasions for resistance, the dignifying resistances of the Thesmophoria and the Adonia, the rituals of the dining room and the bath in the Christian house, the rituals of the night in the Ghetto—rituals which did not destroy the dominant order but created a more complex life for the bodies the dominant order sought to rule in its own image. In our history, the complex relations between the body and the city have carried people beyond the pleasure principle, as Freud described it; these have been troubled bodies, bodies not at rest, bodies aroused by disturbance. How much dissonance and unease can people bear? For two thousand years they sustained a great deal in places to which they had been passionately attached. We might take this record of an active physical life conducted in a center which does not hold as one measure of our present estate.

In the end this historic tension between domination and civilization asks us a question about ourselves. How will we exit from our own bodily passivity—where is the chink in our own system, where is our liberation to come from? It is, I would insist, a peculiarly pressing question for a multi-cultural city, even if it is far from current discourse about group injuries and group rights. For without a disturbed sense of ourselves, what will prompt most of us—who are not heroic figures knocking on the doors of crackhouses—to turn outward toward each other, to experience the Other?

Any society needs strong moral sanctions to make people tolerate, much less experience positively, duality, incompleteness, and otherness. Those moral sanctions arose in Western civilization through the powers of religion. Religious rituals bonded, in Peter Brown's phrase, the body to the city; a pagan ritual like the Thesmophoria did so by literally pushing women out of the boundaries of the house, into a ritual space where both women and men confronted the gendered ambiguities in the meaning of citizenship.

It would be crass to say that we need, in a utilitarian fashion, religious ritual again in order to turn human beings outward—and the history of ritual spaces in the city will not allow us to think of believing in so instrumental a way. As the pagan world disappeared, the Christian found in the making of ritual spaces a new spiritual vocation, a vocation of labor and self-discipline that eventually put its mark upon the city as it had earlier upon the rural sanctuary. The gravity of these ritual spaces lay in ministering to bodies in pain, and the recognition of human suffering inseparably bound in the Christian ethos. By a terrible twist of fate, when Christian communities found they had to live with those unlike themselves, they imposed this conjoint sense of place and the burdens of a suffering body on those, like the Venetian Jews, whom they oppressed.

The French Revolution played out this Christian drama again, and yet not again. The physical environment in which the Revolution imposed suffering, and in which the revolutionaries sought to recuperate a maternal figure incorporating and transforming their own sufferings, had lost the specificity and density of place. The suffering body displayed itself in empty space, a space of abstract freedom but no enduring human connection.

The drama of the revolutionary rituals echoed a pagan drama as well, the attempt deeply rooted in ancient life to deploy ritual, to guide it in the service of the oppressed and the denied. On the Champ de Mars this effort at the design of ritual also aborted; the ancient belief that ritual "comes from somewhere else" now seemed to mean that its powers were beyond design, beyond human agency, inspired by forces which lay beyond the powers of a humane and civilized society.

In its stead, design turned to the shaping of pleasure, in the form of comfort, originally to compensate for fatigue, to lighten the burden of work. But these powers of design which rested the body came as well to lighten its sensory weight, suspending the body in an ever more passive relation to its environment. The trajectory of designed pleasure led the human body to an ever more solitary rest.

If there is a place for faith in mobilizing the powers of civilization against those of domination, it lies in accepting exactly what this solitude seeks to avoid: pain, the kind of lived pain evinced by my friend at the cinema. His shattered hand serves as a witness; lived pain witnesses the body moving beyond the power of society to define; the meanings of pain are always incomplete in the world. The acceptance of pain lies within a realm outside the order human beings make in the world. Wittgenstein bore witness to pain thus in the passage quoted at the beginning of this study. In a magisterial work, *The Body in Pain,* the philosopher Elaine Scarry has drawn upon Wittgenstein's insight. "Though the capacity to experience physical pain is as primal a fact about the human being as is the capacity to hear, to touch, to desire," she writes, pain differs "from every other bodily and psychic event, by not having an object in the external world."[18]

The vast volumes which appear in Boullée's plans serve as one marker of the point at which secular society lost contact with pain. The revolutionaries believed they could fill an empty volume, free of the obstacles and litter of the past, with human meanings, that a space without obstructions could serve the needs of a new society. Pain could be erased by erasing place. This same erasure has served different ends in a later time, the purposes of individual flight from others rather than moving closer toward them. The French Revolution thus marked a profound rupture in our civilization's understanding of pain; David placed the body in pain in the same space that Marianne occupied, an empty, homeless space, a body alone with its pain—and this is an unendurable condition.

Lurking in the civic problems of a multi-cultural city is the moral difficulty of arousing sympathy for those who are Other. And this can only occur, I believe, by understanding why bodily pain requires a place in which it can be acknowledged, and in which its transcendent origins become visible. Such pain has a trajectory in human experience. It disorients and makes incomplete the self, defeats the desire for coherence; the body accepting pain is ready to become a civic body, sensible to the pain of another person, pains present together on the street, at last endurable—even though, in a diverse world, each person cannot explain what he or she is feeling, who he or she is, to the other. But the body can follow this civic trajectory only if it acknowledges that there is no remedy for its sufferings in the contrivings of society, that its unhappiness has come from elsewhere, that its pain derives from God's command to live together as exiles.

NOTES

INTRODUCTION: Body and City

1. Hugo Munsterberg, *The Film: A Psychological Study: The Silent Photoplay in 1916* (New York: Dover Publications, 1970; 1916), 95, 82.
2. Robert Kubey and Mihaly Csikszentmihalyi, *Television and the Quality of Life: How Viewing Shapes Everyday Experience* (Hillsdale, NJ: Lawrence Erlbaum, 1990), 175.
3. M. P. Baumgartner, *The Moral Order of a Suburb* (New York: Oxford University Press, 1988), 127.
4. See, especially, Max Horkheimer and Theodor Adorno, "The Culture Industry: Enlightenment as Mass Deception," *Dialectic of Enlightenment,* trans. John Cummings (New York: Continuum, 1993; 1944), 120–167; Theodor Adorno, "Culture Industry Reconsidered," *New German Critique* 6 (1975): 12–19; and Herbert Marcuse, *One-Dimensional Man: Studies in the Ideology of Advanced Industrial Society* (Boston: Beacon Press, 1964).
5. John of Salisbury, *Policraticus,* ed. C. C. J. Webb (Oxford: Oxford University Press, 1909; original, 1159), pt. 5, no. 2. Because this text is corrupt, quotations from it follow the version used by Jacques Le Goff, "Head or Heart? The Political

Use of Body Metaphors in the Middle Ages," in *Fragments for a History of the Human Body*, Part Three, eds. Michel Feher, Ramona Naddaff, and Nadia Tazi (New York: Zone Books, 1990), 17.

6. See Michel Foucault and Richard Sennett, "Sexuality and Solitude," *Humanities in Review* I.1 (1982): 3–21.

7. Ludwig Wittgenstein, *The Blue and Brown Books: Preliminary Studies for the "Philosophical Investigations"* (New York: Harper Colophon, 1965), 50.

CHAPTER ONE: Nakedness

1. Nicole Loraux, *The Invention of Athens: The Funeral Oration in the Classical City*, trans. Alan Sheridan (Cambridge, MA: Harvard University Press, 1986; Paris, 1981), 113.

2. Thucydides, *History of the Peloponnesian War*, trans. Rex Warner (London: Penguin, 1954), 145.

3. Ibid., 146.

4. Ibid., 147.

5. See Kenneth Clark, *The Nude: A Study in Ideal Form* (Princeton: Princeton University Press, 1956).

6. Thucydides, *History of the Peloponnesian War*, 38.

7. R. E. Wycherley, *The Stones of Athens* (Princeton: Princeton University Press, 1978), 19.

8. Quoted in C. M. Cipolla, *Economic History of Europe*, vol. I (London: Fontana, 1972), 144–145.

9. M. I. Finley, *The Ancient Economy*, 2nd ed. (London: Hogarth Press, 1985), 81.

10. Hesiod, *Works and Days*, 176–178; quoted in Finley, *The Ancient Economy*, 81.

11. J. W. Roberts, *City of Sokrates: An Introduction to Classical Athens* (London and New York: Routledge & Kegan Paul, 1984), 10–11.

12. Aristotle, *Politics*, ed. Richard McKeon, trans. Benjamin Jowett (New York: Random House, 1968), VII, 1330B.

13. Thucydides, *History of the Peloponnesian War*, 120.

14. M. I. Finley, *The Ancient Greeks: An Introduction to Their Life and Thought* (London: Penguin, 1963), 137.

15. E. R. Dodds, *The Greeks and the Irrational* (Berkeley: University of California Press, 1951), 183.

16. Evelyn B. Harrison, "Athena and Athens in the East Pediment of the Parthenon" (1967), in *The Parthenon*, ed. Vincent J. Bruno (New York: Norton, 1974), 226.

17. Philipp Fehl, "Gods and Men in the Parthenon Frieze" (1961), in *The Parthenon*, 321.

18. John Boardman, "Greek Art and Architecture," in *The Oxford History of the Classical World*, eds. John Boardman, Jasper Griffin, Oswyn Murray (New York: Oxford University Press, 1986), 291.

19. See Clark, *The Nude*, 3, 23–24.

20. Peter Brown, *The Body and Society: Men, Women, and Sexual Renunciation in Early Christianity* (New York: Columbia University Press, 1988), 10.

21. Aristotle, *On the Generation of Animals*, II.i, 716a 5; trans. A. L. Peck, Loeb Classical Library (Cambridge, MA: Harvard University Press, 1953), 11.

22. Thomas Laqueur, *Making Sex: Body and Gender from the Greeks to Freud* (Cambridge: Harvard University Press, 1990), 39.

23. Françoise Heritier-Auge, "Semen and Blood: Some Ancient Theories Concerning Their Genesis and Relationship," in *Fragments for a History of the Human Body*, Part Three, 171.

24. Aristotle, *On the Generation of Animals*, II.i, 732a 22–23; trans. Peck, 133.

25. Laqueur, *Making Sex*, 25.

26. Quoted in ibid., 25.

27. See the critique of Empedokles in Aristotle, *On Sense and Sensible Objects*, 437b 25; *On the Soul, Parva Naturalis, On Breath*, trans. W. S. Hett, Loeb Classical Library (Cambridge, MA: Harvard University Press, 1964), 223.

28. Aristotle, *On Sense and Sensible Objects*, 438b; trans. Hett, 225.

29. See for example, the discussion of "Tyranny" in Book Eight in Plato, *The Republic*, trans. Desmond Lee, 2nd ed. (New York: Penguin, 1974), 381–398.

30. See B. M. W. Knox, "Silent Reading in Antiquity," *Greek, Roman, and Byzantinc Studies* 9 (1968): 421–435; and Jesper Svenbro, "La voix intérieure," *Phrasikleia: anthropologie de la lecture en Grèce ancienne* (Paris: Editions la Découverte, 1988), 178–206.

31. Giulia Sissa, "The Sexual Philosophies of Plato and Aristotle," in *A History of Women in the West*. Vol. I: *From Ancient Goddesses to Christian Saints*, ed. Pauline S. Pantel, trans. Arthur Goldhammer (Cambridge, MA: Harvard University Press, 1992; Paris, 1991), 80–81.

32. Joint Association of Classical Teachers, *The World of Athens: An Introduction to Classical Athenian Culture* (Cambridge, UK: Cambridge University Press, 1984), 174.

33. Wycherley, *The Stones of Athens*, 219.

34. Aristophanes, *The Clouds*, 1005ff; paraphrased in ibid., 220.

35. R. E. Wycherley, *How the Greeks Built Cities*, 2nd ed. (New York: Norton, 1976), 146.

36. See Brown, "Body and City," *The Body and Society*, 5–32.

37. Aiskhines, *Prosecution of Timarkhus*, 138ff; quoted in Kenneth Dover, *Greek Homosexuality* (Cambridge, MA: Harvard University Press, 1989)

38. David M. Halperin, *One Hundred Years of Homosexuality* (London: Routledge, 1990), 22.

39. Dover, *Greek Homosexuality*, 100.

40. Quoted in ibid., 106.

41. Homer, *Iliad*, 15.306–10; trans. A. T. Murray, vol. II, Loeb Classical Library (Cambridge, MA: Harvard University Press, 1963), 129.

42. Jan Bremmer, "Walking, Standing, and Sitting in Ancient Greek Culture," in *A Cultural History of Gesture*, eds. Jan Bremmer and Herman Roodenburg (Ithaca, NY: Cornell University Press, 1991), 20. The Homeric quote is from the *Iliad*, 5.778.

43. Alexis, fragment 263; T. Kock, *Comicorum Atticorum fragmenta*, trans. C. B. Gulick (Leipzig, 1880–88); quoted in Bremmer, "Walking, Standing, and Sitting in Greek Culture," 19.

44. Thucydides, *History of the Peloponnesian War*, 149.

45. My thanks to Professor G. W. Bowersock for pointing this out.

46. Birgitta Bergquist, "Sympotic Space: A Functional Aspect of Greek Dining-

Rooms," in *Sympotica: A Symposium on the Symposion,* ed. Oswyn Murray (Oxford: Clarendon Press, 1990), 54.

47. John M. Camp, *The Athenian Agora: Excavations in the Heart of Classical Athens* (London: Thames & Hudson, 1986).

48. Vincent J. Bruno, "The Parthenon and the Theory of Classical Form," in *The Parthenon,* 95.

49. Camp, *The Athenian Agora,* 72.

50. Aristophanes, *The Clouds,* 207; quoted in Wycherley, *The Stones of Athens,* 53.

51. See Johann Joachim Winckelmann, *History of Ancient Art,* trans. Johann Gottfried Herder (New York: Ungar, 1969).

52. Aristotle, *Politics,* trans. Jowett, 310.

53. Ibid.,

54. See the discussion in Josiah Ober, *Mass and Elite in Democratic Athens: Rhetoric, Ideology, and the Power of the People* (Princeton: Princeton University Press, 1989), 299–304.

55. Wycherley, *How the Greeks Built Cities,* 130.

56. Finley, *The Ancient Greeks,* 134.

57. Bremmer, "Walking, Standing, and Sitting in Ancient Greek Culture," 25–26.

58. Froma Zeitlin, "Playing the Other," in *Nothing to Do with Dionysos?,* eds. John J. Winkler and Froma Zeitlin (Princeton: Princeton University Press, 1990), 72.

59. The following account is taken from Xenophon, *Hellenika,* I.7.7–35; *Hellenika,* I–II.3.10, trans. Peter Krentz (Warminster, UK: Aris & Phillips, 1989), 59–67.

60. Hesiod, *Works and Days,* 43; quoted in Joint Association of Classical Teachers, *The World of Athens,* 95.

61. Ober, *Mass and Elite in Democratic Athens,* 175–176.

62. Thucydides, *History of the Peloponnesian War,* 49.

63. Ibid., 242. My emphasis.

64. John. J. Winkler, "The Ephebes' Song," in *Nothing to Do with Dionysos?,* 40–41.

65. For those who wish to pursue this further, see G. R. Stanton and P. J. Bicknell, "Voting in Tribal Groups in the Athenian Assembly," *GRBS* 28 (1987): 51–92; and Mogens Hansen, "The Athenian Ekklesia and the Assembly Place on the Pnyx," *GRBS* 23 (1982): 241–249.

66. Loraux, *The Invention of Athens,* 175. See also Edouard Will, "Bulletin historique," *Revue Historique* 238 (1967): 396–397.

CHAPTER TWO: The Cloak of Darkness

1. Thucydides, *History of the Peloponnesian War,* 151.

2. Ibid., 146.

3. Roberts, *City of Sokrates: An Introduction to Classical Athens,* 128.

4. Erika Simon, *Festivals of Attica: An Archaeological Commentary* (Madison: University of Wisconsin Press, 1983), 18–22.

5. J.-P. Vernant, "Introduction" to Marcel Detienne, *The Gardens of Adonis,* trans. Janet Lloyd (Atlantic Highlands, NJ: The Humanities Press, 1977), xvii–xviii.

6. Sarah Pomeroy, *Goddesses, Whores, Wives, and Slaves: Women in Classical Antiquity* (New York: Schocken Books, 1975), 78.

7. See Roman Jakobson, "Two Types of Language and Two Types of Aphasic Disturbances," in *Fundamentals of Language,* eds. R. Jakobson and Morris Halle (The Hague: Mouton, 1956); and Peter Brooks, *Reading for the Plot* (New York: Knopf, 1984), Chapter 1.

8. Herodotus, *History,* II.35; quoted in François Lissarrague, "Figures of Women," *A History of Women in the West,* vol. I: *From Ancient Goddesses to Christian Saints,* ed. Pauline Schmitt Pantel, 194.

9. Xenophon, *Oikonomikos* 7.35; quoted in Joint Association of Classical Teachers, *The World of Athens: An Introduction to Classical Athenian Culture,* 168.

10. Annick Le Guerer, *Scent,* trans. Richard Miller (New York: Random House, 1992), 8.

11. Aristophanes, *Lysistrata,* 928; quoted by Nicole Loraux, "Herakles: The Super-Male and the Feminine," in *Before Sexuality: The Construction of Erotic Experience in the Ancient Greek World,* eds. David Halperin, John J. Winkler, and Froma I. Zeitlin (Princeton: Princeton University Press, 1990), 31.

12. Alciphron, *Letters,* IV.14; quoted in Detienne, *The Gardens of Adonis,* 65.

13. Dioscorides, *Materia Medica,* II.136.1–3; quoted in ibid., 68.

14. Ibid.

15. Eva Cantarella, *Bisexuality in the Ancient World,* trans. Corma O'Cuilleanain (New Haven: Yale University Press, 1992), 90.

16. Oswyn Murray, "Sympotic History," in *Sympotica: A Symposium on the Symposion,* 7.

17. L. E. Rossi, "Il simposio greco arcaico e classico. . . . , quoted in Ezio Pellizer, "Sympotic Entertainment," trans. Catherine McLaughlin, in *Sympotica,* 183.

18. Sappho, *Greek Lyrics,* vol. 1, trans. David A. Campbell, Loeb Classical Library (Cambridge: Harvard University Press, 1982), 79–80.

19. Plato, *Phaedrus,* 276b; *Phaedrus and Letters VII and VIII,* trans. Walter Hamilton (London: Penguin, 1973), 98.

20. See John J. Winkler, "The Laughter of the Oppressed: Demeter and the Gardens of Adonis," *The Constraints of Desire: The Anthropology of Sex and Gender in Ancient Greece* (New York: Routledge, Chapman & Hall, 1990),

21. Walter Burkert, *Structure and History in Greek Mythology and Ritual* (Berkeley: University of California Press, 1979) 3. *"Ouk emos ho mythos"* is found originally in Euripides, fragment 484. The distinction is pursued in Plato, *Symposium,* 177a, trans. Alexander Nehamas and Paul Woodruff (Indianapolis: Hackett Publishing, 1989), 7; and in *Gorgias,* 523a and 527a, trans. Walter Hamilton (London: Penguin, 1960), 142–143, 148–149.

22. Meyer Fortas, "Ritual and Office," in *Essays on the Ritual of Social Relations,* ed. Max Gluckman (Manchester: Manchester University Press, 1962), 86.

23. Thucydides, *History of the Peloponnesian War,* 152–153.

24. Ibid., 155.

25. Ibid.

26. Plutarch, "Perikles," *The Rise and Fall of Athens: Nine Greek Lives,* trans. Ian Scott-Kilvert (London: Penguin, 1960), 201.

27. Thucydides, *History of the Peloponnesian War,* 604.

28. See Loraux, *The Invention of Athens: The Funeral Oration in the Classical City,* 98–118. The quotation in note 123 is from Thucydides, *History of the Peloponnesian War,* 148.

29. Thucydides, *History of the Peloponnesian War,* 156.

30. Jean-Pierre Vernant, "Dim Body, Dazzling Body," in *Fragments for a History of the Human Body,* Part One, eds. Michel Feher, Ramona Naddaff, and Nadia Tazi (New York: Urzone Books, 1989), 28.

31. Thucydides, *History of the Peloponnesian War,* 147.

CHAPTER THREE: The Obsessive Image

1. Frank E. Brown, *Roman Architecture* (New York: George Braziller, 1972), 35.

2. William L. MacDonald, *The Pantheon* (Cambridge, MA: Harvard University Press, 1976), 88–89.

3. Ibid., 88.

4. Seneca, *Letters to Lucilius,* no 37; quoted in Carlin A. Barton, *The Sorrows of the Ancient Romans* (Princeton: Princeton University Press, 1993), 15–16.

5. Barton, *The Sorrows of the Ancient Romans,* 49.

6. E. H. Gombrich, *Art and Illusion: A Study in the Psychology of Pictorial Representation,* Bollingen Series XXXV.5 (Princeton: Princeton University Press, 1961), 129.

7. Augustine, *Confessions,* X.30; trans. R. S. Pine-Coffin (London: Penguin, 1961), 233. The biblical reference is I John 2:16.

8. Richard Brilliant, *Visual Narratives* (Ithaca, NY: Cornell University Press, 1984), 122.

9. Mary Taliaferro Boatwright, *Hadrian and the City of Rome* (Princeton, Princeton University Press, 1987), 46.

10. Suetonius, "Nero," 31; *The Twelve Caesars,* trans. Robert Graves, rev. ed. (London: Penguin, 1979), 229.

11. Fergus Millar, *The Emperor in the Roman World* (Ithaca: Cornell University Press, 1992), 6.

12. Vitruvius, *The Ten Books of Architecture,* trans. Morris Hicky Morgan (New York: Dover, 1960), 1. I have altered Ms. Morgan's translation slightly.

13. Livy, *Histories,* V.54.4; quoted in *Urbs Roma,* ed. Donald Dudley (London: Phaidon Press, 1967), 5.

14. Spiro Kostof, *A History of Architecture: Settings and Rituals* (Oxford: Oxford University Press, 1985), 191.

15. Ovid, *Fasti,* II.683–684; trans. James George Frazer, Loeb Classical Library (Cambridge, MA: Harvard University Press, 1976), 107. I have altered slightly Frazer's translation.

16. Quoted in Lidia Mazzolani, *The Idea of the City in Roman Thought,* trans. S. O'Donnell (London: Hollis and Carter, 1970), 175.

17. Michael Grant, *History of Rome* (New York: Scribners, 1978), 302.

18. Ibid., 266.

19. Boatwright, *Hadrian and the City of Rome,* 132.

20. Scriptores Historiae Augustae, Hadriani 8.3; quoted in Boatwright, *Hadrian and the City of Rome,* 133.

21. William L. MacDonald, *The Architecture of the Roman Empire*. Vol. I: *An Introductory Study* (New Haven: Yale University Press, 1982), 129.
22. Dio Cassius, *Roman History,* LXIX 4.6; *Dio's Roman History,* vol. 8, trans. Earnest Cary, Loeb Classical Library (Cambridge, MA: Harvard University Press, 1925), 433.
23. Pliny, *Natural History,* xxxv. 64–66; quoted and translated in Norman Bryson, *Vision and Painting* (New Haven: Yale University Press, 1983), 1.
24. Barton, *The Sorrows of the Ancient Romans,* 13.
25. See Keith Hopkins, "Murderous Games," *Death and Renewal* (New York: Cambridge University Press, 1983), 1–30.
26. Quoted in Katherine Welch, "The Roman Amphitheater After Golvin" (Unpublished manuscript, New York University, Institute of Fine Arts), 23. My thanks to Dr. Welch for this and other materials on the amphitheatre.
27. Tertullian, *Apology,* no 15; *Apologetical Works* [and Octavius, *Minucius Felix*], trans. Rudolph Arbesmann, Emily Joseph Daly, and Edwin A. Quain, Fathers of the Church Series, vol. 10 (Washington, D.C.: Catholic University of America Press, 1950), 48.
28. Martial and Welch in Welch, "The Roman Amphitheater After Golvin," 23.
29. Suetonius, "Nero," 39; *The Twelve Caesars,* 243.
30. Ibid.
31. Richard C. Beacham, *The Roman Theater and Its Audience* (Cambridge, MA: Harvard University Press, 1992), 152.
32. Quintilian, *Institutio Oratoria,* 100; quoted and translated by Fritz Graf, "Gestures and Conventions: The Gestures of Roman Actors and Orators," in *A Cultural History of Gesture,* 41.
33. Richard Brilliant, *Gesture and Rank in Roman Art* (New Haven: Connecticut Academy of Arts and Sciences, 1963), 129–130.
34. See Robert Auguet, *Cruelty and Civilization: The Roman Games* (London: Allen & Unwin, 1972).
35. Vitruvius, *The Ten Books of Architecture,* 73.
36. Ibid., 75.
37. Joseph Rykwert, *The Idea of a Town* (Cambridge, MA: MIT Press, 1988), 59.
38. Polybius, *Histories,* VI.31, trans. F. Hultsch and E. S. Shuckburgh (Bloomington: Indiana University Press, 1962), 484; quoted in Spiro Kostof, *The City Shaped: Urban Patterns and Meanings Through History* (London: Thames & Hudson, 1991), 108.
39. Joyce Reynolds, "Cities," in *The Administration of the Roman Empire,* ed. David Braund (Exeter: University of Exeter Press, 1988), 17.
40. Ovid, *Tristia,* V.7.42–46, 49–52; *Ovid,* vol. VI, trans. Arthur Leslie Wheeler, rev. G. P. Gould, 2nd ed., Loeb Classical Library (Cambridge, MA: Harvard University Press, 1988), 239.
41. Tacitus, *Agricola,* 21; Tacitus, *Agricola, Germania, Dialogus,* trans. M. Hutton, rev. R. M. Ogilvie, Loeb Classical Library (Cambridge, MA: Harvard University Press, 1980), 67.
42. Rykwert, *The Idea of a Town,* 62.
43. Plautus, *Curculio,* 466–482; Plautus, vol. II, trans. Paul Nixon, Loeb Classical Library (Cambridge, MA: Harvard University Press, 1977), 239. I have revised this translation slightly.

44. Ramsay MacMullen, *Paganism in the Roman Empire* (New Haven: Yale University Press, 1981), 80.

45. Richard Krautheimer, *Early Christian and Byzantine Architecture,* 4th ed. (New York: Viking-Penguin, 1986), 42.

46. John E. Stambaugh, *The Ancient Roman City* (Baltimore: The Johns Hopkins University Press, 1988), 119.

47. Frank E. Brown, *Roman Architecture,* 13–14.

48. Stambaugh, *The Ancient Roman City,* 44.

49. Malcolm Bell, "Some Observations on Western Greek Stoas," (Unpublished manuscript, American Academy of Rome, 1992), 19–20; see also Marcel Detienne, "En Grèce archaïque: Géométrie Politique et Société," *Annales ESC* 20 (1965): 425–442.

50. Velleius Paterculus, *Compendium of Roman History,* II, trans. Frederick William Shipley (London: Heinemann, 1924), xx, cxxvi, 2–5.

51. Frank E. Brown, *Roman Architecture,* 14.

52. Yvon Thebert, "Private Life and Domestic Architecture in Roman Africa," in *A History of Private Life.* Vol. I: *From Pagan Rome to Byzantium,* ed. Paul Veyne, trans. Arthur Goldhammer (Cambridge, MA: Harvard University Press, 1990), 363.

53. See Mark Girouard, *Life in the English Country House: A Social and Architectural History* (New Haven: Yale University Press, 1978).

54. Peter Brown, *The Body and Society,* 21.

55. Plutarch, *Praecepta conjugalia,* 47.144f; quoted in Peter Brown, *The Body and Society,* 21.

56. Both texts from H. W. Garrod, ed., *The Oxford Book of Latin Verse* (Oxford: Oxford University Press, 1944), Latin on 349, English on 500.

57. Again, my thanks to Professor Bowersock for this suggestion.

58. Marguerite Yourcenar, *Memoirs of Hadrian,* trans. Grace Frick (New York: Farrar, Straus, & Giroux, 1954), 319–320.

59. H. W. Garrod, in *The Oxford Book of Latin Verse,* makes this connection but believes Pope's poem is suggested by Hadrian's, a direct connection which seems tenuous. The poem is printed on pp. 500–501.

CHAPTER FOUR: Time in the Body

1. Origen, *Contra Celsum,* trans. and ed. Henry Chadwick, rev ed. (Cambridge, UK: Cambridge University Press, 1965), 152.

2. Ibid.

3. Ibid.

4. Ibid.

5. Arthur Darby Nock, *Conversion* (Oxford: Oxford University Press, 1969), 227.

6. For both quotes, see Nock, *Conversion,* 8. The reference in James is to *The Varieties of Religious Experience,* 209.

7. See Peter Brown, *The Body and Society,* especially 5–32.

8. The following two paragraphs are adapted and rewritten from my earlier book, *The Conscience of the Eye* (New York: Norton, 1992; 1990), 5–6.

9. Harvey Cox, *The Secular City: Secularization and the Urbanization in Theological Perspective,* rev. ed. (New York: Macmillan, 1966), 49.

10. "Epistle to Diognatus," 7.5; trans. and quoted in Jaroslav Pelikan, *Jesus Through the Centuries* (New Haven: Yale University Press, 1985), 49–50. I have removed here Pelikan's emphasis of the final sentence.

11. Augustine, *The City of God,* XV.1; trans. Gerald G. Walsh, et al., vol. 2, Fathers of the Church Series, vol. 14 (Washington, D.C.: Catholic University of America Press, 1950), 415.

12. Origen, *Contra Celsum,* 313.

13. See I Corinthians 11:2–16; 12:4–13.

14. John Chrysostom, *Homiliae in Matthaeum,* 6.8:72; quoted and discussed in Peter Brown, *The Body and Society,* 315–317.

15. Peter Brown, *The Body and Society,* 316.

16. Origen, *Contra Celsum,* 381.

17. Ibid., 382.

18. Regina Schwartz, "Rethinking Voyeurism and Patriarchy: The Case of *Paradise Lost,*" *Representations* 34 (1991): 87.

19. Dio Cassius, *Roman History,* LIII.27.2; *Dio's Roman History,* vol. VI, trans. Earnest Cary, Loeb Classical Library (Cambridge, MA: Harvard University Press, 1917), 263; quoted in MacDonald, *The Pantheon,* 76. Percy Bysshe Shelley, letter of March 23, 1819, to Thomas Love Peacock, *Letters of Percy Bysshe Shelley,* ed. F. L. Jones, vol. 2 (Oxford: Oxford University Press, 1964), 87–88; quoted in MacDonald, *The Pantheon,* 92.

20. I *Corinthians* 11:20 and 12–14.

21. L. Michael White, *Building God's House in the Roman World: Architectural Adaptation Among Pagans, Jews, and Christians* (Baltimore: Johns Hopkins University Press, 1990), 107, 109.

22. Galatians 3:28.

23. Augustine, *The Confessions,* 229. The biblical reference is Galatians 5:17.

24. Augustine, *The Confessions,* 235.

25. I Corinthians 11:24–25.

26. Quoted and translated in this context by Wayne A. Meeks, *The Moral World of the First Christians* (Philadelphia: Westminster Press, 1986), 113. The biblical references are Colossians 3:9–11 and Ephesians 4:22–24.

27. Seneca, *Moral Epistles,* lvi.1–2; quoted in *Roman Civilization. Vol II: The Empire,* 3rd ed., eds. Naphtali Lewis and Meyer Reinhold (New York: Columbia University Press, 1990), 142.

28. Jerome Carcopino, *Daily Life in Ancient Rome,* trans. E. O. Lorimer (New Haven: Yale University Press, 1968), 263. The Latin may be found in the *Corpus Inscriptionum Latinarum,* VI 15258.

29. Wayne A. Meeks, *The First Urban Christians* (New Haven: Yale University Press, 1983), 153.

30. Jacob Neusner, *A History of the Mishnaic Law of Purities,* Studies in Judaism in Late Antiquity, 6.22: *The Mishnaic System of Uncleanness* (Leiden: Brill, 1977), 83–87.

31. Romans 6:3.

32. Colossians 2:11–12.

33. Krautheimer, *Early Christian and Byzantine Architecture,* 24–25.
34. Richard Krautheimer, *Rome: Profile of a City, 312–1308* (Princeton: Princeton University Press, 1983), 24.
35. Krautheimer, *Early Christian and Byzantine Architecture,* 40.
36. See White, *Building God's House in the Roman World,* 102–123.
37. Ibid.
38. Peter Brown, *Augustine of Hippo* (Berkeley: University of California Press, 1967), 289.
39. Ibid., 321.
40. Augustine, *The City of God,* XIV.1; trans. Gerald G. Walsh, vol. 2, 347.
41. See Friedrich Nietzsche, *On the Genealogy of Morals* I.13, trans. Walter Kaufmann and R. J. Hollingdale (New York: Vintage Books, 1967), 44–46.
42. Ibid., 45.
43. Ibid. Emphasis in original.
44. Ibid., 46.
45. See Louis Dumont, *Homo Hierarchicus: Essai sur le système des castes* (Paris: Gallimard, 1967).

CHAPTER FIVE: Community

1. Georges Duby, *The Age of the Cathedrals: Art and Society, 980–1420,* trans. Eleanor Levieux and Barbara Thompson (Chicago: University of Chicago Press, 1981; Paris, 1976), 112.
2. Max Weber, *The City,* trans. Don Martingale and Gertrud Neuwirth (New York: Macmillan, 1958; Tübingen, 1921), 212–213.
3. Walter Ullmann, *The Individual and Society in the Middle Ages* (Baltimore: Johns Hopkins University Press, 1966), 132.
4. John of Salisbury, *Policraticus,* quoted in Le Goff, "Head or Heart? The Political Use of Body Metaphors in the Middle Ages," in *Fragments for a History of the Human Body,* Part Three, 17.
5. Ullmann, *The Individual and Society in the Middle Ages,* 17.
6. Weber, *The City,* 181–183.
7. Henri Pirenne, *Medieval Cities,* trans. Frank Halsey (Princeton: Princeton University Press, 1946; Paris, 1925), 102.
8. Duby, *The Age of the Cathedrals,* 221. My emphasis.
9. Robert Grinnell, "The Theoretical Attitude Towards Space in the Middle Ages," *Speculum* XXI.2 (April 1946): 148.
10. Jean Berthélemy, *Le Livre de Crainte Amoureuse;* quoted in Johann Huizinga, *The Waning of the Middle Ages,* trans F. Hopman (New York: St. Martin's Press, 1954; Leiden, 1924), 199.
11. Jacques Le Goff, *Medieval Civilization, 400–1500,* trans. Julia Burrows (Cambridge, MA: Basil Blackwell, 1988), 158.
12. Vern Bullough, "Medieval Medical and Scientific Views of Women," *Viator* 4 (1973): 486.
13. Galen, *Ars medica,* preface; quoted and trans. in Owsei Temkin, *Galenism: Rise and Decline of a Medical Philosophy* (Ithaca, NY: Cornell University Press, 1973), 102.

14. Galen, *Ars medica*, 11; quoted in Temkin, *Galenism*, 103.

15. My thanks to Dr. Charles Malek for translating this information.

16. The following account draws upon the work of Marie-Christine Pouchelle, *The Body and Surgery in the Middle Ages*, trans. Rosemary Morris (New Brunswick, NJ: Rutgers University Press, 1990; Paris, 1983).

17. See also the description of de Mondeville in Georges Duby, "The Emergence of the Individual; Solitude: Eleventh to Thirteenth Century," in *A History of Private Life*. Vol. II: *Revelations of the Medieval World*, eds. Philippe Ariès and Georges Duby, trans. Arthur Goldhammer (Cambridge, MA: Harvard University Press, 1988), 522.

18. Henri de Mondeville, *Chirurgie* [of E. Nicaise], 243; and Barthelmey l'Anglais, *Grand Propriétaire* f.xxvj; both quoted in Pouchelle, *The Body and Surgery in the Middle Ages* 115.

19. Ibid.

20. *Ménagier de Paris*, I; quoted in Pouchelle, *The Body and Surgery in the Middle Ages*, 116.

21. Duby, *The Age of the Cathedrals*, 233.

22. John of Salisbury, *Policraticus*, IV.8, "De moderatiore justitiae et elementiae principis"; quoted in Pouchelle, *The Body and Surgery in the Middle Ages*, 203.

23. De Mondeville's image of an internally permeable city resonates with later Italian ideas of urban form; see Françoise Choay, "La ville et le domaine bâti comme corps dans les textes des architectes-théoriciens de la première Renaissance italienne," *Nouvelle Revue de Psychanalyse* 9 (1974).

24. See Caroline Walker Bynum, *Jesus as Mother: Studies in the Spirituality of the High Middle Ages* (Berkeley: University of California Press, 1982), 110–125.

25. See Caroline Walker Bynum, "The Female Body and Religious Practice in the Later Middle Ages," in *Fragments for a History of the Human Body*, Part One, 176–188.

26. Anselm, prayer 10 to St. Paul, *Opera omnia;* quoted in Bynum, *Jesus as Mother*, 114. Anselm's biblical reference is to Matthew 23:37.

27. Bynum, *Jesus as Mother*, 115.

28. Quoted in David Luscombe, "City and Politics Before the Coming of the *Politics:* Some Illustrations," in *Church and City 1000–1500: Essays in Honour of Christopher Brooke*, eds. David Abulafia, Michael Franklin, and Miri Rubin (Cambridge, UK: Cambridge University Press, 1992), 47.

29. See Raymond Klibansky, "Melancholy in the System of the Four Temperaments," in *Saturn and Melancholia*, eds. Raymond Klibansky, Erwin Panofsky, and Fritz Saxl (New York: Basic Books, 1964), 97–123.

30. Duby, *The Age of the Cathedrals*, 228.

31. Philippe Ariès, *Western Attitudes Toward Death: From the Middle Ages to the Present*, trans. Patricia Ranum (Baltimore: Johns Hopkins University Press, 1974), 15.

32. Ibid., 12.

33. Ibid., 12–13.

34. Moshe Barasch, *Gestures of Despair in Medieval and Early Renaissance Art* (New York: New York University Press, 1976), 58.

35. Otto von Simson, *The Gothic Cathedral*, 3rd ed., Bollingen Series XLVIII (Princeton: Princeton University Press, 1988), 138.

36. Achille Luchaire, *Social France at the Time of Philip Augustus,* trans. Edward Krehbiel (London: John Murray, 1912), 145.
37. Allan Temko, *Notre-Dame of Paris* (New York: Viking Press, 1955), 249.
38. Ibid., 250.
39. Howard Saalman, *Medieval Cities* (New York: George Braziller, 1968), 38.
40. Michel Mollat, *The Poor in the Middle Ages,* trans. Arthur Goldhammer (New Haven: Yale University Press, 1986), 41.
41. Lester K. Little, *Religious Poverty and the Profit Economy in Medieval Europe* (London: Paul Elek, 1978), 199.
42. Humbert de Romans, *Sermons,* xl.475–476; quoted in Bede Jarrett, *Social Theories of the Middle Ages 1200–1500* (New York: Frederick Ungar, 1966), 222.
43. Little, *Religious Poverty and the Profit Economy in Medieval Europe,* 67.
44. Ibid., 173.
45. Duby, "The Emergence of the Individual," 509.
46. Marie Luise Gothein, *A History of Garden Art,* vol I, trans. M. Archer-Hind (New York: Hacker, 1966; Heidelberg, 1913), 188.
47. I have revised the translation of Eclogue X in *Virgil's Works,* trans. J. W. Mackail, intro. Charles Durham (New York: Modern Library, 1934), 291.
48. Saalman, *Medieval Cities,* 119, n16.
49. Terry Comito, *The Idea of the Garden in the Renaissance* (New Brunswick, NJ: Rutgers University Press, 1978), 41.
50. Quoted in ibid., 43.
51. Bynum, *Jesus as Mother,* 87.

CHAPTER SIX: "Each Man Is a Devil to Himself"

1. Maurice Lombard, quoted in Jacques Le Goff, "Introduction," *Histoire de la France urbaine.* Vol. II: *La Ville Médiévale,* eds. André Chedeville, Jacques Le Goff, and Jacques Rossiaud (Paris: Le Seuil, 1980), 22. Translated by R.S.
2. Le Goff, *Medieval Civilization, 400–1500,* 207.
3. Ibid., 215.
4. Jacques Heers, *La Ville au Moyen Age* (Paris: Fayard, 1990), 189.
5. Philippe Contamine, "Peasant Hearth to Papal Palace: The Fourteenth and Fifteenth Centuries," in *A History of Private Life.* Vol. II: *Revelations of the Medieval World,* ed. Duby and Ariès, 439.
6. Ibid.
7. Jean-Pierre Leguay, *La rue au Moyen Age* (Rennes, France: Editions Ouest-France, 1984), 156–157.
8. Leguay, *La rue au Moyen Age,* 155.
9. Ibid., 198. Translated by R.S.
10. See Virginia Wylie Egbert, *On the Bridges of Medieval Paris: A Record of Fourteenth-Century Life* (Princeton: Princeton University Press, 1974).
11. Ibid., 26.
12. Robert S. Lopez, *The Commercial Revolution of the Middle Ages, 930–1350* (Englewood Cliffs, NJ: Prentice-Hall, 1971), 88.
13. Ibid., 89.

14. Humbert de Romans, Sermon xcii, *In Merchatis* 562; quoted in Jarrett, *Social Theories of the Middle Ages,* 164.
15. Ibid.
16. Lopez, *The Commercial Revolution of the Middle Ages,* 127.
17. Summerfield Baldwin, *Business in the Middle Ages* (New York: Cooper Square Press, 1968), 58.
18. Lopez, *The Commercial Revolution of the Middle Ages,* 127.
19. Gerald Hodgett, *A Social and Economic History of Medieval Europe* (London: Methuen, 1972), 58.
20. Gordon Leff, *Paris and Oxford Universities in the Thirteenth and Fourteenth Centuries: An Institutional and Intellectual History* (New York: John Wiley & Sons, 1968), 16–17.
21. Jarrett, *Social Theories of the Middle Ages,* 95.
22. Jacques Le Goff, *Your Money or Your Life: Economy and Religion in the Middle Ages,* trans. Patricia Ranum (New York: Zone, 1988), 67.
23. Ernst Kantorowicz, *The King's Two Bodies: A Study in Medieval Political Theology* (Princeton: Princeton University Press, 1981), 316.
24. Leff, *Paris and Oxford Universities in the Thirteenth and Fourteenth Centuries,* 8.
25. Guillaume d'Auxerre, *Summa aurea,* III, 21; the original is in the Biblioteca S. Croce in Florence. These quotations translated by R.S., derive from the printed transcription in Jacques Le Goff, "Temps de l'Eglise et temps du marchand," *Annales ESC* 15 (1960): 417.
26. Etienne de Bourbon, *Tabula Exemplorum,* trans. and ed. J. T. Welter (1926), 139.
27. Guillaume d'Auxerre, *Summa aurea;* "Temps de l'Eglise et temps du marchand," 417.
28. See Norman Cohn, *The Pursuit of the Millennium: Revolutionary Millenarians and Mystical Anarchists of the Middle Ages,* rev. ed. (New York: Oxford University Press, 1972).
29. Le Goff, "Temps de l'Eglise et temps du marchand," 424–425.
30. See David Landes, *Revolution in Time: Clocks and the Making of the Modern World* (Cambridge, MA: Belknap Press, 1983).
31. Quoted in Marie-Dominique Chenu, *La théologie au XIIme siècle* (Paris: J. Vrin, 1957; 1976), 66.
32. Albert Hirschmann, *The Passions and the Interests: Political Arguments for Capitalism Before Its Triumph* (Princeton: Princeton University Press, 1977), 10–11.
33. William of Conches, *Moralis philosophia,* PL. 171.1034–1035; quoted in Jean-Claude Schmitt, "The Ethics of Gesture," *Fragments for a History of the Human Body,* Part Two, eds. Michel Feher, Ramona Naddaff, and Nadia Tazi (New York: Zone Books, 1989), 139.
34. Le Goff, *Your Money or Your Life,* 73.
35. Wolfgang Stechow, *Breughel* (New York: Abrams, 1990), 80.
36. Marilyn Aronberg Lavin, *Piero della Francesca: The Flagellation* (New York: Viking Press, 1972), 71.
37. Philip Guston, "Piero della Francesca: The Impossibility of Painting," *Art News* 64 (1965): 39.
38. Quoted in Stechow, *Breughel,* 51.

39. W. H. Auden, "Musée des Beaux Arts," *Collected Poems,* ed. Edward Mendelson (New York: Random House, 1976), 146–147.

CHAPTER SEVEN: Fear of Touching

1. William Shakespeare, *The Merchant of Venice,* ed. W. Moelwyn Merchant (London: Penguin, 1967), III.3.26.
2. Ibid., IV.1.215–216.
3. Ibid., III.3.27–31.
4. See William H. McNeill, *Venice, The Hinge of Europe, 1081–1797* (Chicago: University of Chicago Press, 1974).
5. Frederick C. Lane, "Family Partnerships and Joint Ventures in the Venetian Republic," *Journal of Economic History* IV (1944): 178.
6. Figures from Ugo Tucci, "The Psychology of the Venetian Merchant in the Sixteenth Century," in *Renaissance Venice,* ed. John Hale (Totowa, NJ: Rowman & Littlefield, 1973), 352.
7. Frederick Lane, *Venice: A Maritime Republic* (Baltimore: Johns Hopkins University Press, 1973), 147.
8. Quoted in Alberto Tenenti, "The Sense of Space and Time in the Venetian World," *Renaissance Venice,* 30.
9. Ibid., 27.
10. Quoted in Brian Pullan, *Rich and Poor in Renaissance Venice* (Oxford: Basil Blackwell, 1971), 484.
11. Felix Gilbert, "Venice in the Crisis of the League of Cambrai," in *Renaissance Venice,* 277.
12. Anna Foa, "The New and the Old: The Spread of Syphilis, 1494–1530," in *Sex and Gender in Historical Perspective,* eds. Edward Muir and Guido Ruggiero (Baltimore: Johns Hopkins University Press, 1990), 29–34.
13. Sigismundo de' Contida Foligno, *La Storie dei suoi tempi dal 1475 al 1510,* vol. 2 (Rome 1883), 271–272; quoted in Foa, "The New and the Old," 36.
14. Gilbert, "Venice in the Crisis of the League of Cambrai," *Renaissance Venice,* 279.
15. Robert Finlay, "The Foundation of the Ghetto: Venice, the Jews, and the War of the League of Cambrai," *Proceedings of the American Philosophical Society* 126.2 (April 1982): 144.
16. See Aristotle, *The Politics,* ed. Richard McKeon, trans. Benjamin Jowett (New York: Modern Library, 1947), Book I, chapter 9.
17. Benjamin N. Nelson, "The Usurer and the Merchant Prince: Italian Businessmen and the Ecclesiastical Law of Restitution, 1100–1500," *Journal of Economic History* VII (1947): 108.
18. Thomas Dekker, *The Seven Deadly Sins of London* (London 1606); quoted in L. C. Knights, *Drama and Society in the Age of Jonson* (London: Chatto & Windus, 1962), 165.
19. Sir Thomas Overbury, "A Devilish Usurer," *Characters* (1614); quoted in Knights, *Drama and Society in the Age of Jonson,* 165.
20. Sander L. Gilman, *Sexuality* (New York: John Wiley & Sons, 1989), 31.

21. Le Geurer, *Scent*, 153, also 159.
22. Quoted in Gilman, *Sexuality*, 86, 87.
23. See Mary Douglas, *Purity and Danger: An Analysis of Concepts of Pollution and Taboo* (London: Routledge & Kegan Paul, 1978).
24. Marino Sanuto, *I Diarii di Marino Sanuto*, ed. Rinaldo Fulin, et al. (Venice 1879–1903), vol. 20, 98; quoted in Finlay, "The Foundation of the Ghetto," 146.
25. Quoted in Pullan, *Rich and Poor in Renaissance Venice*, 495.
26. Ibid., 486.
27. Shakespeare, *The Merchant of Venice*, III.1.76–77.
28. Hugh Honour, *Venice* (London: Collins, 1990), 189.
29. See Douglas's *Purity and Danger* for an entirely convincing, general account of how asceticism can "migrate" into sensuality in the eyes of those it threatens.
30. Norbert Huse and Wolfgang Wolters, *The Art of Renaissance Venice: Architecture, Sculpture, and Painting, 1460–1590*, trans. Edmund Jephcott (Chicago: University of Chicago Press, 1990), 8.
31. Zacaria Dolfin; quoted in Benjamin Ravid, "The Religious, Economic, and Social Background and Context of the Establishment of the Ghetti of Venice" (1983), *Gli Ebrei e Venezia*, ed. Gaetano Cozzi (Milano: Edizioni di Communità, 1987), 215.
32. Brian S. Pullan, *The Jews of Europe and the Inquisition of Venice, 1550–1670* (Totowa, NJ: Barnes & Noble, 1983), 157–158.
33. Quoted in ibid., 158.
34. Johann Burchard, *Liber Notarum* (Cita di Castello, n.p.l., 1906). I have followed, with some minor changes, the translation of Georgina Masson, *Courtesans of the Italian Renaissance* (New York: St. Martin's Press, 1975), 8.
35. Pietro Aretino, *Ragionamenti*, quoted and translated in Masson, *Courtesans of the Italian Renaissance*, 24.
36. Quoted in ibid., 152.
37. Guido Ruggiero, *The Boundaries of Eros: Sex Crime and Sexuality in Renaissance Venice* (New York: Oxford University Press, 1985), 9.
38. Quoted in Masson, *Courtesans of the Italian Renaissance*, 152.
39. Diane Owen Hughes, "Earrings for Circumcision: Distinction and Purification in the Italian Renaissance City," in *Persons in Groups*, ed. Richard Trexler (Binghamton, NY: Medieval and Renaissance Texts and Studies, 1985), 157.
40. Ibid., 163, 165.
41. Quoted in Ravid, "The Religious, Economic and Social Background and Context of the Establishment of the Ghetti of Venice," 215.
42. Carol H. Krinsky, *Synagogues of Europe: Architecture, History, Meaning* (New York: The Architectural History Foundation and MIT Press, 1985), 18.
43. Thomas Coryat, *Coryat's Crudities*, vol. I (Glasgow, 1905), 372–373.
44. Kenneth R. Stow, "Sanctity and the Construction of Space: The Roman Ghetto as Sacred Space," in *Jewish Assimilation, Acculturation and Accommodation: Past Traditions, Current Issues and Future Prospects*, ed. Menachem Mor (Lanham, NE: University Press of America, 1989), 54.
45. My thanks to Joseph Rykwert for pointing this out.
46. See Elliott Horowitz, "Coffee, Coffeehouses, and the Nocturnal Rituals of Early Modern Jewry," *Association for Jewish Studies* 14 (1988): 17–46.

47. Jacob Katz, *Exclusiveness and Tolerance: Studies in Jewish-Gentile Relations in Medieval and Modern Times* (Oxford: Oxford University Press, 1961), 133.

48. Katz, *Exclusiveness and Tolerance*, 138.

49. Howard Adelman, "Leon Modena: The Autobiography and the Man," in *The Autobiography of a Seventeenth-Century Rabbi: Leon Modena's "Life of Judah"*, ed. Mark R. Cohen (Princeton: Princeton University Press, 1988), 28.

50. See Frank Manuel, *The Broken Staff: Judaism Through Christian Eyes* (Cambridge, MA: Harvard University Press, 1992).

51. Adelman, "Leon Modena," 31.

52. Benjamin C. I. Ravid, "The First Charter of the Jewish Merchants of Venice, 1589," *Association for Jewish Studies Review*, I (1976): 207.

53. Natalie Z. Davis, "Fame and Secrecy: Leon Modena's *Life* as an Early Modern Autobiography," in *The Autobiography of a Seventeenth-Century Venetian Rabbi*, 68.

54. Gilman, *Sexuality*, 41.

55. Leon Modena, "Life of Judah," in *The Autobiography of a Seventeenth-Century Venetian Rabbi*, 144.

56. Ibid.

57. Ibid., 162.

58. Shakespeare, *Merchant of Venice*, III.1.53–62.

CHAPTER EIGHT: Moving Bodies

1. William Harvey, *De motu cordis* (Frankfurt, 1628), 165; quoted in Richard Toellner, "Logical and Psychological Aspects of the Discovery of the Circulation of the Blood," *On Scientific Discovery*, eds. Mirko Grmek, Robert Cohen, and Guido Cimino (Boston: Reidel, 1980), 245.

2. Quoted in William Bynum, "The Anatomical Method, Natural Theology, and the Functions of the Brain," *Isis* 64 (December 1973): 453.

3. Thomas Willis, *Two Discourses Concerning the Soul of Brutes* (London, 1684), 44; quoted in Bynum, "The Anatomical Method, Natural Theology, and the Functions of the Brain," 453.

4. See E. T. Carlson and Meribeth Simpson, "Models of the Nervous System in Eighteenth-Century Neurophysiology and Medical Psychology," *Bulletin of the History of Medicine* 44 (1969): 101–115.

5. Barbara Maria Stafford, *Body Criticism: Imaging the Unseen in Enlightenment Art and Medicine* (Cambridge: MIT Press, 1991), 409.

6. Harvey, *De motu cordis*, 165; quoted in Toellner, "Logical and Psychological Aspects of the Discovery of the Circulation of the Blood," 245.

7. Dorinda Outram, *The Body and the French Revolution: Sex, Class and Political Culture* (New Haven: Yale University Press, 1989), 48.

8. Alain Corbin, *The Foul and the Fragrant: Odor and the French Social Imagination* (New York: Berg, 1986; Paris, 1982), 71.

9. Marie-France Morel, "Ville et campagne dans le discours medical sur la petite enfance au XVIII siècle," *Annales* ESC 32 (1977): 1013. Trans. R.S.

10. Outram, *The Body and the French Revolution*, 59.

11. Corbin, *The Foul and the Fragrant,* 91.
12. John W. Reps, *Monumental Washington* (Princeton: Princeton University Press, 1967), 21.
13. Quoted in Elizabeth S. Kite, *L'Enfant and Washington* (Baltimore: Johns Hopkins University Press, 1929), 48.
14. L'Enfant's memorandum is reproduced in H. Paul Caemmerer, *The Life of Pierre Charles L'Enfant* (New York: Da Capo, 1970), 151–154; this quotation on 153.
15. Mona Ozouf, *Festivals of the French Revolution,* trans. Alan Sheridan (Cambridge, MA: Harvard University Press, 1988; Paris, 1976), 148.
16. Robert Harbison, *Eccentric Spaces* (Boston: Godine, 1988), 5.
17. L'Enfant, "Memorandum," in Caemmerer, *Life,* 151.
18. See, for example, "Query VI: Productions Mineral, Vegetable and Animal," in Thomas Jefferson, *Notes on the State of Virginia,* edited with an introduction by William Peden (Chapel Hill: University of North Carolina Press, 1955), 26–72.
19. See Karl Polanyi, *The Great Transformation: The Political and Economic Origins of Our Time* (Boston: Beacon Hill Press, 1957).
20. Adam Smith, *The Wealth of Nations* (New York: Everyman's Library, Knopf, 1991), 4.
21. Ibid., 15.
22. Ibid., 12.
23. See Smith, "How Commerce of the Towns Contributed to the Improvement of the Country," ibid., 362–374.
24. Johann Wolfgang Goethe, *Italian Journey,* trans. W. H. Auden and Elizabeth Mayer (New York: Pantheon, 1962), 124.
25. Goethe, Diary of the Journey from Karlsbad to Rome, September 24, 1786; quoted in T. J. Reed, *Goethe* (Oxford: Oxford University Press, 1984), 35.
26. Goethe, *Italian Journey,* 58.
27. Ibid., 202.
28. Ibid., 124; I have changed Auden and Mayer's excellent translation here, to show more literally the words Goethe uses in the original.
29. Reed, *Goethe* 35, draws attention to this strange usage.
30. Goethe, *Italian Journey,* 124.
31. Léon Cahen, "La Population parisienne au milieu du 18me siècle," *La Revue de Paris* (1919): 146–170.
32. George Rudé, *The Crowd in the French Revolution* (Oxford: Oxford University Press, 1959), 21–22.
33. Charles Tilly, *The Contentious French* (Cambridge, MA: Harvard University Press, 1986) 222.
34. Joan Landes, *Women and the Public Sphere in the Age of the French Revolution* (Ithaca: Cornell University Press, 1988), 109.
35. Rudé, *The Crowd in the French Revolution,* 75–76.
36. Marie-Antoinette, letter of October 10, 1789, to Mercy d'Argenteau; quoted in Simon Schama, *Citizens* (New York: Knopf, 1989), 469.
37. Schama, *Citizens,* 470.
38. See Lynn Hunt, *The Family Romance of the French Revolution* (Berkeley: University of California Press, 1992), especially chapters 1 and 2.

CHAPTER NINE: The Body Set Free

1. Anonymous, *Les Révolutions de Paris,* vol. 17, no. 215 (23–30 brumaire an II, in the revolutionary calendar).
2. Gustave Le Bon, *The Crowd,* intro. Robert K. Merton, no trans. listed (New York: Viking, 1960; Paris, 1895), 33.
3. Ibid., 30.
4. Ibid., 32.
5. François Furet, *Penser la Révolution Française* (Paris: Gallimard, 1978), 48–49. Translated by R.S.
6. Joan Landes, "The Performance of Citizenship: Democracy, Gender and Difference in the French Revolution." Unpublished paper presented at the Conference for the Study of Political Thought (Yale University, April 1993), 2.
7. See Joan Wallach Scott, " 'A Woman Who Has Only Paradoxes to Offer'; Olympe de Gouges Claims Rights for Women," in *Rebel Daughters: Women and the French Revolution,* eds. Sara E. Melzer and Leslie W. Rabine (New York: Oxford University Press, 1992), 102–120.
8. Jean-Jacques Rousseau, *Emile* (Paris: Pleiades, 1971), book V, 247
9. Peter Brooks, *Body Work: Objects of Desire in Modern Narrative* (Cambridge, MA: Harvard University Press, 1993), 59.
10. See Michel Foucault and Richard Sennett, "Sexuality and Solitude," *Humanities in Revue* I.1 (1982): 3–21.
11. Olwen Hufton, *Women and the Limits of Citizenship in the French Revolution* (Toronto: University of Toronto Press, 1992), 64.
12. Michel Vovelle, *La Révolution Française: Images et récits* (Paris: Editions Messidor/Livre Club Diderot, 1986), vol. 2, 139.
13. Edmond Sirel, "Les Lèvres de la Nation," revolutionary broadsheet (Paris, 1792), 6.
14. See Jean Starobinski, *Jean-Jacques Rousseau, la transparence et l'obstacle: Suivi de sept essais sur Rousseau* (Paris: Gallimard, 1971).
15. For Wailly's plan, see Vovelle, *La Révolution Française: Images et récits,* vol. 4, p. 264; for Poyet's plan, see Ministère de la Culture et de la Communication, des Grands Travaux et du Bicentenaire, *Les Architectes de la Liberté, 1789–1799,* exh. cat. (Paris: Ecole Nationale Supérieure des Beaux Arts de Paris, 1789), 216, fig. 154.
16. Quoted in Helen Rosenau, *Boullée and Visionary Architecture* (New York: Harmony Books, 1976), 8.
17. Etienne-Louis Boullée, *Architecture, An Essay on Art,* trans. Sheila de Valle (original MS Français 9153, Bibliothèque Nationale, Paris); reprinted in Rosenau, *Boullée and Visionary Architecture,* 107.
18. Ibid.
19. Ibid., 91.
20. Ibid., 82.
21. Anthony Vidler, *The Architectural Uncanny: Essays in the Modern Unhomely* (Cambridge, MA: MIT Press, 1992). I am also indebted to Professor Vidler for his trenchant analysis of Boullée's work.
22. Emmet Kennedy, *A Cultural History of the French Revolution* (New Haven: Yale University Press, 1989), 197.

23. Anonymous engraving, "Machine proposée à l'Assemblée Nationale pour le Supplice des Criminelles par M. Guillotin," Musée Carnavalet #10–63; reproduced in Daniel Gerould, *Guillotine: Its Legend and Lore* (New York: Blast Books, 1992), 14.

24. Georges Dauban, *Madame Roland et son temps* (Paris, 1864; 1819), 263. Modern historians like Daniel Arasse use a corrupted version of this text; the original is one of the great documents of the Revolution.

25. Daniel Arasse, *The Guillotine and the Terror,* trans. Christopher Miller (London: Allen Lane, 1989), 28.

26. J.-B. Bossuet, *Oeuvres oratoires,* ed. J. Lebourg (Lille and Paris, 1892), vol. 4, 256; quoted in Kantorowicz, *The King's Two Bodies: A Study in Medieval Political Theology,* 409, n. 319. Translated by R.S.

27. Lynn Hunt, *Politics, Culture, and Class in the French Revolution* (Berkeley: University of California Press, 1984), 32.

28. Outram, *The Body and the French Revolution,* 115.

29. Ibid.

30. Ozouf, *Festivals of the French Revolution,* 79.

31. Ibid., 66.

32. David Lloyd Dowd, *Pageant-Master of the Republic: Jacques-Louis David and the French Revolution* (Lincoln: University of Nebraska Press, 1948), 61.

33. *Révolutions de Paris;* quoted in Ozouf, *Festivals of the French Revolution,* 67.

34. *Annales Patriotiques* 108 (April 17, 1792): 478. Dowd, *Pageant-Master of the Republic,* 61, has not translated this quite accurately.

35. Edmond Constantin, *Le Livre des Heureux* (Paris, 1810), 226.

36. I am indebted to Professor Scott for pointing this out to me.

37. "A Boy's Testimony Concerning an Illiterate Woman Signing the Petition at the Champ de Mars, July 17, 1791"; quoted in *Women in Revolutionary Paris, 1789–1795,* eds. Darlene Gay Levy, et al., (Chicago: University of Illinois Press, 1980), 83–84.

38. Mary Jacobus, "Incorruptible Milk: Breast-feeding and the French Revolution," in *Rebel Daughters. Women and the French Revolution,* eds. Sara Melzer and Leslie Rabine (New York: Oxford University Press, 1992), 65.

39. Engraving by Helman, after Monnet, *La Fontaine de la Régénération;* reproduced in Vovelle, *La Révolution Française: Images et Récit,* vol. 4, 142.

40. Marie-Hélène Huet, *Rehearsing the Revolution: The Staging of Marat's Death, 1793–1797* (Berkeley: University of California Press, 1983), 35.

41. Jacobus, "Incorruptible Milk," 65; see also Hunt, *Politics, Culture, and Class in the French Revolution,* 94–98.

42. Hunt, *The Family Romance of the French Revolution,* 80.

43. Anita Brookner, *Jacques-Louis David* (London: Thames & Hudson, 1980), 114.

44. Charles Baudelaire, quoted in Daniel and Guy Wildenstein, *David: Documents supplémentaires au catalogue complèt de l'oeuvre* (Paris: Fondation Wildenstein, 1973); reproduced in Brookner, *David,* 116. Translated by R.S.

45. See Warren Roberts, "David's 'Bara' and the Burdens of the French Revolution," in *Revolutionary Europe, 1750–1850* (Tallahassee, FL: Conference Proceedings, 1990).

CHAPTER TEN: Urban Individualism

1. Raymond Williams, *The Country and the City* (New York: Oxford University Press, 1973), 217.
2. Ibid., 220.
3. E. M. Forster, *Howards End* (New York: Vintage Books, 1989; London, 1910), 112.
4. Judith R. Walkowitz, *City of Dreadful Delight: Narratives of Sexual Danger in Late-Victorian London* (Chicago: University of Chicago Press, 1992), 25.
5. *Housing of the Working Classes,* Royal Commission Report 4402 (1884–85.xxx): 19–20; quoted in Donald J. Olsen, *Town Planning in London: The Eighteenth and Nineteenth Centuries,* 2nd ed. (New Haven: Yale University Press, 1982), 208.
6. See the table on distribution of national capital derived from estate duty statistics in Paul Thompson, *The Edwardians: The Remaking of British Society,* 2nd ed. (New York: Routledge, 1992), 286.
7. Alfred Kazin, "*Howards End* Revisited," *Partisan Review* LIX.1 (1992): 30, 31.
8. See Alexis de Tocqueville, *Democracy in America,* trans. Henry Reeve, 4th ed., vol. II (New York: H. G. Langley, 1845).
9. Virginia Woolf, "The Novels of E. M. Forster," *The Death of the Moth and Other Essays* (New York: Harcourt, Brace, 1970), 172.
10. Bruno Fortier, "La Politique de l'Espace parisien," in *La Politique de l'espace parisien à la fin de l'Ancien Régime,* ed. Fortier (Paris: Editions Fortier, 1975), 59.
11. David Pinckney, *Napoleon III and the Rebuilding of Paris* (Princeton: Princeton University Press, 1958), 25.
12. See G. E. Haussmann, *Mémoires,* vol. 3 (Paris, 1893), 478–483; quoted in Pinckney, *Napoleon III and the Rebuilding of Paris,* 78.
13. Pinckney, *Napoleon III and the Rebuilding of Paris,* 93.
14. Donald Olsen, *The City as a Work of Art: London, Paris, Vienna* (New Haven: Yale University Press, 1986), 92.
15. Walkowitz, *City of Dreadful Delight,* 29.
16. Angelo Masso, *Fatigue,* trans. M. and W. B. Drummond (London, 1906), 156; quoted in Anson Rabinbach, *The Human Motor: Energy, Fatigue, and the Origins of Modernity* (New York: Basic Books, 1990), 136.
17. Roubo; quoted in Sigfried Giedion, *Mechanization Takes Command* (New York: Oxford University Press, 1948), 313.
18. Giedion, *Mechanization Takes Command,* 396.
19. Ibid., 404.
20. Wolfgang Schivelbusch, *The Railway Journey* (Berkeley: University of California Press, 1986), 75.
21. See Richard Sennett, *The Fall of Public Man* (New York: W. W. Norton, 1992; 1976), 81.
22. Ibid., 216.
23. Augustus J. C. Hare, *Paris* (London: Smith, Elder, 1887) 5; quoted in Olsen, *The City as a Work of Art,* 217.
24. See Reyner Banham, *The Well-Tempered Environment,* 2nd ed. (Chicago: University of Chicago Press, 1984), 18–44.

25. Elizabeth Hawes, *New York, New York: How the Apartment House Transformed the Life of the City, 1869–1930* (New York: Knopf, 1993), 231.
26. E. M. Forster, *Two Cheers for Democracy* (London: Edward Arnold, 1972), 66.
27. Forster, *Howards End,* 134.
28. E. M. Forster, *Maurice* (New York: W. W. Norton, 1993), 250 ("terminal note").
29. Anonymous, "The Glorified Spinster," *Macmillan's Magazine* 58 (1888): 371, 374.
30. Forster, *Howards End,* 209–210.
31. Ibid., 210.
32. Ibid., 350.
33. Ibid., 353–354.
34. Both remarks quoted in Alistair M. Duckworth, *Howards End: E. M. Forster's House of Fiction* (New York: Twayne/Macmillan, 1992), 62.
35. Forster, *Howards End,* 113.
36. Letter to Forrest Reid, 13 March 1915, quoted in P. N. Furbank, *E. M. Forster: A Life* (New York: Harcourt Brace Jovanovich, 1978), vol. II, 14.
37. Martin Heidegger, "Building Dwelling Thinking," in Heidegger, *Poetry, Language, Thought,* intro. and trans. Albert Hofstadter (New York: Harper & Row, 1975), 160. Emphasis in original. First given as a lecture in Darmstadt, Germany, on August 5, 1951.
38. Kazin, "*Howards End* Revisited," 32.

CONCLUSION: Civic Bodies

1. See Jane Jacobs, *The Death and Life of Great American Cities* (New York: Random House, 1963).
2. Statistics on the homeless are as shifting as the people they tabulate; nonetheless, in recent years the summer homeless population of Manhattan has hovered around 30,000, the winter population between 10,000 to 12,000; the majority of these displaced persons are single individuals. In the outer boroughs of the city, the numbers of homeless are less, and the percentage of homeless families or family fragments far greater.
3. Lewis Mumford, *The City in History* (New York: Harcourt Brace Jovanovich, 1961), 421.
4. Jean Gottmann, *Megalopolis* (New York: Twentieth Century Fund, 1961), 736.
5. Quoted in Robert Caro, *The Power Broker* (New York: Knopf, 1974), 318.
6. See Caro, *The Power Broker.*
7. Herbert Gans, *The Levittowners* (New York: Pantheon, 1967), 220.
8. Gans, *The Levittowners,* 32.
9. For a succinct statement of these changes, see Melvin M. Webber, "Revolution in Urban Development," in *Housing: Symbol, Structure, Site,* ed. Lisa Taylor (New York: Rizzoli, 1982), 64–65.
10. See, for example, Roland Barthes, *A Lover's Discourse,* trans. Richard Howard (New York: Hill & Wang, 1978).
11. See Kevin Lynch, *The Image of the City* (Cambridge, MA: MIT Press, 1960);

Erving Goffmann, *Relations in Public: Microstudies of the Public Order* (New York: Basic Books, 1971).

12. Alexis de Tocqueville, *Democracy in America,* trans. Edward Reeve (New York: Vintage Books, 1963), Vol. 2, 141.

13. See Robert Jay Lifton, *The Protean Self: Human Resilience in an Age of Fragmentation* (New York: Basic Books, 1993).

14. Sigmund Freud, *Beyond the Pleasure Principle,* trans. James Strachey (New York: W. W. Norton, 1961), 1.

15. Ibid., 21. Emphasis in original.

16. Ibid., 4.

17. Ibid., 5.

18. Elaine Scarry, *The Body in Pain: The Making and Unmaking of the World* (New York: Oxford University Press, 1985), 161.

WORKS CITED

Adelman, Howard. "Leon Modena: The Autobiography and the Man." In *The Auto-biography of a Seventeenth-Century Rabbi: Leon Modena's "Life of Judah."* Ed. Mark Cohen. 19–38.

Adorno, Theodor. "Culture Industry Reconsidered." *New German Critique* 6 (1975): 12–19.

Agulhon, Maurice. *Marianne into Battle: Imagery and Symbolism in France, 1789–1880.* Trans. Janet Lloyd. New York: Cambridge University Press, 1981.

Anonymous. "The Glorified Spinster." *Macmillan's Magazine* 58 (1888): 371, 374.

Arasse, Daniel. *The Guillotine and the Terror.* Trans. Christopher Miller. London: Allen Lane, 1989; Paris, 1987.

Arendt, Hannah. *The Human Condition.* Chicago: University of Chicago Press, 1957.

Ariès, Philippe. *Western Attitudes Toward Death: From the Middle Ages to the Present.* Trans. Patricia Ranum. Baltimore: Johns Hopkins University Press, 1974.

Aristophanes. Vol. I: *The Clouds.* Trans. Benjamin Bickley Rogers. Loeb Classical Library. New York: G. P. Putnam's Sons, 1924.

Aristotle. *De Anima (On the Soul).* Trans. Hugh Lawson-Tancred. London: Penguin, 1986.

————. *Generation of Animals*. Trans. A. L. Peck. Loeb Classical Library. Cambridge, MA: Harvard University Press, 1943.

————. *On Sense and Sensible Objects {De Sensu}*. *On the Soul, Parva Naturalia, On Breath*. Trans. W. S. Hett. Loeb Classical Library. Cambridge, MA: Harvard University Press, 1964.

————. *The Politics*. Ed. Richard McKeon, trans. Benjamin Jowett. New York: Random House, 1968.

Auden, W. H. *Collected Poems*. Ed. Edward Mendelson. New York: Random House, 1976.

Auguet, Robert. *Cruelty and Civilization: The Roman Games*. London: Allen & Unwin, 1972.

Augustine. *The City of God*. Trans. Gerald G. Walsh, S. J., et al. 3 vols. Fathers of the Church series, vol. 14. Washington, D.C.: Catholic University of America Press, 1950.

————. *Confessions*. Trans. R. S. Pine-Coffin. London: Penguin, 1961.

Baldwin, Summerfield. *Business in the Middle Ages*. New York: Cooper Square Publishers, 1968.

Banham, Reyner. *The Well-Tempered Environment*. 2nd ed. Chicago: University of Chicago Press, 1984.

Barasch, Moshe. *Gestures of Despair in Medieval and Early Renaissance Art*. New York: New York University Press, 1976.

Barthes, Roland. *A Lover's Discourse*. Trans. Richard Howard. New York: Hill & Wang, 1978.

Barton, Carlin. *The Sorrows of the Ancient Romans: The Gladiator and the Monster*. Princeton: Princeton University Press, 1993.

Baumgartner, M. P. *The Moral Order of a Suburb*. New York: Oxford University Press, 1988.

Beacham, Richard. *The Roman Theatre and Its Audience*. Cambridge, MA: Harvard University Press, 1992.

Beaucourt, Charles. *Captivité et derniers moments de Louis XVI*. Paris, 1892.

Bell, Malcolm. "Some Observations on Western Greek Stoas." Unpublished manuscript, American Academy in Rome, 1992.

Bergquist, Birgitta. "Sympotic Space: A Functional Aspect of Greek Dining Rooms." In *Sympotica: A Symposium on the Symposion*. Ed. Oswyn Murray.

Berlin, Isaiah. "Two Concepts of Liberty." *Essays on Liberty*. London: Oxford University Press, 1969.

Black, Max. "On Metaphor." *Models and Metaphors: Studies in Language and Philosophy*. Ithaca, NY: Cornell University Press, 1962.

Boardman, John. "Greek Art and Architecture." In *The Oxford History of the Classical World*. Eds. John Boardman with Jasper Griffin and Oswyn Murray. New York: Oxford University Press, 1986.

Boatwright, Mary Taliaferro. *Hadrian and the City of Rome*. Princeton: Princeton University Press, 1987.

Boegehold, Alan L. "Toward a Study of Athenian Voting Procedure." *Hesperia* 32 (1963): 366–374.

Boucher, François. *20,000 Years of Fashion: The History of Costume and Personal Adornment*. New York: Abrams, 1973.

Braund, David. *The Administration of the Roman Empire.* Exeter: University of Exeter Press, 1988.

Bremmer, Jan. "Walking, Standing and Sitting in Ancient Greek Culture." In *A Cultural History of Gesture.* Eds. Jan Bremmer and Herman Roodenburg. Ithaca, NY: Cornell University Press, 1991.

Brilliant, Richard. *Gesture and Rank in Roman Art.* New Haven: Connecticut Academy of Arts and Sciences, 1963.

——. *Visual Narratives.* Ithaca, NY: Cornell University Press, 1984.

Brookner, Anita. *Jacques-Louis David.* London: Thames & Hudson, 1980.

Brooks, Peter. *Body Work: Objects of Desire in Modern Narrative.* Cambridge, MA: Harvard University Press, 1993.

——. *The Melodramatic Imagination.* New Haven: Yale University Press, 1976.

——. *Reading for the Plot: Design and Intention in Narrative.* New York: Knopf, 1984.

Brown, Frank E. *Roman Architecture.* New York: Braziller, 1972.

Brown, Peter. *Augustine of Hippo.* Berkeley: University of California Press, 1967.

——. *The Body and Society: Men, Women, and Sexual Renunciation in Early Christianity.* New York: Columbia University Press, 1988.

Bruno, Vincent J. "The Parthenon and the Theory of Classical Form." In *The Parthenon.* Ed. Vincent J. Bruno. New York: W. W. Norton, 1974.

Bryson, Norman. *Vision and Painting.* New Haven: Yale University Press, 1983.

Burchard, Johann. *Liber Notarum.* Cita di Castello, 1906.

Burkert, Walter. *Structure and History in Greek Mythology and Ritual.* Berkeley: University of California Press, 1979.

Bynum, Caroline Walker. *Jesus as Mother: Studies in the Spirituality of the High Middle Ages.* Berkeley: University of California Press, 1982.

——. "The Female Body and Religious Practice in the Later Middle Ages." In *Fragments for a History of the Human Body, Part One.* Eds. Michel Feher, with Ramona Naddaff and Nadia Tazi.

Bynum, William. "The Anatomical Method, Natural Theology, and the Functions of the Brain." *Isis* 64 (December 1973): 445–468.

Caemmerer, H. Paul. *The Life of Pierre Charles L'Enfant.* New York: Da Capo, 1970.

Cahen, Léon. "La population parisienne au milieu du 18ème siècle." *La Revue de Paris* XI (1919).

Camp, John M. *The Athenian Agora: Excavations in the Heart of Classical Athens.* London: Thames & Hudson, 1986.

Cantarella, Eva. *Bisexuality in the Ancient World.* Trans. Corma O' Cuilleanain. New Haven: Yale University Press, 1992.

Carcopino, Jérôme. *Daily Life in Ancient Rome.* Trans. E. O. Lorimer. New Haven: Yale University Press, 1968; Paris, 1939.

Carlson, E. T., and Meribeth Simpson. "Models of the Nervous System in Eighteenth-Century Neurophysiology and Medical Psychology." *Bulletin of the History of Medicine* 44 (1969): 101–115.

Caro, Robert. *The Power Broker.* New York: Knopf, 1974.

Cave, Roy C., and Herbert H. Coulson. *A Source Book for Medieval Economic History.* New York: Bruce Publishing Co., 1936.

Chédeville, André, Jacques Le Goff, and Jacques Rossiaud, eds. *Histoire de la France urbaine.* Vol. 2: *La ville mediévale.* Paris: Editions du Seuil, 1980.

Chenu, Marie Dominique. *La théologie au XIIme siècle.* Paris: J. Vriu, 1957.

Chenu, Marie Dominique. *La théologie au XIIme siècle.* Paris: J. Vriu, 1957.

Choay, Françoise. "La ville et le domaine bâti comme corps dans les textes des architectes-théoriciens de la première Renaissance italienne." *Nouvelle Revue de Psychanalyse* 9 (1974).

Cipolla, C. M. *The Economic History of Europe.* Vol. I. London: Fontana, 1972.

Clark, Kenneth. *The Nude: A Study in Ideal Form.* Princeton: Princeton University Press, 1956.

Cohen, Mark, ed. *The Autobiography of a Seventeenth-Century Rabbi: Leon Modena's "Life of Judah."* Princeton: Princeton University Press, 1988.

Cohn, Norman. *The Pursuit of the Millennium: Revolutionary Millenarians and Mystical Anarchists of the Middle Ages.* Rev. ed. New York: Oxford University Press, 1972.

Cole, Toby, and Helen Gich Chinoy, eds. *Actors on Acting.* Rev. ed. New York: Crown, 1970.

Comito, Terry. *The Idea of the Garden in the Renaissance.* New Brunswick, NJ: Rutgers University Press, 1978.

Constantin, Edouard. *Le livre des heureux.* Paris, 1810.

Contamine, Philippe. "Peasant Hearth to Papal Palace: The Fourteenth and Fifteenth Centuries." In *A History of Private Life.* Vol. II: *Revelations of the Medieval World.* Eds. Georges Duby and Philippe Ariès.

Corbin, Alain. *The Foul and the Fragrant: Odor and the French Social Imagination.* New York: Berg, 1986; Paris, 1982.

Coryat, Thomas. *Coryat's Crudities.* 2 vols. Ed. James Maclehouse. Glasgow: University of Glasgow Press, 1905; London, 1611.

Cox, Harvey. *The Secular City.* Rev. ed. New York: Macmillan, 1966.

Cozzi, Gaetano, ed. *Gli Ebrei e Venezia. secoli XIV–XVIII.* Milano: Edizioni di Comunità, 1987.

Dauban, Georges. *Madame Roland et son temps.* Paris, 1864; 1819.

Davis, Natalie Z. "Fame and Secrecy: Leon Modena's *Life* as an Early Modern Autobiography." In *The Autobiography of a Seventeenth-Century Rabbi: Leon Modena's "Life of Judah."* Ed. Mark Cohen.

Detienne, Marcel. "En Grèce Archaïque: Géométrie politique et société." *Annales ESC* 20 (1965): 425–442.

———. *The Gardens of Adonis: Spices in Greek Mythology.* Trans. Janet Lloyd. Intro. J.-P. Vernant. Atlantic Highlands, NJ: Humanities Press, 1977; Paris, 1972.

Dio Cassius. *Dio's Roman History.* Vol. VIII. Trans. Earnest Cary. Loeb Classical Library. New York: G. P. Putnam's Sons, 1925.

Dodds, E. R. *The Greeks and the Irrational.* Berkeley: University of California Press, 1951.

Douglas, Mary. *Purity and Danger: An Analysis of Concepts of Pollution and Taboo.* London: Routledge & Kegan Paul, 1978.

Dover, K. J. *Greek Homosexuality.* Cambridge, MA: Harvard University Press, 1989.

Dowd, David. *Pageant-Master of the Republic. Jacques-Louis David and the French Revolution.* Lincoln: University of Nebraska Press, 1948.

Duby, Georges. *The Age of Cathedrals: Art and Society, 980–1420.* Trans. Eleanor Levieux and Barbara Thompson. Chicago: University of Chicago Press, 1981; Paris, 1976.

———. "The Emergence of the Individual; Solitude: Eleventh to Thirteenth Century. " In *A History of Private Life.* Vol. II: *Revelations of the Medieval World.* Eds. Georges Duby and Philippe Ariès. Trans. Arthur Goldhammer. Cambridge, MA: Harvard University Press, 1985; Paris, 1985.

Duckworth, Alistair M. *Howards End: E. M. Forster's House of Fiction.* New York: Twayne / Macmillan, 1992.

Dudley, Donald R., ed. and trans. *Urbs Roma.* London: Phaidon Press, 1967.

Dumesnil, Marie-Françoise. "A Reply to the 'Reflections of Dramatic Art' of Clairon" (1800). Trans. Joseph M. Bernstein. In *Actors on Acting.* Eds. Toby Cole and Helen Crich Chinoy.

Dumont, Louis. *Homo Hierarchicus: Essai sur le système des castes.* Paris: Gallimard, 1967.

Egbert, Virginia Wylie. *On the Bridges of Medieval Paris: A Record of Early Fourteenth-Century Life.* Princeton: Princeton University Press, 1974.

Feher, Michel, with Ramona Naddaff and Nadia Tazi, eds. *Fragments for a History of the Human Body, Parts One, Two, and Three.* New York: Urzone, 1989.

Fehl, Philippe. "Gods and Men in the Parthenon Frieze." In *The Parthenon.* Ed. Vincent J. Bruno.

Finlay, Robert. "The Foundation of the Ghetto: Venice, the Jews, and the War of the League of Cambrai." *Proceedings of the American Philosophical Society* 126.2 (8 April 1982): 140–154.

Finley, M. I. *The Ancient Greeks: An Introduction to their Life and Thought.* London: Penguin, 1963.

———. *The Ancient Economy.* 2nd ed. London: Hogarth Press, 1985.

Foa, Anna. "The New and the Old: The Spread of Syphilis, 1494–1530." In *Sex and Gender in Historical Perspectives,* eds. Edward Muir and Guido Ruggiero. Baltimore: Johns Hopkins University Press, 1990.

Forster, E. M. *Howards End.* New York: Vintage Books, 1989. London, 1910.

———. *Two Cheers for Democracy.* London: Edward Arnold, 1992.

———. *Maurice.* New York: W. W. Norton, 1993.

Fortas, Meyer. "Ritual and Office." In *Essays on the Ritual of Social Relations.* Ed. Max Gluckman. Manchester: Manchester University Press, 1962.

Fortier, Bruno. "La Politique de l'Espace parisien." In *La politique de l'espace parisien à la fin de l'Ancien Régime.* Ed. Bruno Fortier. Paris: Editions Fortier, 1975.

Foucault, Michel. *Discipline and Punish.* New York: Pantheon, 1977; Paris, 1975.

———. *The History of Sexuality.* Vol. 1: *An Introduction.* Trans. Robert Hurley. New York: Vintage Books, 1980; Paris, 1976. Vol. 2: *The Use of Pleasure.* Trans. Robert Hurley. New York: Vintage Books, 1990; Paris, 1984. Vol. 3:

———, and Richard Sennett. "Sexuality and Solitude." *Humanities in Review* I.1 (1982): 3–21.

Freud, Sigmund. *Beyond the Pleasure Principle.* Trans. James Strachey. New York: W. W. Norton, 1961; Vienna, 1923.

Furbank, P. N. *E. M. Forster: A Life.* 2 vols. New York: Harcourt Brace Jovanovich, 1978.

Furet, Française. *Penser la Révolution Française.* Paris: Gallimard, 1978.

Gans, Herbert. *The Levittowners.* New York: Pantheon, 1967.

Garrod, H. W., ed. *The Oxford Book of Latin Verse.* Oxford: Oxford University Press, 1944.

Giedion, Sigfried. *Mechanization Takes Command.* New York: Oxford University Press, 1948.

Gilbert, Felix. " Venice in the Crisis of the League of Cambrai." In *Renaissance Venice.* Ed. John R. Hale.

Gilman, Sander L. *Sexuality.* New York: John Wiley & Sons, 1989.

Giruoard, Mark. *Life in the English Country House: A Social and Architectural History.* New Haven: Yale University Press, 1978.

Goethe, Johann Wolfgang. *Italian Journey, 1786–1788.* Trans. W. H. Auden and E. Mayer. New York: Pantheon, 1962.

Goffmann, Erving. *Relations in Public: Microstudies of the Public Order.* New York: Basic Books, 1971.

Gombrich, E. H. *Art and Illusion: A Study in the Psychology of Pictorial Representation,* Bollingen Series XXXV.5, Princeton: Princeton University Press, 1961.

Gonzales-Crussi, F. *The Five Senses.* New York: Vintage Books, 1991.

Gothein, Marie Luise. *A History of Garden Art.* Vol. I. Trans. M. Archer-Hind. New York: Hacker, 1966; Heidelberg, 1913.

Gottmann, Jean. *Megalopolis.* New York: Twentieth Century Fund, 1961.

Gould, Carol. *Marx's Social Ontology.* Cambridge, MA: MIT Press, 1980.

Graf, Fritz. "Gestures and Conventions: The Gestures of Roman Actors and Orators." In *A Cultural History of Gesture.* Eds. Jan Bremmer and Herman Roodenburg.

Grant, Michael. *History of Rome.* New York: Scribners, 1978.

Grunwald Center for the Graphic Arts, Los Angeles. *French Caricature and the French Revolution, 1789–1799.* Exhibition Catalogue. Los Angeles: University of California Press, 1988.

Guston, Philip. "Piero della Francesca: The Impossibility of Painting." *Art News* 64 (1965): 37.

Habermas, Jurgen. *The Structural Transformation of the Public Sphere: An Inquiry into a Category of Bourgeois Society.* Trans. Thomas Burger, Cambridge, MA: MIT Press, 1989; Darmstadt, 1962.

Hale, John R., ed. *Renaissance Venice.* Totowa, NJ: Rowman & Littlefield, 1973.

Halperin, David. *One Hundred Years of Homosexuality.* London: Routledge, 1990.

Hansen, Mogens. "The Athenian Ekklesia and the Assembly Place on the Pnyx." *Greek Roman Byzantine Studies* 23.3 (Autumn 1982): 241–249.

Harbison, Robert. *Eccentric Spaces.* Boston: Godine, 1988.

Harrison, Evelyn B. "Athena and Athens in the East Pediment of the Parthenon." In *The Parthenon.* Ed. Vincent J. Bruno.

Harvey, David. *Social Justice and the City.* Baltimore and London: Johns Hopkins University Press, 1975.

Harvey, William. *De motu cordis.* Frankfurt, 1628.

Haussmann, G. E. *Mémoires,* vol. 3. Paris, 1893.

Hawes, Elizabeth. *New York, New York: How the Apartment House Transformed the Life of the City, 1869–1930.* New York: Knopf, 1993.

Heers, Jacques. *La ville au Moyen Age.* Paris: Libraire Arthème Fayard, 1990.

Heidegger, Martin. "Building Dwelling Thinking." In *Poetry, Language, Thought.* Intro. and trans. Albert Hofstadter. New York: Harper & Row, 1975.

———. "The Origin of the Work of Art." In *Poetry, Language, Thought.*

Héritier-Augé, Françoise. "Semen and Blood: Some Ancient Theories Concerning

Their Genesis and Relationship." In *Fragments for a History of the Human Body, Part Three.* Eds. Michel Feher, Ramona Naddaff, and Nadia Tazi.

Hesiod. *Works and Days. The Homeric Hymns and Homerica.* Trans. Hugh G. Evelyn-White. Loeb Classical Library. Cambridge, MA: Harvard University Press, 1936.

Hirschmann, Albert. *The Passions and the Interests: Political Arguments for Capitalism Before Its Triumph.* Princeton: Princeton University Press, 1977.

Hodgett, Gerald. *A Social and Economic History of Medieval Europe.* London: Methuen, 1972.

Hollander, Anne. *Moving Pictures.* New York: Knopf, 1989.

Homer. *The Iliad.* 2 vols. Trans. A. T. Murray. Loeb Classical Library. Cambridge, MA: Harvard University Press, 1963; 1925.

Honour, Hugh. *Venice.* London: Collins, 1990.

Hopkins, Keith. *Death and Renewal.* New York: Cambridge University Press, 1983.

Horkheimer, Max, and Theodor Adorno. *Dialectic of Enlightenment.* Trans. John Cummings. New York: Continuum, 1993.

Horowitz, Elliott. "Coffee, Coffeehouses, and the Nocturnal Rituals of Early Modern Jewry." *American Jewish Studies Review* 14 (1988): 17–46.

Huet, Marie-Hélène. *Rehearsing the Revolution: The Staging of Marat's Death, 1793–1797.* Trans. Robert Hurley. Berkeley: University of California Press, 1992.

Hufton, Olwen. *Women and the Limits of Citizenship in the French Revolution.* Toronto: University of Toronto Press, 1992.

Hughes, Diane Owen. "Earrings for Circumcison: Distinction and Purification in the Italian Renaissance City." In *Persons in Groups,* W. Richard Trexler. Binghamton, NY: Medieval and Renaissance Texts and Studies, 1985.

Huizinga, Johan. *The Waning of the Middle Ages.* Trans. F. Hopman. New York: St. Martin's Press, 1954; Leiden, 1919.

Hunt, Lynn. *Politics, Culture, and Class in the French Revolution.* Berkeley: University of California Press, 1984.

———. *The Family Romance of the French Revolution.* Berkeley: University of California Press, 1992.

Huse, Norbert, and Wolfgang Wolters. *The Art of Renaissance Venice: Architecture, Sculpture, and Painting, 1460–1590.* Trans. Edmund Jephcott. Chicago: University of Chicago Press, 1990; Munich, 1986.

Jacobs, Jane. *The Death and Life of Great American Cities.* New York: Random House, 1961.

Jacobus, Mary. "Incorruptible Milk: Breast-feeding and the French Revolution." In *Rebel Daughters: Women and the French Revolution.* Eds. Sara E. Melzer and Leslie Rabine. New York: Oxford University Press, 1992.

Jakobson, Roman. "Two Types of Language and Two Types of Aphasic Disturbances." *Fundamentals of Language.* Eds. Jakobson and Morris Halle. The Hague: Mouton, 1956.

James, E. O. *Seasonal Feasts and Festivals.* New York: Barnes & Noble, 1961.

Jarrett, Bede. *Social Theories of the Middle Ages 1200–1500.* New York: Frederick Ungar, 1966.

Jefferson, Thomas. *Notes on the State of Virginia.* Edited with an Introduction by William Peden. Chapel Hill: University of North Carolina Press, 1955.

John of Salisbury. *Policraticus.* Ed. C. C. J. Webb. Oxford: Oxford University Press, 1909.

Joint Association of Classical Teachers. *The World of Athens: An Introduction to Classical Athenian Culture.* Cambridge, UK: Cambridge University Press, 1984.

Kaminsky, Jack. *Hegel on Art.* Albany, NY: State University of New York Press, 1970.

Kantorowicz, Ernest H. *The King's Two Bodies: A Study in Medieval Political Theology.* Princeton: Princeton University Press, 1957.

Katz, Jacob. *Exclusiveness and Tolerance: Studies in Jewish- Gentile Relations in Medieval and Modern Times.* Oxford: Oxford University Press, 1961.

Kennedy, Emmet. *A Cultural History of the French Revolution.* New Haven: Yale University Press, 1989.

King James Bible. Cambridge, UK: Cambridge University Press, 1988; also New Testament text, New York: Thomas Nelson & Sons, 1925.

Kite, Elizabeth S. *L'Enfant and Washington.* Baltimore: Johns Hopkins University Press, 1929.

Klibansky, Raymond. "Melancholy in the System of The Four Temperaments." In *Saturn and Melancholia,* eds. Raymond Klibansky, Erwin Paustsky, and Fritz Saxl. New York: Basic Books, 1964.

Knights , L. C. *Drama and Society in the Age of Jonson.* London: Chatto & Windus, 1962.

Knox, B. M. W. "Silent Reading in Antiquity." *Greek Roman Byzantine Studies* 9 (1968): 421–435.

Konrad, Gyorgy. *Anti-Politics.* Trans. Richard E. Allen. New York: Harcourt Brace Jovanovich, 1984.

Kostof, Spiro. *A History of Architecture: Settings and Rituals.* Oxford: Oxford University Press, 1985.

———. *The City Shaped: Urban Patterns and Meanings Through History.* London: Thames & Hudson, 1991.

———. *The City Assembled: The Elements of Urban Form Through History.* London: Thames & Hudson, 1992.

Krautheimer, Richard. *Rome: Profile of A City, 312–1308.* Princeton: Princeton University Press, 1980.

———. *Early Christian and Byzantine Architecture.* 4th ed. New York: Viking-Penguin, 1986.

Krinsky, Carol Herselle. *Synagogues of Europe: Architecture, History, Meaning.* New York and Cambridge, MA: The Architectural History Foundation and MIT Press, 1985.

Kubey, Robert, and Mihaly Csikszentmihalyi. *Television and the Quality of Life: How Viewing Shapes Everyday Experience.* Hillsdale, NJ: Lawrene Erlbaum, 1990.

Landes, David. *Revolution in Time: Clocks and the Making of the Modern World.* Cambridge, MA: Belknap Press, 1983.

Landes, Joan B. *Women and the Public Sphere in the Age of the French Revolution.* Ithaca, NY: Cornell University Press, 1988.

———. "The Performance of Citizenship: Democracy, Gender and Difference in the French Revolution." Unpublished paper presented at the Conference for the Study of Political Thought, Yale University, April 1993.

Lane, Frederic Chapin. "Family Partnerships and Joint Ventures in the Venetian Republic." *Journal of Economic History* IV (1944): 178–196.

————. *Venice: A Maritime Republic*. Baltimore: Johns Hopkins University Press, 1973.

Lavin, Marilyn Aronberg. *Piero della Francesca: The Flagellation*. New York: Viking Press, 1972.

Lawrence, A. W. *Greek Architecture*. Additions by R. A. Tomlinson. London: Penguin, 1983.

Le Bon, Gustave. *The Crowd. A Study of the Popular Mind*. Ed. R. Merton. New York: Viking Press, 1960.

Leff, Gordon. *Paris and Oxford Universities in the Thirteenth and Fourteenth Centuries: An Institutional and Intellectual History*. New York: John Wiley & Sons, 1968.

Le Goff, Jacques. "Introduction" to *Histoire de la France Urbaine*. Vol. II: *La Ville Médiévale*. Eds. André Chédeville, Jacques Le Goff, and Jacques Rossiaud. Paris: Editions le Seuil, 1980.

————. *Medieval Civilization, 400–1500*. Trans. Julia Burrows. Cambridge, MA: Basil Blackwell, 1988.

————. *Your Money or Your Life: Economy and Religion in the Middle Ages*. Trans. Patricia Ranum. New York: Zone Books, 1988.

————. "Head or Heart? The Political Use of Body Metaphors in the Middle Ages." In *Fragments for a History of the Human Body, Part Three*. Eds. Michel Feher, Ramona Naddaff, and Nadia Tazi.

————. "Temps de l'Eglise et temps du Marchand." *Annales ESC* 15 (1960):417–433.

Leguay, Jean-Pierre. *La rue au Moyen Age*. Rennes, France: Ouest France, 1984.

Le Guerer, Annick. *Scent*. Trans. Richard Miller. New York: Random House, 1992.

Lenin, V. I. *Materialism and Empiro-Criticism*. New York: International Publishers, 1927; 1908.

Levy, Darlene Gay, Harriet Applewhite, and Mary Johnson, eds. *Women in Revolutionary Paris, 1789–1795*. Chicago: University of Illinois Press, 1980.

Lewis, Naphtali, and Meyer Reinhold, eds. *Roman Civilization: Selected Readings*. Vol. II: *The Empire*. 3rd ed. New York: Columbia University Press, 1990.

Lifton, Robert Jay. *The Protean Self: Human Resilience in an Age of Fragmentation*. New York: Basic Books, 1993.

Lissarrague, François. "Figures of Women." Trans. Arthur Goldhammer. In *A History of Women in the West*. Vol. I: *From Ancient Goddesses to Christian Saints*. Ed. Pauline Schmitt Pantell. Cambridge: Harvard University Press, 1992; Paris, 1991.

Little, Lester K. *Religious Poverty and the Profit Economy in Medieval Europe*. London: Paul Elek, 1978.

Lopez, Robert. *The Commercial Revolution of the Middle Ages, 930–1350*. Englewood Cliffs, NJ: Prentice-Hall, 1971.

Loraux, Nicole. *The Invention of Athens: The Funeral Oration in the Classical City*. Trans. Alan Sheridan. Cambridge, MA: Harvard University Press, 1986.

————. "Herakles: The Super-Male and the Feminine." In *Before Sexuality: The Construction of Erotic Experience in the Ancient Greek World*. Eds. David Halperin, John J. Winkler, and Froma I. Zeitlin. Princeton: Princeton University Press, 1989.

Luchaire, Achille. *Social France at the Time of Philip Augustus*. Trans. Edward Benjamin Krehbiel. London: John Murray, 1912; Paris, 1899.

Luscombe, D. E. "Cities and Politics Before the Coming of the *Politics:* Some Illustrations." In *Church and City 1000–1500: Essays in Honor of Christopher Brooke.* Eds. David Abulafia, Michael Franklin, and Miri Rubin. Cambridge, UK: Cambridge University Press, 1992.

Lykurgos. *Against Leocrates. Minor Attic Orators.* Trans. J. O. Burtt. Loeb Classical Library. Cambridge, MA: Harvard University Press, 1954.

Lynch, Kevin. *The Image of the City.* Cambridge, MA: MIT Press, 1960.

MacDonald, William L. *The Pantheon: Design, Meaning and Progeny.* Cambridge, MA: Harvard University Press, 1976.

————. *The Architecture of the Roman Empire.* Vol. I: *An Introductory Study.* Rev. ed. New Haven: Yale University Press, 1982.

MacMullen, Ramsay. *Paganism in the Roman Empire.* New Haven: Yale University Press, 1981.

Manuel, Frank. *The Broken Staff: Judaism Through Christian Eyes.* Cambridge, MA: Harvard University Press, 1992.

Marcus Aurelius Antoninus. *Meditations.* Trans. G. M. A. Grube. Indianapolis: Hackett Publishing, 1983.

Marcuse, Herbert. *One-Dimensional Man: Studies in the Ideology of Advanced Industrial Society.* Boston: Beacon Press, 1964.

Masson, Georgina. *Courtesans of the Italian Renaissance.* New York: St. Martin's Press, 1975.

Mazzolani, Lidia Storini. *The Idea of the City in Roman Thought: From Walled City to Spiritual Commonwealth.* Trans. S. O'Donnell. Bloomington: Indiana University Press, 1970; Milan, 1967.

McNeill, William. *Venice. The Hinge of Europe, 1081–1797.* Chicago: University of Chicago Press, 1974.

Meeks, Wayne A. *The First Urban Christians: The Social World of the Apostle Paul.* New Haven: Yale University Press, 1983.

————. *The Moral World of the First Christians.* Philadelphia: Westminster Press, 1986.

Melzer, Sara, and Leslie Rabine, eds. *Rebel Daughters. Women and the French Revolution.* New York: Oxford University Press, 1992.

Mercier, Sebastien. *Tableau de Paris.* 12 vols. Amsterdam, NY: 1782–88.

Millar, Fergus. *The Emperor in the Roman World.* Ithaca, NY: Cornell University Press, 1992.

Ministère de la Culture et de la Communication, des Grands Travaux et du Bicentennaire. *Les Architectes de la Liberté 1789–1799.* Exhibition Catalogue. Paris: Ecole Nationale Supérieure des Beaux Arts de Paris, 1989.

Modena, Leon. " Life of Judah." In *The Autobiography of a Seventeenth-Century Rabbi: Leon Modena's "Life of Judah."* Ed. Mark Cohen.

Mollat, Michel. *The Poor in the Middle Ages.* Trans. Arthur Goldhammer. New Haven: Yale University Press, 1986; Paris, 1978.

Morel, Marie-France. "Ville et campagne dans le discours médical sur la petite enfance au XVIIIe siècle." *Annales* ESC 32 (1977): 1007–1024.

Mumford, Lewis. *The City in History.* New York: Harcourt Brace Jovanovich, 1961.

Munsterberg, Hugo. *The Film: A Psychological Study: The Silent Photoplay in 1916.* New York: Dover Publications, 1970; 1916.

Murray, Oswyn. "Sympotic History." In *Sympotica: A Symposium on the Symposiom.* Ed. Oswyn Murray. Oxford: Clarendon Press, 1990.

Nelson, Benjamin N. "The Usurer and the Merchant Prince: Italian Businessmen and the Ecclesiastical Law of Restitution, 1100–1550." *Journal of Economic History* VII (1947): 104–122.

Neusner, Jacob. *A History of the Mishnaic Law of Purities.* Leiden: Brill, 1977.

Nock, Arthur Darby. *Conversion.* Oxford: Oxford University Press, 1969.

Ober, Josiah. *Mass and Elite in Democratic Athens: Rhetoric, Ideology and the Power of the People.* Princeton: Princeton University Press, 1989.

Olsen, Donald J. *Town Planning in London: The Eighteenth and Nineteenth Centuries.* 2nd ed. New Haven: Yale University Press, 1982.

———. *The City as a Work of Art: London, Paris, Vienna.* New Haven: Yale University Press, 1986.

Origen. *Contra Celsum.* Trans. and ed. Henry Chadwick. Cambridge, UK: Cambridge University Press, 1965.

Outram, Dorinda. *The Body and the French Revolution: Sex, Class, and Political Culture.* New Haven: Yale University Press, 1989.

Ovid. *Fasti.* Trans. James George Frazer. Loeb Classical Library. Cambridge, MA: Harvard University Press, 1976.

———. *Tristia.* In Ovid, vol. VI. Trans. Arthur Leslie Wheeler. Rev. G. P. Gould. 2nd ed. Loeb Classical Library. Cambridge, MA: Harvard University Press, 1988.

Ozouf, Mona. *Festivals and the French Revolution.* Trans. Alan Sheridan. Cambridge, MA: Harvard University Press, 1988; Paris, 1976.

Pantel, Pauline Schmitt, ed. *A History of Women in the West.* Vol. I: *From Ancient Goddesses to Christian Saints,* trans. Arthur Goldhammer. Cambridge, MA: Harvard University Press, 1992; Paris, 1991.

Paterculus, Velleius. *Compendium of Roman History II.* Trans. Frederick William Shipley. London: W. Heinemann, 1924.

Pelikan, Jaroslav. *Jesus Through the Centuries.* New Haven: Yale University Press, 1985.

Pellizer, Ezio. "Sympotic Entertainment." In *Sympotica: A Symposium on the Symposion.* Ed. Oswyn Murray.

Pinckney, David. *Napoleon III and the Building of Paris.* Princeton: Princeton University Press, 1958.

Pirenne, Henri. *Medieval Cities: Their Origins and the Revival of Trade.* Trans. Frank D. Halsey. Princeton: Princeton University Press, 1946.

Plato. *Gorgias.* Trans. and intro. Walter Hamilton. London: Penguin, 1960.

———. *Symposium.* Trans. and intro. Alexander Nehamas and Paul Woodruff. Indianapolis: Hackett Publishing, 1989.

Plautus. Vol. VII: *Curculio.* Trans. Paul Nixon. Loeb Classical Library. Cambridge, MA: Harvard University Press, 1977.

Plutarch. "Perikles." *The Rise and Fall of Athens: Nine Greek Lives.* Trans. Ian Scott-Kilvert. London: Penguin, 1960.

Polanyi, Karl. *The Great Transformation: The Political and Economic Origins of Our Time.* Boston: Beacon Hill Press, 1957.

Polybius. *Histories.* 6 vols. Trans. W. R. Paton. Loeb Classical Library. Cambridge, MA: Harvard University Press, 1980.

Pomeroy, Sarah. *Goddesses, Whores, Wives , and Slaves: Women in Classical Antiquity.* New York: Schocken Books, 1975.

Pouchelle, Marie-Christine. *The Body and Surgery in the Middle Ages.* Trans. Rosemary Morris. New Brunswick, NJ: Rutgers University Press, 1990; Paris, 1983.

Pullan, Brian S. *Rich and Poor in Renaissance Venice.* Oxford: Basil Blackwell, 1971.

———. *The Jews of Europe and the Inquisition of Venice, 1550–1670.* Totowa, NJ: Barnes & Noble, 1983.

Rabinbach, Anson. *The Human Motor: Energy, Fatigue, and the Origins of Modernity.* New York: Basic Books, 1990.

Ravid, Benjamin. "The First Charter of the Jewish Merchants of Venice, 1589." *Association for Jewish Studies Review* I (1976): 187–222.

———. "The Religious, Economic, and Social Background and Context of the Establishment of the Ghetti of Venice." In *Gli Ebrei e Venezia, secoli XIV– XVIII.* Ed. Gaetano Cozzi.

Reed, T. J. *Goethe.* Oxford: Oxford University Press, 1984.

Reps, John. *Monumental Washington.* Princeton: Princeton University Press, 1967.

Reynolds, Joyce. "Cities." In *The Administration of the Roman Empire.* Ed. David Braund.

Roberts, J. W. *City of Sokrates: An Introduction to Classical Athens.* New York: Routledge & Kegan Paul, 1984.

Roberts, Warren. "David's 'Bara' and the Burdens of the French Revolution." In *Revolutionary Europe 1750–1850.* Tallahassee, FL: Conference Proceedings, 1990.

Rosenau, Helen. *Boullée and Visionary Architecture.* New York: Harmony Books, 1976.

Rousseau, Jean-Jacques. *Emile, ou Traité de L'Éducation.* Paris: Gallimard, 1971; 1762.

Rudé, George. *The Crowd in the French Revolution.* New York: Oxford University Press, 1959.

Ruggiero, Guido. *The Boundaries of Eros: Sex Crime and Sexuality in Renaissance Venice.* New York: Oxford University Press, 1985.

Rykwert, Joseph. *The Idea of a Town: The Anthropology of Urban Form in Rome, Italy and the Ancient World.* Cambridge, MA: MIT Press, 1988.

Saalman, Howard. *Medieval Cities.* New York: George Braziller, 1968.

Sade, D. A. F, Marquis de. *Three Complete Novels (Justine, Philosophy in the Bedroom, Eugénie de Franval).* Trans. Richard Seaver and Austryn Wainhouse. New York: Grove Press, 1966.

Sappho. *Greek Lyrics.* Trans. David A. Campbell. Loeb Classical Library. Cambridge, MA: Harvard University Press, 1982.

Scarry, Elaine. *The Body in Pain: The Making and Unmaking of the World.* New York: Oxford University Press, 1985.

Schama, Simon. *Citizens.* New York: Vintage Books, 1989.

Schivelbusch, Wolfgang. *The Railway Journey.* Berkeley: University of California Press, 1986.

Schmitt, Jean-Claude. "The Ethics of Gesture." In *Fragments for a History of the Human Body, Part Two.* Eds. Michel Feher, Ramona Naddaff, and Nadia Tazi.

Schwartz, Regina. "Rethinking Voyeurism and Patriarchy: The Case of *Paradise Lost.*" *Representations* 34 (1991): 85–103.

Scott, Joan Wallach. " 'A Woman Who has Only Paradoxes to Offer'; Olympe de

Gouges Claims Rights for Women." In *Rebel Daughters: Women and the French Revolution*. Eds. Sara E. Melzer and Leslie Rabine.

Seneca. *Seneca's Letters to Lucilius*. 2 vols. Trans. E. Phillips Barker. Oxford: Clarendon Press, 1932.

———. *Seneca: Moral Epistles*. Trans. and intro. Anna Lydia Motto. Chico, CA: Scholars Press, 1985.

Sennett, Richard. *The Fall of Public Man*. New York: W. W. Norton, 1992; 1976.

———. *The Conscience of the Eye*. New York: W. W. Norton, 1992; 1990.

Shakespeare, William. *The Merchant of Venice*. Ed. W. M. Merchant. London: Penguin, 1967.

Simon, Erika. *Festivals of Attica: An Archaeological Commentary*. Madison: University of Wisconsin Press, 1983.

Simson, Otto von. *The Gothic Cathedral: Origins of Gothic Architecture and the Medieval Concept of Order*. 3rd ed., Bollingen Series XLVIII. Princeton: Princeton University Press, 1988.

Sirel, Edmund. "Les Lèvres de la Nation." Paris, 1792.

Sissa, Giulia. "The Sexual Philosophies of Plato and Aristotle." In *A History of Women in the West*. Vol. I: *From Ancient Goddesses to Christian Saints*. Ed. Pauline Schmitt Pantel. Trans. Arthur Goldhammer. Cambridge, MA: Harvard University Press, 1992; Paris, 1991.

Smith, Adam. *The Wealth of Nations*. New York: Everyman's Library, Knopf, 1991; London, 1776.

Stafford, Barbara Maria. *Body Criticism: Imaging the Unseen in Enlightenment Art and Medicine*. Cambridge, MA: MIT Press, 1991.

Stambaugh, John E. *The Ancient Roman City*. Baltimore: Johns Hopkins University Press, 1988.

Stanton, G. R., and Bicknell, P. J. "Voting in Tribal Groups in the Athenian Assembly." *Greek Roman and Byzantine Studies* 28 (1987).

Starobinski, Jean. *Jean-Jacques Rousseau, la transparence et l'obstacle: Suivi de sept essais sur Rousseau*. Paris: Gallimard, 1971.

Stechow, Wolfgang. *Breughel*. New York: Abrams, 1990.

Stow, Kenneth R. "Sanctity and the Construction of Space: The Roman Ghetto as Sacred Space." In *Jewish Assimilation, Acculturation and Accommodation: Past Traditions, Current Issues and Future Prospects*. Ed. Menachem Mor. Lanham, University Press of America, 1989.

Strauss, Leo. *The City and Man*. Chicago: Rand-McNally, 1964.

Suetonius. *The Twelve Caesars*. Trans. Robert Graves. Rev. ed. London: Penguin, 1979.

Svenbro, Jesper. "La voix intérieure." *Phrasikleia: anthropologie de la lecture en Grèce ancienne*. Paris: Editions de la Découverte, 1988.

Symonds, J. A. *Memoirs*. New York: Viking Press, 1984.

Tacitus. *Agricola*. Trans. M. Hutton. Rev. R. M. Ogilvie. *Agricola, Germania, Dialogus*. Loeb Classical Library. Cambridge, MA: Harvard University Press, 1970.

Talma, François-Joseph. "Grandeur Without Pomp" (1825). In *Actors on Acting*. Eds. Toby Cole and Helen Crich Chinoy.

Temkin, Owsei. *Galenism: Rise and Decline of a Medical Philosophy*. Ithaca, NY: Cornell University Press, 1973.

Temko, Allan. *Notre Dame of Paris*. New York: Viking Press, 1955.

Tenenti, Alberto. "The Sense of Space and Time in the Venetian World." In *Renaissance Venice*. Ed. John R. Hale.

Tertullian. *Apologetical Works* [and Octavius, *Minucius Felix*]. Trans. Rudolph Arbesmann, Emily Joseph Daly, and Edwin A. Quain. The Fathers of the Church Series, vol. 10. Washington, DC: Catholic University of America Press, 1950.

Thebert, Yvon . "Private Life and Domestic Architecture in Roman Africa." In *A History of Private Life*. Vol. I: *From Pagan Rome to Byzantium*. Ed. Paul Veyne. Cambridge, MA: Harvard University Press, 1990; Paris, 1985.

Thompson, Paul. *The Edwardians: The Remaking of British Society*. 2nd ed. New York: Routledge, 1992.

Thucydides. *History of the Peloponnesian War*. Trans. Rex Warner, intro. M. I. Finley . London: Penguin, 1954.

Tilly, Charles. *The Contentious French*. Cambridge, MA: Harvard University Press, 1986.

Toellner, Richard. "Logical and Psychological Aspects of the Discovery of the Circulation of the Blood." In *On Scientific Discovery*. Eds. Mirko Grmek, Robert Cohen, and Guido Cimino. Boston: Reidel, 1980.

Tucci, Ugo. "The Psychology of the Venetian Merchant in the Sixteenth Century." In *Renaissance Venice*. Ed. John R. Hale.

Ullmann, Walter. *The Individual and Society in the Middle Ages*. Baltimore: Johns Hopkins Press, 1966.

Vernant, Jean-Pierre. "Introduction" to Marcel Detienne, *The Gardens of Adonis*.

———. "Dim Body, Dazzling Body." In *Fragments for a History of the Human Body, Part One*. Eds. Michel Feher, Ramona Naddaff, and Nadia Tazi.

Veyne, Paul. *Bread and Circuses*. Abridged and trans. Brian Pearce. London: Allen Lane / Penguin, 1990; Paris, 1976.

Vidler, Anthony. *The Architectural Uncanny: Essays in the Modern Unhomely*. Cambridge, MA: MIT Press, 1992.

Virgil, *Eclogues*. *Virgil's Works*. Trans. J. W. Mackail. Intro. Charles Durham. New York: Modern Library, 1934.

Vitruvius. *The Ten Books of Architecture*. Trans. Morris Vicky Morgan. New York: Dover Publications, 1960.

Vovelle, Michel. *La Révolution Française: Images et récits*. 5 vols. Paris: Messidor / livre Club Diderot, 1986.

Walkowitz, Judith R. *City of Dreadful Delight: Narratives of Sexual Danger in Late-Victorian London*. Chicago : University of Chicago Press, 1992.

Weber, Max. *The City*. Trans. Don Martindale and Gertrud Neuwirth. New York: The Free Press, 1958; Tübingen, 1921.

Webber, Melvin. "Revolution in Urban Development ." In *Housing: Symbol, Structure, Site*. Ed. Lisa Taylor. New York: Rizzoli, 1982.

Welch, Katherine. "The Roman Amphitheatre after Golvin." Unpublished manuscript, New York University Institute of Fine Arts, 1992.

White, Michael L. *Building God's House in the Roman World: Architectural Adaptation Among Pagans, Jews, and Christians*. Baltimore: Johns Hopkins University Press, 1990.

Whyte, William. *City: Rediscovering the Center*. Garden City, NY: Doubleday, 1988.

Wildenstein, Daniel and Guy. *David: Documents supplémentaires au catalogue complèt de l'oeuvre*. Paris: Fondation Wildenstein, 1973.

Williams, Raymond. *The Country and the City.* New York: Oxford University Press, 1973.

Willis, Thomas. *Two Discourses Concerning the Soul of Brutes.* London, 1684.

Winckelmann, Johann Joachim. *History of Ancient Art.* Trans. Johann Gottfried Herder. New York: Ungar, 1969.

Winkler, John J. *The Constraints of Desire: The Anthropology of Sex and Gender in Ancient Greece.* New York: Routledge, Chapman & Hall, 1990.

———. "The Ephebes' Song." In *Nothing to Do with Dionysos?* Eds. John Winkler and Froma Zeitlin. Princeton: Princeton University Press, 1990.

Wittgenstein, Ludwig. *The Blue and Brown Books: Preliminary Studies for the "Philosophical Investigations."* New York: Harper Colophon, 1965.

Woolf, Virginia. "The Novels of E. M. Forster." *The Death of the Moth and Other Essays.* New York: Harcourt, Brace, 1970.

Wycherley, R. E. *How the Greeks Built Cities: The Relationship of Architecture and Town Planning to Everyday Life in Ancient Greece.* 2nd ed. New York: W. W. Norton, 1976.

———. *The Stones of Athens.* Princeton: Princeton University Press, 1978.

Xenophon. *Hellenika I–II.310.* Ed. and trans. Peter Krentz. Warminster, UK: Aris & Phillips, 1989.

Yourcenar, Marguerite. *Memoirs of Hadrian.* Trans. Grace Frick. New York: Farrar, Straus & Giroux, 1954.

Zanker, Paul. *The Power of Images in the Age of Augustus.* Trans. Alan Shapiro. Ann Arbor: University of Michigan Press, 1990.

Zeitlin, Froma. "Playing the Other: Theatre, Theatricality, and the Feminine in Greek Drama." In *Nothing to Do with Dionysos?* Eds. John Winkler and Froma Zeitlin.

Zucker, Paul. *Town and Square: From the Agora to the Village Green.* New York: Columbia University Press, 1969.

INDEX

Page numbers in *italics* refer to illustrations.